MOON

T0373023

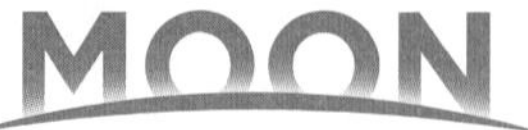

PRAGUE & BEYOND

AUBURN SCALLON

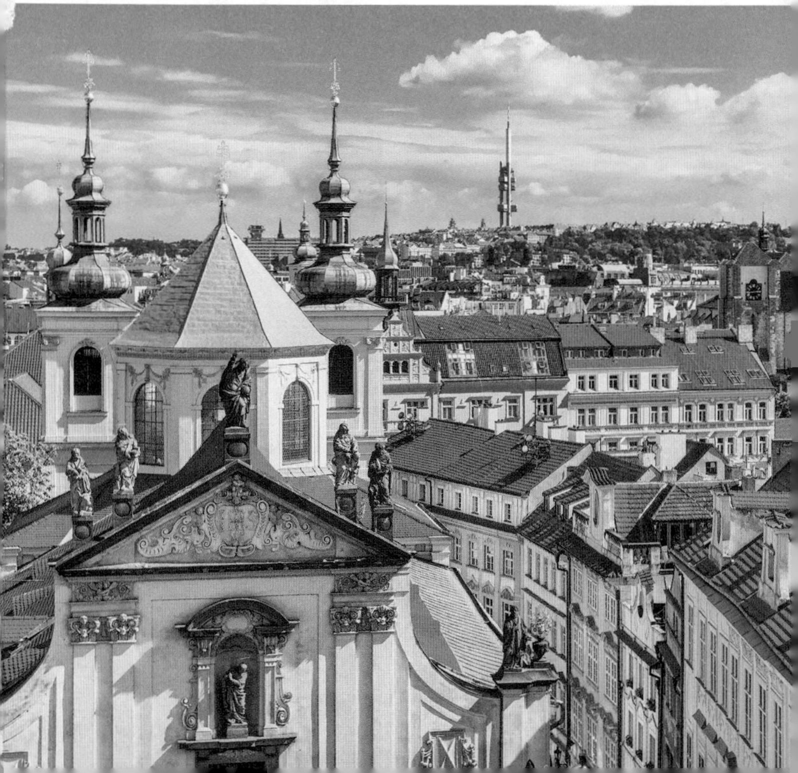

CONTENTS

1 Karlovy Vary's Mill Colonnade

2 chlebíčky are a perfect picnic treat

3 spring in Prague

4 vineyard in Moravia

5 traditional decorated eggs at an Easter Market

6 Charles Bridge Tower

DISCOVER
PRAGUE & BEYOND

Some Czechs like to joke, with a characteristically self-deprecating wit, that everyone has heard of Prague but many have no idea that it's in the Czech Republic. Prague has certainly earned its share of attention, along with various nicknames, through the centuries. "The Golden City" reflects the red-orange rooftops, the crowned National Theater, and the pastel facades bathed in sunlight. "The City of a Hundred Spires" (or a thousand, depending on who's counting) captures the complexity of the skyline viewed from numerous towers and viewpoints across town. "The Heart of Europe" might be one of the most important monikers, reminding visitors that geographic location puts the Czech capital smack in the center of the continent (and Prague being referred to as "Eastern European" while located west of Vienna is definitely a sore spot for many).

Prague certainly is a captivating city, but taking a few steps off the typical tourist path will open up a country filled with pleasant surprises. Architectural wonders range from mountaintop towers in Liberec and manicured gardens in Mikulov to artfully arranged human bones in Kutná Hora and Brno. The famous fairy-tale vibe in Český Krumlov complements the town's artistic scene. World-famous breweries in Pilsen organize guided tours, while innovative microbrewers set up shop in repurposed industrial spaces. Exhibits of history, royalty, and occupying forces in Olomouc or Brno are intertwined with a modern generation of Czechs bringing innovation to the dining and nightlife scenes. Taking in the natural beauty of Bohemian Paradise or a spa weekend in Karlovy Vary can offer an escape from the stresses of modern life. There is no one right way to explore the beauty and complexity of this country, but there are plenty of options to fill itineraries for different tastes.

MY FAVORITE EXPERIENCES

1 Wandering the vast complex of Prague's **Vyšehrad,** which is no less impressive (and much less crowded) than the Prague Castle (page 99).

2 Sipping a foam-topped *pivo* (beer) in one of Prague's **beer gardens** (page 107).

3 Surveying the landscape from the mountaintop **Ještěd Hotel and TV Tower** in Liberec. The sweeping view reaches all the way to the German and Polish borders (page 178).

4 Dining and drinking in **Prague's outer neighborhoods,** where you can still get a sense of the undiscovered vibe the city was once known for (page 98).

5 Taking in the panoramic view from Český Krumlov's **Castle Tower**—equally beautiful in summer (when the city teems with tourists) and winter (when the city is quieter, and snow blankets the landscape) (page 239).

>>>

6 Melting stress away in the relaxing salt caves of **Elisabeth Spa** in Karlovy Vary (page 202).

>>>

7 Admiring the **Baroque fountains** scattered across Olomouc. Searching for them creates a fun scavenger hunt across the city (page 296).

8 Comparing the lager at **Pilsner Urquell Brewery** (page 219) with those at inventive **microbreweries** in Pilsen (page 227).

9 Tasting the country's best wines surrounded by aristocratic glamour in the **Czech National Wine Cellar** at Valtice Château (page 282).

10 Watching the sunset from **Holy Hill** as the light fades over the picturesque town of Mikulov (page 277).

11 Wandering through the "bone church" at the **Sedlec Ossuary,** which contains the artfully arranged bones of more than 40,000 human skeletons (page 166).

EXPLORE PRAGUE & BEYOND

A two- or three-day tour of Prague will give you a solid first impression of the city. After that, there are excellent options for day trips or longer excursions. **Kutná Hora, Liberec,** and **Bohemian Paradise** are all easily doable as day trips by train or bus. An overnight stay will help to make the most out of **Karlovy Vary, Pilsen,** or **Český Krumlov,** balancing travel time without feeling rushed. If you head east to the Moravian region, it's worth spending 2-3 days (or more) traveling between **Olomouc, Brno,** and the **Lednice-Valtice Area.** All three cities are easily connected to each other and to Prague by regular trains and buses or highways.

BEST OF PRAGUE

An ideal itinerary in Prague varies wildly based on the weather. A sunny day opens the doors to manicured gardens and outdoor beer gardens, while winter requires more indoor entertainment. These two days provide a base for you to modify according to your interests, no matter the weather.

>DAY 1: EARLY 20TH-CENTURY ELEGANCE

This day centers largely around the glamour of Prague's early 20th century, one of my favorite eras that often receives less attention than Prague's Communist history and beer halls. Browse the programs at Prague's National Theater and concert halls when booking your accommodation. Make your reservation at Café Louvre a few days before arrival. Note that the sights of the Jewish Quarter are closed on Saturdays.

- Arrive in the morning to check into your hotel or drop off luggage. Refuel with coffee and cake at Old Town's Cubist-themed **Grand Café Orient.**
- Head to the **Alfons Mucha Museum** to get to know an Art Nouveau master.
- Next, walk through Wenceslas Square to **Palac Lucerna** for a cold *pivo* (beer) or hot mug of *svařák* (spiced wine) in **Kavárna Lucerna,** and get a pic of the upside-down horse statue.

Prague's Cubist Grand Café Orient

The Old Jewish Cemetery is next to the Pinkas Synagogue.

- Exit through the Franciscan Gardens and hop on a tram to the **Jewish Quarter's** Pinkas Synagogue and Old Jewish Cemetery. Afterwards, head back to your hotel to change into theater attire.
- Book an early evening dinner at **Café Louvre** for a Czech meal of *svíčková* or roast duck.
- Arrive early to admire the ceilings and find your seat for an opera, ballet, or classical music concert at Prague's **National Theater or concert halls.**
- After the show, walk through a peaceful (and safe) **Old Town Square** at night, followed by a stroll over the **Charles Bridge** for a view of the spotlights on the Prague Castle before heading home to bed.

Prague's National Theater

>DAY 2: PRAGUE BEYOND THE CITY CENTER

This itinerary aims to avoid crowds, learn about local history, and get to know life outside Old Town. Make a reservation for dinner at **Martin's Bistro** and drinks at both **Oblaca Bar** and **Bukowski Bar** a few days in advance. Note that the **National Monument to the Heroes of the Heydrich Terror** and **New Town Hall Tower** are closed on Mondays, and Martin's Bistro is only open for lunch (10am-4pm) on Sundays.

- After a hotel breakfast, jump on the metro to **Vyšehrad,** a peaceful complex with an ornate cemetery of Czech legends, a Gothic Cathedral that opens at 10am, and hillside views over the river. On a sunny day, grab a drink and a snack at the **Hospůdka Na Hradbach** beer garden.
- Walk downhill and along the river to the **Dancing House** for a beverage at the rooftop Glass Bar with panoramic city views.
- Step inside the **National Monument to the Heroes of the Heydrich Terror** around the corner for a free history lesson on a fascinating story of Czech resistance efforts during World War II.
- Walk through the park at Karlovo náměstí and climb the **New Town Hall Tower,** site of the first Prague Defenestration.

SIGHTSEEING WITHOUT THE CROWDS

When it comes to finding a quiet moment in tourist hot spots, the common refrain among photographers is to arrive before sunrise. The most famous sights can be pretty crowded from morning to evening during summer and Christmas seasons. Saving these sights for weekdays instead of weekends, arriving first thing in the morning, or waiting until nighttime can give you a different experience with fewer crowds. Otherwise, just be patient and take your time at the sights you choose to visit. Wait for the crowds to rise and disperse around you, and watch for the moment to get a good view or picture as you immerse yourself in the moment.

- Jump on a tram to **Martin's Bistro** for a dinner of international dishes fresh from the neighborhood farmers market.

Dancing House or Fred and Ginger building

- In spring, summer, or autumn, you should be able to catch a sunset (or twilight) drink at the **Žižkov TV Tower**'s Oblaca Bar.
- Close out the night with beers or cocktails over candlelight at the laid-back **Bukowski Bar.**

DAY 3: DAY TRIP TO KUTNÁ HORA

You can stay in Prague one more day to explore the Prague Castle and the Malá Strana neighborhood in detail, or you can jump on a train for a quieter, less crowded tour of Kutná Hora's visually impressive churches and contemporary art. Kutná Hora travelers should make a reservation for lunch at **Staročeská restaurace V Ruthardce** the day before. Note that the Church of the Assumption opens late at 11am on Sundays. Apply at least three weeks in advance for permission to take photos at the Church of the Assumption and Sedlec Ossuary.

- Have breakfast, check out of your hotel, and stash your luggage at the main train station (Praha hl. n). Then jump on a train around 8am to **Kutná Hora hl. n** (about 60 minutes). Book your train tickets in advance at www.cd.cz or in person at the station—they're unlikely to sell out.
- Walk to the luminescent **Church of the Assumption** and pick up a combined ticket for the Sedlec Ossuary and St. Barbara's Cathedral.
- Continue to the **Sedlec Ossuary** to peruse the Church of All Saints, the "bone church," and the surrounding cemetery.
- Take the tourist shuttle to **Staročeská restaurace V Ruthardce** for a hearty Czech lunch (try the *kulajda* soup).
- Walk through town and along a statue-lined footbridge to the **GASK Gallery of the Central Bohemian Region.** Take in the creatively curated permanent exhibit "States of Mind – Beyond the Image."
- Head next door to marvel at the interior and exterior beauty of **St. Barbara's Cathedral** and complete your combined church ticket.

St. Barbara's Cathedral in Kutná Hora

- Walk back to the tiny **Chocolate Museum and Chocolaterie** and ask the staff to call you a taxi while you browse souvenirs or enjoy a hot chocolate.
- Allow 15-20 minutes for the journey back to **Kutná Hora hl. n.** Then catch a late-afternoon or early-evening train back to Prague, leaving almost every hour.

LIBEREC AND BOHEMIAN PARADISE

Get a taste of North Bohemia's natural beauty and architectural charm, surrounded by mountain ranges and protected forests.

BEFORE YOU GO

- **Hotel reservations:** Book nights 1 and 2 at a hotel in Liberec. (Return to Prague at the end of day 3.)
- **Restaurant reservations:** For day 1, make reservations at **Balada** (lunch) and **Masa Buka** (dinner; closed Sun. and Mon.) at least 24 hours in advance. For day 2, make dinner reservations at **Radniční Sklípek** a few days in advance. For day 3, make brunch reservations at **Mykina.** All restaurants located in Liberec.
- **Transit:** Book your return from Liberec to Prague by bus at least 24 hours in advance.
- **Don't forget:** Bring comfortable hiking shoes and sunscreen to explore Bohemian Paradise.

DAY 1: PRAGUE TO LIBEREC

- Have breakfast, check out of your hotel, and jump on an hourly **Regiojet bus** (60 minutes) to Liberec in the morning. Check into your hotel and settle in or stash your luggage.
- Walk to the main square of Náměstí Dr. E. Beneše to find the Neo-Renaissance **Town Hall.** Take a few photos and climb the tower.
- Take a quick peek behind the Town Hall at the exterior of the **F. X. Šalda Theatre,** and seek out the **Giant's Feast** sculpture, which is on top of a bus stop.
- Backtrack through the square and downhill to **Balada** for a casual Czech lunch.
- Move your luggage into your room (if you couldn't earlier) and walk

Liberec Town Hall

Ještěd Hotel and TV Tower

sandstone rocks at Jan's Viewpoint in Bohemian Paradise

to the **Fügnerova bus station** to pick up one 24-hour tourist ticket (50 CZK each) for today and three single rides (20 CZK each) for the following days.

- Jump on a tram (15-20 minutes) to Horní Hanychov and take the cable car to **Ještěd Hotel and TV Tower** for 360-degree views and a drink or snack in the retro-futuristic café.
- Head back down on the cable car any time before 6pm. Take the tram to Fügnerova and bus #15 or #19 to Technická univerzita to reach the **Liberec Reservoir.** Kick back with a Svijany beer from the outdoor pub or walk across the turret-lined dam for a lap around the water.
- Walk to **Masa Buka** for a Greek dinner and then head back to your hotel for a good night's sleep.

>DAY 2: DAY TRIP TO BOHEMIAN PARADISE

You're coming back to Liberec, so no need to check out of your accommodation. Stop by an ATM for some local currency before leaving Liberec, and wear your hiking gear on the train. Comfortable shoes or sport sandals are enough for these well-worn paths, as long as you don't mind them getting dirty.

- Enjoy a hotel breakfast and hop on a tram to the **Liberec Train Station** around 9:30am. Trains to Turnov (30-45 minutes) leave at least once an hour. English-speaking staff at this station may be limited, so book your round-trip train tickets online in advance at www.cd.cz.
- From the Turnov Train Station, follow the yellow and green trails through the town of **Turnov** and pick up some hiking snacks at any local shop.
- When you reach the residential Turnov město train station, follow the red trail into Bohemian

EXPLORE

WHERE TO GO FROM PRAGUE

If You Want...	Destination	Why Go?	Distance/ Travel Time from Prague	How Long to Stay
Bone churches	Kutná Hora (page 161)	Marvel at a famous ossuary that's adorned with more than 40,000 human skeletons.	1 hour by train	one day
	Brno (page 249)	Admire a bone church that's larger than Kutná Hora's, then relax at a lively pub or craft cocktail bar.	2.5 hours by train	two days
Local life	Liberec (page 174)	Survey the city and countryside from a mountaintop tower, then join the locals at a reservoir.	1 hour by bus	one day
	Olomouc (page 285)	Wander through a picturesque Old Town of fountains and religious monuments in Moravia's spiritual capital.	2 hours by train	two days
Hiking	Bohemian Paradise (Český Ráj) (page 186)	Trek past castle ruins and sandstone formations, pausing at lookout points to survey the Czech landscape.	2 hours by train	one day
Spas and thermal springs	Karlovy Vary (page 196)	Fill your cup at the free-flowing thermal springs across town and make a spa appointment to be pampered, Czech-style.	2 hours by bus	overnight
Beer	Pilsen (page 212)	Visit the Pilsner Urquell brewery and local brew pubs, then soak in hops at a "beer spa."	1 hour by bus or train	overnight
Castles and châteaux	Český Krumlov (page 232)	Explore the medieval town and 13th-century castle, then spend a day rafting down the Vlatva River.	3 hours by train or bus	2-3 days
	Lednice and Valtice Châteaux (page 268)	Explore a châteaux that once housed the aristocracy of the Austro-Hungarian Empire, then taste wine from the surrounding vineyards.	4 hours by train	2-3 days

Paradise to the **Hlavatice Lookout Tower.** Climb the spiral staircase and try to spot Ještěd in the distance.

- Continue along the red trail to **Hospůdka U Hradu** and grab a snack or a drink on the picnic grounds.
- Wander across the statue-lined bridge to peek inside the courtyard of **Valdštejn Castle.**
- Follow the red and blue trails onward to **Jan's Viewpoint** and spot the Czech flag flying over a landscape of sandstone rocks.
- Around late afternoon, turn back and follow the red path out of the nature reserve and through town (about 90 minutes) to the **Turnov Train Station.** Trains back to Liberec (30-45 minutes) depart roughly once an hour.
- From the Liberec Train Station take a tram (7-10 minutes) back to the Town Hall for dinner in the underground beer hall **Radniční Sklípek.**
- After dinner, grab a drink at **Jimmy's** nightclub underneath the F. X. Šalda Theatre before turning in.

John of Nepomuk at the Valdštejn Castle

>DAY 3: LIBEREC TO PRAGUE

This is an easy itinerary to relax after two jam-packed days. Allow yourself a lazy morning before checking out of your hotel and storing your luggage. Book your Prague bus online at least 24 hours in advance.

- Walk to **Mykina** for a breakfast of open-faced sandwiches and specialty coffee.

chlebíčky from Mykina for breakfast

- Stop into **Lázně Regional Art Gallery** to browse the latest art exhibit.
- Continue up **Masarykova Street** for an easy walk along a tree-lined row of historical villas.
- When you reach the Zoo tram stop, grab a ride back to your hotel to pick up your luggage. Within a 40-minute window, you can also jump back on the tram to the Fügnerova bus station with the same ticket.
- Take an afternoon Regiojet bus back to Prague.

NAVIGATING OUTSIDE PRAGUE

Trains and buses are the easiest way to venture beyond Prague. An integrated public transport system of trains and buses, plus private companies, all offer comfortable, reliable, and affordable service to basically anywhere you want to go. Renting a car may provide a little more freedom of movement, but it also comes with often confusing rules for parking that vary from city to city, plus paying for highway access with requirements not always explained in English. Sit back and let someone else do the driving while you enjoy the views of the Czech countryside.

RENTING A CAR

An international license is required to drive in the Czech Republic. To access the highways, you'll need to purchase a sticker at a border crossing point, post office, or gas station and display it on your windshield. Prague's highways, particularly the D1 highway connecting Prague and Brno, are notorious for heavy traffic and construction delays. Satellite navigation or GPS is recommended for visitors navigating the Czech Republic by car.

Budget Rental Car (www.budget.com) is available for pickup and drop-off at the Prague Airport. Prices range from around 900 CZK per day (compact, manual transmission) to 1,600 CZK per day (sedan, automatic transmission) or 2,500-5,000 CZK per day (family-sized van, manual or automatic transmissions), plus gas, insurance, highway permits, and parking.

LUGGAGE STORAGE

You can store your luggage at Prague's **Main Train Station** (Praha hlavní nádraží) or **Florenc bus station** for up to 24 hours for 60-100 CZK per day. For longer, multi-day trips, try **Luggage Storage Prague** (www.luggagestorageprague.com), which maintains three locations near Náměstí Republiky, Praha hlavní nádraží, and Národní třída. Prices start at 150 CZK per piece for one day, with discounted rates of 105 CZK per piece for 2-7 days.

ČESKÝ KRUMLOV AND PILSEN

Get to know South Bohemia with a peaceful trip to Český Krumlov, famous for its castle views with a lesser-known artistic side, followed by Pilsen's beer-focused nightlife. This itinerary is designed either for shoulder seasons or for a winter visit, when Český Krumlov in particular is less crowded, and both cities have the chance of being blanketed in snow.

>BEFORE YOU GO

- **Hotel reservations:** Book accommodation for night 1 in Český Krumlov and nights 2 & 3 in Pilsen. (Return to Prague at the end of day 4.)
- **Restaurant reservations:** For day 1, make lunch reservations for **U dwau Maryí.** For Day 2, make dinner reservations at **Nero.** For Day 3, make lunch reservations at **Pivstro** (closed Sun-Mon), dinner at **U Mansfelda,** and drinks at **Beer Factory** in Pilsen, all at least 24 hours in advance.

view from the Český Krumlov Castle

- **Sight reservations:** Make reservations for the **Pilsner Urquell Brewery** and **Pilsen Underground** at least a week in advance. Add a reservation at **Fotoatelier Seidel** if you want a private photo shoot in the studio.
- **Transit:** Book your train or bus tickets from Prague to Český Krumlov, train from Český Krumlov to Pilsen (changing in České Budějovice), and bus or train from Pilsen to Prague about a week in advance.
- **Don't forget:** Clothing you can layer for various temperatures, comfortable shoes for lots of walking, and your camera (or smartphone) to take in the views.

>DAY 1: PRAGUE TO ČESKÝ KRUMLOV

Layer your clothing for a day of sightseeing, both indoors and outdoors.

- Have breakfast in Prague before jumping on a three-hour morning bus ride to Český Krumlov.
- After checking into your hotel, walk through town to **U dwau Maryí** for an Old Bohemian Feast beside the river.
- Stop into the **Fotoatelier Seidel** photography museum for a glimpse into the 19th-century life of a local photographer. Make reservations in advance for a photo shoot complete with period costumes in the light-filled photo studio.
- Take an easy walk to **Seminární zahrada** and use your photographic inspiration to capture a few last city views from this quiet viewpoint.
- Head towards the **Český Krumlov Castle** and walk through the five courtyards to get a feel for the size and layout of the grounds, with photo-worthy views in the fifth courtyard. Skip the crowds at the tower for now (you'll be back tomorrow).
- Take some time in the evening to relax and regroup at your hotel, or wander the charming streets as they become quieter in the evening. Then head to **Nonna Gina** for an Italian dinner before turning in for the night.

Nonna Gina's quiet side street

>DAY 2: ČESKÝ KRUMLOV TO PILSEN

Dress comfortably for lots of walking and an afternoon train journey.

- Grab a quick, early hotel breakfast, check out of your hotel, and stash your luggage at your accommodation.
- Head straight to the **Český Krumlov Castle Tower and Museum** for an overview of the history and some of the most coveted city views.

St. Bartholomew's Cathedral in the main square of Pilsen with the golden fountain

- As tour groups begin to arrive at the castle grounds, head to the **Egon Schiele Gallery** to admire the paintings and art exhibits.
- Have an early lunch at **Restaurace na Ostrove** with the rushing river as a soundtrack.
- Give yourself plenty of time to pick up luggage and book a taxi from your hotel to the **Český Krumlov Train Station** in order to catch the only train to Pilsen at around 2pm (changing in České Budějovice) to arrive around 6:30pm.
- From the Pilsen train station, check into your hotel and head to **Nero** for a Mediterranean-inspired dinner.
- After dinner, walk through **Republic Square (Náměstí Republiky)** for some nighttime photos of the three golden fountains glowing against the shadowy backdrop of the Cathedral of St. Bartholomew.

>DAY 3: EXPLORE PILSEN

Layer your clothes because the brewery cellars can be chilly and you'll be out until the sun goes down.

- Take it easy after a few days of heavy travel. Enjoy a leisurely hotel breakfast and a late start.
- When you're ready, head to the **Great Synagogue (Velká synagoga)** and spend an hour admiring the architecture and browsing the art exhibit.

the Great Synagogue in Pilsen

- Cross the street for lunch and a microbrew at **Pivstro.**

fresh food and brews at Pivstro

- Walk to Pilsen's central **Republic Square (Náměstí Republiky)** to see the golden fountains and Marion plague column in daylight, and pick up one or two tram tickets at the information center.
- Climb to the top of the tallest church tower in the country at the **Cathedral of St. Bartholomew** and enjoy a 360-degree view of the city.
- Take a long walk or a tram ride to the **Pilsner Urquell Brewery** to make the 3:45pm tour in English.
- After the tour, jump on a tram back into town and refuel with a hearty Czech dinner at **U Mansfelda.**
- Finish the night by sampling microbrews at **Beer Factory** before heading to bed.

EXPLORE

DAY 4: PILSEN TO PRAGUE

Make sure you've got cash for entrance to the Patton Memorial (closed Monday and Tuesday). Layer your clothing to transition between a chilly Pilsen Underground tour and heated restaurants and public transportation.

- Have breakfast at your hotel before checking out and storing your luggage.
- Spend an hour learning about the US Army's role in liberating this region from Nazi control during World War II at the **Patton Memorial.**
- Walk along the main road of sady Pětatřicátníků, pausing to look at the Patton Monument in front of the Great Synagogue before continuing up the road to see the **"Thank You, America!" Memorial.**
- Stop into **Měšťanská Beseda** for lunch in a historical café atmosphere.
- After lunch, try an afternoon microbrew at **Pivotečka,** but keep an eye on the time.
- Arrive at the **Pilsen Underground** a few minutes before your 2:20pm reservation for an English tour.
- Finish the day by using your voucher for one last small beer and snack if needed at the adjoining **Na Parkánu** pub.
- Head back to your hotel to pick up luggage and catch an early evening bus or train back to Prague (1 hour).

OLOMOUC, BRNO, MIKULOV, AND VALTICE CHÂTEAUX

Contrast Brno's vibrant nightlife with the peaceful streets of Olomouc and the grand châteaux of Mikulov and the Lednice-Valtice area during this introduction to the Czech Republic's eastern region. These distinctive Moravian towns have each housed royalty and weathered wars in previous centuries, giving them plenty of stories to tell.

>BEFORE YOU GO

- **Hotel reservations:** Book accommodation for night 1 in Olomouc, nights 2 & 3 in Brno, and nights 4 & 5 in Mikulov. (Return to Prague in the morning on day 6.)
- **Restaurant reservations:** For day 1, make reservations at **Hanácká hospoda** (dinner) in Olomouc at least 24 hours in advance. For day 3, make reservations at **Soul Bistro** (dinner) and **Bar Který Neexistuje** (drinks) in Brno a few days in advance. For day 5, make reservations at **Restaurace Marcela Ihnačáka** (dinner) in Mikulov a few days in advance.
- **Sight reservations:** Make reservations online for **English-language château tours in Valtice** for Day 5 roughly one month in advance, especially during peak seasons. Make Day 3 reservations for Brno's **Ossuary at St. James Church** and **10-Z Bunker Tour** (both closed Mondays) a few days in advance.

Mikulov with Holy Hill in the background

- **Transit:** Book your Day 2 bus ticket from Olomouc to Brno, your Day 4 train from Brno to Mikulov, and your Day 6 train from Mikulov to Prague, at least 24 hours in advance (all available online).
- **Don't forget:** Comfortable shoes for lots of walking in Olomouc and Brno, a phone charger or backup battery to ensure access to smartphone apps in Olomouc, and footwear that you don't mind getting a little dirty for hiking in Mikulov, plus a little space reserved in your luggage to take home some Moravian wine. Note that several sights on this itinerary are **closed on Mondays,** so plan accordingly.

>DAY 1: PRAGUE TO OLOMOUC

Before leaving Prague, download the Olomouc UNESCO app plus the audio guides to the Archdiocesan Museum and the Museum of Modern Art on a solid Wi-Fi connection. Have some local currency on hand for taxis, or download the Liftago app for ease of getting around. Note that the Archdiocesan Museum is free on Sundays and closed on Mondays.

- Enjoy some coffee and a snack on a morning Regiojet train (just over 2 hours) from Prague to Olomouc. Jump in a taxi from the train station (Olomouc hl. n.) to check in and drop off any luggage at your accommodation.
- Use your audio guide on a self-guided tour of the **Archdiocesan Museum** (closed Mon.) for an overview of Olomouc's religious and aristocratic history.
- Stop by **Wenceslas Cathedral,** ideally on a Wednesday so you can catch an organ demonstration every hour between 9am and 4pm except noon.
- Grab a light lunch at Long Story Short Hostel's **Cooking Bar Café,** preferably on the summer terrace if the weather allows.
- Go on a scavenger hunt to find the six **Baroque fountains** scattered throughout town, ending in the **Upper Square** (known locally as Horní náměstí).
- Use your Olomouc UNESCO app to find the meaning behind every sculpture on the **Holy Trinity Column** and take a close look at the **Astronomical Clock,** decorated in Socialist Realism style.

Astronomical Clock in Socialist Realism style

- Head back to your hotel, move your baggage into the room, and relax. Then try some Olomouc cheese with your dinner at **Hanácká hospoda.**
- Finish the night with drinks alongside a rowdy crowd at **Vertigo** in the university district (all ages welcome) before heading to bed.

>DAY 2: OLOMOUC TO BRNO

Note that the Museum of Modern Art is free on Sundays and closed on Mondays. Brno's Super Panda Circus is also closed on Sundays.

- After a late night, breakfast at **Miss Sophie's Café** is worth getting out of bed for. Check out of your hotel, stash your luggage, and revive yourself with specialty coffee and waffles, and treat yourself to a few minutes in the backyard hammock.
- Take a few steps up the street to appreciate the curated graffiti in the passageway across from the **Modern Art Museum** and **David Černý's "Man Hanging Out"** sculpture on the building's exterior. Then head inside for the organized art collection and a rooftop viewpoint.
- Pop back to the hotel, pick up your luggage, and take a taxi to the train station (Olomouc hl. n.) around noon. Find your bus platform outside the train station for a one-hour Regiojet or Flixbus ride to **Brno's Hotel Grand bus stop.** Most accommodation options are less than a 10-minute walk, or you can jump in a taxi.

quiet streets of Olomouc

- After checking into your hotel, stop by **4pokoje** for a late lunch.
- Walk up to **Saints Peter and Paul's Cathedral** and survey the town from the hilltop church tower.
- Circle back to the **Town Hall** to see the legendary Brno "dragon," the wagon wheel, and the crooked spire before climbing another tower for a central perspective.
- Wander through **Náměstí Svobody (Freedom Square)** for a glimpse of the Plague Column, and check out Brno's modern and somewhat comical Astronomical Clock. They swear it's meant to resemble a bullet . . .
- Head over to **Pivnice Pub Pegas** for some classic Czech food at the oldest on-site microbrewery in Moravia.
- Use the moonlight (and the streetlights) to find the hidden entrance to **Super Panda Circus** and enter a psychedelic fairy-tale setting with a playful approach to ordering cocktails. Fall into bed afterwards without setting any alarms.

>DAY 3: EXPLORE BRNO

Note that Brno's Ossuary at St. James and 10-Z Bunker are closed on Mondays.

- Take it slow this morning and head to **Bavard Café and Bar** when you're ready for a leisurely brunch of eggs Benedict.
- Meander over to **St. James Church** and admire the serene, vanilla-colored walls of the building's interior. Then step outside to giggle at the tiny sculpted man mooning onlookers from an exterior church window.

Basilica of Saints Peter and Paul in Brno

- Keep an eye on the time for your reservation at the **Ossuary at St. James Church** to examine the artfully arranged bones.
- Continue the eerie atmosphere with a guided tour of **10-Z Bunker,** a former bomb shelter turned hostel and museum of military history with multimedia storytelling.
- Step back into daylight and head to **SKOG** for coffee and a snack if needed. Take some down time in the café or your hotel to write postcards, post photos, check emails, or just relax.
- In the late afternoon or early evening, walk to **Výčep Na stojáka,** sample some Czech craft beer, and watch the streets around Jakubské náměstí fill up with groups of friends and foam-topped glasses.
- When you've worked up an appetite, pop over to **Soul Bistro** for dinner.
- Shortly after sunset, walk down to the courtyard outside **Janacek Theater** and grab a bench to watch the colorful light show projected onto the outdoor fountain.
- After a few cocktails at **Bar Který Neexistuje,** use some liquid courage to try a few Czech phrases (found in the back of this book) while ordering, paying your tab, or saying goodbye.

The crowd at Výčep Na stojáka regularly spills into the square.

>DAY 4: BRNO TO MIKULOV

Wear your most comfortable shoes and pack super light to take advantage of the regional buses connecting these towns. Double-check schedules for the day at www.idsjmk.cz. If you've got large luggage, book your train ticket from Brno to Mikulov online in advance at www.cd.cz. Make sure you've got cash to pay for dinner at Amici Miei.

- After checking out of your hotel and stashing your luggage, climb the hill to **Špilberk Castle and Museum.** Spend a couple of hours perusing the exhibits and savoring the unobstructed views from the surrounding park.
- Grab lunch at **Forky's.** Bonus points if you can snag the picture-window table upstairs, where a small charitable donation added to your bill gets you an ideal people-watching perspective over Jakubské náměstí.
- After lunch, pick up your luggage and head to the main train station, **Brno hlavní nádraží**, for just over an hour's ride to Mikulov. Alternatively, Brno dolní nádraží is an additional 10-minute walk from the main train station.

Špilberk Castle and Museum

escape the crowds in Mikulov

St. Sebastian's Chapel and Bell Tower on Holy Hill

- When you arrive at the Mikulov na Moravě train station, call a taxi or walk 15-20 minutes to most hotels to check in.
- Walk through town to the gates of the **Mikulov Château** grounds. Spend some time wandering the gardens and getting lost in the pathways and courtyards surrounding the building.
- Head next door to the **Church Tower of St. Wenceslas** for a bit of history, 360-degree balcony views, and a tiny interior art gallery.
- Enjoy some early evening down time until roughly one hour before sunset (or have dinner first). Then hike up **Holy Hill** and stake out a seat in the grass to watch the sky change colors over the town.
- Follow the path back downhill to finish the day with a few glasses of *Pálava* wine and Italian cuisine at **Amici Miei.**

ravioli and wine at Amici Miei

DAY 5: DAY TRIP TO VALTICE

Before heading out, ask your hotel to break any large bills into small change to pay for two regional buses. Note that château tour schedules vary by month, and that both Avalon Keltic restaurant and the National Wine Cellar are closed on Mondays.

- Have breakfast at your hotel before catching **regional bus** 585 around 8:30am (confirm times and fares at www.idsjmk.cz) for a 20-30 minute ride to Valtice.
- Check in for your tour of **Valtice Château,** usually starting at 10am (for an English-language tour, reserve in advance).
- Exit the grounds and cross the street to **Avalon Keltic** for a hearty lunch of Czech cuisine in the ivy-covered courtyard.
- Cross back to the château grounds and head underground to the **National Wine Cellar.** Show your château tour ticket for a 10% discount, and spend up to 120 minutes sampling the 100 best wines in the country. Choose a few favorite bottles to take home as souvenirs.

TRAVEL LIKE A LOCAL

The subtle differences of a new culture are often easy to miss at first glance. These tips will help you avoid drawing attention to yourself as a tourist and help you prepare for the interactions you're likely to experience, such as dining out or riding public transport.

get to know life outside the center

- **Explore Prague's outer neighborhoods.** Spoiler alert: most Czech residents don't live in castles or pay the tourist prices in Old Town Square and Malá Strana. Definitely enjoy the beauty of historical center, then jump on public transport to find the independent restaurants, peaceful parks, and interesting sights of modern Prague in neighborhoods like Karlín, Vinohrady, Žižkov, and Holešovice. Practice your polite greetings in the local language as you enter these more residential spaces.
- **Follow public transport etiquette.** Conversations are generally kept to a low whisper on trams, buses, and the metro. It's also customary to give up your seat for older adults, pregnant women, or very small children.
- **Stand on the right, walk on the left.** Most metro stations use escalators to enter and exit. Keep your luggage and your friends from blocking the left-hand lane unless you're willing to keep pace with the many residents who use these services daily.
- **Reservations are a way of life.** Sitting down for afternoon coffee? Make a reservation. Dinner at a popular restaurant? Make a reservation. Table at a pub or cocktail bar? You guessed it. There may be space for walk-ins, but both meals and nightlife are usually planned in advance.
- **Order like a local.** You'll likely be asked what you'd like to drink within seconds of sitting down—feel free to ask for more time, or walk in with an idea in mind. Beers come in large (0.5-liter) or small (0.3-liter) sizes, and wine is often ordered by deciliters (0.1 for a small glass, 0.2 for an average glass), so be prepared for these follow-up questions. Substituting ingredients or requesting things on the side is not common, but is more tolerated at vegetarian or vegan restaurants.
- **Learn the meaning of monuments.** Knowing that one Charles Bridge plaque is actually a tribute to a martyred saint, that the John Lennon Wall began with messages of peace and freedom (not just random graffiti), and that love locks are removed monthly to maintain the structural integrity of centuries-old bridges will change the way you interact with those sights.
- **Practice a few formal phrases.** Make an effort to use *"dobrý den"* (Good day) instead of *"ahoj"* (hi!), or *"Moc děkuji"* (thank you very much) instead of *"Díky"* (thanks!), with anyone who isn't family or a very close friend. Even if you don't say them perfectly, the effort is a sign of respect for a culture that values the difference between formality and informality.
- **Smiles are rare and genuine.** Don't be put off by straight-faced pedestrians or matter-of-fact shopkeepers. This isn't usually a sign or rudeness or dislike, but simply the reflection of a culture that takes a more measured approach to expressing emotions.

- Exit the wine cellar and take some photos of the grounds until it's time for your reserved tour of the **Baroque Palace Theater,** usually at 3pm in English.
- Pick up any last-minute souvenirs at the gift shop before heading back to the bus stop around 5pm (confirm times at www.idsjmk.cz) and catch **bus 585** back to Mikulov.
- Drop off any souvenirs and wine bottles at your hotel and relax as needed. Then walk to **Restaurace Marcela Ihnačáka** for dinner and drinks before turning in for the night.

>DAY 6: MIKULOV TO PRAGUE

Note that the Jewish Cemetery is closed from Nov-March and on Mondays in April and October.

- Have breakfast at your hotel before checking out and storing your luggage. Then walk up to the **Jewish Cemetery** and spend some time appreciating the ornate headstones and expansive grounds of this site, especially in comparison to Prague's tragically crowded Old Jewish Cemetery.
- Continue uphill to take in the unobstructed city views from the **Goat Tower,** a former military lookout.
- Have a farewell lunch at **Starý Špitál,** then pick up your luggage from the hotel and walk or taxi to the train station for a roughly four-hour ride back to Prague.

Valtice Château courtyard

BEFORE YOU GO

WHEN TO GO

Bohemian Paradise and **the Mikulov-Lednice-Valtice area** are very much seasonal destinations, best visited in good weather from April to October. Summers in **Český Krumlov** have been bordering on overtourism in recent years, but the town is still a peaceful destination in spring, winter, and autumn.

HIGH SEASON (JUNE-AUG. AND DEC.)

Summers can be sweltering (sometimes rising above 35°C/95°F), with strings of humid days broken up by summer storms complete with thunder and lightning. Aim for June if possible, when the crowds are a little lighter and performing arts companies haven't gone on their summer vacations. Skip July and August if you want to avoid the crowds, especially in Prague, or take these months to unwind with a rafting trip along the Vltava River or a weekend in quieter Moravian towns. December, when the Christmas markets set up shop, is a busy time in Prague, but other Czech cities also offer plenty of holiday magic and markets.

SHOULDER SEASON (APRIL-MAY AND SEPT.-NOV.)

Spring and fall are my absolute favorite seasons in the Czech

rafting on the Vltava River in Český Krumlov

WHAT YOU NEED TO KNOW

- **Currency:** Czech Crown (or "koruna" in Czech), abbreviated **CZK** or **kc.**
- **Conversion rate:** at the time of writing, 1 USD=23 CZK, 1 CAD=17.5 CZK, 1 GBP=28 CZK, 1 EUR=17.5 CZK, 1 AUD=15.75 CZK, 1 NZD=15 CZK, and 1 ZAR=1.57 CZK. Alternately, 20 CZK=roughly 0.85 USD; 1.13 CAD; 0.69 GBP; 0.77 EUR; 1.26 AUD; 1.35 NZD; and 12.96 ZAR.
- **Entry Requirements:** Travelers from the United States, Canada, Australia, New Zealand, or other EU countries do not need a visa to enter the Czech Republic for less than 90 days. To enter Europe, all you need is a passport that's valid at least three months after your departure from the EU. A visa is required for travelers from South Africa. At the time of writing, the UK was still a member of the EU.
- **Emergency number:** 112
- **Time Zone:** GMT+1 (Central European Time) or GMT+2 (Central European Summer Time)
- **Electrical system:** 220-240 V

Republic. You get to escape the summer humidity and the layers required to survive winter (but keep an umbrella in your bag). There's also the added bonus of more time and space to appreciate tourist hot spots.

Springtime brings colorful flowers to life in parks and gardens while food, drink, and music festivals start popping up around town. Sunshine can often stick around through September, followed by a palette of autumn colors decorating the trees. Late summer and autumn months also bring wine festivals to Prague parks and Moravian vineyards. National pride is high in autumn, with the anniversary of Czechoslovak Independence on October 28 and celebrations of Freedom and Democracy on Nov 17. Food fans will love St. Martin's Day (Nov 11), known for a traditional feast of roast goose, red cabbage, and dumplings served with a special wine that is opened at 11:11am on the 11th day of the 11th month.

LOW SEASON (JAN.-MAR.)

Winters in Prague can be mild, but can also dip down to subzero temperatures (as low as -15°C/5°F), with surrounding cities often experiencing more snow than the capital. That said, Czech cities are beautiful with a blanket of snow, and public transportation keeps running. When the temperatures drop, you can escape to a museum,

Christmas Market on the Old Town Square in Prague

pub, or a cozy café with a cast of local characters. Going during the off-season can also be easier on your budget, with lower prices for flights and hotel rooms. I've enjoyed almost every day trip in this book, excluding Bohemian Paradise and Mikulov, in the dead of winter. Some destinations, like Český Krumlov Castle or the Lednice and Valtice châteaux, may have limited hours or fewer open areas, but the tradeoff also includes fewer visitors jostling for space and the chance of photos with snow-covered backdrops.

GETTING THERE

Almost all international arrivals will fly into Prague's **Vaclav Havel Airport** (PRG; Aviatická; +420 220 111 888; www.prg.aero), formerly known as Prague Ruzyně International Airport. There are multiple direct flights from the UK and Europe, and some seasonal direct service from US east-coast cities in the summer. There are no direct flights from Australia, New Zealand, or South Africa.

You will arrive and depart from Terminal 1 for countries outside the Schengen area (e.g., North America, the UK, Asia, Africa, and the Middle East). Terminal 2 serves flights from within Europe's Schengen countries. Note that you will depart from Terminal 2 if your flight path includes changing planes in a Schengen airport, like Frankfurt or Amsterdam, before continuing to your final destination. Prague's airport is small and reasonably easy to navigate, and the public Wi-Fi is hit-or-miss.

GETTING AROUND

IN PRAGUE

Prague's city center is incredibly walkable (if you have comfortable shoes), and public transport easily connects almost every neighborhood. The most popular sights are clustered in a few areas—the condensed Old Town, the ring of New Town wrapping around it, and the Malá Strana neighborhood sitting below the Prague Castle. Most surrounding neighborhoods, such as Vinohrady, Žižkov, Letná, or Karlín, are just one or two metro or tram stops outside the city center, making them easy to access or use as your home base.

tram in front of St. Nicholas Church in Malá Strana

BUDGETING

- **Beer:** 35-65 CZK domestic, 50-100 CZK microbrews and imported
- **Glass of wine:** 35-150 CZK
- **Cocktail:** 100-300 CZK
- **Soft drink:** 45-75 CZK
- **Latte or cappuccino:** 50-85 CZK
- **Lunch or dinner:** 150-500 CZK per person
- **Hostel dorm bed:** 150-750 CZK per night
- **Hotel room:** 1,500-10,000 CZK per night
- **Car rental:** 900-5,000 CZK per day
- **Gasoline:** 30-35 CZK per liter, 100-150 CZK per gallon
- **Parking:** 25-100 CZK per hour, 200-1,000 CZK per day
- **Public Transport Pass:** 110 CZK per day

One possible pitfall is that Prague's streets are not arranged in a grid, so make sure to carry a printed map (or download an offline one) to avoid getting turned around, especially in Old Town. Also note that a small group of dishonest taxi drivers have a history of overcharging tourists in Prague. Avoid hailing a cab on the streets, especially near popular tourist sights. If you need a taxi, ask your hotel or restaurant to order for you and to give you an estimate of the price. Rideshare apps like **Liftago, Uber,** or **Bolt** have become popular alternatives in recent years. Public transport and walking are your best bet overall, with two exceptions: transporting large luggage, or staying somewhere difficult to access on night tram service after midnight.

OUTSIDE PRAGUE

Train and bus service makes it easy and affordable to visit cities across the country without renting a car. The multiple companies offering comfortable train and bus rides, plus the national rail service, are my ideal options to avoid worrying about gas prices, confusing parking rules in different towns, and required highway stickers for various routes.

Most Czech towns are extremely walkable, and tram service is available in university towns like Liberec, Pilsen, Brno, and Olomouc. You won't find many cars in the center of Český Krumlov, Karlovy Vary, or Mikulov, adding to their peaceful appeal. The Czech countryside also has a wide range of cycling paths for more athletic travelers, detailed at www.czechtrails.com.

WHAT TO PACK

No matter the season, layers are the way to go when packing for Central Europe. Winters can be mild or freezing, spring can arrive early or late, and snow is unusual but not impossible in October or April. An extra sweater, plus an **umbrella or rain coat,** might come in handy all year long. Focus on **comfortable footwear** that won't slip or twist any ankles on cobblestone streets, particularly sandals in summer rain storms.

Day-to-day fashion is fairly casual—sports jerseys, baseball caps, and large company logos will quickly identify you as an outsider—and one semi-formal outfit is a must if you're interested in classical music or the performing arts. Otherwise, **smart-casual attire** and **plenty of layers** works for almost every activity. Add a **swimsuit,** even in winter, if you're traveling to a spa town. Large scarves also come in handy and can double as picnic blankets in Prague's many parks. A **smaller bag or backpack** might be useful for consolidating and storing luggage for day trips.

If you're coming from the UK or the States, make sure you pack an **adapter** so you can use your electronics in Continental Europe. Plugs in Central Europe use two round prongs with a voltage of 220V. You will definitely want a camera or at least a good quality phone to snap pics, and don't forget your charger or battery pack for long days of sightseeing. **Earbuds or headphones** can be useful for accessing museum audio guides that you can download onto your phone, or to enjoy entertainment on longer bus or train rides.

Bring a supply of any **cosmetics or toiletries** that you regularly depend on. Pharmacies are unlikely to stock some overseas brands, such as Ibuprofen or Nyquil, or certain allergy medications. Non-applicator tampons are more prevalent in small corner stores, but you'll find wider selections in supermarkets. Bug spray can also be helpful in the summer, as A/C is scarce and windows rarely have screens. Many hotels provide shampoo and body wash, sometimes in 2-in-1 bottles, but conditioner is a rare luxury even in high-end places. Don't forget a **refillable water bottle** to stay hydrated with Prague's clean, safe tap water.

KEY RESERVATIONS

IN PRAGUE

Many of Prague's sights require buying tickets or arranging tours onsite. Two that you can book online in advance are a guided tour of the **Prague Castle** (via email at info@hrad.cz) and a guided tour of the **Strahov Library** (via email at erika@strahovskyklaster.cz). The Prague Castle availability is usually open to accommodate requests, but the Strahov Library is limited to a strict number of visitors per year, so send your request or questions as soon as (or before) you book your dates if you want to see the building's ornately painted ceilings up close.

OUTSIDE PRAGUE

A tour of **Villa Tugendhat,** Brno's UNESCO-protected jewel of modern architecture, requires at least six months of advance notice to experience.

Book your tickets to see the interiors of the **Lednice and Valtice Châteaux** or tours of the **Český Krumlov Castle** at least a month in advance to ensure the availability of English tours.

SIGHTSEEING PASSES

IN PRAGUE

A **Prague Card** (www.praguecard.com) offers free admission or discounts on many of the city's attractions, including certain areas of the Prague Castle, Petřín Tower, the Jewish Museum, the Charles Bridge Towers, St. Nicholas's Town Belfry, and the Mucha Museum. Cards can be purchased for two days (1,550 CZK), three days (about 1,810 CZK), or four days (about 2,080 CZK). The card also works as a valid ticket for all public transport in Prague (e.g., buses, trams, and the metro), but must be presented along with an ID if inspected. The card can be purchased in person, or ordered online and collected at Tourist Information Centers at the Prague Airport (8am-8pm) or at the two centers in their Old Town locations (9am-7pm).

The Prague card is definitely useful, but not an essential tool for exploring the city. It provides many valuable discounts, but usually doesn't offer priority entry or exclusive access. A basic three-day public transport pass costs 310 CZK, and the average entrance to Prague's sights ranges from free to around 250 CZK. However, if you combine the Jewish Museum with access to multiple tower views where you only spend half an hour, plus a classical music concert at Lobkowicz Palace, these admissions can add up. Getting value for your purchase depends on how many of the included sights are on your preferred itinerary, so peruse the list before purchasing.

Charles Bridge from the Kampa waterfront

DAILY REMINDERS

farmers market on Náplavka in Prague

IN PRAGUE

The importance of work-life balance in Czech culture means that many cafés, restaurants, and independent shops have limited hours on weekends, especially **Sundays** and sometimes **Mondays.** There are still plenty of restaurants focused on an international clientele where you can find a good meal. Cafés also open later in the day as opposed to early mornings, so save your coffee breaks for the afternoons.

SATURDAY

- The sights of the **Jewish quarter are** closed.
- **New Jewish Cemetery** and **Olšany Cemetery** are closed.
- A weekly farmers market is held at **Náplavka.**

SUNDAY

- **St. Vitus Cathedral** has limited hours (noon-4pm).
- **Church of Our Lady Before Týn** has limited hours (10am-noon).
- **St. Nicholas Church** has limited hours (noon-4pm).
- Many **shops** have limited hours.

One ticket that does offer faster entrance to a popular sight is the mobile ticket to the **Old Town Hall and Astronomical Clock Tower** (prague.mobiletickets.cz, 210 CZK). This provides the combined benefit of discounted admission and allowing visitors to skip the line of tourists purchasing tickets on-site. A **Town Hall Pass** (350 CZK) provides access to the Old Town Hall (2x) and New Town Hall (1x) over a period of three days, and includes skipping the lines. The Town Hall Pass is available for purchase in person at both locations.

MONDAY
The following sights are closed:

- **New Town Hall**
- **National Museum**
- **Church of Our Lady Before Týn**
- **Convent of St. Agnes of Bohemia**
- **National Monument to the Heroes of the Heydrich Terror**
- **National Gallery—Trade Fair Palace**
- **Rudolfinum Gallery**

TUESDAY

- **DOX Center for Contemporary Art** is closed.

WEDNESDAY

- **Convent of St. Agnes** has extended hours (10am-8pm)
- **National Gallery—Trade Fair Palace** has extended hours (10am-8pm).

THURSDAY

- **Rudolfinum Gallery** has extended hours (10am-8pm).
- **DOX Center for Contemporary Art** has extended hours (10am-9pm).

FRIDAY

- **Olšany Cemetery** has limited hours (10am-2pm).
- Prague's **New Jewish Cemetery** has limited hours (9am-2pm).

BEYOND PRAGUE
A number of attractions are closed on **Mondays,** including Brno's **10-Z Bunker, Ossuary at St. James,** and **Villa Tugendhat. Mikulov, Lednice,** and **Valtice Châteaux** are also closed Mondays (except in July and August). Český Krumlov's **Tour Route II** and **Baroque Theater Tour** are unavailable on Mondays.

Brno's **Villa Tugendhat** is also closed Tuesdays in January and February.

Student travelers should invest in an **ISIC card** (www.isic.org) to take advantage of any available discounts. Some sights and museums offer discounts to international students, while public transport requires valid ID from a Czech university to qualify for student rates. Most places will not accept a student ID card from a college or university abroad as proof of student status.

OUTSIDE PRAGUE

Passes for additional destinations, including **Český Krumlov, Brno,** and **Olomouc,** are covered in the destination chapters.

PRAGUE

Since the turn of the century, Prague has moved from an undiscovered darling to a popular European destination. The city's architectural landscape, from the church spires of Old Town to repurposed industrial spaces in Holešovice, provides a visual timeline of art history, with Gothic towers, Cubist lampposts, and Communist functionalism all punctuating the pastel buildings and cobblestoned streets. These postcard-worthy structures are a perfect backdrop for dreamy walks or watching the sunset from a vantage point above it all.

HIGHLIGHTS

✪ **OLD TOWN SQUARE:** Church towers to your right, a 15th-century astronomical clock to your left, and a Baroque church across the square. Old Town Square (Staroměstské náměstí) also plays host to holiday markets at Easter and Christmas (page 57).

✪ **JEWISH QUARTER (JOSEFOV):** One of the most intact Jewish quarters in Central Europe includes a historic cemetery, a powerful Holocaust memorial, and the oldest active synagogue in Europe (page 63).

✪ **WENCESLAS SQUARE:** The center of political and commercial life in Prague, this square has plenty of stories to tell (page 69).

✪ **DANCING HOUSE:** A whimsically curved building from the early 1990s, inspired by Fred Astaire and Ginger Rogers, symbolizes a blend of East meets West and old and new ideas (page 75).

✪ **CHARLES BRIDGE:** Take a walk along more than 650 years of history while enjoying sweeping city views from the towers, plus street musicians and souvenir stands (page 76).

✪ **JOHN LENNON WALL:** Admire this living, breathing graffiti wall, which has been consistently covered with Beatles lyrics, John Lennon portraits, and messages of peace and protest since the 1980s (as of 2019, tourists are no longer allowed to add to it themselves) (page 77).

✪ **PRAGUE CASTLE:** The world's largest castle complex includes the Gothic glory of St. Vitus Cathedral, expansive manicured gardens, and the royal elegance of the Lubkowicz Palace (page 80).

✪ **PETŘÍN LOOKOUT TOWER:** Prague's mini-Eiffel Tower may not be taller, but its perch on top of Petřín Hill technically makes it higher than its French inspiration (page 90).

✪ **VYŠEHRAD COMPLEX:** Prague's "other castle" offers a more peaceful vibe than the Prague Castle. The cemetery provides the resting place of some local legends, while today's locals enjoy the beer garden in the summer (page 99).

✪ **PRAGUE'S BEER GARDENS:** Czechs famously drink more *pivo* (beer) per capita than any other nation in the world. A summer afternoon in one of Prague's beer gardens will show you why (page 107).

✪ **PRAGUE'S NATIONAL THEATER:** This golden beauty, home to ballet, opera, and theater performances, was partially crowd-funded by Czech citizens in the 1800s (page 115).

Prague

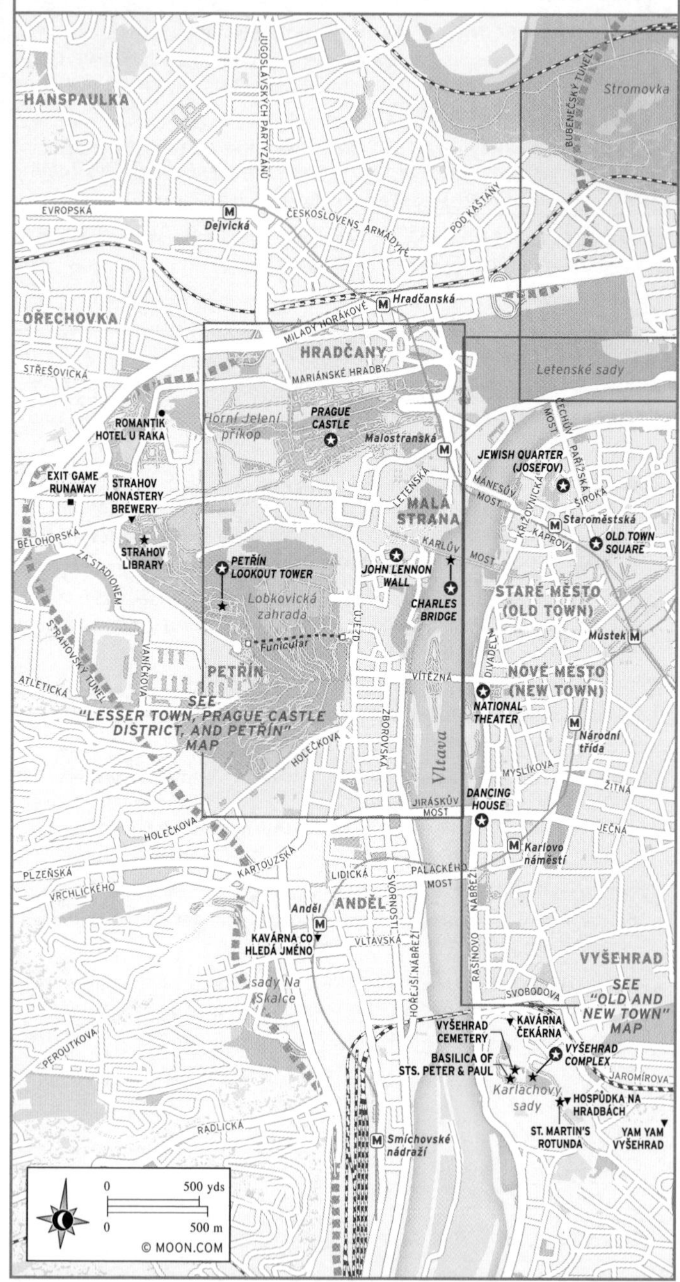
HANSPAULKA
JUGOSLÁVSKÝCH PARTYZÁNŮ
Stromovka
BUBENEČSKÝ TUNEL
EVROPSKÁ
Dejvická
ČESKOSLOVENS ARMÁDY
POD KAŠTANY
Hradčanská
MILADY HORÁKOVÉ
OŘECHOVKA
HRADČANY
MARIÁNSKÉ HRADBY
STŘEŠOVICKÁ
Letenské sady
ROMANTIK HOTEL U RAKA
Horní Jelení příkop
PRAGUE CASTLE
Malostranská
ČECHŮV MOST
PAŘÍŽSKÁ
EXIT GAME RUNAWAY
STRAHOV MONASTERY BREWERY
JEWISH QUARTER (JOSEFOV)
MÁNESŮV MOST
KŘIŽOVNICKÁ
ŠIROKÁ
LETENSKÁ
MALÁ STRANA
Staroměstská
KAPROVA
OLD TOWN SQUARE
BĚLOHORSKÁ
STRAHOV LIBRARY
KARLŮV MOST
ZA STADIONEM
PETŘÍN LOOKOUT TOWER
JOHN LENNON WALL
Lobkovická zahrada
CHARLES BRIDGE
STARÉ MĚSTO (OLD TOWN)
STRAHOVSKÝ TUNEL
Funicular
ÚJEZD
Můstek
DIVADELNÍ
PETŘÍN
VÍTĚZNÁ
NOVÉ MĚSTO (NEW TOWN)
VANÍČKOVA
ATLETICKÁ
NATIONAL THEATER
SEE "LESSER TOWN, PRAGUE CASTLE DISTRICT, AND PETŘÍN" MAP
ZBOROVSKÁ
Národní třída
HOLEČKOVA
Vltava
MYSLÍKOVA
ŽITNÁ
DANCING HOUSE
JIRÁSKŮV MOST
JEČNÁ
HOLEČKOVA
Karlovo náměstí
KARTOUZSKÁ
PLZEŇSKÁ
LIDICKÁ
PALACKÉHO MOST
VRCHLICKÉHO
SVORNOSTI
NÁBŘEŽÍ
Anděl
ANDĚL
KAVÁRNA CO HLEDÁ JMÉNO
VLTAVSKÁ
RAŠÍNOVO
HOŘEJŠÍ NÁBŘEŽÍ
VYŠEHRAD
sady Na Skalce
SVOBODOVA
SEE "OLD AND NEW TOWN" MAP
KAVÁRNA ČEKÁRNA
VYŠEHRAD CEMETERY
PEROUTKOVA
VYŠEHRAD COMPLEX
BASILICA OF STS. PETER & PAUL
JAROMÍROVA
Karlachovy sady
HOSPŮDKA NA HRADBÁCH
RADLICKÁ
ST. MARTIN'S ROTUNDA
YAM YAM VYŠEHRAD
Smíchovské nádraží
0
500 yds
0
500 m
© MOON.COM

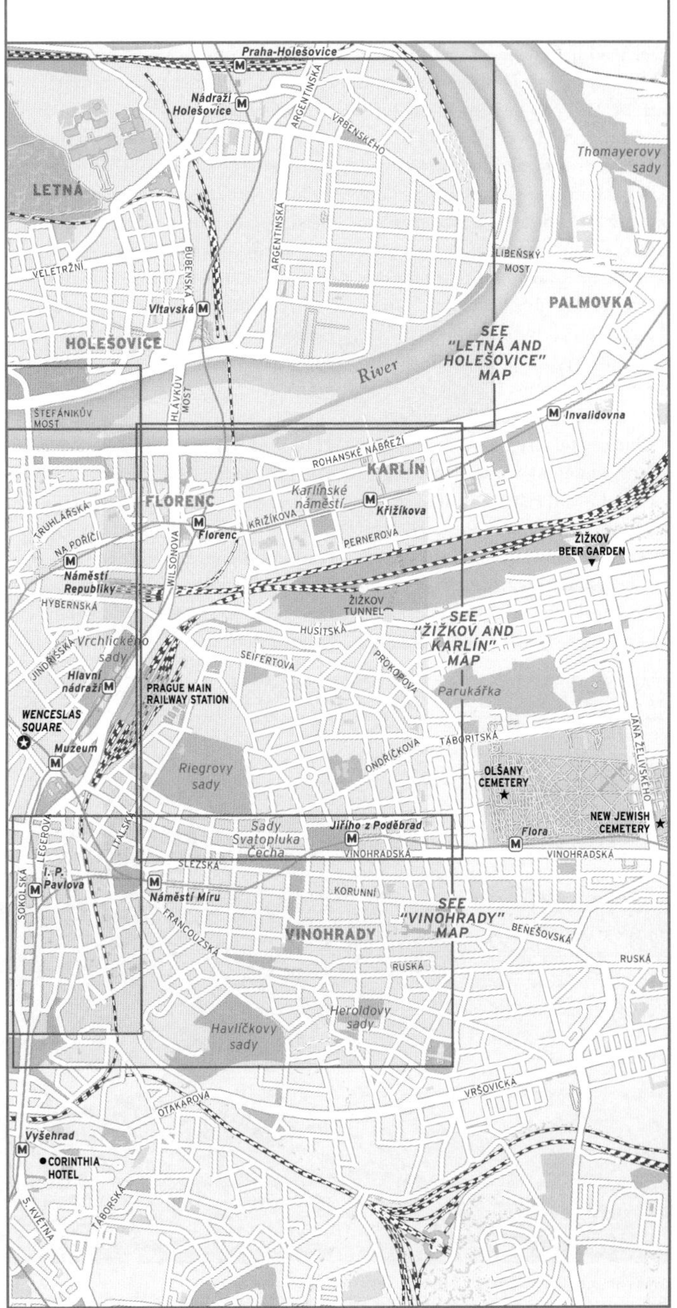
Praha-Holešovice
Nádraží Holešovice
ARGENTINSKÁ
VRBENSKÉHO
Thomayerovy sady
LETNÁ
BUBENSKÁ
ARGENTINSKÁ
VELETRŽNÍ
LIBEŇSKÝ MOST
PALMOVKA
Vltavská
HOLEŠOVICE
SEE "LETNÁ AND HOLEŠOVICE" MAP
River
ŠTEFÁNIKŮV MOST
HLÁVKŮV MOST
Invalidovna
ROHANSKÉ NÁBŘEŽÍ
KARLÍN
Karlínské náměstí
Křižíkova
FLORENC
TRUHLÁŘSKÁ
Florenc
KŘIŽÍKOVA
PERNEROVA
NA POŘÍČÍ
Náměstí Republiky
WILSONOVA
ŽIŽKOV BEER GARDEN
HYBERNSKÁ
ŽIŽKOV TUNNEL
HUSITSKÁ
SEE "ŽIŽKOV AND KARLÍN" MAP
JINDŘIŠSKÁ
Vrchlického sady
SEIFERTOVA
PROKOPOVA
Hlavní nádraží
PRAGUE MAIN RAILWAY STATION
Parukářka
WENCESLAS SQUARE
JANA ŽELIVSKÉHO
Muzeum
TÁBORITSKÁ
ONDŘÍČKOVA
Riegrovy sady
OLŠANY CEMETERY
LEGEROVA
ITALSKÁ
Sady Svatopluka Čecha
Jiřího z Poděbrad
NEW JEWISH CEMETERY
Flora
VINOHRADSKÁ
SLEZSKÁ
I. P. Pavlova
SOKOLSKÁ
Náměstí Míru
KORUNNÍ
FRANCOUZSKÁ
VINOHRADY
SEE "VINOHRADY" MAP
BENEŠOVSKÁ
RUSKÁ
Heroldovy sady
Havlíčkovy sady
VRŠOVICKÁ
OTAKAROVA
Vyšehrad
CORINTHIA HOTEL
TÁBORSKÁ
5. KVĚTNA

Along with Prague's often-described fairy-tale atmosphere, Czech culture includes an affinity for whimsy and ideals of freedom and beauty. This can be seen in the John Lennon graffiti wall, David Černý's often controversial public art pieces, or adults unironically wearing hoodies with animal ears—although, to be fair, the dark humor and cautiously pessimistic local character resembles a Brothers Grimm story more closely than a lighthearted cartoon. Replace ". . . they all lived happily ever after" with the national motto of "truth prevails," and you'll start to get the picture.

The capital city is still defining its rapidly changing identity, maintaining an old-world charm while embracing 21st-century innovation. Historic exteriors often hold modern design inside restaurants, coffee shops, and office buildings. An entrepreneurial spirit has led to a wave of small businesses trying new concepts, like computer-focused museums or cafés centered around cats or cryptocurrency, all within steps of centuries-old structures.

This multi-dimensional culture can please an entire spectrum of interests: architecture, fine arts and culture, culinary curiosities, niche museums, and rowdy or sophisticated nightlife options. There is a laid-back, live-and-let-live attitude, and a strong sense of enjoying your free time with as much enthusiasm as you spend striving for professional success.

HISTORY

The Prague fairy tale begins around the year 870, when the Přemyslid dynasty (Prague's earliest line of ruling families) founded the Prague Castle. This remained the seat of power until the 11th century, when Vratislav II, King of Bohemia, chose to rule from

swans on the Vltava River add to the fairy-tale atmosphere

Vyšehrad instead. These two hillside fortified complexes on opposite sides of the Vltava River helped to ensure the safety and prominence of Prague's early aristocracy.

Wenceslas I (known as Vaclav in Czech), now the patron saint of the Czech Republic and inspiration for the Christmas carol "Good King Wenceslas," ruled as the Duke of Bohemia from 922-935. He was known for being a devout Christian in an era when paganism was still quite popular. Wenceslas died a martyr's death on September 28, 935, killed by his own brother, Boleslav the Cruel. You can pay your respects to the good king at his chapel inside St. Vitus Cathedral, or at the enormous statue of the saint on horseback at the top of Wenceslas Square.

Another hero of Czech history arrives centuries later. After the Přemyslid dynasty failed to produce an heir in the early 1300s, the title was passed to John of Luxembourg and then to his son Charles IV, who ruled over Prague's Golden Age during the 14th century. Charles (Karel in Czech) was named both King of Bohemia and Holy Roman Emperor, giving his seat in Prague even more importance. Charles's legacy includes the establishment of the New Town and the founding of Charles University in 1348, plus the construction of the Charles Bridge in 1357.

The early 14th century was a time of religious conflict led by Jan Hus, the religious leader behind the Hussite movement. Hus stood up to the Catholic Church by giving sermons on reformation directly to the people in their local language. This didn't go over well and he was burned at the stake in 1415. A statue of Jan Hus and his followers now dominates the center of Old Town Square, and July 6 is a public holiday in his honor.

view from the Charles Bridge Tower

Defenestration (the act of throwing authority figures out of high windows) is notorious in Prague for starting wars. The First Defenestration of 1419 was carried out by a group of Hus's followers who stormed the New Town Hall and demanded the release of prisoners. When their demands were refused, they took it out on the officials in the tower that now stands on Charles Square (Karlovo náměstí). This act began the Hussite Wars that lasted until 1434.

The Habsburg dynasty took over in 1526, moving the seat of power to Vienna and solidifying Prague's connection with the surrounding regions of Austria and Hungary for the next few centuries. Prague enjoyed a brief resurgence in the late 16th century.

The Second Defenestration took place in 1618 at the Prague Castle, and is marked with a plaque both inside and outside of the tower. Tossing two officials out this window was a Protestant response to Emperor Ferdinand II attempting to impose Catholicism as the law of the land.

This act led to the Thirty Years' War that raged across Europe from 1618-1648.

The 18th and 19th centuries brought a movement of increased pride in the local language and culture known as the Czech National Revival. This led to the foundation of the National Museum (1818), the National Theater (1868), and the eventual break from the Austro-Hungarian Empire to become the independent state of Czechoslovakia on October 28, 1918. The First Republic era (1918-1938) under President Tomas G. Masaryk saw the rise of café culture, preserved today in Café Louvre and Kavarna Slavia.

The 20th century then turned to the horrors of World War II (1939-1945), followed by decades of isolation from the outside world under Communist rule from 1945-1989. There was a brief loosening of restrictions on things such as the press, travel, and freedom of speech in 1968, called the Prague Spring, but this was met with a brutal Soviet invasion and crackdown later that year. A Soviet presence remained in Prague until 1989. You can find deeper insights into these events at sights such as the Jewish Museum, the Museum of Communism, and the Town Belfry by St. Nicholas Church.

Prague's modern life began in 1989, when the Velvet Revolution marked the end of Soviet occupation and the re-establishment of an independent Czechoslovakia. This was followed by the Velvet Divorce just a few short years later in 1993, when the Czech Republic and Slovakia peacefully divided into two countries. The word "Velvet" refers to the peaceful nature of these dissolutions, and acknowledges the affinity of Czech president Václav Havel for the band the Velvet Underground.

Orientation and Planning

ORIENTATION

The historic center of Prague is packed with history and interesting sights, but it can also be packed with people vying for the best photographs. For a deeper sense of the city, split your time between visiting monuments and getting to know the surrounding neighborhoods of Holešovice, Letná, Karlín, Vinohrady, Vršovice, or Žižkov.

OLD TOWN (STARÉ MĚSTO)

The **cobblestoned streets** and **century-spanning architecture** of this neighborhood inspired the UNESCO World Heritage Center to crown the entire Historic Center of Prague a protected site in 1992. This twisted maze of streets around **Old Town Square** can get a bit crowded. Early mornings and off-seasons are a great time to enjoy this area with a little more breathing room. The Jewish quarter known as **Josefov** sits in the northwest corner of Old Town, surrounded by the curve of the Vltava River.

NEW TOWN (NOVÉ MĚSTO)

The name New Town applies to a large semi-circle that wraps from one edge of the Vltava River, around the Old

view from the Old Town Hall Tower

Town, to the other side of the river bend. Charles IV founded this neighborhood along with Charles University in 1348 (not exactly "new" by today's standards) in order to expand the size and influence of the city toward his grand dreams. Walking from the **Municipal House and Powder Tower** on one edge to the **National Theater** and **Dancing House** on the other could take half an hour (without stopping to sightsee). Three microneighborhoods are centered around New Town's main squares: **Náměstí Republiky, Václavské náměstí,** and **Karlovo náměstí.**

Prague skyline from the Powder Tower

LESSER TOWN (MALÁ STRANA)

Malá Strana, the Czech name for the neighborhood sprawled around the base of the Prague Castle, loosely translates to "Lesser Town" or "Little Quarter," but it deserves far more credit than this nickname implies. Long before joining Hradčany, Old Town, and New Town to form a unified Prague in 1784, this eighth-century market area was **Prague's oldest settlement.** Situated between two of the city's most popular tourist attractions (**Charles Bridge** and the Prague Castle), these cobblestoned streets were an essential part of the Royal Route during the processions of newly ordained kings. These days, the area's **historic charm** is tempered with a fairly heavy presence of touristy souvenir shops and camera-wielding tourists. However, the history and beauty surrounding these cobblestoned streets are worth taking a few side steps around the crowds to discover semi-hidden sights, such as the Wallenstein Gardens and John Lennon Wall. As you head south along the base of Petřín Park, historic Malá Strana blends into the more modern dining district of Anděl.

PRAGUE CASTLE DISTRICT (HRADČANY)

The hillside castle district of Hradčany, across the Vltava River from Old Town and above Malá Strana, is dominated by the Prague Castle grounds and surrounding gardens, with a few luxury hotels and cafés dotting the residential area behind it. Beware that a deceptively easy walk plotted on a map may actually take double the time you anticipate; you may have to climb stairs or find one of a few hard-to-spot entrances among the fortified castle walls. This area is more of a destination than a place to get lost among the streets, so choose your entry point, note your tram stops, and enjoy the view from the geographical vantage point that drew the royal residence in the first place.

PETŘÍN

The massive green hillside on the western side of the Vltava River separates the historic castle district of Hradčany to the north from the bustling cosmopolitan life around the Anděl neighborhood in the sprawling southern district of Smichov. Largely dominated by Petřín Park, this quiet side of Prague is an ideal place for an outdoor picnic, a romantic (if a bit strenuous) walk through the park, or just a chance to sprawl out on the grass and admire the city skyline.

VINOHRADY

This popular home for international residents is filled with restaurants that reflect that diversity, and bars that cater to the wide-ranging clientele. The surrounding parks such as Havlíčkovy sady and Riegrovy Sady often host food and wine festivals during warmer months, and the Christmas market at Náměstí Miru is a local favorite. Just southeast of Wenceslas Square, Karlovo náměstí, and the edges of New Town, these are easy baby steps off the traditional tourist path. The southeastern edge of Vinohrady blends into neighboring Vršovice, best known for the nightlife destination of Krymská Street.

ŽIŽKOV

This formerly working-class neighborhood, stretching from Prague's main train station (Hlavní Nádraží) in New Town along the northern edge of Vinohrady, may be rapidly changing, but it hasn't completely lost its gritty, take-it-or-leave-it spirit. Case in point: you shouldn't necessarily expect an English menu or a smiling server in every establishment. You can pinpoint Žižkov from almost anywhere in Prague thanks to the rocket-shaped TV Tower dominating the city skyline. The pub-heavy neighborhood was named for Hussite hero Jan Žižka, whose statue sits atop neighboring Vítkov Hill.

KARLÍN

After massive flooding in 2002, Karlín experienced an extensive revitalization effort. Today this sophisticated neighborhood is better known for its culinary scene, wine bars, and prime location for house-hunting young families. The artsy vibe is less dance party and more conversations over Cabernet, with recently opened **repurposed spaces** such as **Přístav 18600** and **Kasarna Karlín** adding more life to the changing landscape. Karlín stretches east from the edge of New Town and Florenc bus station along the banks of the Vltava River.

LETNÁ AND HOLEŠOVICE

Letná, located across the river to the north of Old Town and west of Hradčany, is best known for the massive **Letná Park** that lines its southern edge. The **Letná beer garden** inside the park is a major summertime hot spot, and the surrounding **trendy residential streets** are lined with cafés, international restaurants, and the **National Gallery's Trade Fair Palace.**

There are no ideas too weird for the **industrial** neighborhood of Holešovice to the east of Letná. Theatrical space in a former slaughterhouse? Check. Dance club covered in pipes and gears? Sure. Crypto-anarchist coffee shop that only accepts virtual currencies? Why not? From **street art** to a **contemporary arts center** focused on socially conscious exhibitions, this neighborhood is full of surprises.

VYŠEHRAD

The area around Vyšehrad (meaning "high castle") south of New Town walks a fine line—it's not quite the center of town, but not quite the suburbs—and includes **the Vyšehrad Complex,** a major tourist attraction that doubles as a locally loved destination for relaxation. The beauty and importance of the Vyšehrad Complex rivals the Prague Castle, but draws a fraction of the crowds, and the surrounding streets and restaurants showcase more **local life** than souvenir stands.

PLANNING YOUR TIME

You could do a whirlwind tour of Prague in a fast-paced **two days** by picking and choosing the sights most important to you. A **long weekend** will give you the extra time needed to explore the lesser-known sights and neighborhoods for the less-crowded corners of character and culture. Add a day trip to one of the surrounding towns, such as Kutná Horá or Liberec. **One week** in the Czech Republic is a great way to compare the cosmopolitan life of Prague with a second destination, such as the spa town of Karlovy Vary or the wine region surrounding the town of Mikulov.

Summer, Easter, and **Christmas** holidays are peak times, and around Christmas, in particular, you will receive an incredibly festive atmosphere in exchange for longer lines at most major sights. It's best to arrange hotel reservations, tickets to performances, and even restaurant reservations as far in advance as possible for the best selection and rates.

Itinerary Ideas

DAY 1

Before you set out for the day, book a mobile ticket to skip the line for the Old Town Hall Tower views above Prague's Astronomical Clock.

1 Start the day with a healthy açai bowl or hearty breakfast bagel at **Cacao,** a casual café just off Náměstí Republiky.

2 Pause to admire the architectural diversity of the Municipal House, Powder Tower, and Hybernia Theater from the corner of Na Příkopě street along your 10-minute walk to the **Alfons Mucha Museum.** Spend around 90 minutes exploring the swirling style of an Art Nouveau master before browsing the gift shop.

3 Just five minutes further west, Jindřišská Street opens up onto **Wenceslas Square.** Find the cross in bricks in front of the National Museum, stand under the horseback statue of St. Wenceslas, peruse the quotes on benches lining the center, and imagine thousands of citizens shaking their keys in the air in 1989 as then-Czechoslovakia regained its independence.

4 Take a deep breath before a crowded, 10-minute, cobblestoned walk from the base of Wenceslas Square to the postcard views of **Old Town Square.** Using your mobile ticket booked in advance, skip the line to the Old Town Hall Tower and proceed straight to the 360-degree views from above the Astronomical Clock.

5 Walk 10 minutes east along Dlouhá street to **Sisters Bistro** to fuel up on *chlebíčky* (open-faced sandwiches).

6 How tired are your feet? You can either walk 20 minutes across the Vltava River and uphill through the park to **Letná Beer Garden,** or jump on tram 8 or 26 from Dlouhá třída to Letenské náměstí and enjoy an easy 10-minute walk south. Either way, you'll be rewarded with a cold pilsner and panoramic views from one of Prague's most popular warm-weather escapes. After a couple beers, head back to your hotel or hostel to regroup and get dressed for a night at the theater.

7 A yellow Metro line to the Národní třída stop or a tram to the Národní divadlo stop will drop you near the **National Theater,** symbolizing the importance of the arts to Czech culture as part of the National Revival in the early 20th century.

8 Make a reservation for a post-show dinner in the elegant First Republic-style of the early 1900s at **Café Louvre,** just a three-minute walk east of the National Theater. A riverside walk after dinner includes a lit view of the Prague Castle, courtesy of the Rolling Stones.

DAY 2

The Malá Strana neghborhood is home to a few lesser-known sights scattered among the most popular tourist attractions. Before you leave for the day, make reservations for dinner at **U modré kachničky.**

1 Start with coffee and a fluffy Benedict soufflé for breakfast at **Kavárna co hledá jméno,** a local favorite hidden inside a parking lot in the Anděl neighborhood.

2 After brunch, jump on a 15-minute tram from the Anděl tram stop to Malostranská to explore the **Wallenstein Gardens**—keep an eye out for free-roaming peacocks between the fountains, statues, and labyrinth-like hedges.

3 Exit the Wallenstein Gardens near Malostranská and walk along the riverfront, underneath the Charles Bridge, and across Kampa Island for about 10 minutes to find the **John Lennon Wall.** Since 2019, tourists are no longer allowed to add to the wall, but should feel free to hum a Beatles song.

4 Follow Lázeňská street north for two minutes to Mostecká Street. Instead of crossing the Charles Bridge (don't worry, you will later), spend half an hour climbing the **Lesser Town Bridge Tower** for a bird's eye view of the afternoon crowds.

5 Head a few steps back into Malá Strana to grab a coffee or beer and a bite to eat at **Roesel—Beer & Cake,** a friendly local café tucked just off this touristy street.

6 After your light lunch, walk around the corner to Malostranské náměstí and catch tram 22 to the Prague Castle. Jump off at tram stop Královský letohrádek to enter through the Royal Summer Gardens and find **St. Vitus Cathedral.** You'll want to spend at least half an hour admiring both the interior and exterior of this iconic monument.

7 To get a glimpse of aristocratic atmosphere at your own pace, walk five minutes east to **Lobkowicz Palace,** where you can take an audio-guided tour of a 16th-century royal residence. Give yourself 60-90 minutes to peruse the portrait gallery, porcelain collection, classical music artifacts, and an impressive balcony view.

Itinerary Ideas

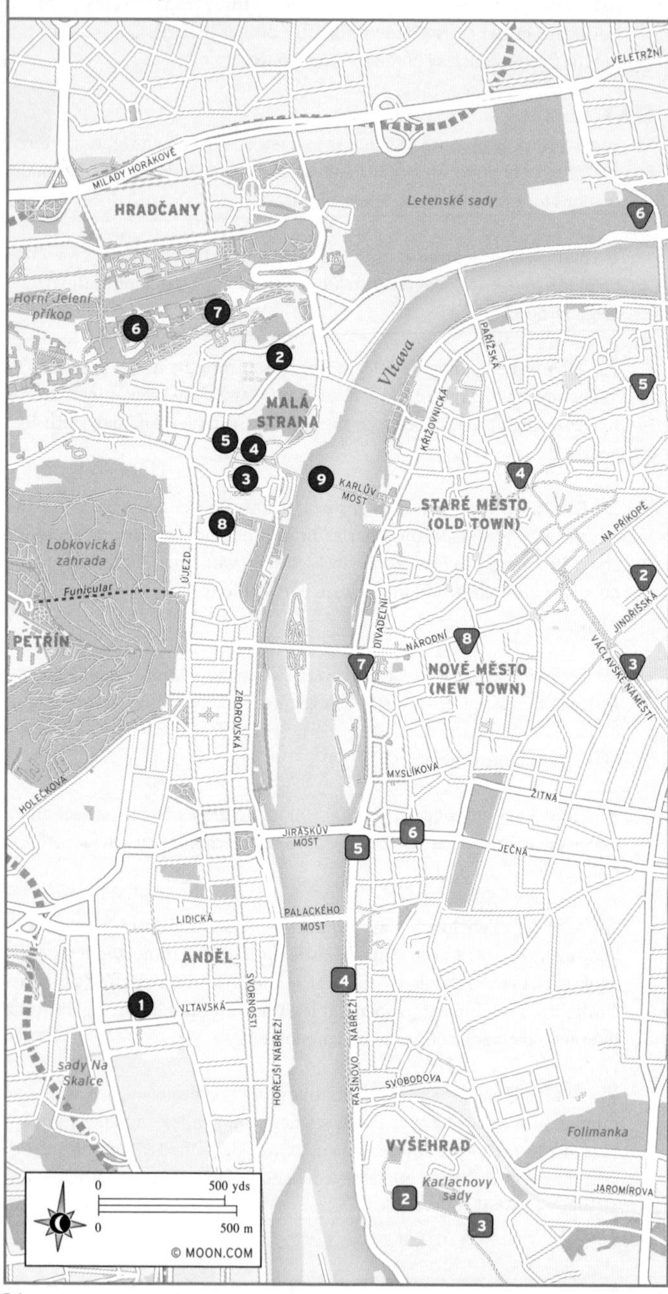

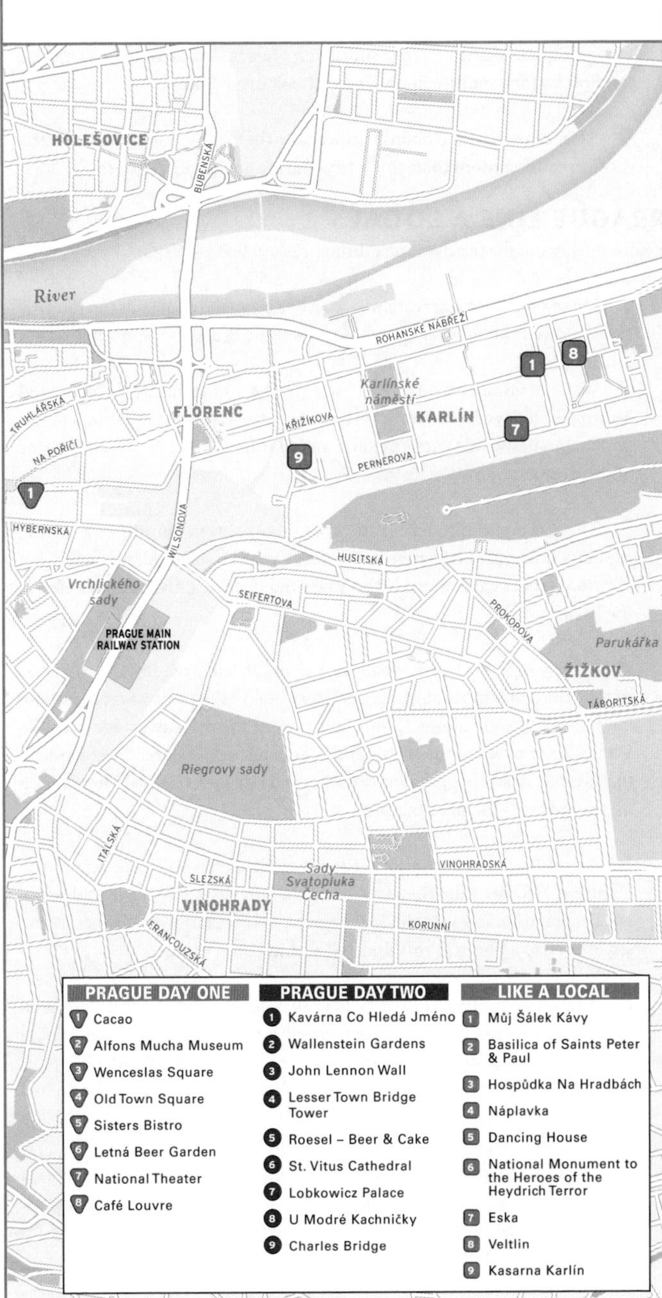
HOLEŠOVICE
BUBENSKÁ
River
ROHANSKÉ NÁBŘEŽÍ
Karlínské náměstí
KARLÍN
FLORENC
TRUHLÁŘSKÁ
NA POŘÍČÍ
KŘIŽÍKOVA
PERNEROVA
HYBERNSKÁ
WILSONOVA
HUSITSKÁ
Vrchlického sady
SEIFERTOVA
PROKOPOVA
PRAGUE MAIN RAILWAY STATION
Parukářka
ŽIŽKOV
TÁBORITSKÁ
Riegrovy sady
ITALSKÁ
VINOHRADSKÁ
SLEZSKÁ
Sady Svatopluka Čecha
VINOHRADY
KORUNNÍ
FRANCOUZSKÁ
PRAGUE DAY ONE
1 Cacao
2 Alfons Mucha Museum
3 Wenceslas Square
4 Old Town Square
5 Sisters Bistro
6 Letná Beer Garden
7 National Theater
8 Café Louvre
PRAGUE DAY TWO
1 Kavárna Co Hledá Jméno
2 Wallenstein Gardens
3 John Lennon Wall
4 Lesser Town Bridge Tower
5 Roesel – Beer & Cake
6 St. Vitus Cathedral
7 Lobkowicz Palace
8 U Modré Kachničky
9 Charles Bridge
LIKE A LOCAL
1 Můj Šálek Kávy
2 Basilica of Saints Peter & Paul
3 Hospůdka Na Hradbách
4 Náplavka
5 Dancing House
6 National Monument to the Heroes of the Heydrich Terror
7 Eska
8 Veltlin
9 Kasarna Karlín

8 Exit the Prague Castle by heading west through the South Gardens, stopping for a few panoramic photos. Follow the stairs downhill and head east on Thunovská street, then south into Malá Strana to arrive at **U modré kachničky** for a multi-course dinner (book in advance).

9 After dinner, take a moonlit walk across the **Charles Bridge** with a little more breathing room than you'll find during any daylight hours.

PRAGUE LIKE A LOCAL

Before setting out for the day, book dinner reservations at **Eska.**

1 Make a weekday reservation or arrive early on the weekends (no reservations allowed) for expertly prepared coffee and brunch at **Můj šálek kávy.**

2 Walk 15 minutes west to Florenc and take a 10-minute ride on the red Metro line to Vyšehrad. Walk through the parks, pay your respects to the famous names inside the cemetery, and admire the Art Nouveau interior of the **Basilica of Saints Peter & Paul.**

3 There is no need to be bashful about day drinking in this beer-loving capital. Grab a cold beverage and a snack at the laid-back **Hospůdka Na Hradbách** beer garden inside the Vyšehrad Complex, five minutes east of the basilica.

4 After your beer break, head west through the park toward the river to find the stairs in front of the cemetery and basilica entrance. Continue downhill and walk about 15 minutes toward the railway bridge over the Vltava River to reach the **Náplavka** boardwalk below street level. Smile at the overfed swans begging for crumbs, and add an extra hour here if you hit the Saturday farmer's market.

5 An additional 15-minute walk along Náplavka will take you to the **Dancing House.** Take the elevator to the top-floor Glass Bar and order any beverage for access to the 360-degree viewing platform. Then cross the street to snap a photo of this unusual architectural wonder.

6 Add a touch of local history to your afternoon at the free **National Monument to the Heroes of the Heydrich Terror,** just a three-minute walk up Resslova Street. You can absorb the story of the World War II heroes, who are the reason for the bullet holes in these church walls, in less than an hour.

7 Walk two minutes to the Karlovo náměstí stop for a 20-minute ride on the yellow Metro line back to Karlín. Exit the metro at Křižíkova and walk five minutes south to **Eska** (book in advance) to enjoy a modern take on Czech cuisine in a minimalist, industrial environment.

8 Prague may be known for beer, but Karlín is home to the Czech wine scene. After dinner, walk five minutes northeast from Eska to sample *vino* from across the former Austro-Hungarian region at **Veltlin.**

9 For more lively entertainment, walk 15 minutes west to the edge of the neighborhood to **Kasarna Karlín.** You'll find an artsy, international crowd enjoying open-air bars, live music, an outdoor summer cinema, and a variety of effortlessly cool events.

Sights

OLD TOWN (STARÉ MĚSTO)

✪ OLD TOWN SQUARE (STAROMĚSTSKÉ NÁMĚSTÍ)

Metro: Staroměstská or Můstek

If you've ever seen a postcard of Prague, there's a good chance it was taken in Old Town Square, a pedestrian square known for its attractive church spires, Gothic towers, and pastel palette. Stunning views and festive holiday markets make this eternally photogenic location worth a visit, especially in the quieter early mornings or late evenings. Stake out some bench space at the base of the Jan Hus monument to admire the architecture on all sides.

Try to avoid patronizing any plush dancing animals or floating carpet

Staroměstské náměstí

Old and New Town

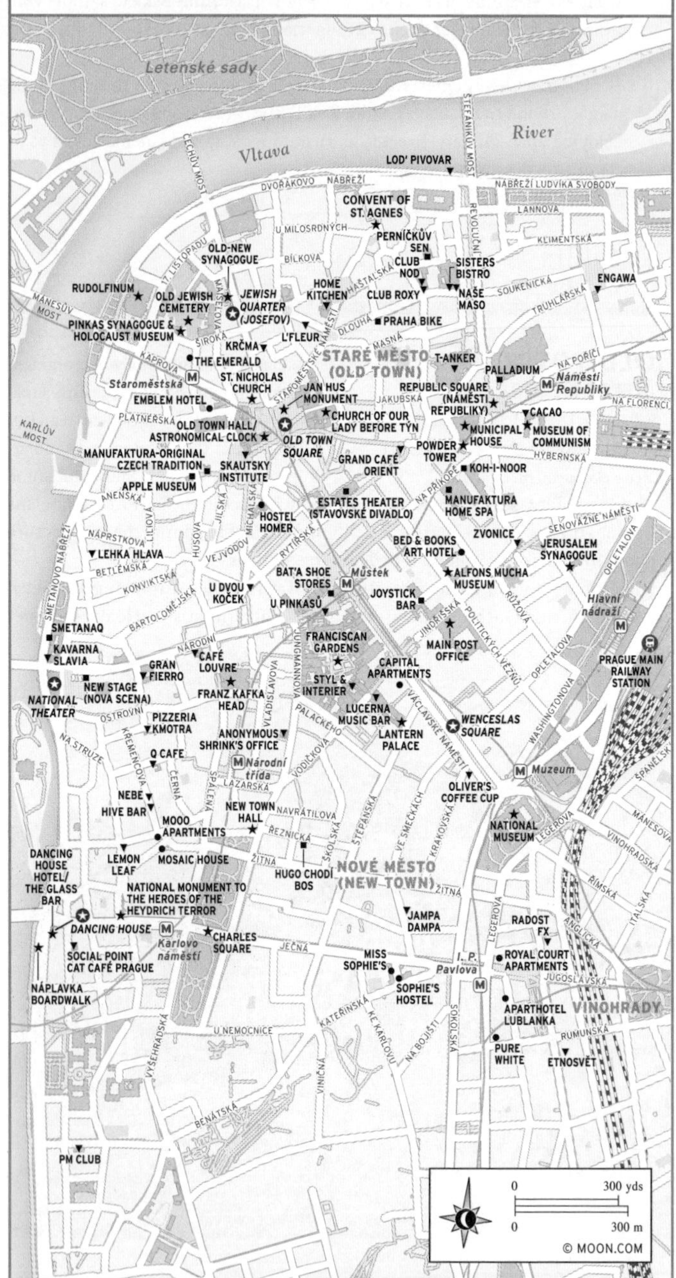

illusionists detracting from the historic significance of the area. Also, it's best to skip the food stands (beware of heaping piles of Prague ham deceptively priced by weight, not portion) and largely overpriced restaurants lining the perimeter.

Tip: For friendly service and a reasonably priced snack in the area, venture left of the Old Town Hall, underneath the etched scenes in the Renaissance façade of the "House at the Minute" (Dum U Minuty), to find the semi-hidden entrance to the **Skautsky Institut.**

OLD TOWN HALL (STAROMĚSTSKÁ RADNICE)

Staroměstské náměstí 1; +420 775 400 052; www.staromestskaradnicepraha.cz/en; 9am-10pm Tues-Sat, 11am-10pm Sun; 250 CZK; metro stops Staroměstská or Můstek

The only remaining pieces of Prague's 14th-century Old Town Hall are the Gothic Tower of the Astronomical Clock and a sliver of burgundy wall across from the Church of Our Lady Before Týn. The remainder of the building was destroyed in the Prague Uprising against German occupation at the end of World War II. A series of white crosses in the bricks around the base mark the execution place of 27 noblemen and followers of Jan Hus. These men led a Protestant revolt in the early 1600s with Prague's Second Defenestration (throwing someone out a window) at the Prague Castle.

Admission to the Old Town Hall includes a bird's eye view from the top of the **clock tower**—accessible via elevator—coupled with access to a few historical interior halls and the Chapel of the Virgin Mary. A pre-purchased electronic ticket (prague.mobiletickets.cz, 210 CZK) allows you to save some money and skip the lines. For true tower fans, a **Town Hall Pass** (350 CZK) provides access to the Old Town Hall (twice) and New Town Hall (once) over a period of three days, and also includes skipping the lines. Two-hour English-language tours (250 CZK) are also available on select scheduled evenings, often on Saturdays.

ASTRONOMICAL CLOCK

Prague's Astronomical Clock (known as "Orloj" in Czech) is more than 600 years old. It's often said that clock master Hanuš was blinded so that he couldn't replicate its beauty for any other city; however, this myth has been debunked by documentation from 1410 that gives actual credit to clockmaker Mikuláš of Kadaň and an astronomy and math professor Jan Šindel (who each kept their eyes). The façade and machinery got a careful restorative makeover to repair some residual damage from World War II and present its best face for the 2018 celebrations of Czechoslovakia's 100th anniversary.

The amount of information held on the colorful faces is as impressive as

the sun, the moon, the stars . . . Prague's Astronomical Clock

the fact that this 15th-century timepiece is still ticking today. The golden swirls of the upper circle track a 12-hour and 24-hour clock, the time of sunrise and sunset, the current zodiac sign, and a variety of other historic time systems.

When the hour is approaching, crowds gather on the street in front of the clock in anticipation. When the bells chime hourly 9am-11pm, the four characters on either side come to life, with vanity staring in a mirror, greed holding a purse full of money, a skeleton (death) ringing his bell, and a musical Turk shaking his head in denial. A parade of the 12 apostles rotates through the doors above the clock face. Full disclaimer: despite its fame, many find the just-under-a-minute animation underwhelming, so feel free to skip the show and arrive between the hours. Then wait for the masses to disperse to admire the impressive external beauty of the clock faces up close.

The stationary statues flanking the lower face are known as the Philosopher, the Archangel Michael, the Astronomer, and the Chronicler. Inside the ring, a 365-day calendar fans out around the paintings of zodiac signs. If you look closely, you'll see a name or two written beside each number, representing a Czech name day (or "svátek"). That's right—most Czechs have one of these traditional names, and parents who want to deviate have to register for official government permission. As a result, Czechs get two yearly excuses to celebrate: the day they were born, and the day that their name falls on the calendar. You'll find Adam and Eva on December 24 (in connection with Christmas), and Czechs take their name for New Year's Eve, "Silvestr," from December 31.

JAN HUS MONUMENT

The dominant stone figure in the center of Old Town Square represents an early 14th-century figure of rebellion against the Catholic Church. Jan Hus may not have the international name recognition of Martin Luther, but he was fighting for religious reform roughly a century before the Protestant Reformation gained momentum. Sadly, like so many enemies of the Catholic church, Hus was burned at the stake on July 6, 1415. This statue was unveiled in 1915, exactly 500 years after his execution, and July 6 remains a Czech national holiday in his honor. The base of the statue is engraved with multiple quotes, including one from Hus himself: "Love each other, and wish the truth to everyone" (*Milujte se, pravdy každému přejte*).

CHURCH OF OUR LADY BEFORE TÝN (CHRÁM MATKY BOŽÍ PŘED TÝNEM)

Staroměstské náměstí 604; +420 222 318 186 or +420 602 204 213; www.tyn.cz; 10am-1pm and 3pm-5pm Tues-Sat, 10am-noon Sun; admission by donation; metro stops Staroměstská or Můstek

The twin Gothic towers of the Church of Our Lady Before Týn, called Adam and Eve, are an iconic symbol of Old Town Square. If you look closely, you'll see that the pair are not symmetrical, an unintended result of decades-long construction delays from the mid-14th and continued renovations over the centuries.

The history of the decoration also speaks of Prague's religious turmoil. The church was adorned first with a statue of the Virgin Mary, then replaced during the Hussite era with a golden chalice and statue of the first

Hussite King George of Poděbrad. When Catholics regained control, the chalice was melted down and Mary retook her place of power. Walk around the church to the right to see a replica of the Virgin Mary.

The interior of the church is visible only through a gate just inside the entryway, which serves as a small viewing area for visitors; photography is prohibited. Architecture fans might enjoy a quick peek at the Baroque design, golden touches, and the oldest organ in all of Prague. The entrance is hidden beneath the arches below, tucked between art galleries and restaurants. Otherwise, this church is best admired from across the square, particularly when overlooking seasonal Christmas and Easter markets.

ST. NICHOLAS CHURCH (CHRÁM SV. MIKULÁŠE)

Staroměstské náměstí 1101; +420 224 190 990; www.svmikulas.cz; 10am-4pm Mon-Sat, noon-4pm Sun; free; metro and tram stop Staroměstská

The towering Baroque beauty with green domed rooftops in the corner of Old Town Square is best known for hosting nightly classical-music concerts (400-500 CZK), usually at 5pm or 8pm. The tourist-friendly program focuses on international favorites such as Mozart, Vivaldi, and Pachelbel with the occasional inclusion of local names such as Antonin Dvořák. Tickets are available online through the Prague Ticket Office (www.pragueticketoffice.com) or at the Via Musika shop near the entrance of the Church of Our Lady Before Týn. Even if classical music isn't your thing, poke your head inside long enough to admire the crystal chandelier and gold details of the church interior.

To avoid confusion, note that the Church of St. Nicholas shares a name with another Church of St. Nicholas (Kostel sv. Mikuláše) across town in the Malá Strana neighborhood.

CONVENT OF ST. AGNES (KLÁŠTER SV. ANEŽKY ČESKÉ)

U Milosrdných 17; +420 778 725 086; www.ngprague.cz; 10am-6pm Tues-Sun, 10am-8pm Wed; 220 CZK; tram stop Dlouhá třída

One of the National Gallery's most peaceful properties houses a vast collection of religious art and a relaxing sculpture garden that wraps around the building. This is one of Old Town's less frequented sights, providing a mellow experience compared to the nearby sights in Old Town Square.

The namesake of this convent and member of the Přemyslid dynasty shares an anniversary with the country itself—St. Agnes of Bohemia was canonized in 1989, the same year then-Czechoslovakia gained independence from Communist rule. She helped to found this site in the early 13th century. The lower level of the museum includes her grave, with signage explaining the legend of her missing remains, and interactive touchscreens detailing the history of various rooms. The floor also includes a children's

St. Agnes Convent and sculpture garden

room with coloring pages, stencils, stamps, and artistic activites that might appeal to any age, and 12 sculpture fragments that visitors are able to touch (intended to provide a tactile experience for blind visitors).

The upper levels of the museum contain a vast collection of medieval religious art from 1200-1550, such as 30+ representations of madonnas (in a wide range of skin tones) ranging from gentle knowing smiles or nursing mothers to a fierce protectress standing on top of a lion. Descriptions in Czech and English offer explanations of symbolism. The 15 rooms of artistic pieces would take at least 90 minutes to pause and appreciate every installation, and can get overwhelming. Choose your pace based on interest and stamina, skip ahead when desired, and take breaks on cushioned benches spread throughout the exhibit as needed.

St. Agnes's outdoor sculpture gardens, renovated in 2016, actually qualify as a hidden gem of Prague, so go now before they're discovered en masse. Entrance is free to the public from a gate along the riverbank, just west of Loď Pivovar (a restaurant and brewery on a boat), or near the main entrance of the convent. The benches and grass near the convent entrance are a popular place to relax after a visit, but don't miss a walk all the way around the building to find hidden sculptures from Czech artists tucked under trees and into corners. The garden is open year round (as weather allows) from 10am-4pm Nov-Feb, 10am-6pm March-May and Sept-Oct, and extended summertime hours from June-Aug from 10am-10pm Sun-Thurs and 10am-midnight on Friday and Saturday. To refuel after a visit, stop by nearby Sisters Bistro for open-faced sandwiches called *chlebíčky* or Perníčkův sen for a gingerbread pick-me-up.

Rudolfinum is full of legends.

RUDOLFINUM

Alšovo nábřeží 12; +420 227 059 227; www.rudolfinum.cz; tram or metro stop Staroměstská

This concert hall has played host to more than just incredible symphonies. After hosting classical concerts and gallery exhibitions from 1885 to 1918, the Rudolfinum became the home of the new Czechoslovakian parliament. Concert halls were renovated into meeting rooms and didn't return to a home of culture until the midst of World War II, when it housed the German Philharmonic from 1942-1945 and served as a meeting place for Nazi officials.

This period of German occupation spawned a legend around the statues lining the rooftop. In the novel *Mendelssohn Is on the Roof*, Reinhard Heydrich (one of Hitler's high-ranking deputies) orders the statue of Jewish composer Felix Mendelssohn-Bartholdy to be removed. The fictional plot sends two workers to the roof who don't know which one Mendelssohn is, and they almost demolish Richard Wagner, one of Hitler's favorite German composers, because of his large nose. While this story is often repeated as factual by walking-tour guides, none of them are able to point out the statue of Wagner on the rooftop. Wagner was never actually part of the crowd, but you can find Bach, Beethoven, Mendelssohn, and Mozart.

Today this building is home to the Czech Philharmonic Orchestra and serves as one of the premiere venues of the Prague Spring Festival. The lower floors of the building hold a free gallery space (www.galerierudolfinum.cz) and children's interactive exhibitions, as well as a column-lined café (www.rudolfinumcafe.cz), accessible on the lower left side of the building while facing the entrance.

✪ JEWISH QUARTER (JOSEFOV)

Prague's Jewish Quarter, tucked into the river bend around Old Town, has roots as early as the 10th century. This former ghetto was officially walled in after a 13th-century decree requiring the separation of Jewish and Christian communities. Restrictions lightened in the 16th century under Rudolf II, who worked with many Jewish banking families, then tightened again under Maria-Theresa in the 17th century. An Edict of Tolerance was finally granted in 1781 by Emperor Josef II, namesake of the neighborhood.

One of the darker reasons that Prague's Jewish Quarter is more intact than its Central European neighbors was Hitler's affinity for Prague. The Nazi dictator's plans to establish a "monument to an extinguished race" kept the bombs of World War II from demolishing the area. This created the bittersweet result of preserving centuries-old streets and synagogues from an inhumane era of occupation, so that today's visitors can focus on the rich, vast history of the Jewish community in Prague.

the Old-New Synagogue and Jewish Town Hall

The majority of sights, including the Old Jewish Cemetery and Pinkas Synagogue, are managed by the **Jewish Museum** (www.jewishmuseum.cz), which includes packaged admission (350 CZK) to a collection of seven buildings and sites. A combination ticket to the Jewish Town of Prague (500 CZK) also includes admission to the Old-New Synagogue, which is the only sight available to purchase individually (200 CZK). Tickets may be purchased at the Pinkas Synagogue, the Klausen Synagogue, the Information and Reservations Center located at Maiselova 15, or online. At the time of writing, the Spanish Synagogue usually included in the Jewish Museum was closed for long-term renovations.

Interested parties could easily spend multiple days exploring Josefov. There is a quiet air of reverence and remembrance around the individual sights and synagogues, but the surrounding streets are full of modern life, hotels, and some of the city's most high-end shopping on Pařížská Street. Most religious sites around the neighborhood are closed on Saturdays, but the restaurants, cafés, and designer shops remain open. The seclusion of previous centuries has faded away, with the area now existing as a part of tourist trails and daily cosmopolitan life in the city center.

Many sights below are closed on Jewish holidays. Note that shoulders should be covered, and men will be required to wear a head covering in some locations.

OLD-NEW SYNAGOGUE (STARONOVÁ SYNAGOGA)

Červená; +420 224 800 812 or +420 224 800 813; www.synagogue.cz; Nov-Mar, 9am-5pm Sun-Thurs; April-Oct, 9am-6pm Sun-Thurs; open Fridays until one hour before Shabbat, closed Saturdays and Jewish holidays; 200 CZK; metro and tram stop Staroměstská

The Old-New Synagogue holds the title of oldest working synagogue in all of Europe. Originally known as "New" or "Great" when it was built in the 13th century, the ironic name developed when younger buildings popped up in the 16th century. The simplicity of the high ceilings, arched Gothic windows, and dark ironwork inside provide a contrast to the more ornate embellishments of its neighbors.

Legend surrounds the attic, which is said to house a giant clay creature created by Rabbi Löw sometime around 1590. The Rabbi supposedly created the mythical Golem to protect the Jewish community from harm, and then put him to bed every Friday night to rest for the Sabbath. When the Golem's temper began to turn more Frankenstein than friend, the Rabbi put him into long-term hibernation in the attic, where he waits to be awakened if needed again. The attic remains off limits to visitors today, so consider yourself safe. The building is also rumored to have survived for so long, through fires and wars, under the protective cover of angel wings transformed into doves.

Guided tours (80 CZK) held in English around 10:30am or 2pm (other times available upon request) can help to add context and legend to the experience. Visit the Information and Reservations Center, located at Maiselova 15, in person to confirm that day's availability.

The Old-New Synagogue is not part of the Jewish museum, but entrance can be combined with entrance to all Jewish Museum sights under the Jewish Town of Prague ticket (500

CZK). You can purchase an advanced ticket (180 CZK) to just the Old-New Synagogue online at www.synagogue.cz. The Old-New Synagogue can also be combined with a ticket to the colorful Jerusalem (also known as "Jubilee") Synagogue near Prague's Main Train Station (Hlavní nádraží) and the Alfons Mucha Museum. The combined Old-New Synagogue and Jerusalem Synagogue ticket (270 CZK) is available for purchase from the Jerusalem Synagogue.

the crooked headstones of the Old Jewish Cemetery

OLD JEWISH CEMETERY (STARÝ ŽIDOVSKÝ HŘBITOV)

Široká 3; +420 222 749 211; www.jewishmuseum.cz; Nov-Mar, 9am-4:30pm; Apr-Oct, 9am-6pm; closed Saturdays and Jewish holidays; entry covered by Jewish Museum ticket; metro and tram stop Staroměstská

Roughly 12,000 crooked headstones are crowded into the Old Jewish Cemetery, likely representing thousands more buried below. Many of the gravestones, ranging from the early 15th century to 1787, are marked with symbols connected to their occupations or family names. You're likely to find a crowd around Rabbi Löw in connection with the tale of the Golem at the Old-New Synagogue. Wandering the narrow paths through the graves is both a peaceful and powerful experience, illustrating the confinement that this community endured along with a warm reverence of maintaining the tradition of honoring these lives. Instead of flowers, you may spot evidence of the Jewish tradition of leaving small rocks on top of individual headstones. This historic resting place is tucked just off the Vltava riverbank near the Rudolfinum Concert Hall.

PINKAS SYNAGOGUE AND HOLOCAUST MUSEUM (PINKASOVA SYNAGOGA)

Široká 3; +420 222 749 211; www.jewishmuseum.cz; Nov-Mar, 9am-4:30pm; Apr-Oct, 9am-6pm, closed Saturdays and Jewish holidays; entry covered by Jewish Museum ticket; metro and tram stop Staroměstská

The second-oldest synagogue in Prague, built in 1535, now functions as a somber memorial to nearly 80,000 victims of the Shoah (a Hebrew word meaning calamity or destruction, and now used as a preferred term by many in the Jewish community for "the Holocaust"). The names, grouped both by family name and the victims' Bohemian and Moravian hometowns, were handwritten on the synagogue's interior walls between 1992-1996 to create this moving site of remembrance.

Continue through a hall of drawings made by children who were held at the Jewish ghetto of Terezín while en route to the concentration camps at Treblinka or Auschwitz. The pictures were saved by Friedl Dicker-Brandeis, who taught art classes while also held at Terezín (1942-1944) to help the youngest residents process their emotions. She hid the drawings in two suitcases when she was transported from the premises, resulting in their preservation. The drawings are a heart-wrenching (and, for many, tear-inducing) combination of happy memories and expressions of despair.

A visit to the Pinkas Synagogue may be emotional, but it is important. It embodies the notion from philosopher George Santayana that "Those who cannot remember the past are condemned to repeat it."

NEW TOWN (NOVÉ MĚSTO)

REPUBLIC SQUARE (NÁMĚSTÍ REPUBLIKY)

This northeastern side of New Town holds an incredible collection of original architectural styles. From the curve of Na Příkopě street you are surrounded by the dark Gothic stone of the Powder Tower, the swirling Art Nouveau elegance of the Municipal House, the columned entrance of the Empire-style Hybernia Theater, the sturdy International façade of the Czech National Bank, and the stark grey cement of the KB banking building.

As a language note, while Old Town Square and Wenceslas Square have become relatively common English translations, Náměstí Republiky (and most names including "Náměstí," pronounced "NAHM-yes-tee") sound odd in any form other than Czech, even to the resident English speakers—imagine someone looking for Los Angeles asking how to get to "The Angels." Think of these square names as a chance to practice the local dialect. Remembering their original form will help you decipher maps, find the correct public transport stops, and ask directions across the city.

POWDER TOWER (PRAŠNÁ BRÁNA)

Náměstí Republiky 5; +420 725 847 875; www.muzeumprahy.cz/prasna-brana; Nov-Feb, 10am-6pm; April and Oct, 10am-8pm; May-Aug, 10am-10pm; 100 CZK; tram or metro stop Náměstí Republiky

The Powder Tower is named for one of its many previous uses: storing gunpowder in the 18th century. Centuries before, this 1475 Gothic tower marked the historical entrance to Old Town and the beginning of the royal coronation route to the Prague Castle. Admission gains you access to a spiral staircase of 186 stone steps and an overview of the Old Town that is often less crowded, and shared less often on social media, than the iconic bird's eye view from Charles Bridge Towers. Otherwise, and if there are no cars coming, take a quick detour off the sidewalk and strut underneath the arch connecting New Town to Old Town with your best royal posture.

MUNICIPAL HOUSE (OBECNÍ DŮM)

Náměstí Republiky 5; +420 222 002 101; www.obecnidum.cz; 10am-8pm; tours 290 CZK; tram or metro stop Náměstí Republiky

This modern-day concert hall has been instrumental in the country's political history. On October 28, 1918, the independent state of Czechoslovakia was announced from its balcony, and later Václav Havel, first president of the Czech Republic, held his early meetings with Communist-era Prime Minister Ladislav Adamec inside these halls.

The Municipal House was built on the site of the King's Court in the 14th and 15th centuries, which served as the residence of Bohemian kings during that period. The Art Nouveau exterior reflects the decadence of the

Prague's Art Nouveau Municipal House and Gothic Powder Tower

early 20th century and symbolizes part of the Czech National Revival leading up to the First Republic of Czechoslovakia. The swirling exterior includes a mosaic entitled an "Homage to Prague" framed by a quote from Svatopluk Čech, proclaiming, "Hail to you Prague! Defy time and malice as you have weathered all storms throughout the ages!"

The interior holds a number of concert spaces, most notably **Smetana Hall**, which serves as home to the Prague Symphony Orchestra (FOK) and where the Prague Spring Music Festival kicks off each year. Access to the upstairs halls require concert tickets or guided tours (300-600 CZK) that you can book online (www.obecnidum.cz) or at the Municipal House box office on the left side of the ground floor between 10am-8pm. Feel free to wander the bottom floors to admire the Art Nouveau details in the pricey, ornately decorated restaurant and café (beers around 100 CZK).

MUSEUM OF COMMUNISM (MUZEUM KOMUNISMU)

V Celnici 4; +420 224 212 966; www.muzeumkomunismu.cz; 9am-8pm; 290 CZK; tram or metro stop Náměstí Republiky

It can be hard for an outsider to imagine life under the Communist rule imposed from the 1940s to 1989. The personal collection inside the Museum of Communism helps put the personal touches and propaganda of the era into perspective. Re-creations include a school classroom, a child's bedroom, a workshop, and an interrogation room alongside exhibits and photos chronicling decades of occupation. Give yourself time to read the descriptions along the walls to get a more nuanced picture of everyday life, from healthcare and education to local police and major military events.

This large warehouse-style exhibition space is rarely overcrowded. You'll find the building tucked just off Náměstí Republiky, behind the Hybernia Theater and the weekday farmers markets that surround the metro entrance.

JERUSALEM SYNAGOGUE (JERUZALÉMSKÁ SYNAGOGA)

Jeruzalémská 7; +420 224 800 812 or +420 224 800 813; www.synagogue.cz; 10am-5pm Sun-Fri; 80 CZK; tram stop Jindřišska

Also called the **Jubilee Synagogue** to commemorate the 50th anniversary of Franz Josef's rule, this youngest of Prague's Jewish houses of worship was built from 1905-1906. The brightly hued exterior combined Moorish structural design with an Art Nouveau interior. Visitors interested in Jewish history should head inside for a permanent exhibition, "Jewish Monuments and their Reconstruction after 1989," as well as temporary exhibitions often focused on modern, postwar history.

To find this off-the-beaten-path beauty, take the scenic route from Náměstí Republiky toward Wenceslas Square, down Senovážná street instead of Na Příkopě going toward Jindřišska Tower. You'll first see the Church of Svatý Jindřich a svatá Kunhuta near the tram stop. Behind this church on the left-hand side, you'll find Jerusalem Synagogue hiding down quiet Jeruzalemska street.

PRAGUE MAIN RAILWAY STATION (PRAHA HLAVNÍ NÁDRAŽÍ)

Wilsonova 8; +420 221 111 122; www.cd.cz, ticket counters 3:20am-12:30am Mon-Fri, 2:00am-2:30am and 3:20am-12:30am Sat-Sun; metro or tram stop Hlavní nádraží

Prague's Main Railway Station is surrounded by a long stretch of green grass presided over by a statue of US president Woodrow Wilson, who supported the establishment of Czechoslovakia. A plaque to the left of his statue includes another famous US politician, Madeleine Albright, who discovered her Czech roots late in life. This outdoor area is one of few places in Prague to avoid (or at least be alert) after dark.

The ground floor of the station is your typical, modern collection of fast food and convenience shops, but the second floor holds a few interesting sights even for travelers who don't plan to use its transport services. Look for the domed ceiling and Art Nouveau design, including a carved stone face of Prague, Mother of Cities. A more paternal figure, Sir Nicholas Winton, is memorialized on Platform 1. The bronze statue of the British hero, standing beside a suitcase and holding two young children, symbolizes Winton's efforts to save 669 Jewish children during the Holocaust by arranging transport out of the country to Britain on "kindertrains." In 2014, Winton was awarded the Order of the White Lion, the highest Czech honor, at age 105, just a few months before his death.

Art Nouveau lobby of the Prague Main Railway Station

Wenceslas Square, the cosmopolitan heart of the city

ALFONS MUCHA MUSEUM

Panská 7; +420 224 216 415; www.mucha.cz; 10am-6pm; 300 CZK; tram stop Jindřišska or metro stop Můstek

While the Art Nouveau movement is generally associated with Paris, one of its original innovators is an undeniably local hero, Alfons Mucha. This three-room museum offers an easy introduction to one of the most revered Czech artists, whose work contributed to the beauty of the Municipal House and St. Vitus Cathedral.

After growing up in the South Moravian region of the Czech Republic, Mucha made his name doing interior decoration for the aristocracy of the Austro-Hungarian Empire and designing theatrical posters in Paris that ultimately established his signature swirling designs. Later in life, he returned to his homeland to focus on more political works that captured the essence of the Czech character.

Admire the theatrical posters in the front of the museum, and don't miss the 30-minute video about his life tucked into the rear of the building. Before you leave, stop by the adjoining gift shop for a wide range of sophisticated souvenirs to delight the art fan in your life.

✪ WENCESLAS SQUARE (VÁCLAVSKÉ NÁMĚSTÍ)

This center of economic activity and political change may not look like much at first glance, but the streets around this long rectangular "square" have witnessed some world-changing history. The only hints of its early 14th-century days as *Koňský trh* (a "Horse Market") are the massive statue of St. Wenceslas, the patron saint of the Czech Republic, on horseback at the top of the square. The highway dividing the square from the National Museum was renamed Wilsonova in 1989, a symbolic departure from its previous *Vítězného února* ("Victorious February") that marked the Communist takeover in 1948.

Today the busy square holds pieces of past and present influences.

International shopping outlets, tourist-focused restaurants, and fast-food chains occupy many of the historic buildings. The city has plans to revitalize this pedestrian space and bring local life back to the center. For now, take a walk through the benches engraved with inspirational quotes that line the center islands and absorb the years of political protests that marked this space over the years. As recently as 2019, Czech citizens packed these streets to express their discontent with their local government.

NATIONAL MUSEUM (NÁRODNÍ MUSEUM)

Václavské náměstí 68; +420 224 497 111; www.nm.cz; 10am-6pm daily; 260 CZK (special ticket 350 CZK); metro stop Muzeum

Located at the top of Wenceslas Square, the National Museum has undergone long-term renovations for nearly a decade. Some exhibits have reopened as additional work continues. The observation deck in the domed roof is popular with photographers for a view over the square from above. Access requires a combined ticket to the museum and dome (350 CZK) that can only be purchased onsite on the day of visiting. Even if you don't make it inside, do take a moment to admire the newly polished exterior of this late 19th-century Renaissance beauty, which had its place in the Czech National Revival movement. The domed rooftop and arched windows were built alongside the National Theater and Municipal House in an effort to reclaim a sense of national pride and cultural identity. This eventually led to the establishment of the glamorous First Republic of an independent Czechoslovakia in 1918. These days, the building attracts the glitterati of Hollywood, appearing in films such as *Casino Royale* and *Mission: Impossible*.

The National Museum has had a long history of delays. The museum and its collection were established in 1818 and housed in Hradčany in the early 1800s. New locations were considered in the 1840s and the 1860s, but it wasn't until the late 1800s that the current location was approved. The current building officially opened in 1891—after half a century of discussions and negotiations!

MAIN POST OFFICE (HLAVNÍ POŠTA)

Jindřišská 14; +420 221 131 111; 2am-midnight; free; tram stop Václavské náměstí and metro stops Muzeum or Můstek

Even if you have nothing to mail, the Main Post Office is worth a look inside, but you have to look up. Swirling frescoed designs line the walls around arched windows beneath a vaulted glass ceiling. A shop in the corner sells stationery, stickers, and packing materials. Stop in almost any time—the building only closes between midnight and 2am—but stick to mental pictures to avoid a reprimand from the security staff. Photography is not allowed inside this government building.

LANTERN PALACE (PALAC LUCERNA)

Štěpánská 61; +420 224 224 537; www.lucerna.cz; free; passage open 24 hours; tram stop Václavské náměstí

Prague's city center is filled with covered passageways, known as *pasáž* in Czech, that connect the cafés, shops, and venues housed in the buildings that surround them. In the early 1900s, Palac Lucerna was the first of these shopping and culture centers built in the Czech Republic. The design and construction were carried

STUDENT PROTESTS AND OCCUPATIONS

Political demonstrations and celebrations have often centered around Wenceslas Square and the surrounding streets of New Town.

Monument to Freedom and Democracy at Národní třída

- **Celebration of Czechoslovakia's Independence (Oct. 28, 1918):** Crowds gathered on Wenceslas Square to celebrate the newfound independence of Czechoslovakia from the Austro-Hungarian Empire. This day remains a national holiday, and 2018 marked joyful celebrations of the 100th anniversary, even though Czechoslovakia doesn't technically exist today.

- **Student protests against German invasion (Oct. 28, 1939):** Student protesters marked the anniversary of Czech independence by taking to the streets, including Old Town Square and Wenceslas Square, to express outrage against the growing German occupation of Czechoslovakia. When German soldiers tried to get the crowds under control, a young medical student, Jan Opletal, was shot in the stomach and died in the hospital.

- **Anti-Nazi protests (Nov. 15, 1939):** A funeral for Jan Opletal, the man who was killed in protests just weeks earlier, turned into another spontaneous anti-Nazi protest. In response, German soldiers raided the dormitories and executed nine of the student organizers behind the events on November 17, 1939. Nazi occupation continued until the end of World War II. Opletalova Street, running from Wenceslas Square to Prague's main train station (Hlavní nádraží), is named after the man who sacrificed his life, and November 17 became known as International Students' Day.

- **Student protests against the Soviet occupation (1969):** To protest the restrictive Soviet occupation under the Communist government, young philosophy student Jan Palach lit himself on fire in Wenceslas Square on January 16, 1969. A second act of self-immolation, by student Jan Zajíc, occurred on February 25, 1969. Despite their extreme efforts, Soviet occupation continued for another 20 years. A cross in bricks in front of the National Museum marks the spot where Palach lit himself on fire, and a sculptural memorial near Rudolfinum commemorates both Palach and his mother's grief.

- **International Students' Day Anniversary (Nov. 1989):** By November 17, 1989, the Berlin Wall had crumbled and Communist regimes were falling around Europe. Students gathered at Vyšehrad for a demonstration to mark the 50th anniversary of their outspoken predecessors and to express their desire for independence. Thousands of citizens joined the march along the Vltava River toward Wenceslas Square, but were stopped and brutally attacked by riot police. A memorial of hands reaching out from Národní třída street pays tribute to this massacre.

- **Celebrations of Independence from Communism (Dec. 1989):** The November demonstrations led to the formation of the Civic Forum and its elected leader Václav Havel. Demonstrations continued for weeks in Wenceslas Square, with protesters jingling their keys in the air to symbolize time for the Communist government to go home. Top officials resigned within weeks, and Havel was officially elected president on December 29, 1989. Chants of "*Havel na hrad*" (Havel to the castle) marked the end of the Velvet Revolution, named for its casualty-free (if not entirely peaceful) transition of power.

out by Vácslav Havel, grandfather of future president Václav Havel. Today, one of the biggest draws for visitors is the highly photographable David Černý sculpture hanging from its domed ceiling. In contrast to the proud statue of St. Wenceslas on the square outside, Černý's rider sits astride an upside-down horse, with rumors that the saint's face resembles various modern politicians.

The hallways surrounding the sculpture lead to the historic 1909 **Kino Lucerna** cinema, a glamorous First Republic-style café in **Kavárna Lucerna,** and one of Prague's longest-running dance clubs, **Lucerna Music Bar.** In the summer, a new rooftop bar (www.strechalucerny.cz, 100 CZK entry) draws lad-back crowds to enjoy the views from this central vantage point from 3pm-10pm Sat-Mon.

FRANCISCAN GARDENS (FRANTIŠKÁNSKÁ ZAHRADA)

Jungmannovo náměstí; +420 221 097 231; Oct-Apr, 8am-7pm; Apr-Sept 7am-10pm; Sept-Oct 7am-8pm; free; tram stop Václavské náměstí

This peaceful, relaxing outdoor garden hidden in an inner courtyard provides an escape from busy Wenceslas Square. The pace of life is slow in this little oasis, with families enjoying ice cream on benches surrounded by latticed fences covered in rose vines. The tall, arched windows and red rooftops of the massive Church of Our Lady of the Snows watches over the children's playground near its base. Take a moment to imagine the Prague landscape if this house of worship extended all the way to the Vltava River's edge, as originally planned. Lighthearted sculptures and a bubbling fountain round out the overall sense of calm.

The Franciscan Gardens are accessible from the Svetozor Passage on Vodičkova Street or an unmarked gate tucked into the back corner of Jungmannovo náměstí.

FRANZ KAFKA HEAD

Spálená 22; free; tram or metro stops Národní třída

As you head from Wenceslas Square toward Prague's National Theater, you'll come across an artistic tribute to a local literary genius from renowned local sculptor David Černý. A giant mirrored head of Franz Kafka installed in 2014 rotates in 42 layers, slowly turning the author's profile in circles in a courtyard just off Národní třída street in front of the Quadrio shopping center. The profile moves in different patterns every few seconds, so split your group into spots around the statue and see who can snap the first picture of a completed profile. This statue also has a twin at Whitehall Technology Park in Charlotte, North Carolina.

the rotating face of Franz Kafka by David Černý

CHARLES SQUARE (KARLOVO NÁMĚSTÍ)

The most residential part of New Town stretches from Prague's National Theater along the Vltava riverbank and around the larger rectangular park of Karlovo náměstí, yet another site named for the beloved King Charles IV. The square, established in 1348, was also known as the Cattle Market (Dobytčí trh) or the New Town Square, for its proximity to the New Town Hall (Novoměstská radnice).

park in Charles Square

These days, the square is more likely to serve as a site of relaxation than radical protest. The two rectangular halves of green space are divided by busy streets of tram tracks and traffic, but inside the border of trees and flowered gardens a Baroque fountain, curving pathways, and benches to rest your feet cultivate a peaceful vibe.

NEW TOWN HALL (NOVOMĚSTSKÁ RADNICE)

Karlovo náměstí 1; +420 224 948 225; www.novomestskaradnice.cz; Tues-Sun 10am-6pm from spring to autumn (dependent on weather); 60 CZK; tram stop Novoměstská radnice or metro stop Karlovo náměstí

The Gothic Tower of the New Town Hall in the corner of Karlovo náměstí was the site of Prague's First Defenestration (the act of throwing someone, usually an authority figure, out a window). In 1419, an angry crowd of Jan Hus's followers demanded the release of Protestant prisoners before tossing seven council members from the tower, an early act of the religious conflict that led to the Hussite Wars.

Visitors can get an up-close look at the site of the historic action, plus views of the surrounding area, by climbing the tower's 221 wooden steps. Entrance also includes an exhibit on the history of the area in a former guard's apartment and a small art gallery. A combined **Town Hall Pass** (350 CZK), which provides access to the Old Town Hall (twice) and New Town Hall (once) over a period of three days and also includes skipping the lines, will benefit most visitors. The pass can be purchased onsite at either location.

NATIONAL MONUMENT TO THE HEROES OF THE HEYDRICH TERROR (NÁRODNÍ PAMÁTNÍK HRDINŮ HEYDRICHIÁDY)

Resslova 9a; +420 222 540 718 or +420 720 988 421; 9am-5pm Tues-Sun; free; tram or metro stops Karlovo náměstí

The National Monument to the Heroes of the Heydrich Terror is a moving tribute to one brave act of World War II resistance efforts. The memorial is in the basement of the Baroque Church of Saints Cyril and Methodius, which played an important role in the story. After successfully assassinating Reinhard Heydrich, one of Hitler's top deputies, the small group of men who carried out the plan took refuge inside this church, where they hid for weeks from a city-wide manhunt. This

HEROES OF THE RESISTANCE: THE ANTHROPOID MISSION

the Church of Saints Cyril and Methodius holds a World War II memorial

Prague is known for its history of foreign rulers and occupations, but the local character is also defined by acts of resistance from brave, everyday citizens standing up to injustice in the face of impossible odds. The Anthropoid mission of 1942 is one of these stories, recently catching Hollywood's attention with two English-language films (the painstakingly researched *Anthropoid* in 2016 and Heydrich-focused *The Man with the Iron Heart* in 2017). Spoilers ahead, in case you want to watch them first.

A pair of paratroopers living in exile during World War II were sent back to Czechoslovakia in late 1941 with a daunting task—to assassinate Reinhard Heydrich, one of Hitler's cruelest deputies who was nicknamed "The Butcher of Prague." Josef Gabčík and Jan Kubiš teamed up with a small group of fellow dissidents, who often risked their lives to house or meet with the men. The group observed the Nazi leader's movements and concocted a plan.

On May 27, 1942, they stopped Heydrich's car in the outskirts of the city, en route to the Prague Castle. Josef Gabčík jumped in front of the car and attempted to shoot Heydrich, but his gun failed. Jan Kubiš turned to Plan B and tossed a grenade toward the car. Its blast lodged a piece of metal into Heydrich's body. The Anthropoid team retreated and Heydrich was taken to the hospital, where he died from infection roughly one week later.

A seven-man team went into hiding, eventually given sanctuary inside the Church of Saints Cyril and Methodius. Their location was given up by a fellow paratrooper, Karel Čurda, resulting in a standoff at the church on June 18, 1942. The men opened fire on the Nazi army when they entered, and took refuge in the basement, where they were attacked with tear gas and rising water. Five men saved their last bullets to take their own lives and avoid capture. Many of the families who housed them turned to cyanide capsules to avoid interrogation. Nazi retaliation for the assassination wiped out the village of Lidice and killed hundreds more.

Prague's **Naked Tour Guide** (+420 778 030 508, www.nakedtourguideprague.com) offers an excellent in-depth Anthropoid Movie Tour (1,000 CZK), including a film screening in an art-house cinema, discussion of the differences between Hollywood representations and actual history, locations of safe houses in Žižkov, and lots of historical context.

eventually led to a standoff with the Nazi army that ended in their deaths. You'll find a plaque that describes the events (in Czech) flanked by small statues of a paratrooper and a priest outside the church above original bullet holes on the church wall. The year 1942 is also embedded in the sidewalk below the plaque.

Inside the free memorial is a small exhibition of letters and photos in glass cases that tell the stories of the soldiers in both Czech and English. Visitors may also enter the crypt where most of the men ultimately lost their lives. The Church of Saints Cyril and Methodius itself is only open during Orthodox masses on Sundays. The separate entrance to the memorial is located at street level beside steps to the church itself.

✪ DANCING HOUSE (TANČÍCÍ DŮM)

Jiraskovo Namesti 6; +420 720 983 172; www.tadu.cz; observation deck 9am-midnight; tram stop Jiráskovo náměstí

The twisted glass-and-stone walls of the Dancing House look like a hand reached out of the clouds and squeezed one corner of the skyline, yet somehow it blends seamlessly into the city landscape. The architectural landmark stands on a site accidentally bombed by the American army in 1945, which stood empty until after the Velvet Revolution. The modern collaboration between two 20th-century architects, Canadian-American Frank Gehry and Croatian-Czech Vlado Milunić, was inspired by the shape of famous dancing couple Fred Astaire and Ginger Rogers, after whom the top-floor restaurant is named. Its tension and intertwined embrace between the materials also represents the mid-1990s state of the Czech Republic, blending respect for the past while charging optimistically into the future, navigating cultural influences of East and West.

The ground floor houses a small gallery, with the boutique Dancing House Hotel and office space occupying the middle floors. The top two levels house the fine dining Fred and Ginger restaurant, the Glass Bar, and an observation deck (wrapped around the twisted metal orb on top of the building) that offers 360-degree views of the Vltava River, the Prague Castle, and city skylines. The small observation platform, with binoculars on the edges and limited bench seating in the center, can get crowded on summer afternoons but is often peaceful in the morning, after dark, and during off-seasons.

the twisted silhouette of the Dancing House

NÁPLAVKA BOARDWALK

Náplavka; +420 222 013 618; www.prazskenaplavky.cz; free; tram stop Palackého náměstí or metro stop Karlovo náměstí

Whether it's for a Saturday farmers market, a food festival, or a midweek evening stroll, the Rašín boardwalk, better known as Náplavka, draws locals and visitors to its cobblestoned paths year-round. This below-street-level embankment is lined with boat bars and restaurants, occasional live music or permitted buskers, and swans begging for food from anyone dangling their legs over the edge. Access is possible via ramps and stairs at various points along the street, from around the Dancing House to the railway bridge just below Vyšehrad. You can also catch a five-minute ride on one of the small summer ferry boats here, included in the Prague public transport system, to the opposite riverbank of Náplavka Smíchov (another prime swan-spotting destination). Ferries run every 10-15 minutes from 8am to 8pm, April through October.

LESSER TOWN (MALÁ STRANA)

✪ CHARLES BRIDGE (KARLŮV MOST)

Karlův most; free; tram stops Malostranské náměstí or Staroměstská

Construction of the Charles Bridge famously began in 1357 on July 9 at 5:31am, based on Charles IV's belief (from numerology and astrology) that 1-3-5-7-9-7-5-3-1 would bring good luck. Whether he was right, or whether the rumored combination of eggs, wine, or milk mixed into the foundations kept the oldest of Prague's bridges safe for centuries, is one of the structure's many secrets.

Crossing the bridge begins by passing through glorious Gothic splendor under the arches of the **Old Town Bridge Tower (Staroměstská mostecká věž)** on one side and the **Lesser Town Bridge Towers (Malostranské mostecké věže)** of Malá Strana on the

Climb the Charles Bridge Towers for an incredible view.

other. Entrance to either tower (www.muzeumprahy.cz, 100 CZK each) is accessible from 10am to roughly sunset, depending on the time of year, offering a coveted bird's-eye view over the hordes of tourists below. Both towers offer incredible views, so decide whether you want a better view of Malá Strana or Old Town before you make the climb, or splurge on both perspectives by documenting the city with photographs of every direction.

Thirty Baroque statues along the edges of the bridge were installed between the late 17th century and 1928, upping the landmark's visual appeal. These famous figures include Saint Wenceslas in prayer on your right as you enter from Malá Strana, and Sts. Cyril and Methodius, credited for bringing Christianity to the area, baptizing the Czechs and Slovaks. They're the fifth statue on your right entering from Old Town.

By far the most popular statue is **St. John of Nepomuk,** crowned with a golden halo of five stars near the center of the bridge. St. John was famously martyred by King Wenceslas IV for either jealousy or politics—protecting the confessional secrets of Queen Sofia, or disrespecting Wenceslas by confirming a monastery without his permission—depending on who you ask. It has become a tourist ritual to rub the image of Sofia at the base of his statue, as well as an unrelated dog engraved on the left side, to bring good luck or a return visit to Prague.

An ornate plaque of swirling iron a few steps to the right of St. John of Nepomuk's statue marks the site where his body was thrown into the Vltava River on Wenceslas's orders. Please don't attach any "love locks" to this essential grave marker—or really on any historical bridge in the city. A local preservation group removes them monthly to maintain structural integrity, and a photo is a much better way to commemorate a romantic moment.

To cross the bridge with any breathing room, you'll need to be up at dawn with the photographers, stumbling home in the early morning hours, or visiting on an off-peak weekday in questionable weather. This popular pedestrian bridge is generally packed with people jostling for a photo, browsing souvenir stands of jewelry and skyline sketches, or crowded around a tour guide explaining one of the bridge's many legends. Crossing the bridge can take anywhere from 7-20 minutes, depending on your ability to dodge selfie sticks.

memorial to St. John of Nepomuk (no love locks, please!)

✪ JOHN LENNON WALL (ZEĎ JOHNA LENNONA)

Velkopřevorské náměstí; free; tram stop Malostranské náměstí or Hellichova

John Lennon never visited Czechoslovakia, but his messages of peace and rebellious spirit still managed to reach the hearts of its residents. The John Lennon Wall was born shortly after Lennon's assassination in 1980, when an unknown artist covered the wall surrounding a courtyard with Beatles lyrics alongside the singer's likeness. Under Communist rule, which prohibited Western music and influences, this was a criminal act. The wall was painted over multiple times, but never stayed blank for very long.

In November of 2014, 25 years after the Velvet Revolution, the wall was completely whitewashed by a group of local art students who left only the words "Wall Is Over." The group later released a statement saying that they were opening "free space for new messages of the current generation." Prague's art community responded to the challenge, and within days of the event, the interactive monument was covered again with its latest incarnation of peaceful words and political grievances. The Beatles imagery was refreshed again by local artists in March of 2019 to mark the anniversary of the Velvet Revolution and then covered with messages about climate change by environmental activists in April 2019.

the John Lennon Wall, a monument to peace and freedom

The Knights of Malta (who own this private property) and the city officials have grown increasingly frustrated that the original character of the wall, with portraits of its namesake musician alongside Beatles lyrics and messages of hope, had been overtaken by random graffiti, Instagram handles, and vulgar phrases. As of 2019, new rules forbid any unauthorized tourist contributions to this site, which will be monitored by security cameras. A more static memorial created by professional artists was in progress at the time of writing.

The city and Knights of Malta are working on preserving the site and adding information in multiple languages to explain its significance. The monument to freedom and artistic expression is certainly still worth a visit. Street musicians are usually present to serenade the selfie takers with Beatles covers, but busking for money is forbidden.

TOWN BELFRY BY ST. NICHOLAS CHURCH (SVATOMIKULÁŠSKÁ MĚSTSKÁ ZVONICE)

Malostranské náměstí 556/29; +420 725 847 927; en.muzeumprahy.cz/the-town-belfrey-by-st-nicholas-church; Nov-Feb, 10am-6pm; Mar, 10am-8pm; Apr-Sept, 10am-10pm; Oct, 10am-8pm; 100 CZK; tram stop Malostranské náměstí

The six floors or platforms of this belfry (which is not actually part of the domed house of worship next door), spread across 215 steps, take you through a decade-by-decade tour of Czech history. Climb the stairs from the bedrooms of 18th-century watchmen, through a shadowy bell tower, all the way up to recreated holographic conversations of the top floor, which was used as a Communist spy center in the 1980s. A multimedia presentation just below the spy center tells the story of Lesser Town (Malá Strana's) role in resistance efforts from May 5-9, 1945 that led to the end of World War II. Take advantage of 360-degree views of the Charles Bridge and the Prague Castle on both the outdoor

PRAGUE'S MUSICAL HISTORY

Music has long been intertwined with Czech culture, from classical composers such as Antonín Dvořák and Bedřich Smetana to the music festivals that fill the countryside each summer. The influence of music has also made its mark on modern-day politics and tourism. Here are a few of my favorite pieces of Czech musical trivia:

- Austria may be able to claim Mozart's birthplace, but the **statue outside the Estates Theater,** where he premiered the opera *Don Giovanni*, is a testament to his notorious love (and, some would argue, preference) for Prague audiences.
- The arrest of the psychedelic band **Plastic People of the Universe** for disturbing the peace under Communist Czechoslovakia helped to inspire the Charter 77 petition of 1976. These signatures became a who's who of political dissidents, many of whom received government retaliation for speaking up for personal freedoms (and for the right to rock and roll).
- Two charismatic political leaders took the stage at **Reduta Jazz Club** for an impromptu saxophone jam session in 1994. A plaque marks the site where Czech President Havel joined US President Bill Clinton onstage for the joy of making music in a democratic society.
- You can thank the **Rolling Stones** for keeping the Prague Castle visible throughout the night. As one of the first rock bands to play in Prague after the fall of Communism, and as friends of President Václav Havel, the band designed and financed the lighting design in 1995.
- Prague has even made its mark on contemporary pop music. The dance club at **Radost FX** was featured in Rihanna's music video for the song "Please Don't Stop the Music" in 2007.
- **Metallica** won local praise in 2018 when they performed a cover of 1970s Czech folk classic *Jožin z bažin* ("Jožin of the Swamp") for a packed house. A quick online search for the video, with English subtitles and iconic dance moves, will introduce you to one of the greatest quirky fairy tales ever told in song, and also give you a taste of Czech humor.

gallery level and covered windows of the top floor. This monument, which reopened in 2017 after the Prague City Museum took over operations and carried out renovations, is still fairly undiscovered by tourist standards, so you can enjoy some breathing room while you explore.

Malá Strana from the Town Belfry by St. Nicholas

VRTBA GARDEN (VRTBOVSKÁ ZAHRADA)

Letenská 4; +420 272 088 350 or +420 603 233 912; www.vrtbovska.cz; Apr-Oct only, 10am-7pm; 80 CZK; tram or metro stop Malostranské náměstí

Fans of landscape architecture should visit the Italian-style terraces of the Vrtba Garden, with the added bonus of a raised viewpoint over panoramic city skylines and an almost eye-level perspective of the Prague Castle. This quiet, 18th-century oasis decorated with swirling grass, expressive statues of Roman gods, and a curved staircase leading to a hillside pavilion is a popular site for weddings and engagement photos. The entrance, down an unassuming driveway on your right while walking away from St. Nicholas Church on Karmelitská street, can be easy to miss, so keep your eyes peeled for the small sign.

expressive statues of Roman gods in the Vrtba Garden

KAMPA MUSEUM

U Sovových mlýnů 2; +420 257 286 147; www.museumkampa.cz; 10am-6pm; 330 CZK; tram stop Hellichova

You can spot Kampa Museum, housed in a former mill inside Park Kampa, from the opposite side of the Vltava River thanks to its line of glowing yellow penguins. The collection of modern art, curated by Jan and Meda Mládek, focuses on Central European artists expressing the struggles of working under oppression in the second half of the 20th century, as well as temporary exhibitions on modern themes. You could spend as little as one hour or an entire afternoon in this space. As you leave, don't miss a photo op with three of David Černý's creepy-but-cute bronze babies with bar codes for faces, crawling in the grass beside the museum. Discounted tickets offering limited access to specific exhibitions are available.

FRANZ KAFKA MUSEUM

Cihelná 2b; +420 257 535 507; www.kafkamuseum.cz; 10am-6pm; 260 CZK; tram or metro stops Malostranská

Inside this museum, fans of this complicated literary legend will find letters, diaries, photographs, music, and installations that explore the connection between his most famous works and their underlying connections to the city of his birth. Kafka was raised by German-speaking Jewish parents and was educated in both German and Czech schools in the Czech Republic. Many of his novels were written in German, but he was able to speak and write both languages. A thorough read of extracts from the letters and manuscripts that have been translated into English could take a couple of hours if you want to fully immerse yourself. Even if you don't step foot inside the museum, it's worth visiting the courtyard, which holds one of David Černý's many controversial sculptures—two men pissing into a pool in the shape of the Czech Republic.

To get here, take a riverside walk just north of the Charles Bridge.

PRAGUE CASTLE DISTRICT (HRADČANY)

✪ PRAGUE CASTLE (PRAŽSKÝ HRAD)

Pražský hrad; +420 224 372 423 or +420 224 371 111; www.hrad.cz; upper tram stops Královský letohrádek, Pražský hrad, or Pohořelec; lower metro stops Malostranská or Malostranské náměstí

SUNSET OVER PRAGUE

Thanks to a spire-filled skyline, a hilly landscape, and a local affinity for nature and being outdoors, watching the sunset on a summer evening in Prague is a spectacular experience. Sunsets in Prague happen around 9pm in June and July and roughly 4pm in December or January. Grab a picnic and a partner (or go solo and peaceful) and try any of these prime viewing spots.

SIGHTS WITH VIEWS

You'll have to pay to catch views at these sights, but the memorable experience is worth the price.

- **Charles Bridge Towers:** It may require patience to get a prime spot in either the Old Town Bridge Tower or the Lesser Town Bridge Towers near Malá Strana, but these views are worth the wait. Stick to Old Town for a direct view of the Prague Castle over the River and Malá Strana for a slightly less crowded experience.
- **The Dancing House:** If you prefer an aerial perch, head to the viewing platform on the top floor of the Dancing House. Entrance fees are waived with purchase of a cocktail (125-200 CZK) or non-alcoholic drink (55-75 CZK) at the adjoining Glass Bar. An off-season evening in spring or autumn offers a more peaceful atmosphere around this popular landmark, while sunset marks the lively beginning of nightlife in summer.

PARKS AND OUTDOOR SPACES

Join the locals in a park or riverside boardwalk for a free visual feast as evening approaches.

- **Náplavka:** Dangle your legs over the edge of this riverside boardwalk between the southern edge of New Town and Vyšehrad and admire the swans on the Vltava River as the evening turns to night.
- **Riegrovy Sady:** The great sloping lawn of this Vinohrady park offers a tree-framed sunset view of the Prague Castle over a sea of red roofs. In the early evening, open space becomes scarce in between couples and families on picnic blankets, dogs curled beside their people, and the occasional Frisbee player or acoustic guitarist setting a soft soundtrack.
- **Vítkov Hill:** My personal favorite sunset spot requires a 20-minute gentle climb from the edge of Žižkov up to the courtyard outside the National Memorial on Vítkov Hill (U Památníku, www.nm.cz). Find a seat on the stairs or stand underneath the massive equestrian statue of Jan Žižka and survey the lands of Old Town, New Town, Karlín, and Malá Strana. This lesser-known vantage point in the outskirts of Prague provides a quieter experience to end the day.

The name Prague Castle can be a bit misleading. The "castle" is not one building of turrets and royal residences, but actually refers to a massive fortified area of government buildings, churches, museums, and manicured gardens. This roughly 70,000-square-meter area (more than 17 acres/750,000 square feet) holds the Guinness World Record for the largest castle complex in the world.

The castle's history covers roughly a century of royal families and architectural styles. Duke of Bohemia Bořivoj I and his wife Ludmila founded the castle around the year 880. Future residents included their grandson Wenceslas I (later known as St. Wenceslas), members of the Habsburg royal family, and Thomas Garrigue Masaryk, the first president of Czechoslovakia in 1918. The Prague Castle remains the seat of the Czech president today, with the flag flying on days he (or she) is in town. The stone-faced, unmovable castle guards outside the main Matthias Gates put on a "Changing of the Guards" ceremony at noon, with a smaller version happening every hour from 7am.

The mixed-and-matched architectural style—from the Gothic-Renaissance-Baroque blend of the St. Vitus Cathedral to the Baroque exterior and Romanesque interior of St. George's Basilica—chronicles an ongoing "home improvement" project that stretched from 880 to the early 1900s. You can spot the more modern elements of Slovenian architect Josip Plečnik's 20th-century touches around the grounds.

Visiting the Prague Castle

The Prague Castle can easily be a multi-hour excursion, and visiting every corner would take multiple days. That said, you can pick and choose the areas that interest you most to customize your exploration, and a combination of 2-4 buildings and gardens can be enough to give you a taste of the castle experience. Those in a hurry or on a budget can take a peek inside St. Vitus Cathedral followed by a walk along the South Garden's panoramic city views, both for free. Add on an hour-long visit to the Lobkowicz Palace for a single-admission entrance to explore aristocratic interiors and an enviable balcony view, plus the optional add-on of an afternoon classical-music concert.

The castle grounds themselves are open from 6am-10pm, while the buildings and museums have shorter hours. Be prepared for a steady stream of tour groups from open to close in high seasons, with slightly more breathing room during off seasons and weekdays.

Ticket options include **Prague Castle—Circuit A** (350 CZK, valid for 2 days), which comprises St. Vitus Cathedral, the Old Royal Palace, "The Story of Prague Castle" exhibition, St. George's Basilica, Golden Lane with the Daliborka Tower, and Rosenberg Palace. **Prague Castle—Circuit B** (250 CZK, valid for 2 days), which includes St. Vitus Cathedral, the Old Royal Palace, St. George's Basilica, and Golden Lane with the Daliborka Tower. A pass to photograph the interiors of the Prague Castle requires an additional 50 CZK ticket.

An official **tour guide** in English (100 CZK per person, per hour, minimum 400 CZK) adds much more color and personalized explanations than an **audioguide** (350 CZK per device for 3 hours, 450 CZK per device per day). To book a guide, visit the information center in the Third Courtyard near the entrance to St. Vitus Cathedral or email info@hrad.cz.

Increased security measures were implemented after protest art group Ztohoven snuck onto the grounds in 2015 and replaced the Czech flag with a giant pair of red boxer shorts. Entrances now require a security checkpoint, no large bags are allowed inside, and drones are prohibited from flying overhead.

ROYAL SUMMER PALACE AND GARDENS (LETOHRÁDEK KRÁLOVNY ANNY)

Mariánské hradby 1; +420 224 372 434 or +420 224 372 415; www.hrad.cz; Apr-Oct only, 10am-6pm; free; tram stop Královský letohrádek

For a peaceful start to your castle tour during the warmer months, use the smaller entrance one tram stop before the main entrance at **Queen Anne's**

Lesser Town, Prague Castle District, and Petřín

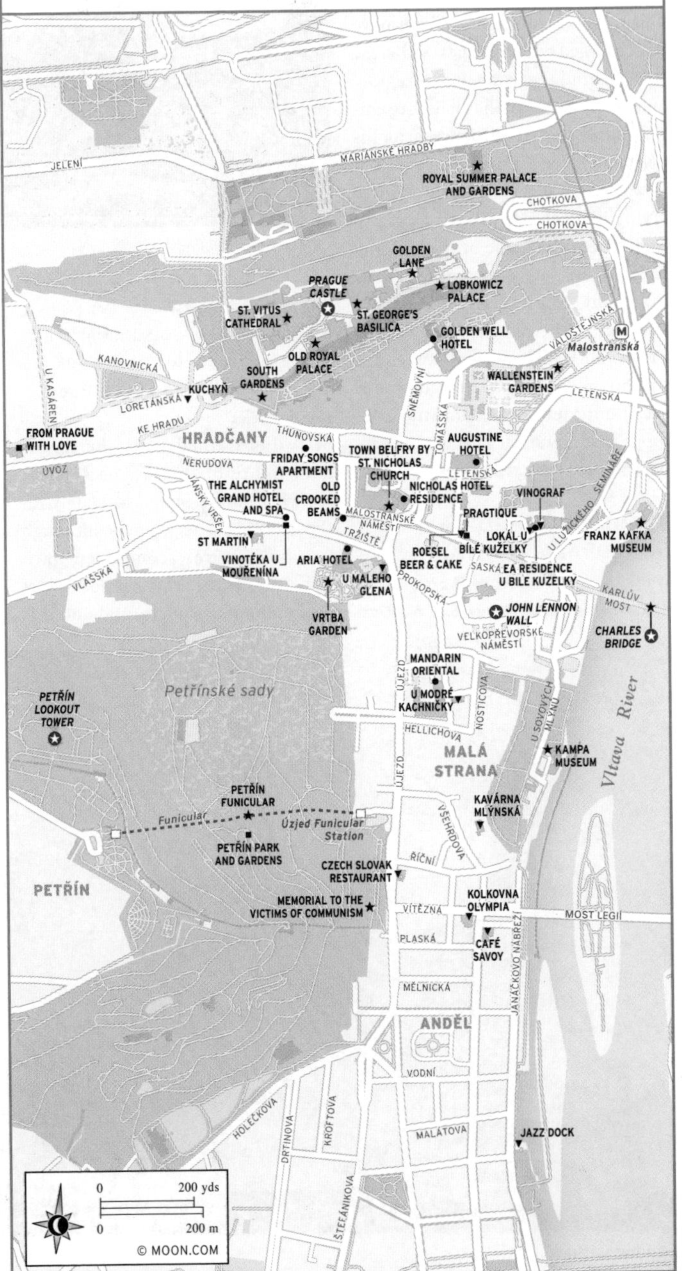

Summer Palace and Royal Gardens. The 16th-century Italian Renaissance villa is etched with scenes of love above its columned terrace arches. Sadly, the story behind that romance is tragic—King Ferdinand I of the Habsburg empire family started construction for his beloved Queen Anne, but she passed away before it was completed after giving birth to her 15th (!) child. To understand the name of the "singing fountain" in the courtyard, you have to actually crouch underneath and put your ear to the cement basin to hear the vibrations. Then peek between the trees in the corner for a first glimpse of the hilltop views over Malá Strana before a leisurely stroll through the gardens toward the castle gates.

ST. VITUS CATHEDRAL (KATEDRÁLA SV. VÍTA)

Pražský hrad-III. nádvoří; +420 224 372 423; www.katedralasvatehovita.cz; Apr-Oct,

Queen Anne's Summer Palace and Royal Gardens

9am-5pm Mon-Sat, noon-4pm Sun; Nov-Mar, 9am-4pm Mon-Sat, noon-4pm Sun; limited free access, full access with Circuit A (350 CZK) or B (250 CZK); tram stop Pohořelec

St. Vitus Cathedral is the dominant figure of the Prague skyline. It's what most people associate with the historic castle grounds, although it wasn't entirely completed until the 20th century. Wenceslas I first built a Romanesque rotunda on this

St. Vitus Cathedral

spot in the 10th century. Charles IV began construction of the Gothic beauty, whose official full name is the Cathedral of St. Vitus, Václav and Vojtěch, in 1344. The long name recognizes the man who founded it (Vaclav or Wenceslas). An arm bone of the Sicilian St. Vitus—the patron saint of dancers and performing artists, who also protects against dog bites, lightning, and oversleeping—is buried in St. Wenceslas's tomb. The third name, Vojtěch, represents a Bohemian bishop killed during missionary work and also buried on this site, although with far less name recognition and fanfare than his famous counterparts.

Construction began in the 14th century but wasn't finished for 600 years. Work on the cathedral was interrupted or damaged throughout the centuries by events like the 15th-century Hussite wars, 16th-century fires, the Thirty Years' War in the 17th century, multiple conflicts under Maria Theresa's 18th-century rule, and neglect by the Habsburgs in the 19th century. It took the spirit of the Czech National Revival and the creation of the Association for the Completion of the St. Vitus Temple in 1859 to see the project through to consecration in 1929.

Exterior: The intricate façade over the western entrance to St. Vitus has a historical look, but this area was actually part of the building's finishing touches. For example, both the rose window and the decorative doors covered with images from the cathedral's storied history weren't completed until the mid-1900s. The four proud architects of this final construction era also weren't shy about adding statues of themselves just below the rose window.

Around the corner to the right of the church exterior lies the truly historical 14th-century **Golden Gate,** on the southern side of the building. The tall pointed doorways of this former entrance, no longer in use, sit underneath mosaics of the Last Judgement, made with around one million individual pieces of glass and marble around 1370.

Interior: The entrance to the cathedral is on the left-hand side of the Western façade, with lines often wrapped around the corner of the building. Both ticketed and non-ticketed visitors stand in the same line. The rear of the church just inside the entryway is as far as non-ticketed visitors are allowed to go, so waves of tour groups come inside to get one shot of the church layout bathed in the light of stained glass. Photos without ticketed permission are not technically allowed, but the prohibition is loosely enforced in this area.

The first perk for ticketed visitors, just past the turnstiles on your left, is an unobstructed view of Alfons Mucha's window scene depicting Christianity coming to the Czech lands. It's painted, not stained glass, which sets it apart from the remaining windows, all done by different Czech artists.

Continuing down the left aisle, the center of the cathedral marks the border between old and new construction, with this expansion shifting the organ to this unusual position on a side wall. The wooden relief on the right side of the aisle depicts four areas (Malá Strana, Hradčany, Old Town, and New Town) that were united in 1784 to form the city of Prague—this feature is often overlooked, but it can be fun to pick out city sights or where you're staying. Crowds generally form a bottleneck at the rear curve of the cathedral and shuffle slowly around the two-ton silver sculpture that tops St. John of Nepomuk's coffin.

St. Wenceslas Chapel lies on this opposite side of the building. It's worth craning your neck to see, through the doorways, the rectangular area that's restricted to all visitors. This chapel also serves as the entrance to the crown jewel storage area, but they're on strict lockdown and only displayed to the public on rare special occasions and anniversaries. Opening the door requires seven keys that are split between public figures, including the Czech president, the Prime Minister, and the Archbishop.

Tickets and tours: The quick, budget-friendly way to see St. Vitus Cathedral is a free peek from just inside the neo-Gothic entryway (which requires waiting in line with ticketed visitors). Any of the sights beyond the entryway of the church require a packaged castle ticket, either Circuit A (350 CZK) or Circuit B (250 CZK). If you decide on an all-access castle ticket, splurge on a tour guide (100 CZK per person, per hour, minimum 400 CZK) for detailed stories that add color to the historic figures represented inside all of the buildings. You can book a guide in person at the information center in the Third Courtyard near the entrance to St. Vitus Cathedral or via email to info@hrad.cz.

OLD ROYAL PALACE (STARÝ KRÁLOVSKÝ PALÁC)

Třetí nádvoří Pražského hradu 2; +420 224 372 434; www.hrad.cz; Apr-Oct, 9am-5pm; Nov-Mar, 9am-4pm; admission only with Circuit A (350 CZK) or B (250 CZK); tram stop Pohořelec or Pražský hrad

The Old Royal Palace, one of the castle's earliest buildings (from the 12th century), is a fun stop for history buffs. The former royal residence and receiving area only retains a few small glimpses of its former glamour, but is best known as the site of war-causing conflict. The intricately webbed ceiling of Vradislav Hall covers a long central corridor that was historically used for jousting matches, and can be seen in the wide "Rider's Staircase" used to exit the room. The palace tower also marks the site of the Second (more famous) Defenestration of Prague in 1618. Another religious rebellion, this time in response to the closure of Protestant chapels in Bohemia by Catholic Emperor Ferdinand II of the Habsburgs, saw two government officials and their secretary tossed out the window. The fall was not fatal—as legend has it, they landed in a pile of excrement before being taken in by Polyxena Lubkowitz at her nearby palace—but that doesn't mean it didn't have consequences. The act is credited for starting the Thirty Years' War that wreaked havoc on Central Europe. The window is marked inside and also marked by a ground-level plaque, and is visible free of charge from the Southern Gardens.

ST. GEORGE'S BASILICA (BAZILIKA SV. JIŘÍ)

Náměstí U Svatého Jiří; +420 224 372 434; www.hrad.cz; Apr-Oct, 9am-5pm; Nov-Mar, 9am-4pm; admission only with Circuit A (350 CZK) or B (250 CZK); tram stop Pohořelec or Pražský hrad

Entrance to St. George's Basilica gives architecture buffs a chance to compare the orange-red Baroque exterior with the minimalist Romanesque arched ceilings inside (and also offers tired tourists a seat in the pews to rest their feet). The large stone coffin in the center of the chapel holds Boleslav I, also known as Boleslav the Cruel, the younger brother of Wenceslas who

St. George's Basilica inside the Prague Castle grounds

was responsible for his murder. It also holds the chapel of St. Ludmila, grandmother of Boleslav and Wenceslas, on the right side of the central staircases. Ludmila's figure is usually depicted with a scarf or veil around her neck to symbolize her death by strangulation, rumored to have been ordered by her daughter-in-law Drahomira. Ludmila raised Wenceslas as a Christian, while Drahomira was loyal to the pagans of Bohemia: yet another instance of Czech resentment over the imposition of a dominant religion.

St. George's Basilica also holds fairly regular evening concerts of classical favorites.

LOBKOWICZ PALACE (LOBKOWICZKÝ PALÁC)

Jiřská 3; +420 702 201 145; www.lobkowicz.com; 10am-6pm; 295 CZK; tram stops Pohořelec or Pražský hrad, metro stop Malostranská

The 16th-century Lobkowicz Palace is the only privately owned building in the castle complex. After centuries of housing one of Prague's early noble families, the building now serves as a museum offering a taste of aristocratic elegance as well as an impressive collection of memorabilia showcasing the family's patronage toward artists and musicians. This is also the house where Polyxena Lobkowicz took in survivors of the 1618 Prague Defenstration from the Old Royal Palace.

Getting to the palace is possible without a castle ticket—just head downhill from St. George's Basilica on Jiřská street parallel to Golden Lane—but visitors will need to buy a ticket to enter the palace itself. Plan at least an hour to immerse yourself in the aristocratic atmosphere.

Inside, descendants of the 700-years-and-counting Lobkowicz family line take great pride in describing their family collection via the audio guide included with admission. The building and its elements were seized in recent decades by both the Nazis and Communists before finally returning to the family. Twenty-two decadent rooms include a massive collection of portraits (of both people and animals) as well as porcelain dishes, an armory of rifles, and chandelier-topped rooms draped with curtains. You may want to skip past some of the detailed family descriptions of the portraits in the first two rooms, simply pausing to admire and learn more about any that catch your eye.

Classical music fans will appreciate the music room, which displays Josef František Maxmilián's patronage of composers such as Mozart, Beethoven, and Handel. Find written symphonies dedicated to the Lobkowicz prince alongside portraits of the composers and historical musical instruments. Time your visit around 1pm to join the audience for daily classical concerts (390 CZK concert or 590 CZK concert + museum) under a frescoed ceiling in the intimate Baroque concert hall, or wander the exhibitions during that hour without crowds.

The museum route ends with a panoramic balcony view of Prague.

Golden Lane in the Prague Castle

GOLDEN LANE (ZLATÁ ULIČKA)

Zlatá ulička; +420 224 372 423; www.hrad.cz; Apr-Oct, 9am-5pm; Nov-Mar, 9am-4pm; admission only with Circuit A (350 CZK) or B (250 CZK); tram stops Pohořelec or Pražský hrad, metro stop Malostranská

For a kitschy glimpse at 16th-century life in this area, choose a castle ticket that includes access to Golden Lane. The rows of 16 small houses built into the fortifying wall were inhabited by goldsmiths and members of the castle guard from the 16th century. Many tour guides offer speculation about alchemists' workshops in the area dedicated to fulfilling the whims of occult enthusiast Rudolph II, but these legends should be taken with a healthy dose of skepticism. The preserved and recreated residences now include Franz Kafka's former writing haunt (number 22) alongside souvenir and toy shops. Number 14 was the home of internationally renowned tarot-card reader Matylda Průšová, also known as "Madame de Thebes," who was arrested and died in custody for predicting the end of the Nazi regime. Climb the stairs into the White Tower (Bílá věž) to view suits of armor and a small torture chamber of brutal instruments.

The entire street is restricted by a ticketed turnstile during opening hours. Free access to walk down Golden Lane without entry to the buildings is possible only after 6pm.

SOUTH GARDENS (JIŽNÍ ZAHRADY)

Pražský hrad; www.hrad.cz; Apr-Oct only, 6am-10pm; free; tram stops Pohořelec or Pražský hrad, metro stops Malostranská or Malostranské náměstí

For panoramic city views with no surcharge, head to the South Gardens. This long strip of manicured lawns and rounded staircases provides an obstacle-free view (if you ignore the selfie-takers) over Malá Strana's red-orange roofs, the Vltava River, Old Town, and the city beyond. Look along the castle walls outside the Old Royal

Palace for the plaque at the base of the tower from which the officials were tossed during the Defenestration of Prague in 1618.

Prague Castle gardens

Those on a free castle tour can access these gardens through the Bull Staircase from the third courtyard beside St. Vitus Cathedral, and opposite the Golden Gate, while those on a full tour can get here from the end of Golden Lane or Jiřská street after visiting the Lobkowicz Palace. The eastern end of these gardens marks the entrance to **St. Wenceslas' Vineyard,** named for the patron saint of the Czech lands, where you can recap your visit over a bottle of Riesling or Pinot Noir (500-900 CZK). You can also exit the South Gardens to the west onto Hradčanské náměstí and walk toward the Strahov Library, Strahov Brewery, or Petřín Park and Lookout Tower.

STRAHOV LIBRARY (STRAHOVSKÁ KNIHOVNA)

Strahovské nádvoří 1; +420 233 107 718; www.strahovskyklaster.cz; 9am-noon and 1pm-5pm; 120 CZK; tram stop Pohořelec

The Strahov Library, with its ceiling murals, ornate globes, and book-lined walls, is the crown jewel of the early 12th-century Strahov Monastery complex, which also includes a gallery and basilica. Inside the library, the intricately decorated Theological Hall and Philosophical Hall feature regularly on "Most Beautiful Libraries in the World" lists—and, unlike the similarly opulent library in Old Town's Klemintinum, which prohibits photos, photography is allowed in Strahov Library for an extra 50 CZK. The Strahov Library is worth a stop for photography fans and architecture buffs, while less-enthusiastic members of any travel group can wait patiently over a beer at the nearby Strahov Monastery Brewery.

The library accepts a limited number of visitors per year to protect the books, and visitors are not allowed to step foot inside the two halls without a guided tour, which must be reserved months in advance. (Book individually via email: erika@strahovskyklaster.cz.) Admission comes with a printed guide in English to provide some history and context. During your visit, if you opt for the tour, be aware that you will likely appear in many visitors' photographs as you walk through the rooms.

The Strahov Monastery was established on this site in the 12th century, but the buildings suffered from centuries of fires and attacks. Ongoing restoration efforts have preserved the 17th-century Baroque style of the Theological Hall, and

the interior of Strahov Library

the Philosophical Hall maintains brighter Classicist elements of the late 18th century.

In addition to angling for photos, you can explore the Cabinet of Curiosities, a full corridor outside the two halls that is lined with artifacts seen as exotic in previous centuries—unusual animals for a landlocked area (crab, turtle, and seashells), the remains of a now-extinct Dodo bird, jeweled books, and Asian statues of warriors and aristocrats.

PETŘÍN

✪ PETŘÍN LOOKOUT TOWER (PETŘÍNSKÁ ROZHLEDNA)

Petřínské sady; +420 257 320 112; www.muzeumprahy.cz; Apr-Sept, 10am-10pm; Nov-Feb, 10am-6pm; March and Oct, 10am-8pm; 150 CZK; tram stop Újezd + Funicular ride

After visiting the newly unveiled Parisian Eiffel Tower in 1889, the Czech Tourist Club decided that the Prague skyline was missing something. The Petřín Lookout Tower was created for the General Land Centennial Exhibition in 1891, serving as a replica in tribute and admiration for its French inspiration. The tower also holds cheeky bragging rights as being technically higher than the Eiffel Tower due to its hilltop location. Climbing the 299 steps to the observation deck gives you one of the highest viewpoints in the city. There is an elevator (60 CZK), but it is seen more as an option for limited mobility and elderly visitors than for tired tourists.

Petřín Lookout Tower

The easiest way to reach the tower is an uphill funicular ride from the Petřín station located inside the park near the Újezd tram stop, and requires the same rules as a ride on any form of Prague's public transport—have a ticket and be sure to validate it before entering. For a simple, cost-free option, you could also walk through the park from the top of the hill after a visit to the Prague Castle or Strahov Monastery, both near the Pohořelec tram stop.

PETŘÍN FUNICULAR

Petřínské sady; www.dpp.cz; 9am-11:30pm; brief closures in March and Oct; 24 CZK; tram stop Újezd

This land-based version of a cable car is more than just the simplest way to ascend Petřín Hill. The Petřín Funicular offers panoramic window views from the base of the hill to the Petřín Lookout Tower, with a stop at one platform in between. This nostalgic hillside transport first ran on a water-based system in 1891, halting operations during World War I before switching to an electrical system when it resumed in 1932. The system took another 20-year break after a landslide in 1965. Since reopening in 1985, the ride has been part of the city's public network; access is included within a valid Prague transport ticket. Carriages leave every 15 minutes from November to March and every 10 minutes from April to October. Look for the Petřín funicular station just inside the grounds of the park when entering near the Újezd tram stop.

The Petřín Funicular is part of Prague's public transport system. There is a ticket machine on site, and a single ride (24 CZK) requires first buying a ticket and then stamping it in the yellow validation machines before boarding the funicular, to avoid a hefty fine from the controllers checking at either side of the ride.

the stark Memorial to the Victims of Communism by Olbram Zoubek

MEMORIAL TO THE VICTIMS OF COMMUNISM

Petřínské sady; free; tram stop Újezd

Seven crumbling bronze men by sculptor Olbram Zoubek line the steps to Petřín Park as a Memorial to the Victims of Communism unveiled in 2002. The first man appears whole, while successive statues are each missing parts of their bodies, symbolizing a commitment to perseverance in the face of the damage inflicted from 1948-1989. The statistics running along the stairs spell out the effects in stark numbers: 205,486 people convicted, 248 executed, 4,500 died in prison, 327 died during illegal border crossings, and 170,938 people left their homes behind to emigrate. The figures are particularly harrowing when lit from below in the evening.

VINOHRADY

PEACE SQUARE (NÁMĚSTÍ MÍRU)

free; metro stop Náměstí Míru

This square is defined by the towering spires of the Neo-Gothic **Church of St. Ludmila** (Kostel svaté Ludmily). The church is best admired from the outside, alongside the residents reading or relaxing on the benches as pedestrians crisscross the bright, flower-lined paths. Easter and Christmas markets in this square are among the city's most popular, when wooden stands fill the air with the sweet smell of crêpes (*palačinky*) and hot honey wine (*medovina*).

Church of St. Ludmila at Náměstí Míru

Vinohrady

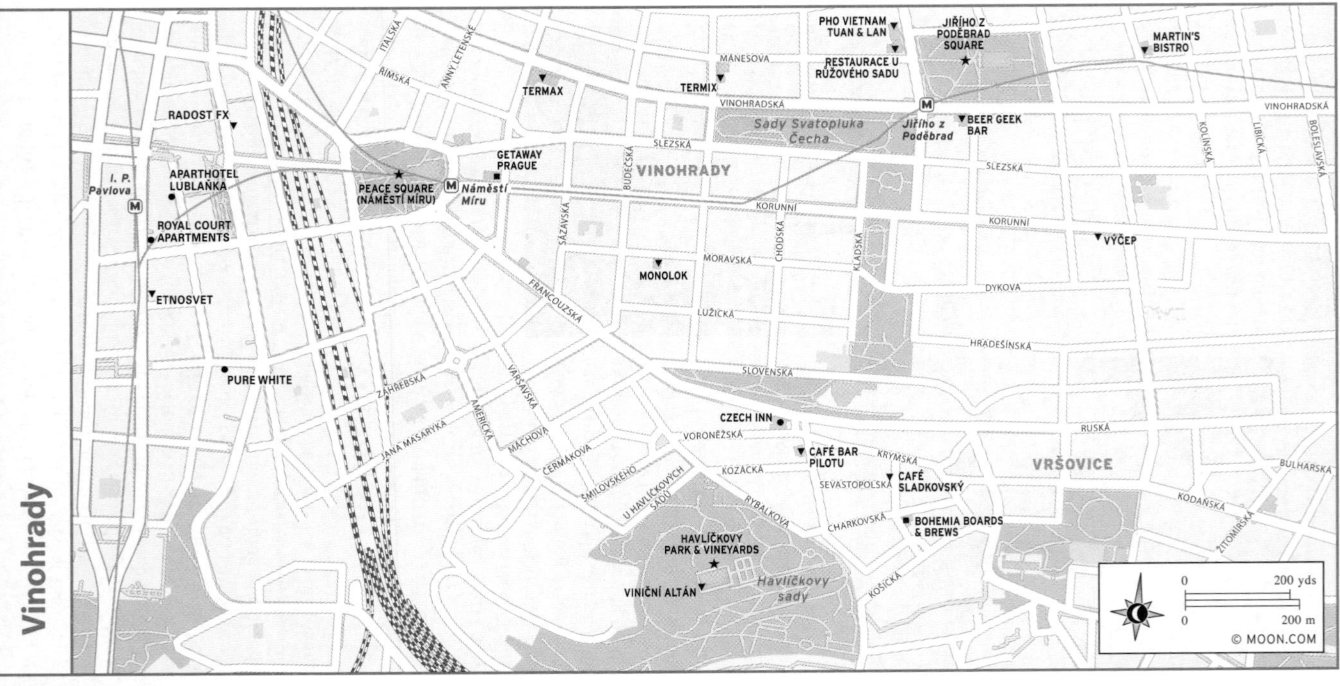
I. P. Pavlova
RADOST FX
APARTHOTEL LUBLAŇKA
ROYAL COURT APARTMENTS
ETNOSVET
PURE WHITE
ITALSKÁ
ŘÍMSKÁ
ANNY LETENSKÉ
PEACE SQUARE (NÁMĚSTÍ MÍRU)
Náměstí Míru
GETAWAY PRAGUE
TERMAX
TERMIX
MÁNESOVA
VINOHRADSKÁ
PHO VIETNAM TUAN & LAN
RESTAURACE U RŮŽOVÉHO SADU
JIŘÍHO Z PODĚBRAD SQUARE
MARTIN'S BISTRO
Sady Svatopluka Čecha
Jiřího z Poděbrad
BEER GEEK BAR
SLEZSKÁ
BUDEČSKÁ
VINOHRADY
KORUNNÍ
SÁZAVSKÁ
CHODSKÁ
KLADSKÁ
VÝČEP
KOLÍNSKÁ
LIBICKÁ
BOLESLAVSKÁ
MORAVSKÁ
MONOLOK
DYKOVA
FRANCOUZSKÁ
LUŽICKÁ
HRADEŠÍNSKÁ
SLOVENSKÁ
ZÁHŘEBSKÁ
VARŠAVSKÁ
AMERICKÁ
JANA MASARYKA
MÁCHOVA
ČERMÁKOVA
ŠMILOVSKÉHO
U HAVLÍČKOVÝCH SADŮ
CZECH INN
VORONĚŽSKÁ
RUSKÁ
CAFÉ BAR PILOTU
KRYMSKÁ
KOZÁCKÁ
SEVASTOPOLSKÁ
CAFÉ SLADKOVSKÝ
VRŠOVICE
BULHARSKÁ
RYBALKOVA
CHARKOVSKÁ
BOHEMIA BOARDS & BREWS
KODAŇSKÁ
ŽITOMÍRSKÁ
HAVLÍČKOVY PARK & VINEYARDS
VINIČNÍ ALTÁN
Havlíčkovy sady
KOŠICKÁ
0 200 yds
0 200 m
© MOON.COM

JIŘÍHO Z PODĚBRAD SQUARE

Free; metro stop Jiřího z Poděbrad

Jiřího z Poděbrad Square is a popular outdoor hangout to enjoy a takeaway meal, browse the farmers market, admire the architecture, or toss a Frisbee in the grass in the heart of neighborhood life in Prague. The large clock face of the modern brown and white Catholic **Church of the Most Sacred Heart of Our Lord** (Kostel Nejsvětějšího Srdce Páně) marks the border where Vinohrady begins to blend into the neighborhood of Žižkov. Take a poll among your group to see how the majority feel about this love-it-or-hate-it piece of early 20th-century architecture. A farmers market of fresh vegetables and flowers, plus ready-to-eat snacks, covers half the square from morning to late afternoon, every Wednesday through Saturday. The area is also surrounded by independent restaurants and coffee shops frequented by the neighborhood's international residents. Grab a seat on the benches lining the central path for some prime people-and-puppy watching before crossing the street to Beer Geek for a microbrew or to Pho Vietnam Tuan & Lan for some takeout Vietnamese food.

Jiřího z Poděbrad Square in Vinohrady

ŽIŽKOV

ŽIŽKOV TV TOWER (ŽIŽKOVSKÝ VYSÍLAČ)

Mahlerovy sady 1; +420 210 320 081; www.towerpark.cz; 9am-midnight; observation deck 250 CZK; tram stop Lipanská or tram and metro stops Jiřího z Poděbrad

It is a fitting testament to Prague's growth and fluctuation that the defining structure of the Žižkov neighborhood offers an array of posh experiences in an area known for its rough-and-tumble reputation. The Žižkov TV Tower, built between 1985 and 1992, holds the title of the tallest building in Prague, at more than 700 feet (216 meters). The interior contains an observation deck with panoramic views as well as an exclusive **One Room Hotel** and the **Oblaca** fine dining restaurant and cocktail bar. Ten of David Černý's giant baby sculptures (similar to those beside Kampa Museum in Malá Strana) can be seen climbing its walls.

OLŠANY CEMETERY AND NEW JEWISH CEMETERY (OLŠANSKÉ HŘBITOVY/ NOVÝ ŽIDOVSKÝ HŘBITOV)

tram and metro stops Želivského

Two important burial grounds serving Prague's Jewish community are located on the outside edge of Žižkov. The massive Olšany Cemetery (Vinohradská 153; +420 272 011 126; www.hrbitovy.cz; May-Sept, 8am-7pm; Mar-Apr and Oct, 8am-5pm Fri; Nov-Feb, 8am-4pm; free) was established in 1680 in response to the Plague epidemic sweeping Europe. Prague's oldest and largest graveyard holds the body of student protester Jan Palach. Across the road, Prague's New Jewish Cemetery (Izraelská 1; +420 224 800 812; www.synagogue.

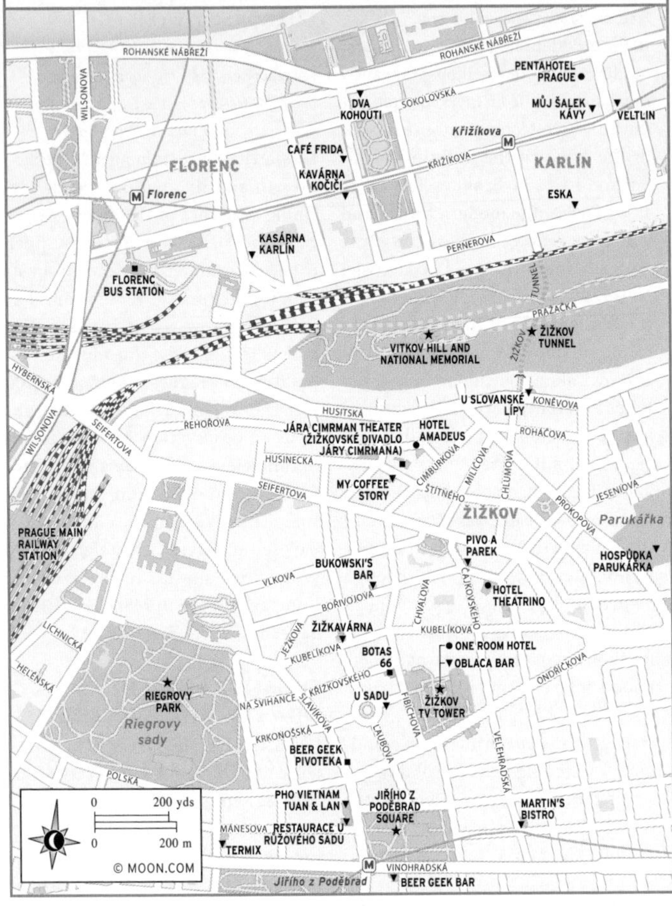

cz; Apr-Oct, 9am-5pm Sun-Thurs, 9am-2pm Fri; Nov-Mar, 9am-4pm Sun-Thurs, 9am-2pm Fri; free), established in 1890, is best known for housing the grave of writer Franz Kafka and his parents (tombstone number 21-14-21) along with a memorial to the Czechoslovak Jews killed during the Holocaust.

VÍTKOV HILL AND NATIONAL MEMORIAL (NÁRODNÍ PAMÁTNÍK NA VÍTKOVĚ)

U Památníku; +420 732 947 509; www.nm.cz; Nov-Mar, 10am-6pm Thurs-Sun; Apr-Oct, 10am-6pm Wed-Sun; memorial 120 CZK; tram stop Biskupcova or bus stop Ohrada

One of the most beautiful places to watch the sunset over Prague is from the National Memorial at Vítkov Hill. A roughly 20-minute walk up the hill from the Žižkov beer garden on the edge of Žižkov treats visitors to an open platform around a towering statue of Jan Žižka on horseback, with the Czech flag flying to your left and the Prague Castle framed by trees directly in front of you. History fans may want to peek inside the National Memorial for the exhibition on important events in 20th-century Czech history. Otherwise, skip the entrance fee and simply enjoy the view.

ŽIŽKOV TUNNEL (ŽIŽKOVSKÝ TUNEL)

Žižkovský Tunel; free; bus stop Tachovské náměstí

The nearly 1,000-foot-long (300-meter) Žižkov Tunnel connects the Žižkov neighborhood with Karlín, whose residents prefer to call it the Karlín Tunnel, underneath Vítkov Hill. The lengthy path is perfectly safe, even though you can't see from one side to the other, and is limited to pedestrians and bicycles. It was originally built for shelter from nuclear fallout. The echo is powerful, and you may often hear shouts or even music on your pilgrimage between the two very different districts of Prague. The tunnel is well lit at night, making it an easy connection for dinner at nearby U Slovanské Lípy on the Žižkov side and an evening drink at one of Karlín's sophisticated wine bars.

LETNÁ AND HOLEŠOVICE

METRONOME

Nábřeží Edvarda Beneše; free; tram stop Čechův most

The giant red Metronome keeping time over Prague is a fairly modern

A towering statue of Jan Žižka watches over the neighborhood named after him.

THE NOTORIOUS DAVID ČERNÝ

Three of David Černý's "Babies" stand outside of Kampa Museum.

If you see a public sculpture in Prague, there is a good chance that David Černý is the artist behind it. The controversial artist was born just before the Prague Spring of 1968 and grew up in the subsequent era of Communist crackdown. When the Velvet Revolution opened Czechoslovakia's borders, Černý seized the opportunity to study in Switzerland and New York City.

The young artist grabbed attention in 1991 by painting a Soviet tank and war memorial bright pink. This earned him an arrest at age 23, but members of parliament repainted the tank pink in protest. Černý didn't stay imprisoned long and the tank was removed. The artist's work (and political statements) continue to decorate and provoke the city—he sent a giant blue middle finger entitled "Gesture" down the Vltava River when President Miloš Zeman was elected in 2013. Below are some of his pieces worth seeking out:

- A seven-foot Sigmund Freud entitled **"Man Hanging Out"** grips a rooftop outside the building at Na Perštýně 14 in Old Town (don't be fooled by the similar man hanging from an umbrella in front of the Mosaic House Hotel).
- The **saint riding an upside-down horse** suspended from the rooftop of Palac Lucerna in Wenceslas Square is also a David Černý creation.
- **"Piss"**—two mechanical men urinating into a Czech Republic-shaped pool in front of the Franz Kafka musem—embodies his cheeky, provocative style.
- Three of his bronze **"Babies"** with barcodes for faces sit beside the Kampa Museum, while 10 of their siblings crawl the sides of the Žižkov TV Tower.
- Černý's latest installation is a rotating, mirrored **head of Franz Kafka** near the National Theater.
- A day trip to Liberec includes his **"Giant's Feast,"** a severed head and beverages decorating the top of a bus stop.
- Head to Olomouc to see **"Adam & Eve"** inside the Museum of Modern Art, or **"Robber"** hanging onto a ledge outside the same building.

monument, built in 1991. The largest statue of Joseph Stalin in the world previously held this perch, keeping a symbolic watchful eye over the city until the Communist-era monument was blown to bits with dynamite in 1962. If you want an up-close look these days, you'll have to dodge the skateboarders who have claimed the cement platform around the metronome and its surrounding ledges. Pop-up beverage/beer stands and occasional concerts cater to the crowds of summer.

Letná and Holešovice

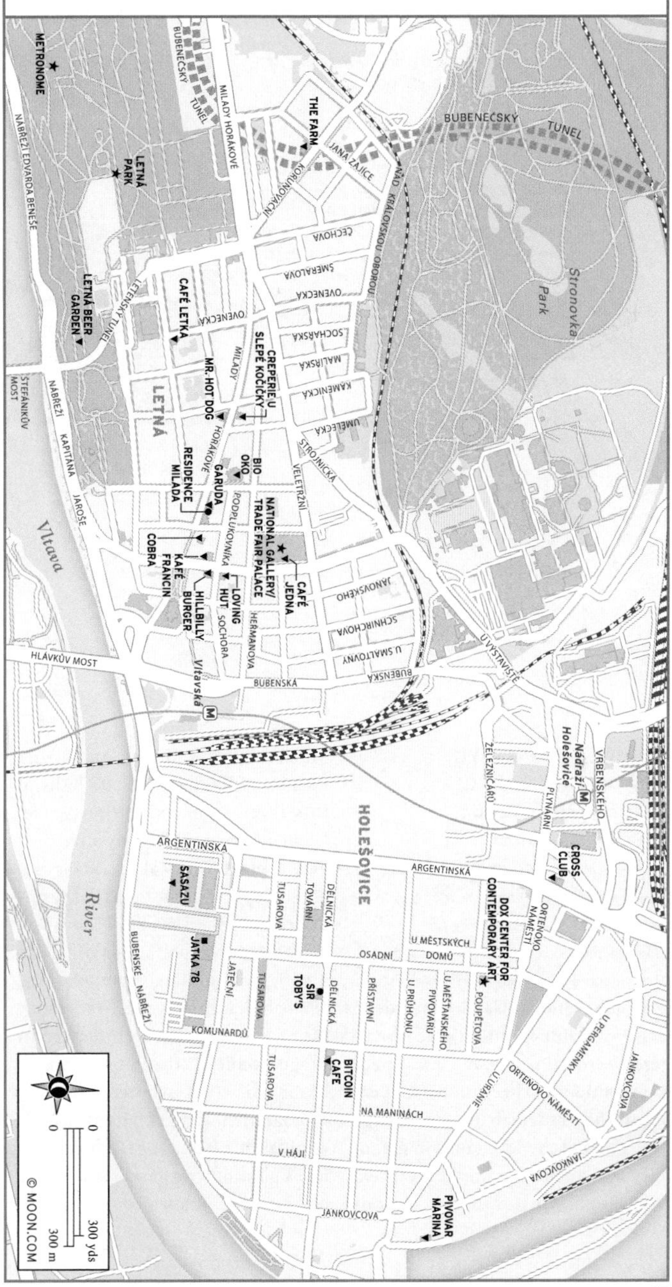

TOP EXPERIENCE

PRAGUE OFF THE BEATEN PATH

Prague's major sights are worth seeing, but the central neighborhoods can be packed with tourists. A good strategy is to visit the top sights that you can't bear to miss for as long as you can stand the crowds—then head to some of the lesser-known neighborhoods for the more undiscovered vibe that backpackers often associated with Prague of the 1990s and early 2000s. This adventure into fewer English-language menus, signage, and tourist-friendly customer service can give a more authentic picture of local life in Prague when approached with patience, preparation, and respect for the space.

Here's what some of Prague's lesser-known neighborhoods have to offer:

Prague's surrounding neighborhoods are full of color and character.

- **Vinohrady:** International, and just baby steps off the tourist path.
- **Žižkov:** Rowdy, and rumored to have the most bars per capita of any European district.
- **Karlín:** Sophisticated, and known for its food and wine bars, Karlín also embodies a spirit of revitalization, with repurposed spaces holding markets and entertainment venues.
- **Holešovice:** Industrial and offbeat. Think: Theatrical space in a former slaughterhouse, or crypto-anarchist coffee shop.

NATIONAL GALLERY—TRADE FAIR PALACE (VELETRŽNÍ PALÁC - NÁRODNÍ GALERIE)

Dukelských hrdinů 47; +420 224 301 122; www.ngprague.cz; 10am-6pm Tues-Sun, 10am-8pm Wed; 220 CZK; free for children and visitors under 26; tram stops Strossmayerovo náměstí or Veletržní palác

Prague's National Gallery includes a collection of exposition places scattered across Prague, but most people mentioning the National Gallery mean the Trade Fair Palace. A large collection of modern and contemporary art—including work by Vincent van Gogh, Gustav Klimt, Alfons Mucha, Claude Monet, and Pablo Picasso—fills the walls and halls of this three-story exhibition space. Contemporary exhibitions often provide context for local life, such as a photography exhibit to mark the anniversary of the 1968 Soviet invasion or painted interpretations of Czech identity and national symbols. The 1920s building was the first example of Functionalist architecture in Prague, built for the Prague Sample Trade Fairs that inspired its name. Join families and art fans at the adjoining Café Jedna to relax over coffee, a glass of wine, and some of the best hummus in town.

DOX CENTER FOR CONTEMPORARY ART

Poupětova 1; +420 295 568 123; www.dox.cz; 10am-6pm Sat-Mon, 11am-7pm Wed and Fri, 11am-9pm Thurs; 180 CZK; tram stop Ortenovo náměstí

The mission of DOX Center for Contemporary Art includes using a variety of art forms to "create a space for research, presentation, and debate on important social issues." Thought-provoking exhibitions provide the starting point for panel discussions, film screenings, and interactive community events on topics ranging from big data and migration to the portrayal of war-torn countries. Recent exhibitions include Chinese contemporary artist Ai Weiwei's statement on refugees and human rights. This former 19th-century industrial space was converted to its present-day incarnation at the beginning of the millennium. Come with an open mind and decompress with a post-excursion discussion at the nearby Bitcoin Café. This place embodies a modern Czech sensibility, both literally and figuratively—Czechs of all ages aren't shy about talking politics or world events over a beer, and the space shows repurposed spaces and art among industry that characterizes the Holešovice neighborhood.

VYŠEHRAD

TOP EXPERIENCE

✪ VYŠEHRAD COMPLEX

V Pevnosti 159/5b; +420 261 225 304; www.praha-vysehrad.cz; free; metro stop Vyšehrad

Legend has it that this vast complex (and the city of Prague itself) was constructed after Princess Libuše looked out over the undeveloped landscape around the 8th century and declared,

walking the grounds of Vyšehrad Complex

"Behold, I see a great city, whose fame will touch the stars."

You can enter the large grass-filled grounds of the Vyšehrad Complex after a short walk from the Vyšehrad metro, taking the exit toward the Congress Center and following the brown street signs pointing the way through a few residential streets. The grounds themselves include a maze of green spaces dotted with statues, alongside some of the city's oldest historic monuments. This quiet complex is far less crowded or touristy than the Prague Castle across the river, but filled with comparable levels of history and beauty. Wander the edges of the park complex for stunning city-wide viewpoints from an alternate angle to those of Old Town or Malá Strana.

Visitors to both Vyšehrad (meaning "high castle") and the Prague Castle are often confused by the lack of Disneyland-style turrets and princess-worthy bedrooms. The term "castle" in Prague is not necessarily a single ornate building, but is used to describe fortified walls surrounding a seat of power, such as this royal base of King Vratislav II in the 11th century.

ST. MARTIN'S ROTUNDA (ROTUNDA SV. MARTINA)

V Pevnosti; +420 224 911 353; www.kkvys.cz; free; metro stop Vyšehrad

Shortly beyond the brick entrance of the Vyšehrad Complex you'll come upon a large circular building seemingly sprouting from the ground. St. Martin's Rotunda is arguably Prague's oldest intact building, dating from the 11th century. It has seen its fair share of battles, after being used as gunpowder storage during the Thirty Years' War from 1618-1648 (much like the Powder Tower of New Town in later years). The rotunda still holds a cannonball in its walls from the Prussians during the Battle of Prague in 1757. These days it maintains a more peaceful existence and is used for occasional religious services. It is not open to tourists, but signage in English in the surrounding courtyard can add context to the view. If you're ready for a break, the entrance to the **Hospůdka Na Hradbách** beer garden is hiding just behind the rotunda.

One of the oldest structures in Prague is St. Martin's Rotunda.

BASILICA OF SAINTS PETER AND PAUL (BAZILIKA SV. PETRA A PAVLA)

Štulcova; +420 224 911 353; www.kkvys.cz; 50 CZK; metro stop Vyšehrad

The tall neo-Gothic towers of the Basilica of Saints Peter and Paul mirror the Prague Castle's St. Vitus Cathedral across the river. The interior of this 19th-century version (damaged and remodeled multiple times since its 11th-century founding by King Vratislav II) contains gorgeous Art Nouveau-style depictions of saints along its columns, along with flowered ceilings and stained-glass windows. Give yourself at least half an hour to browse the eye-catching decoration in soft, muted colors on every wall.

The church was given the status of a "basilica minor" by Pope John Paul II, engraved in a plaque near the ornate doors, as a sign of its importance (as opposed to its architectural style).

The church is accessible to the public from 10am daily (except for 10:30am after mass on Sundays), and stays open until 5pm in winter and 6pm on summer evenings except Thursday, when it shuts at 5:30 to prepare for evening mass. This ornate beauty is far less crowded and more accessible than St. Vitus, drawing visitors on a tight schedule and those wanting to experience a slice of history without elbowing their way through tour groups.

VYŠEHRAD CEMETERY

Štulcova; +420 224 911 353; www.slavin.cz; May-Sept, 8am-7pm; Nov-Feb, 8am-5pm; Mar-Apr and Oct, 8am-6pm; free; metro stop Vyšehrad

Many of Prague's final resting places are artfully decorated with intricate headstones and designed for visitors. In fact, the aisles of Vyšehrad's Cemetery hold many of Prague's celebrities who may enjoy an audience beyond the grave as much as they did while walking the earth. You can enter the cemetery through a gate to the left of the Basilica of Saints Peter and Paul, where a list of famous graves is detailed by number, or from the back of the cemetery after a walk from the Vyšehrad metro station. Some of the names you may recognize include the classical composer Bedřich Smetana, whose resting place is surrounded by towering obelisks. A bust of Antonín Dvořák stands behind a gate along the northern wall. Art Nouveau painter Alfons Mucha's plaque is tucked into a corner of the Slavin Tomb at the top of the stairs near the eastern entrance, and romantic poet Karel Hynek Mácha's name is written in gold on a headstone among the aisles. Literary fans take note that the Kafka buried here is Czech sculptor Bohumil Kafka, not the writer Franz Kafka, whose grave is in the New Jewish Cemetery in Žižkov. Also, "Rodina" is not the most popular Czech surname, but it means "family," so you'll find it on many of the tombstones marking familial plots.

Bars and Nightlife

"Nightlife" is almost the wrong term to use for Prague's beverage scene, considering a cold beer with lunch or an afternoon drinking in a beer garden is as much a part of life as a night on the town. Hikes and cycling trips include multiple pub stops along the way, and a steaming-hot adult beverage at an outdoor holiday market isn't limited to roped-off areas or wristbands. Recreation with a drink in hand is integrated into all hours of daily life.

That prevalence of adult beverages doesn't necessarily translate to a rowdy, shouty landscape. Prague overall has more of a mellow pub culture than a massive club scene (but there are definitely places to dance if desired). Most wine, beer, and cocktail bars apart from the dance clubs stick to table service all night, as opposed to mingling around a bar and communicating directly with a bartender. Budget 30-65 CZK for a domestic beer,

LOCAL LEGENDS

These names are legendary among the local community, but are not necessarily household names to tourists unless you're a fine-arts aficionado. Here is a short rundown of some famous Czechs that locals would be shocked to know you've never heard of.

You will be forgiven for not knowing romantic poet **Karel Hynek Mácha** (1810-1836), but he will be familiar to anyone who visited his statue in Petřín Park. Mácha's most famous work, "Maj" ("May"), uses nature to share stories of life and love, and was translated into English on the 200th anniversary of the poet's birth in 2010.

grave of classical music legend Bedřich Smetana

The music of **Bedřich Smetana** (1824-1884) is celebrated in his hometown of Litomyšl, about two hours east of Prague, with a festival every summer. The classical composer also lends his name to the great concert hall inside the Municipal House. This father of Bohemian music is best known for "Má vlast" ("My Homeland"), which opens the Prague Spring Music Festival each year and includes odes to the Vltava River and Vyšehrad.

Smetana's younger contemporary, **Antonín Dvořák** (1841-1904), gained international, or you could even say intergalactic, recognition for his classical compositions infused with Czech folk influences. Dvořák's "New World Symphony" accompanied American astronauts Neil Armstrong and Buzz Aldrin on their trip to the moon in 1969.

Even if you don't immediately recognize his name, the swirling designs of Art Nouveau painter **Alfons Mucha** (1860-1939) will likely look familiar. While the artistic style is often connected to France, this hero of the movement is undeniably Czech. Mucha's work graces a window in St. Vitus Cathedral, the ceiling murals of Smetana Hall in the Municipal House, and an entire museum in New Town devoted to his posters, paintings, and interesting life story.

Jaromir Jagr (1972-present), one of the most beloved ice-hockey heroes of the modern Czech nation (even though he played many years for the NHL in the US), is an artist on the ice. The Kladno-born god of the sport went pro in the Czech Republic at age 15 and won two Stanley Cup championships with the Pittsburgh Penguins. You can also thank Jagr for helping to popularize the mullet hairstyle in the early 1990s, still embraced by some older Czech men to this day.

depending on the neighborhood, and 50-100 CZK for craft beer and imported microbrews. A glass of wine can vary from 35-150 CZK, and specialty cocktails generally fall into the 150-300 CZK range.

Servers often keep a tally of the drinks on a piece of paper at your table in a traditional pub, or use an automated system in other venues. Separate checks are expected, but it is the responsibility of the patrons to remember what they had and tell the server which food or drinks they want to pay for at the end of the night—something to note if you're the last one of your group to pay the bill! Credit cards are accepted in maybe 65 percent of venues, but many systems don't allow tips on cards, so carrying cash in the local currency is always a good backup plan. Euros may be accepted in some touristy pubs around the center, but usually at an abysmal exchange rate.

The pub scene starts in the early

RESERVATIONS . . . AT THE BAR?

Visitors may be surprised to find that local nightlife requires reservations. For a seat in a popular pub or a table at a wine or cocktail bar, channel your inner planner and call ahead with a name, time, and number in your party, or check the venue's website for an online reservation system. It is possible to bounce from bar to bar, but be prepared for about 50 percent of the places you try to have no seats available. Standing at the bar or in the aisles of a pub isn't generally done. But don't worry—this doesn't mean you have to spend your whole night sitting at a table. Music venues such as Cross Club, Cobra, Nebe, or Lucerna Music Bar, or alternative spaces such as Kasarna Karlín or Přístav 18600—or any of the city's beer gardens—are your best chances to interact with younger locals and meet fellow international visitors.

Make a reservation for "just one beer" (and try to keep it!).

evening around 4-7pm. Many venues and restaurants then transition from dinner to late-night drinks without much change to the atmosphere. A recent smoking ban has also put more patrons on the sidewalks in front of pubs and clubs, so noise ordinances in residential areas usually limit these hours to 11pm or midnight.

Dance clubs may ask for ID to get in the door, and non-EU residents often have to show their passport (not just a copy). Cover charges aren't prevalent, but live music venues may ask for a 50-200 CZK entry fee, depending on the entertainment of the evening. Nightlife in Prague is also fairly casual, and people generally don't worry about changing clothes to go from work, school, or the park to the pub.

NIGHTLIFE DISTRICTS

The international crowd is likely to liven up most establishments around the center. Old Town dance clubs generally cater to a young crowd of college students, tourists, and international bachelor/bachelorette parties looking to down drinks without being 100 percent sure where they're going to wake up.

The pubs and small clubs lining Krymská street in the Vršovice district get a steady stream of business from the large Czech Inn hostel at the top of the hill and the local residents who live in the surrounding area. Lots of pubs spread across the Žižkov neighborhood make for a wide array of choices, but aren't consolidated around a single street.

Wine bars in Karlín and craft-beer pubs in Vinohrady allow for conversation over a quality beverage, while the music venues of Holešovice, from DJs and concerts at Sasazu to hip-hop and electronic music at Cross Club, attract an eclectic crowd.

Try a mini-pub crawl from Letná beer garden to Café Letka to Bio Oko's cinema bar, ending with a cocktail at Cobra to experience the walkable diversity of this neighborhood's nightlife scene.

PUBS

OLD TOWN (STARÉ MĚSTO)

✪ Skautsky Institute

Staroměstské náměstí 4; +420 732 947 509; www.skautskyinstitut.cz; 1pm-10pm Tues, Wed, and Fri; 3pm-10pm Sat and Sun; 1pm-midnight Mon and Thurs

Skautsky Institute is a peaceful escape from Old Town crowds. The laid-back space, run by young adult members of Prague's local Boy and Girl Scouts organization, extends from the light-filled interior with minimalist wooden furniture to the wrap-around balcony in the quiet center of the building. Coffee, craft beer on draft, and light snacks are surprisingly budget-friendly for Old Town Square. This secret hideout is popular with students and location-independent workers.

Skautsky Institute's inner courtyard

T-Anker

Náměstí Republiky 8; +420 722 445 474; www.t-anker.cz; 11am-10pm

For a nostalgic trip through Prague's modern history, take the escalators through the 1970s Kotva Shopping Center up to the modern crowd enjoying a rooftop beer at T-Anker. Nine rotating taps and a full menu keep local office workers and international visitors coming back to this lookout on the eastern edge between Old and New Towns for lunch and after-work drinks. Elevator access direct to the pub is available on the left-hand side when facing the building.

NEW TOWN (NOVÉ MĚSTO)

U Pinkasů

Jungmannovo náměstí 16; +420 221 111 152; www.upinkasu.com; 10am-11pm

Bartenders have kept the regulars of U Pinkasů supplied with foam-topped pints of Pilsner—well, technically half-liters—since the mid-1800s. The pub has expanded over the decades, along with the crowds, into multiple floors of arched ceilings and wooden pub furniture. Try the afternoon for a coveted seat in the Gothic Summer Beer Garden between the stone walls. Reservations strongly recommended.

LESSER TOWN (MALÁ STRANA)

✪ Lokál U Bílé kuželky

Míšeňská 12; +420 257 212 014; www.lokal-ubilekuzelky.ambi.cz; 11:30am-midnight Sun-Thurs, 11:30am-1am Fri-Sat

Multiple Lokál locations across the city take a traditional, casual Czech beer hall and give it a trendy, minimalist twist. Reservations are recommended for a seat in the long halls of Lokál U Bílé kuželky just off the Charles Bridge in Malá Strana. The pours of various foam-levels are largely a gimmick, so stick to a full glass of *pivo* (beer) with locally sourced sausage or marinated cheese as a snack.

Kavárna Mlýnská

Všehrdova 14; +420 257 313 222; noon-midnight

Kavárna Mlýnská on the edge of Park Kampa attracts a mellow, artsy crowd that occasionally includes notorious local artist David Černý. The muraled walls, cozy size, and affordable drinks create a fairly local space, so pull out a few Czech phrases, keep your conversations to a moderate volume, and pay in cash (no cards accepted) to blend in with the crowd.

PRAGUE CASTLE DISTRICT (HRADČANY)

Strahov Monastery Brewery

Strahovské nádvoří 301; +420 233 353 155; www.klasterni-pivovar.cz; 10am-10pm

From the monks who brought you the gorgeous halls of the Strahov Library comes the centuries-old, but refurbished in this millennium, Strahov Monastery Brewery, known locally as "Klášterní pivovar Strahov." While admittedly a little touristy, the 230-seat restaurant and beer hall serves delicious seasonal brews and Czech food with efficient, multi-lingual service and plenty of indoor and outdoor seating.

VINOHRADY

✪ Beer Geek Bar

Vinohradská 62; +420 776-827-068; www.beergeek.cz; 3pm-2am

Beer Geek Bar was one of the earliest purveyors of microbrew culture in Prague. The 32 rotating taps across the street from Jiřího z Poděbrad square still draw an international crowd of locals and travelers to this mid-sized underground pub lined with banquette seating in primary colors. Order your beers and snacks (including 11 flavors of chicken wings from an American head chef) at the bar. The bottle shop of the same name two streets away (at Slavíkova 10) stocks a wide selection of souvenirs for the beer lover in your life. Reservations recommended by phone or email at rezervace@beergeek.cz.

thirty-two microbrews on tap at Beer Geek

Výčep

Korunní 92; +420 720 120 100; www.vycepkorunni.cz; 11am-11pm Mon-Thurs, 11am-midnight Friday, noon-midnight Sat, noon-10pm Sun

This casual new addition to the Vinohrady neighborhood is a rare Bohemian pub serving delicious Moravian beer from the Dalešice brewery. Part pub, part restaurant, the refreshing soundtrack of folk music instead of international pop tunes draws a slightly older crowd of neighborhood residents and tourists in for a drink or a meal. A semi-upscale selection of Moravian wine, homemade lemonades, and specialty coffee offer non-beer choices for mixed crowds. Reservations recommended.

ŽIŽKOV

Pivo a Parek

Bořivojova 58; +420 734 201 195; 2pm-10pm Mon-Fri, 4pm-10pm Sat-Sun

The limited menu of Pivo a Parek is as simple as translating the name "beer and hot dogs." That casual simplicity extends to the chalkboard-menu-and-wooden-table interior of this mid-sized staple. A lively summer beer garden in the inner courtyard has a residential feel in the shadow of the Žižkov TV Tower. If the 10pm closing

THE BEST CZECH BEVERAGES

In Prague, the local custom is to stick to the deliciously simple beer or wine by the glass, or indulge in high-end cocktails heavy on flair and presentation. Ordering a rum and Coke in a traditional Czech pub is likely to get you a shot of rum plus a bottle of cola (charged for both), and maybe a glass of ice to mix them yourself! (If you're looking for cocktails, choose a place specializing in mixology.)

Homemade lemonades *(domácí limonády)* come in all kinds of flavors.

BEER

Beer is the local beverage of choice, and cheaper than water (!) on most menus. A beer in Prague can range from 30 CZK for a half-liter in small neighborhood pubs, rising to around 50 CZK in more touristy areas around the city center or Malá Strana, and up to 75-100 CZK for an imported microbrew. Most locals prefer a foam-topped **Pilsner Urquell,** although the growing microbrewery scene caters to a broadening array of tastes—*Matuška* and *Únětice* are some popular up-and-coming brands.

WINE

Central Europe's climate and geography favor white wines and lighter, fruit-forward reds, with the eastern region of Moravia producing some of the best domestic labels.

Burčák is a sweet young wine similar to Beaujolais nouveau. You won't find it on a lot of wine menus, but it starts to pop up in plastic bottles and wine festivals from around September until the end of November. Warning: this easy-to-drink autumn treat packs a killer headache upon overconsumption.

When the weather turns cold, gloved hands begin to clutch glasses of ***svařák,*** the local take on mulled wine sold at most Christmas markets and some traditional Czech pubs in winter. *Svařák* is less sweet and more citrusy than traditional mulled wine, and is often spiked with Czech rum or brandy.

To satisfy a sweet tooth at Christmas or Easter markets, try a small glass of ***medovina,*** a sugar-packed honey wine that can be served hot or cold.

SPIRITS

For a taste of local spirits, skip the absinthe and order a throat-burning shot of ***slivovice,*** a clear plum brandy. Alternatively you could try some ***Becharovka,*** an herbal liqueur with hints of cinnamon and pine from a distillery in Karlovy Vary, best described with the phrase "it tastes like Christmas." In warmer weather, order it with tonic and a slice of lime to create a "Beton" cocktail.

NON-ALCOHOLIC

Domácí limonády translates literally to "homemade lemonade" but means a freshly mixed, sparkling drink infused with fresh fruit, cucumber, ginger, or mint, to name a few flavors. Prague's rapidly growing **specialty coffee scene** has sparked a generation of baristas who embrace the craft as a passion beyond a profession.

time is early for your tastes, grab some takeaway bottles from their well-stocked beer fridges or head down the street to Bukowski's Bar for a late-night cocktail.

KARLÍN

Dva Kohouti

Sokolovská 55; +420 604 611 001; www.dvakohouti.cz; 4pm-2am Mon-Fri, noon-2am Sat, noon-10pm Sun

The young guys behind the "two cocks" (as the name loosely translates) are well known in the local brewery scene, drawing crowds from the moment they opened in late 2018. The interior of this brewery and taproom is simple—wooden benches and tables on one side of the warehouse-style space, standing tables and exposed tanks on the other. The fence-enclosed cement beer garden attracts young professionals from the area in summer and smokers in winter. No reservations are taken, so arrive before 5pm on weekdays or try a weekend afternoon if you want a seat.

Dva Kohouti brewery and pub in Karlín

LETNÁ AND HOLEŠOVICE

Café Letka

Letohradská 44; +420 777 444 035; www.cafeletka.cz; 8am-midnight Mon-Fri, 10am-midnight Sat, 10am-10pm Sun; cash only

Prague bars are usually split into two camps: great beer and a nondescript house wine, or an impressive wine selection and one decent beer. Café Letka serves the best of both worlds in an intimate setting of distressed wood, pillow-lined windows, and pastel accents. Quality coffee and a breakfast menu bring a morning crowd that blends seamlessly into leisurely lunches and post-work crowds unwinding over adult beverages and late-night snacks. This is a sophisticated alternative to the nearby Letná beer garden. Cash only; weekend reservations recommended.

TOP EXPERIENCE

✪ BEER GARDENS

The phrase *Česká pohoda* is one of those tricky, untranslatable ideas, but is basically used to describe enjoying life in good weather. Combine two essential elements of Czech social life—beer and being in nature—and you've got the idea. The opening of beer gardens in nearly every neighborhood is a sure sign that the season of sunshine has arrived. Each of the city's beer gardens has a distinct character.

ŽIŽKOV

Žižkov Beer Garden

Koněvova; +420 774 567 367; May-Sept (usually), 11am-midnight daily, depending on weather

Žižkov Beer Garden, at the base of Vítkov Hill near the Ohrada bus stop, feels more like an outdoor barbeque or family reunion. Pop music from recent decades blasts from speakers of questionable quality and neighborhood dogs run free in the surrounding grass while local residents sip Staropramen

KASARNA KARLÍN & PŘÍSTAV 18600

Kasarna Karlín, former army barracks turned bar and event space

The Karlín neighborhood is known for food, wine, and being an ideal place to live, but is also a neighborhood in transition: there is construction around the neighborhood, such as the rebuilding of a bridge of railway tracks into shops that will fill the stone arches underneath it. (At the time of writing, they were covered in scaffolding.)

Kasarna Karlín (Prvního Pluku 2; www.kasarnakarlin.cz; 1pm-11:30pm), which opened in June 2017, is part of the early generation making the neighborhood an up-and-coming destination. Every corner of the outdoor space, located inside repurposed industrial barracks, is packed with entertainment, with rotating options like a volleyball court, outdoor cinema, view tower, and a metallic unicorn statue in the summer or an ice rink in winter. Mini-art galleries, cafés, bars, and live music are tucked into the various doorways surrounding the square, making it easy to drift from one space to the next for a change of scenery. This year-round hot spot attracts an ultra-cool international crowd. Come for a drink, or catch some unstructured live music performances. The live music shows are more like seeing a band in a friend's basement than a concert venue—people wander into the room, listen to a song, and then wander back out to the courtyard.

Přístav 18600 (Rohanský ostrov 8; www.18600.cz; late April-Sept, noon-10:30pm, weather permitting): Tucked behind rows of industrial office buildings and down a dirt path beside the Vltava River lies an oasis of outdoor beer stands and picnic tables, with a volleyball court and a playground for families. A group of young architects created the laid-back hangout in 2014 to relax among wild plantlife instead of pristine parks. For added fun, take a summertime ferry ride from Holešovice below street level near the Pražská Tržnice tram stop to arrive after an afternoon at DOX Contemporary Art Center or while staying at Sir Toby's Hostel. Bring cash for a reusable-cup deposit.

under beach umbrellas. This residential favorite feels endearingly stuck in a previous era and makes for a perfect stop before or after climbing Vítkov Hill to admire the view.

Hospůdka Parukářka

Vrch sv. Kříže Parukářka; +420 776 366 410; www.parukarka.cz; May-Sept (usually), 1pm-11pm daily, depending on weather

The outdoor patio of this smallish pub-in-a-park has a relaxed, neighborhood vibe. Leave a 50 CZK deposit for your glass and grab a spot in the grass. The hilly landscape of the surrounding park includes impressive views of the Žižkov TV Tower and the city center in the distance. Time your visit around June when this park hosts the **Žižkovské pivobraní**, a neighborhood microbrew festival with multiple tents and live bands that draws an all-ages crowd.

LETNÁ AND HOLEŠOVICE

✪ Letná Beer Garden

Letenské sady 341; +420 233 378 200; May-Sept, 11am-midnight daily, depending on weather

You can tell that Prague summer has begun when the drinks start flowing around Letná Beer Garden, located inside the park of the same name, with arguably the best view in town over the

a beer garden with a view at Letná Park

Vltava River and Old Town. Hundreds of international visitors pack the rows of picnic tables along the edge of the hillside park, with dogs and their humans often stopping here for a break on a walk through the park. Carts and stands along the edges serve primarily beer, with some vendors also offering cider, wine, and shots of liquor. Available snacks are largely meat-based dishes like grilled sausages. Feel free to bring a deck of cards or entertainment for your group, but no outside food or drink is allowed, so step into the grassy lawn of the surrounding park if you want to bring a picnic or vegetarian snacks.

VYŠEHRAD

Hospůdka Na Hradbách

V Pevnosti 2; +420 734 112 214; 2pm-midnight Mon-Fri, noon-midnight Sat-Sun, indoor pub open year-round with garden depending on weather

This beer garden tucked inside the Vyšehrad Complex just behind St. Martin's Rotunda is a laid-back, all-ages space popular among locals. Picnic tables lining the outer edges offer a view of the city if you peek over the hedges. The center area of the two-tiered lawn offers more tables surrounding an open play space, drawing families and the stroller set to enjoy a drink within eyesight of their young ones. Beverage stands along the edges offer a wide selection of beer, wine, cider, and *domácí limonády* (a sparkling soft drink in various fruit and herb flavors), plus grilled meats and snacks. The small indoor pub on site can provide refuge in a rainstorm, but the beer garden is the star of this space.

COCKTAIL BARS

OLD TOWN (STARÉ MĚSTO)

L'Fleur

V Kolkovně 5; +420 734 255 665; www.lfleur.cz; 6pm-3am; cocktails 175-250 CZK

Most of Old Town's cocktail bars center around speakeasy style, prohibition, or a bygone era of New York City, complete with suspendered staff and Manhattan prices. L'Fleur, with its stained-glass windows, exposed brick walls, and cozy banquette seating, offers a different twist. The staff are both knowledgeable and refreshingly unpretentious. The cocktail list takes inspiration from museums and artistic eras, like Art Nouveau-named drinks served in glasses with swirling designs, and the presentation strikes the right balance of cute without falling into kitsch. Try a Thé Vert and Passiflore ("green tea and passionflower") or go for the current featured cocktail, usually based around a seasonal fruit or herb. L'Fleur is praised equally for its champagne list alongside its mixology, and an unpublicized food menu is available upon request. Reservations recommended.

Club NoD

Dlouhá 33; +420 733 307 600; www.nod.roxy.cz; 1pm-1am Mon-Fri, 4pm-1am Sat-Sun; cocktails 100-130 CZK

Housed inside a progressive experimental theater, Club NoD serves simple-but-good drinks in a visually

LOCAL BEER CULTURE

As one of the oldest brewing cultures around, Czechs take *pivo* (beer) very seriously, and the country ranks among the highest per-capita consumption rates in the world. A few things you should know:

Try a Svijany if you get a chance.

- **Pilsner is king.** While local microbrews are starting to expand the national palate, don't expect to find stouts, reds, or IPAs outside of select beer pubs. Try a Pilsner Urquell for the classic experience, and if you spot a Svijany sign (my personal favorite beer) outside any neighborhood pubs, duck inside for at least one.
- **Foam is a sign of freshness.** You haven't been shortchanged if the liquid doesn't reach the brim of your glass. A typical pour has a frothy head that leaves rings below the rim with each sip.
- **Choose your size.** When ordering a beer, you'll be asked if you want a large (*velké*), which is a half-liter (almost 17 ounces), or small (*malé*) one of 0.3 liters (just over 10 ounces), particularly if you appear to be female.
- **Practice your toast.** The Czech version of "cheers" is "*Na zdraví*" (literally meaning "to health") and pronounced roughly "NAH-straw-vee." Emphasizing the first syllable is important to differentiate it from the Russian "*na zDROvvje*" (being lumped in or confused with other Slavic-speaking countries is a pet peeve among many Czechs). Toasting in a Czech pub is common for the first round. To toast, each person at the table should make eye contact while clinking glasses. Reaching over or under another set of arms is not allowed. Yes, this takes some time for each pair to acknowledge everyone else—it's a ritual that highlights the personal connection of sharing a beverage.
- **Drink to your health.** If you share a *pivo* with a local, you might be surprised to hear people describe it as "healthy." Many Czechs like to tout the level of vitamins in their favorite beverage and will counter any health-conscious criticisms by pointing out the amount of sugar in most non-alcoholic options.
- **Take your time.** Prague is not a binge-drinking city, and you won't win any points for chugging in record time. In fact, many young people find it strange that the losers in American drinking games are punished with sips. In true Czech style, beer is to be enjoyed, savored, and revered all day long over lunch, dinner, and evenings with friends.

stimulating environment of rotating art exhibitions, from photography and paintings to light installations, to explore with your beverage of choice in hand. This café-by-day becomes a pre-and-post-theater bar by night. The mid-sized room of white booths and wood tables is populated with an all-ages crowd discussing the latest gallery exhibit or enjoying a pre-party drink before heading next door to dance at Club Roxy.

NEW TOWN (NOVÉ MĚSTO)

Anonymous Shrink's Office

Jungmannova 11; +420 608 911 884; 6pm-2am Sun-Thurs, 6pm-3am Mon-Fri; cocktails 235 CZK

The ingredients may be a mystery, but that's half the fun of ordering "cocktail therapy" based on a Rorschach-test menu at Anonymous Shrink's Office. Settle into a high-backed, brown leather chair in this candlelit, underground brick cave—or, if you're looking for a private table and you ask nicely as you enter, the bar staff might show you the secret room hidden behind a bookshelf. This newcomer to the Prague cocktail scene attracts young professionals and international travelers, but the doorbell required for entry ensures that it's never overcrowded. Reservations recommended.

Hive Bar

Křemencova 8; +420 739 238 258; www.hivebar.cz; 6pm-2am Tues-Sun; cocktails 100-150 CZK

Formerly the Funky Bee, this recently renovated cocktail space now focuses on rum- and honey-based drinks, on a lively street of dance clubs and bars targeting international crowds. This intimate, dimly lit venue works as a meeting point for a pre-party cocktail before heading to nearby Nebe dance club. One quirky discount for athletic travelers: beach volleyball players receive 10 percent off if they can show a photo of where they play.

✪ Glass Bar

Jiráskovo Náměstí 6; +420 703 651 330; www.glassbar.cz; 10am-midnight; cocktails 125-200 CZK

To access the 360-degree views from the rooftop of the Dancing House you can: 1) stay at the Dancing House Hotel, 2) pay 100 CZK for terrace access, or 3) order a cocktail (125-200 CZK) or non-alcoholic drink (55-75 CZK) at the Glass Bar with entry included. The cozy, window-lined indoor space on the top floor of this architectural masterpiece offers quiet elegance in the off-season. Summer months bring a livelier vibe to the summer terrace surrounding the twisted metal orb atop the building.

VINOHRADY

✪ Café Bar Pilotu

Dónská 19; +420 739 765 694; 5pm-midnight Mon-Thurs, 5pm-1am Sat-Sun; cocktails 150-200 CZK; tram and bus stop Krymská

For craft cocktails and a casual atmosphere, head to Café Bar Pilotu near the top of bar-lined Krymská street in the trendy Vršovice neighborhood. Bookshelves and a grand piano establish a living-room vibe hosted by inventive mixologists. The creative cocktail list is inspired by neighboring businesses—think fresh ingredients for a vegetarian restaurant or an everything-on-the-shelves approach for the convenience shop.

ŽIŽKOV

Bukowski's Bar

Bořijovova 86; +420 773 445 280; 7pm-3am; cocktails 90-150 CZK

Bukowski's Bar is cool for all the same reasons as the Žižkov neighborhood. It's affordable, comfortable, nonjudgmental, a little grungy, and always up for a party. The friendly staff at this long-standing, all-ages, local favorite know their way around the bar. Dim lighting and a candle-lined bookshelf covering one wall set a homey atmosphere to the multi-room venue, with conversations varying from intimate whispers to slurred debates from table to table.

Oblaca Bar

Mahlerovy sady 1; +420 210 320 086; www.towerpark.cz; 7pm-3am; cocktails 250 CZK

For a more upscale experience, try a cocktail with a panoramic view at Oblaca Bar inside the Žižkov TV Tower. The unofficial dress code in this sophisticated crowd is fashion forward, and you'll need to check in with a hostess on the ground floor to be allowed access to the elevator. Reservations required, especially on weekends or during peak seasons.

LETNÁ AND HOLEŠOVICE

Cobra

Milady Horákové 8; +420 778 470 515; www.barcobra.cz; 8am-2am Mon-Fri, 10am-2am Sat, 10am-midnight Sun; wine 50-150 CZK

The bar staff at Cobra like to get creative, so make sure to investigate the latest specialty cocktail list. This trendy, minimalist environment of exposed lightbulbs and bar-stool seating includes a rotating set of DJs from Thursday-Saturday nights. Take note of the address or look for the small door sign of this otherwise unmarked and easy-to-miss venue.

CLUBS AND LIVE MUSIC

Dance clubs start to fill up around 10pm and "last call" is generally up to the venue, with no legally required closing times.

OLD TOWN (STARÉ MĚSTO)

Club Roxy

Dlouhá 33; +420 608 060 745; www.nod.roxy.cz; 10pm-5am; cocktails 90-140 CZK

Club Roxy has been packing the dance floor since 1992, as long as the independent Czech Republic has existed. The underground Art Deco concert space hosts an international lineup of electronic music, hip-hop, and rock shows that draw a mixed crowd on any given night of the week. Tickets and cover charges vary, so browse the lineup to see what's on during your stay.

NEW TOWN (NOVÉ MĚSTO)

Nebe

Křemencova 1; +420 608 644 784; www.nebepraha.cz; 6pm-3am Tues, 6pm-4am Wed-Thurs, 6pm-5am Fri-Sat; cocktails 100-125 CZK

For a dressed-up night of drinking and dancing, head to any of Nebe's three locations across Náměstí Republiky, Václavské náměstí, and Karlovo náměstí. The underground club near Karlovo náměstí attracts a young, lively bunch bouncing to current Top 40 hits well into the pre-dawn hours. Reservations recommended for early evening cocktails or a table to call home base.

✪ Lucerna Music Bar

Vodičkova 36; +420 224 217 108; www.musicbar.cz; cocktails 100 CZK

Friday and Saturday nights at Lucerna Music Bar flash back to the tunes from the 1980s and '90s—decades that Communist Czechoslovakia only partially got to experience. The crowd at this massive dance hall spans decades, but every one of them can pull out the moves to "(I've Had the) Time of My Life" and "Greased Lightning" on cue when these crowd favorites hit the speakers. Weekdays offer an international live music lineup of slightly more current artists. Hours vary per event, but the box office is open for questions from 9am to 7pm on weekdays.

LGBTQ+ PRAGUE

Prague's live-and-let-live attitude ranges from tolerance to celebration for the gay and lesbian community, with a popular Pride parade each summer, a Mezipatra film festival (www.mezipatra.cz) each fall, and Queer balls (www.queerball.cz) held in Prague and Brno in February or March. Czech culture is generally less accepting but usually not actively hostile or aggressive toward trans individuals. The overall landscape is generally safe for LGBTQ+ residents to enter any pub, dance in any nightclub, or hold hands while walking down the streets, but a romantic advance toward another patron outside of a designated gay club may not be well received. **Prague Pride** (www.praguepride.cz) keeps a list of recommended hotels and bars where visitors should be welcomed with open arms.

Prague's cis gay male club scene has historically centered around the Vinohrady neighborhood but has expanded into multiple neighborhoods. The small, neon-lit dance floor at Vinohrady's **Termix** (Třebízského 4a; +420 222 710 462; www.club-termix.cz; 10pm-6am Wed-Sat) is generally packed with young men dancing to Top 40 hits, while **Termax** (Vinohradská 40; +420 222 710 462; www.club-max.cz; 10pm-6am Fri-Sat), just a few streets away, claims the title of Prague's largest gay bar.

- **Freedom Night** parties (www.freedomnight.cz) cater to a cis lesbian crowd with monthly DJ dance parties around Prague every third Friday, plus additional events in Brno, Pilsen, and Bratislava, Slovakia. The Prague party is often hosted at **PM Club** (Trojická 10; +420 222 518 097; www.pmclub.net; 4pm-4am daily) near the Vltava River and the base of Vyšehrad hill. **Jampa Dampa** (V Tůních 10; +420 604 774 959; www.jampadampaprague.cz; 8pm-3am Wed, 8pm-5am Sat-Sun) in New Town is also known to welcome a lesbian crowd.

- For a quieter vibe during daylight hours, head to **Q Cafe** (Opatovická 12; +420 776 856 361; www.q-cafe.cz; 1pm-2am daily) for a relaxing atmosphere with subtle rainbow-themed touches around the bar and bench seating. This New Town location near Karlovo náměstí welcomes a mixed crowd of the LGBTQ+ community and allies.

- For further questions or advice, try **Trans*parent** (www.transparentprague.cz) for the trans community or Brno-based STUD (www.stud.cz) for the wider LGBT community.

LESSER TOWN (MALÁ STRANA)

U Maleho Glena

Karmelitská 23; +420 257 531 717; www.malyglen.cz; 7:30pm-2am; 200 CZK cover charge downstairs

The intimate underground jazz club at U Maleho Glena draws a packed house nearly every night of the week for live music on a small stage, so reservations are recommended. The main floor restaurant above the performance area offers a menu of Tex-Mex, Czech classics, American burgers, and vegetarian options, also available downstairs, so come early for dinner to get a great seat for the 9pm nightly shows.

Jazz Dock

Janáčkovo nábřeží 2; +420 774 058 838; www.jazzdock.cz; tickets 175-375 CZK

Prague's favorite jazz club sits on the water, lined with windows, hosting live jazz concerts late into every night of the week. Jazz Dock opened in 2009 on the Smichov riverbank to create an affordable alternative to more expensive tourist venues in the city center, where at least half of the scheduled performers are Czech musicians. Tickets are sold in two levels, with one price guaranteeing a seat and another for standing room only. Jazz dock is open until 4am most nights and 2am on Sundays. Doors open earlier from April-Sept, starting at 1pm Fri-Sun and 3pm Mon-Thurs. In the colder months of Oct-Mar the party starts at 3pm Fri-Sun and 5pm Mon-Thurs.

VINOHRADY

Radost Fx

Bělehradská 120; +420 224 254 776; www.radostfx.cz; 11pm-5am Thurs-Sat; cocktails 100-150 CZK

A late-night party at Radost FX can keep the dance floor packed until 5am on a good night. The mid-sized dance floor, with partitioned areas of lounge seating around it and intricate lighting, sets an atmosphere of casual elegance. Rihanna's video for "Please Don't Stop the Music," shot here in 2007, will give you a stylized glimpse inside. Thursdays are a hip-hop party, Friday nights have house or electronic beats, and Saturdays blast R&B and trap to keep the crowds energized.

Cross Club's steampunk exterior

LETNÁ AND HOLEŠOVICE

Cross Club

Plynární 23; +420 736 535 010; www.crossclub.cz; 6pm-5am Sun-Thurs, 6pm-7am Fri-Sat; cocktails around 100 CZK

The steampunk décor of mechanical sculpture and moving gears make **Cross Club** easy to spot on the streets of Holešovice. Two stages of hip-hop, dubstep, drum and bass, and electronic music draw a rowdy crowd until all hours. Weekends often come with a cover charge around 100 CZK.

Performing Arts

With glamorous interiors, affordable prices, and a rich history of classical music, there's good reason that Prague is ranked one of Europe's top cultural and creative destinations.

CLASSICAL MUSIC

Municipal House

Náměstí Republiky 5; +420 222 002 101; www.obecnidum.cz; tickets 500-1,500 CZK depending on event; tram or metro stop Náměstí Republiky

Smetana Hall inside the Municipal House has the honor of opening the Prague Spring concert each year with a performance of its namesake's symphony *Má vlast* ("My Country"). Gorgeous murals encircle the domed ceiling of this home to the Prague Symphony Orchestra (FOK). More than 1,250 seats line the floor and surrounding balconies, with fantastic acoustics no matter which you choose. The smaller 300-seat **Sladkovsky Hall** and 150-seat **Gregr Hall** provide more intimate settings for chamber concerts.

Rudolfinum

Alšovo nábřeží 12; +420 227 059 227; www.rudolfinum.cz; box office Sept-June, 10am-6pm Mon-Fri; July-Aug, 10am-3pm

DRESSING FOR A NIGHT AT THE THEATER

When it comes to fashion in the Czech Republic, a sense of appropriateness often trumps being trendy. At theaters and concert halls, tourists won't be turned away for wearing jeans or shorts, but they're definitely likely to get a few sideways glances. Instead, aim for wedding-appropriate attire when visiting the ornate halls of the national theaters and concert venues. Cocktail dresses and a suit and tie (at least a collared shirt or unwrinkled top and trousers) are a safe bet. Opening nights and premieres may even inspire floor-length gowns and tuxedos among some regular theater-goers. The more avant-garde theaters (e.g., Nová scéna or Jatka 78) can be a little more casual, but overall a night of entertainment is treated with a sense of reverence.

Now, this doesn't mean that Czech theaters are elitist environments. On the contrary, Prague is one of the most affordable European capitals to take in a show. Enjoyment and appreciation for fine arts is an ingrained element of Czech culture—this is, after all, a country that elected a playwright as their first president. Dressing up is simply a sign of respect, so throw a special occasion outfit into your suitcase to complement the beauty of your theatrical surroundings.

Mon-Fri; tickets 300-3,000 CZK depending on event; tram or metro stop Staroměstská

There are two concert halls housed inside the Rudolfinum—the stately Dvořák Hall, named for the renowned composer Antonin Dvořák, who conducted the first Czech Philharmonic concert in 1896, and the smaller chandeliered ceiling of the Suk Hall, added during the 1940s renovations. This home of the Czech Philharmonic also hosts concerts by the Prague Symphony Orchestra (FOK), Prague Philharmonia (PKF), smaller chamber ensembles, and visiting musicians during the Prague Spring Festival.

THEATER, DANCE, AND OPERA

✪ National Theater

Národní 2; +420 224 901 448; www.narodni-divadlo.cz; tickets 100-1,500 CZK depending on event; tram stop Národní divadlo or metro stop Národní třída

You can spot the golden-crowned rooftop of the National Theater from almost any point along the Vltava River. This queen of the cultural scene was built in the late 1800s, along with the National Museum, as part of the Czech National Revival—a movement that focused on reclaiming the Czech language and cultural identity from the creeping influences of the surrounding empires. Inside the columned walls of this Renaissance Revival building, the rows of plush red seats, the painted ceiling, and the golden detailed opera boxes create an aura of pure elegance. Get your tickets for ballet, opera, and theater performances online or at the box office next door, inside the New Stage.

New Stage (Nová Scéna)

Národní 4; +420 224 901 448; www.narodni-divadlo.cz; tickets 250-700 CZK depending on event; tram stop Národní divadlo or metro stop Národní třída

The beehive-like glass building beside Prague's National Theater is the New Stage. A little more experimental than its stately neighbor, this theater started as the home of circus-arts troupe Laterna Magika before both were adopted by the National Theater in 2010. Today the stage is shared between dance, drama, and circus performances in a modern, intimate setting. Young artistic types and audience members congregate at the casual (and Wi-Fi-free) Café Nona on the second floor. Stop by Václav

Havel Square, the courtyard between the New Stage and National Theater, to see the glowing red heart memorial and signature of the first Czech president—appropriately surrounded by performance spaces, as Havel was a former playwright.

Estates Theater (Stavovské Divadlo)

Železná; +420 224 901 448; www.narodni-divadlo.cz; tickets 100-2,000 CZK depending on event; metro stop Můstek

Don't let anyone convince you that the cloaked statue outside of the Estates Theatre is connected to a *Harry Potter* dementor or to Emperor Palpatine from *Star Wars*. It actually represents the 1787 premiere of Mozart's opera *Don Giovanni* inside this Neoclassical 18th-century building. The Estates Theater was also the first place that the Czech national anthem "Where Is My Home?" was sung in 1843—marked by a plaque on the wall to the right of the main entrance. Today, the luxurious pale blue and gold interior hosts a full program of ballet, theater, and opera.

Jatka 78

Bubenské nábřeží 306; +420 773 217 127; www.jatka78.cz; 10am-midnight Mon-Fri, 9am-midnight Sat; tickets 100-550 CZK depending on event; tram stop Pražská tržnice or metro stop Vltavská

Jatka 78 takes its playful name from the building's former life as a slaughterhouse. This gritty, multi-use performance space with an emphasis on circus performances opened its doors in 2015 inside the grounds of Holešovice's Prague City Market (Pražská tržnice). The artfully curated warehouse now houses resident theater, dance, and circus-arts companies, plus a bar and bistro.

National Theater (Národní divadlo)

Jára Cimrman Theater (Žižkovské Divadlo Járy Cimrmana)

Štítného 5; +420 222 781 860 or +420 222 783 260; www.zdjc.cz; cimrmanenglishstudio@gmail.com; tickets 200-350 CZK; tram stops Husinecká or Tachovské náměstí

Czech-language plays have traditionally been inaccessible for an English-speaking audience. Fortunately, a small group of drama lovers took on the challenge of translating the country's most beloved fictional character in 2014. The Cimrman English Theatre company performs comedic shows of the Czech's most interesting man in the world at the Jára Cimrman Theater in Žižkov. Czech-language versions of Jára Cimrman's antics—named "the Greatest Czech" in a 2005 national poll—have been gracing this stage since 1967.

Festivals and Events

New Year's Eve (Silvestr)

The local name for New Year's Eve, "Silvestr," takes its name from the Czech saints' days calendar (which can be found on the lower clock face of the Astronomical Clock in Old Town Square). Fireworks are the centerpiece of the party—teenagers and young adults shoot bottle rockets at each other in the main squares, turning them into a bit of a war zone. Tons of bars and restaurants across the city, especially those lining the **Vltava River,** put on their own unofficial fireworks shows at midnight on December 31 (bundle up and head to **Letná Park** for a great view). As of 2019, the city government of Prague has decided to replace the official fireworks, usually held in the evening on January 1, with a videomapping show on the National Theater out of respect and safety concerns for local wildlife.

Čarodejnice ("Witches Day")

April 30 is a family-friendly event marking the end of winter in the Czech Republic. Many of Prague's parks, particularly **Ladronka Park** just west of the Anděl neighborhood, prepare bonfires topped with a wooden figure dressed in witch's clothing. Many local children attending the celebrations also don their pointed black hats and cloaks as part of the fun. From around noon to early evening, the area around the fires entertains the crowds with beer stands, grilled sausages, and free concert stages of local Czech bands. Around sundown everyone circles around the witch to watch the pile go up in flames and bid farewell to the cold months of winter.

Prague Spring (Pražské Jaro)

The Prague Spring International Music Festival (www.festival.cz) centers around a number of significant dates. It began in 1946 to celebrate one peaceful year since the end of World War II. A performance of Bedřich Smetana's *Má vlast* ("My Country") kicks things off in the **Municipal House's Smetana Hall** every year on the anniversary of the composer's May

CZECH HOLIDAY TRADITIONS

In addition to festive markets that pop up around the city, Christmas and Easter are commemorated with some noteworthy local traditions.

Christmas carp markets

EASTER

For a largely non-religious country, Easter (*Velikonoce* in Czech, which comes from *"velká noc"* meaning "great night") is a really big deal, with festive markets popping up around town. Many of the local traditions have roots in paganism rather than Christianity, so the holiday often feels more like a celebration of spring.

Easter in Prague is also accompanied by an unusual tradition. On Easter Monday (not Sunday) before noon, boys and men take braided, ribbon-covered whips made from young saplings and visit the women in their lives. They knock on their neighbors' doors and sing *"Hody, hody doprovody, dejte vejce malovaný, nedáte-li malovaný, dejte aspoň bílý, slepička vám snese jiný . . ."* which means roughly "Give me a painted egg, or at least a plain one. The hen will give you another."

The boys then (gently) whip the women to ensure beauty, health, and fertility for the next year, and are rewarded with eggs, chocolate, or a shot of liquor for teens and fathers. The rules vary slightly between regions, but some also dictate that guys visiting after noon will be greeted with a bucket of water in the face rather than a reward.

While this tradition makes my feminist blood boil a bit (a feeling echoed by some Czech female friends), I am assured by other locals that the intention is lighthearted and nostalgic. You're unlikely to witness the tradition in the city center, but might spot groups of young men with their decorated sticks on some of the outer neighborhood streets or day-trip towns.

CHRISTMAS

Prague's Christmas season kicks off on December 5, which is the name day for St. Mikulaš (the Czech version of St. Nicholas). You might spot the costumed saint, accompanied by an angel and a devil, hanging around Prague's streets or shopping malls. In more residential neighborhoods, the trio goes door to door visiting children. Czech kids sing a song or recite a poem to show they've behaved and are rewarded with candy. The devil comes along to see if naughty children show fear (because good kids should have nothing to hide).

Another staple of Prague's street corners around Christmas, visible from about mid-December through the 24th, are fishmongers with mini-swimming pools of carp. These fish, breaded and fried, serve as the main course of a traditional Czech Christmas dinner, celebrated on the evening of December 24. Some families bring the fish home to live in the bathtub until the big day, while others have the fishmonger do the scaling and beheading right there on the corner (so watch your step in the messy sidewalks around these stands).

12 passing. The following three weeks fill Prague's concert halls, from the Rudolfinum to the National Theater, with international symphony orchestras and up-and-coming young musicians competing for prizes. Tickets (200-2,000 CZK depending on the show) for this late spring festival generally go on sale around Christmas the year before, so feel free to book early and up the anticipation factor for your trip.

Prague Fringe Festival

Fans of avant-garde theater, comedy, and cabaret should think about a trip in late May or early June to catch the Prague Fringe Festival (www.praguefringe.com). This English-language festival takes over the Malá Strana neighborhood for nine days of comedy, cabaret, music, dance, and theater. Performers come from England, America, Australia, and all across Europe to play in various spaces from traditional theaters to cafés and cave-like cellars. The shows (150-200 CZK) are roughly an hour long, with some family-friendly content in the afternoon and adults-only entertainment stretching into the evenings. Inspired by the Edinburgh Fringe, the Prague version is an intimate event where audiences and artists mingle until all hours at the bar inside Malostranská beseda (Malostranské náměstí 21; +420 257 409 112; www.malostranska-beseda.cz) after the program finishes.

Prague Signal Festival

The Czech Republic's largest cultural event takes place on the streets of Prague for one long weekend (usually Thursday-Sunday) each October. Signal Festival (www.signalfestival.com) brings millions of visitors to witness the light installations and video-mapping shows projected onto some of Prague's architectural beauties around the city. Vendors offering hot wine, beer, and snacks surround the most popular venues. Most of the exhibitions are free to enjoy, with a mobile app leading foot traffic through the various sites across Vinohrady, New Town, Old Town, Malá Strana, and Karlín. Some interactive events require a small admission price (50-100 CZK). The video mapping on the Cathedral of St. Ludmila at Náměstí Míru is always a crowd favorite, repeating between 7pm and midnight throughout the night.

St. Martin's Day

The legend of St. Martin has historical roots, but the local wine and dining traditions have only developed in recent decades. According to the story, St. Martin rides into town on a white horse every November 11 (his name day) and is meant to bring with him the first snow of the season. Winemakers and sommeliers across the country also pay close attention to the time—at 11:11am on November 11 they open and pour the first taste of that year's *Svatomartinské* young wine, which is on the sweet side. Almost every Czech restaurant in town offers a special menu of the St. Martin's meal: roast goose served with red cabbage and dumplings (usually 150-500 CZK depending on the venue).

Recreation and Activities

Being in nature is a national Czech pastime. Whenever the weather is nice (and sometimes even when it isn't), a significant portion of Prague clears out of the city to spend time amongst the trees.

PARKS

LESSER TOWN (MALÁ STRANA)

Wallenstein Gardens (Valdštejnská Zahrada)

Letenská 4; +420 257 075 707; www.senat.cz; Apr-May and Oct, 7:30am-6pm Mon-Fri, 10am-6pm Sat-Sun; Jun-Sept, 7:30am-7pm Mon-Fri, 10am-7pm Sat-Sun; closed Nov-Feb; free; tram or metro stop Malostranská

Reasons to visit the manicured, Baroque-style Wallenstein Gardens: free-roaming peacocks, a peaceful carp-filled pond, a wall of gargoyle-like faces in a stalactite rock wall, an aviary of owls, outdoor summer evening concerts, the frescoed ceiling of Greek/Roman gods and Trojan War scenes in the Sala Pavilion, and a quiet respite from Malá Strana's busy streets. The tall hedges lining the paths provide a labyrinth-like atmosphere between the pond and fountain at one end of this secluded garden and the open courtyard and bench seating at the other. Do be on your best behavior—the buildings surrounding these gardens also house today's government officials of the Czech Senate. The entrance is tucked back from the street on the left side when facing the Malostranská metro station.

view of the Prague Castle from Wallenstein Gardens

PETŘÍN

Petřín Park and Gardens (Petřínské Sady)

You could easily get lost for an afternoon among the curving pathways throughout this park that stretches across roughly 8 hectares (20 acres) of land. Start with a visit to the rose gardens surrounding the base of the Petřín Lookout Tower. Heading downhill, you'll pass a statue of Czech poet Karel Hynek Mácha, who wrote the locally famous poem "*Maj*" ("May"). Couples come to share a kiss in his presence (preferably under a birch or cherry tree) on the first of May, the day on which Czechs celebrate love, but with way less pressure or commercialization than Valentine's Day. The quiet Kinsky gardens cover the southern area of the park, divided by a castle fortification known as the Hunger Wall. This fortification was commissioned by Charles IV in the mid-14th century and named for the jobs providing an income to poor communities of the time.

VINOHRADY

Riegrovy Park (Riegrovy Sady)

One of the most popular places to watch the sunset, alongside nature-loving folks and couples cuddling on blankets, is the great lawn of Riegrovy Sady. The distant view of the Prague Castle over iconic red-orange rooftops in Malá Strana sets a peaceful scene, particularly since the city's largest beer garden (formerly nearby) closed in 2019. Puppies and their human companions frequent the surrounding paths, which stretch from the main train station (*hlavní nádraží*) uphill toward Jiřího z Poděbrad Square.

Havlíčkovy Park and Vineyards (Havlíčkovy Sady)

You might hear Havlíčkovy sady, the name of the park, and **Grébovka,** the internal vineyards, used interchangeably to describe this hilly green area on the southern edge of Vinohrady. The Stone Grotto's curved walls, arched doorways, and sculpted fountain are a photographer's dream. The summer and autumn months bring a variety of wine festivals to the grounds, and the **Viniční Altán** gazebo wine bar and **Pavilon Grébovka** restaurant (Havlíčkovy sady 2188; +420 725 000 334; www.vinicni-altan.cz; 10am-10pm daily; wine 60-100 CZK; tram and bus stop Krymská) pours drinks all year long. This area offers a relaxing, sophisticated alternative for outdoor entertainment.

the stone grotto at Havlíčkovy sady

LETNÁ AND HOLEŠOVICE

Letná Park (Letenské Sady)

Letenské sady; www.letenskyzamecek.cz; beer garden 11am-11pm; tram stops Čechův most, Letenské náměstí, or Strossmayerovo náměstí

The main draw for many of Letná Park's visitors is one of the city's largest beer gardens overlooking the

Vltava River and the rooftops of Old Town. Outside of those imbibing around the rows of picnic benches, local residents come to the park to walk their dogs, admire the blooming flower beds, or tie a slackline between two trees and spend an afternoon testing their balance. Entrance to the park is possible via an uphill hike from the Vltava River banks near the Čechův most tram stop, or a more leisurely walk from the opposite side of the park around tram stops Letenské náměstí or Strossmayerovo náměstí.

CYCLING

If you're okay with the bumps of some cobblestone streets, cycling can be a fun way to get around Prague.

BIKE TOURS AND RENTALS

Praha Bike

Dlouha 24; +420 732 388 880; www.prahabike.cz; Mar 15-Oct 15, 9am-8pm; Oct 16-Mar 14, 10am-5pm

You can get an overview of the city with Praha Bike offering tours around the Prague Castle, the Vyšehrad Complex, beer gardens, or panoramic viewpoints (650-1250 CZK), or just rent a bike (220 CZK for two hours) and explore on your own.

BIKE SHARING

Rekola

www.rekola.cz

You'll also find pink ridesharing Rekola (www.rekola.cz) bikes around the city. These are available for rent by downloading a mobile app. Don't worry if the first two screens ask for your email and password in Czech—you can set the default language to English as soon as you're registered. The first 15 minutes are free and then users are charged 24 CZK per hour on their credit card.

SPECTATOR SPORTS

Many Czechs are more likely to play a sport themselves than to spend much time watching them. Lots of adults participate in organized leagues for ice hockey, floorball, soccer, and other active hobbies (with the requisite meeting in the pub afterward). However, when it comes to national and international championships or intercity rivalries, there are a few local sports that result in locals donning jerseys and hitting the streets.

ICE HOCKEY

Ice hockey is a top contender for the most popular national sport. Jaromir Jagr of NHL fame is a national hero, despite leaving the Czech Republic to play across the pond. Every pub in town will have multiple screens devoted to matches during the Winter Olympics or the World Hockey Championships in May—Czechs broke IHF attendance records with more than 11,000 fans per game when they hosted these championships in 2015.

Prague's two main teams are HC Sparta Praha (www.hcsparta.cz) and HC Slavia Praha (www.hc-slavia.cz), who play in the Tipsport Arena (Za Elektrárnou 419/1; +420 266 727 411; www.tipsportarena-praha.cz; tickets 100-300 CZK) in Holešovice or the O2 Arena (Českomoravská 2345/17; +420 266 771 351; www.o2arena.cz; tickets 100-300 CZK) east of the city center.

FOOTBALL

On the world stage where "football" means soccer, you'll know when the two biggest rivals in Prague are playing. Fans of SK Slavia Praha (www.slavia.cz) and AC Sparta Prague (www.sparta.cz) often get a police escort to march through the city before the match. Slavia's home stadium is the

CATS AND DOGS

Cuddle up with some coffee and kittens.

The Czech Republic is a dog-loving country, with one of the highest canine ownership rates in all of Europe. Don't be surprised to see these furry companions on public transport (with a muzzle), in pubs and restaurants, or with their ears flopping in the wind while racing across Prague's many parks. Czech dogs are well trained and owners are very responsible for their pets' behavior and pretty good about cleaning up their poo on the sidewalks.

But what about the cat lovers? Prague has experienced a surge in cat cafés, creating feline-friendly spaces in almost every neighborhood.

CAT CAFÉS

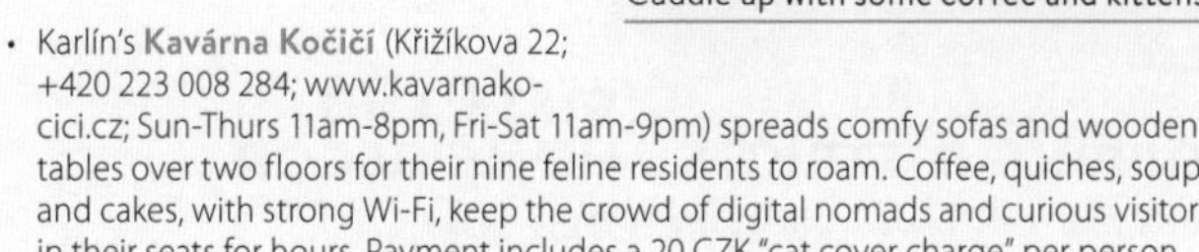

- Karlín's **Kavárna Kočičí** (Křižíkova 22; +420 223 008 284; www.kavarnakocici.cz; Sun-Thurs 11am-8pm, Fri-Sat 11am-9pm) spreads comfy sofas and wooden tables over two floors for their nine feline residents to roam. Coffee, quiches, soups, and cakes, with strong Wi-Fi, keep the crowd of digital nomads and curious visitors in their seats for hours. Payment includes a 20 CZK "cat cover charge" per person.

- At **Social Point Cat Café Prague** (Gorazdova 20; +420 776 610 627; www.catcafe-prague.com; 10am-8pm), just behind the Dancing House in New Town, visitors pay 120 CZK for the first hour and 1 CZK per additional minute for unlimited access to self-serve coffee, tea, light snacks, and multiple rooms of sofas, board games, video games—and the company of cats, of course.

- If someone in your travel group has allergies, or you love cat-themed décor but want to eat and drink in peace, there are options for you, too. Letná's **Creperie U slepé Kočičky** (Milady Horákové 38; +420 233 371 855; www.slepakocicka.cz; 11am-11pm daily) is decked out in adorably kitschy cat style and serves sweet and savory crêpes (75-175 CZK), and the Old Town pub **U Dvou Koček** (Uhelný trh 10; +420 224 229 982; www.udvoukocek.cz; 11am-11pm daily) is a beer and cat lover's paradise serving traditional Czech cuisine (entrées 100-300 CZK).

Sinobo Stadium (U Slavie 1540/2a; +420 725 875 438; www.slavia.cz; tickets 200-1,000 CZK), formerly known as Eden Arena, in Vršovice while AC Sparta calls Letná's **Generali Arena** (Milady Horakove 1066/98; +420 296 111 400; www.sparta.cz/en; tickets cost about 170-500 CZK) their home base. Rivalry games are a rowdy, beer-fueled glimpse into local fandom from an otherwise fairly subdued national character.

ESCAPE GAMES

Getaway Prague

Blanická 9; +420 776 084 796; www.gtwy.cz; Mon-Fri 11am-10pm, Sat-Sun 11am-11pm; 1,000-1,200 CZK per team

Getaway Prague, near the square at Náměstí Miru, provides a historic vibe of being locked up in a historic prison or investigating a crime scene. Celebrate your escape in under an hour over craft beers in the Vinohrady or Vršovice neighborhoods.

Exit Game Runaway

Parléřova 7; +420 602 666 668; www.runaway.cz; 9am-7pm; 1,200-1,400 CZK per team

The scenarios at Exit Game RunAway cross borders and decades, with themes from Christopher Columbus to Al Capone, Alchemy to an Escape from Guantanamo Bay. The multi-room challenges in this space near the Strahov Monastery Brewery will test the minds and imaginations of teams from 2-4 players.

Shopping

The retail landscape is not necessarily Prague's main attraction, but there are a few places worth heading to if you're looking for retail therapy or a souvenir.

SHOPPING DISTRICTS

Prague's one well-known shopping destination is **Pařížská ulice** (www.parizskastreet.cz), which fittingly translates to "Parisian street," where the most famous names in luxury fashion line the storefronts. The high-end shopping lane branches off from Old Town Square between St. Nicholas Church and the Tourist Information Center and runs through the Jewish Quarter of Josefov. Pařížská is where the visiting European fashion elite, decked out in designer shades in the summer and fur coats in winter, peruse collections from Tiffany's jewelers, Prada handbags, and Louis Vuitton luggage.

A walk around the edges of **Wenceslas Square** or **Na Příkopě street,** dividing Old Town and New Town, might be fun for some window shopping of Czech names interspersed with international chain stores that show Prague's identity as a modern cosmopolitan city as much as a historical European capital. Many of the souvenir shops around Old Town and Malá Strana fall distinctly into the tourist-trap category, so stick to recommendations below for truly local gifts and memorabilia hiding in plain sight in these areas.

GIFTS AND HOME DECOR

OLD TOWN (STARÉ MĚSTO)

Manufaktura—Original Czech Tradition

Karlova 26; +420 601 310 605; www.manufaktura.cz; 10am-8pm Sun-Thurs, 10am-9pm Fri-Sat; 100-1,000 CZK

The Manufaktura—Original Czech Tradition concept grew out of a desire to offer truly local souvenirs. The company began in 1991 by collecting handmade goods from small towns across the country. More than 25 years later, they have kept a network of independent producers of wooden toys, candles, cosmetics, and household accessories in business and accessible to Prague tourists wanting to support local craftspeople.

LESSER TOWN (MALÁ STRANA)

Pragtique

Mostecka Street 20; www.pragtique.cz; 10am-8pm daily; 50-500 CZK

For a gift that supports local, independent designers, try Pragtique just off the Malá Strana side of the

GEEK CULTURE IN PRAGUE

Historical Prague was all about the kings and castles, but modern-day Czech life embraces technology in all its many forms. The city has a thriving startup scene and pockets of the counterculture vibe can be found among the crowds of its annual Comic Con. Fans of video games, innovation, or an evening of Settlers of Catan all have a place in Prague.

The unofficial **Apple Museum** (Husova 21; +420 774 414 775; www.applemuseum.com; 240 CZK; 10am-10pm daily), just off Old Town Square, is a tribute to the complicated genius of Steve Jobs. The space claims to be the largest private collection of Apple products in the world, from 1980s desktops to limited-edition iPods. A mobile app guides visitors through Jobs' career, from Macintosh to Pixar, plus a café and a pop-art gallery housed in the basement.

New Town's **Joystick Bar** (Jindřišská 5; +420 732 473 788; www.joystickbar.cz) serves one of Prague's favorite microbrews, Uněticky Pivovar, in a room filled with classic arcade games and pinball machines (10 CZK). This old-school gamers bar is open from 4pm to 2am Tuesday to Saturday, closing at midnight on Sundays and Mondays.

Prague's **Bitcoin Café** (Dělnická 43; www.paralenipolis.cz; 8am-8pm Mon-Fri, noon-9pm Sat-Sun; prices vary with currency) in Holešovice provides a home for the local crypto-anarchist crew devoted to an open and decentralized internet. They don't take cash or cards, but the staff will teach you how to buy cryptocurrency using their onsite machine to pay for your specialty coffee and cake.

Bohemia Boards & Brews (Charkovská 18; +420 252 548 435; www.bohemiaboardsandbrews.com; 5pm-11pm Mon-Fri, 4pm-11pm Sat-Sun) in Vršovice has a massive collection of board games available for a 60 CZK cover charge. A menu of sandwiches, snacks, and beverages ensure that players don't have to take a hunger break in between turns.

Charles Bridge. This trendy boutique is self-described as "where love for Prague meets a sense of style." Modern designs on t-shirts, onesies, notebooks, postcards, magnets, tote bags, posters, and accessories are inspired by classic Czech symbols such as the Astronomical Clock, the Prague Castle, Golem, and the Týn Church in Old Town. Stop into neighboring Roesel—Beer and Cake for a post-shopping snack. You can find a **second location** (Národní 37) in between Old Town Square and Wenceslas Square.

PRAGUE CASTLE DISTRICT (HRADČANY)

From Prague With Love

Loretánská 13; +420 736 751 012; www.frompraguewithlove.eu; 10:30am-6pm Tues-Sun; 100-2,000 CZK

Want to grab a locally made t-shirt, tote bag, or kitchen accessories near the Prague Castle? Stop in From Prague with Love, just a few streets away from the main castle gates near Hradčanské náměstí. The family-owned shop of screen-printed cotton, porcelain, and wooden goods uses simple line drawings of Prague symbols, city maps, or the souvenir-appropriate name of their brand.

BEAUTY PRODUCTS

NEW TOWN (NOVÉ MĚSTO)

Manufaktura Home Spa

Na Příkopě 16a; +420 601 310 645; www.manufaktura.cz; 10am-8pm daily; 150-500 CZK

In 2005, the Manufaktura team took the idea that beer and natural ingredients are good for your hair and skin and expanded it into an entire brand of shampoo, cosmetics, and home spa

BEST SOUVENIRS

Take home some Czech gingerbread from Perníčkův sen.

There are some great options to bring a piece of Czech culture home with you:

- **Gingerbread:** Gingerbread has a local history dating at least to the 16th century, with the Czech recipe originating in the Pardubice region. You won't find a household without at least a few different designs around Christmas time, often baked in huge batches and shared with friends, neighbors, and coworkers in the weeks before the holiday season. Visit the family-owned **Perníčkův sen** (Haštalská 21; +420 607 773 350; www.pernickuvsen.cz; 10am-6pm daily) in Old Town for a wide selection of adorably hand-designed sweets.
- **Pilsner Beer or Becherovka:** You can find bottles from most of the bigger breweries in any local supermarket, or hold off until duty-free shopping on your trip home.

treatments. The Manufaktura Home Spa makes their products from natural local ingredients, including beer, wine, herbs, and minerals, and are not tested on animals. You can find additional Manufaktura Home Spa shops in shopping malls such as Náměstí Republiky's Palladium mall, the Flora shopping mall in Žižkov, the Nový Smíchov mall in Anděl, and inside Prague's main train station (Hlavní Nádraží).

SHOES

NEW TOWN (NOVÉ MĚSTO)

Bat'a Shoe Stores

Václavské náměstí 6; +420 221 088 478; www.bata.cz; 9am-9pm Mon-Sat, 10am-9pm Sun; 1,000-5,000 CZK

One of the country's biggest names in fashion, Tomáš Baťa, came from generations of shoemakers in the South Moravian town of Zlín. Shoppers can browse his styles today in Bat'a shoe stores. Baťa established the brand in

Many of the Czech Republic's big-name distilleries (e.g., Becherovka, Žufánek) are based in cities outside of Prague, so a supermarket or the airport is your best bet for spirits.

- **Wine:** Your best bet for wine in Prague is choosing from the wine bar scene, where most of those you taste are also available to take home. **Vinograf** (www.vinograf.cz) has locations in Malá Strana and New Town, while **Veltlin** (www.veltlin.cz) in the Karlín neighborhood focuses on small, independent wine producers. Gala wines are one of the most trusted names on the Czech wine landscape, available at **Vinotéka U Mouřenína** (www.vinotekaumourenina.cz) in Malá Strana.

- **Cider:** For a more unusual (but delicious) alternative to beer, try some local cider or non-alcoholic juices from **F.H. Prager** (Bořivojova 81; www.pragercider.cz; 4pm-10pm Wed-Sat), with a retail shop and tasting room in Žižkov. Prague's cider scene is on the rise, with cider festivals lining the Náplavka riverbanks at least once every summer.

- **No. 2 Pencils:** Czechs also had a hand in the popularity of #2 pencils. The 18th-century art supply company **Koh-i-noor** (Na Příkopě 26; +420 739 329 019; www.koh-i-noor.cz; 10am-8pm daily) patented the blend of lead inside and made the pencil yellow, which spread to copycats and became the industry standard. Their colored pencils and art supplies remain incredibly popular, particularly for fans of children's or adults' coloring books.

- **"The Little Mole":** An authentic choice for young ones is Krtek (or Krteček), the locally loved cartoon character known as "the Little Mole." In 2009, NASA astronaut Andrew Feustel, who is married to a Czech woman, took a toy version of Krtek into space in honor of a 1965 episode detailing a similar adventure. This Czech alternative to Mickey Mouse entered into a Chinese partnership in 2016, giving the character a modern reboot and new location, but the vintage look still dominates Czech toy shops. Buy the Little Mole and other toys at **Rocking Horse Toy Shop** (Loretánské náměstí 3; +420 220 512 234 or +420 603 515 745; 11am-6pm daily; 50-500 CZK) near the Prague Castle or at **Hugo chodí bos** (Řeznická 12; +420 602 834 930; 10am-6pm Mon-Fri; 100-600 CZK) in New Town.

One particular plea is to avoid purchasing the Soviet-era memorabilia that's sold in a number of shops. Czechoslovakia was forcefully occupied by the Soviet Union from 1968-1989 so any investment in Russian nesting dolls or trinkets and t-shirts with a hammer-and-sickle insignia is ultimately celebrating the oppression of Czech people. In other words, just don't do it.

1894 and improved production processes around the turn of the century after witnessing US assembly-line production techniques. Baťa was also known for creating communities around his factories through urban planning that focused on residences and green space for his workers in the areas around the factories. Today, his mid-range styles are sold in shopping malls around the world, and the Tomáš Baťa institute in his hometown trains future generations of entrepreneurs. You can find additional locations in New Town at the Palladium mall on Náměstí Republiky and in Žižkov at the Flora shopping mall.

ŽIŽKOV

Botas 66

Křížkovského 18; +420 774 981 418; www.botas66.com; 11am-7pm Mon-Fri, 11am-5pm Sat; 1,800-2,100 CZK

The casual, independent style of Botas 66 represents a more modern name in local shoe design that fits perfectly

EASTER AND CHRISTMAS MARKETS

Old Town Square Christmas market

Prague is magical all year round, but the holiday markets around Christmas and Easter turn the volume up to eleven. Wooden stands fill every square in town with the smells of warm spiced wine (*svařák*), hot honey wine (*medovina*), and street-food blends of meats and potatoes. Old Town Square and Wenceslas Square Christmas markets run through most of December and into the New Year, while some of the smaller neighborhood markets may have more limited runs. The landscape is equally festive during the week before Easter in the same locations, just swapping Christmas decorations for pastel colors.

Prague's holiday markets are generally cheerful and family-friendly, with tourists dominating Old Town Square and locals often stopping by locations near metro stops (e.g., Náměstí Miru, Náměstí Republiky, or Anděl) for a festive pre-commute drink or snack. Most market visitors spend their time browsing and chatting while occasionally picking up some presents. Delicately carved ornaments of wooden scenes and Christmas symbols (around 50-300 CZK) are traditional trinkets. At the Easter markets, you'll find intricately painted wooden eggs called *kraslice* (100-500 CZK) alongside one unusual element: a braided, ribbon-covered whip made from young saplings (50-300 CZK). (Wondering how this whip is used? See page 118.)

Holiday market stalls generally come to life around 10am and stay busy until 10pm, with food and drinks served in the city center until midnight. Details can change from year to year. Prague Markets (www.trhypraha.cz) and Prague Tourism (www.prage.eu) are good resources to double-check the dates and times around your visit.

into the effortlessly cool Žižkov neighborhood. The Botas brand has deep local roots, founded in the late 1940s, and their iconic Botas Classic brand gained popularity in the 1960s. The slang word "botasky" was added to the Czech dictionary as a catch-all term for sport shoes, but the brand had more of an old-fashioned, nostalgic appeal until 2008. Two students, Jan Kloss and Jakub Korouš, gave the design a reboot with the Botas 66 line as part of a school project. The company embraced the update, and the brand's popularity has grown among a new generation of sneakerheads. There is also **another location** (Skořepka 4) tucked among the busy streets of Old Town.

WINE, BEER, AND SPIRITS

LESSER TOWN (MALÁ STRANA)

Vinotéka U Mouřenína

Tržiště 17; +420 606 483 087; www.vinotekaumourenina.cz; 2pm-10pm daily; bottles 200-5,000 CZK

The wooden cabinets lining the walls of Vinotéka U Mouřenína are stocked with Czech, Italian, and French wines and cognacs in a wide range of price points, with a few small tables in the front and rear of the store for tasting.

OLD TOWN SQUARE
(STAROMĚSTSKÉ NÁMĚSTÍ)

The markets on Old Town Square are the most crowded and commercial of the bunch, with a strong focus on consumable goods like sweets, hot drinks, and street food. The layout is designed for photo ops, including a large Christmas tree in front of the towers of the Church of Our Lady Before Týn plus stairs to a festive viewing platform in the center of it all.

WENCESLAS SQUARE
(VÁCLAVSKÉ NÁMĚSTÍ)

Wenceslas Square's market is a low-key experience, usually lined with more food and beverage stands than gifts or trinkets. There is room to enjoy a warm drink and a bite if you can find a spot at the few standing tables.

REPUBLIC SQUARE
(NÁMĚSTÍ REPUBLIKY)

Náměstí Republiky adds a lighthearted presence in front of the busy Palladium shopping mall. This medium-sized market wraps around a busy transportation corner and caters to shoppers grabbing a quick drink, bite, or small gift among their holiday errands at the mall. If you spot a Včelcovina stand, try a glass of their hot honey wine (*medovina*).

PEACE SQUARE
(NÁMĚSTÍ MÍRU)

The local favorite is usually Náměstí Míru with a mix of treats and handmade crafts, plus a small Christmas tree, in the shadow of the Church of St. Ludmila. The pace at this market is slower, made for eating, browsing, and absorbing the atmosphere.

AROUND ANDĚL METRO STATION

The streets around the Anděl metro station host a crowded market of their own. The aisles are narrow and hurried workers from the surrounding offices may channel their inner Grinch when annoyed by the crowds, but a small petting zoo and street musicians still draw families here to keep young ones entertained.

When in doubt, look for bottles by Gala, one of the country's most celebrated winemakers. International shipping is available in store or on their website (only in Czech, so you'll need your preferred translation tool).

VINOHRADY

Beer Geek Pivoteka

Slavíkova 10; +420 775-260-871; pivoteka.beergeek.cz; 1pm-9pm Mon-Fri, 11am-9pm Sat, 3pm-9pm Sun; bottles 60-400 CZK

Beer Geek Pivoteka is the place for microbrews in Prague. This beer-lover's boutique, arranged on shelves by country of origin, stocks over 500 different bottles from across Europe and the US. A few local Czech favorites include anything by Clock, Matuška, Raven, or Zichovec. You can find many of the local bottles on tap at nearby Beer Geek Pub if you want to try before you buy. International shipping is available online (only in Czech, so you'll need your preferred translation tool).

MARKETS

The most current Czech designs don't have a permanent home, but they do have a presence. **Mint Design Market** (www.mintmarket.cz) is an independent pop-up concept of fashion, design, and food that has been bouncing around the country—from Brno to Pilsen to Prague and beyond—since 2015. The collection of young and independent designers runs an e-shop and offers information on the time and location of their events on their website.

OLD TOWN (STARÉ MĚSTO)

SmetanaQ

Smetanovo nábřeží 4; www.smetanaq.cz; 10am-8pm; tram stop Národní divadlo

The SmetenaQ complex, which opened in 2016, houses a young group of independent furniture and accessories designers on its second floor, and a small Deelive Design Store selling their ideas come to life on the ground floor. The riverfront spot also includes a popular café and a gallery on the top level. Located next to Prague's prestigious FAMU school of TV and film, the crowd skews young, hip, and artsy.

Food

Traditional Czech cuisine is hearty, meaty, and often covered in sauce. Local meals (including most daily lunch specials) are divided into grilled meats (pork, beef, game, chicken, or duck) with some form of potatoes or dumplings on the side. Vegetables are scarce and seafood is uncommon (or pricey) in this landlocked country. Enjoy the indulgence of comfort foods like *svíčková* (a national favorite) or a rich roast duck, or grab some *chlebíčky* for a lighter lunch.

OLD TOWN (STARÉ MĚSTO)

CZECH

✪ Sisters Bistro

Dlouhá 39; +420 775 991 975; www.chlebicky-praha.cz; 8am-8pm Mon-Fri, 8am-6pm Sat, 8am-4pm Sun; sandwiches 50-75 CZK

When all you need is a quick bite between sightseeing, stop into Sisters Bistro for a fresh, modern take on traditional Czech *chlebíčky* (open-faced sandwiches). Instead of the old-fashioned classic of ham and potato salad on white bread, these artisan updates include beetroot with goat cheese or roast beef with sprouts, not to mention service with a smile. Mix and match to make a meal or take a selection across the river for a picnic in Letná Park.

✪ Naše Maso

Dlouhá 39; +420 222 311 378; www.nasemaso.cz; 10am-8pm Mon-Fri, 10am-6pm Sat; entrées 75-200 CZK

With a staff committed to traditional butchery techniques and cooperation with Czech farmers, this carnivore's favorite is accurately named "Our Meat." Be bold and work your way to the counter to order—the tiny butcher shop is generally packed with residents doing their grocery shopping, food tours sampling Prague ham and sausages, and a lunch crowd enjoying burgers and beef tartare. Two beverages, beer and water, flow from self-service taps on the wall. Meat enthusiasts will want to reserve a seat for dinner with the butcher Mondays to Wednesdays at 7pm. Bring your appetite and your questions—he speaks five languages (including English).

Krčma

Kostečná 4; +420 725 157 262; www.krcma.cz; 11am-11pm; entrées 175-300 CZK

Krčma is an underground den of deliciousness just steps from Old Town Square. Enjoy hearty portions of grilled meats, sauces, and dumplings in a medieval setting of cave-like brick walls. Vegetarian options are minimal in this old-style, traditional Czech tavern.

Lod' Pivovar

Dvořákovo nábřeží, kotviště č. 19; +420 773 778 788; www.pivolod.cz; 11:30am-11pm Sun-Thurs, 11:30am-midnight Fri-Sat; entrées 200-300 CZK

This microbrewery is on a boat! The top-floor restaurant of Lod' Pivovar offers fresh, modern takes on Czech cuisine—think rabbit, duck, or pork knee accompanied by more vegetables than you'd find in a traditional pub. The below-deck seating area strikes a more casual pub vibe, serving beer snacks and in-house microbrews.

INTERNATIONAL

Home Kitchen

Kozí 5; +420 774 905 802; www.homekitchen.cz; 7:30am-10pm Mon-Fri, 8am-10pm Sat; entrées 200-300 CZK

On a cold day, the selection of soups at Home Kitchen will warm you up from the inside out. Browse the display of main courses (e.g., grilled meats and pastas), starters (e.g., hummus or soup), and salads to inspire your appetite. The trendy staff in skinny jeans and well-groomed facial hair cater to a casual clientele of leisurely lunchers alongside tourists finishing up tours of the Jewish Quarter in this mid-sized bistro. Reservations recommended.

Engawa

Petrském náměstí 5; +420 775 383 999; www.engawapraha.cz; 11am-11pm Mon-Sat, noon-10pm Sun; entrées 250-600 CZK

As a bona fide sushi snob raised in Seattle, I had forgotten the flavor of fresh fish until my first bite of Engawa sushi. The staff at this casually elegant, multi-room Japanese restaurant take quality seafood seriously, even in a landlocked country. The extensive menu includes grilled meats and Japanese hot pots alongside sushi sets and a la carte sashimi on a quiet square near the eastern edge of Old Town.

VEGETARIAN

✪ Lehka Hlava

Boršov 2; +420 222 220 665; www.lehkahlava.cz; 11:30am-11:30pm Mon-Fri, noon-11:30pm Sat-Sun; entrées 225-275 CZK

In a meat-heavy country, Lehka Hlava ("Clear Head") is a vegetarian oasis. The intimate dining room includes a dark blue ceiling, twinkling star lights, and calming fish tank to set the scene for a mellow meal. Browse the meat-free menu from Thai curry to quesadillas, with a glossary of potentially unfamiliar terms like tempeh or seitan. Reservations required.

COFFEE, TEA, AND SWEETS

Grand Café Orient

Ovocný trh 19; +420 224 224 240; www.grandcafeorient.cz; 9am-10pm Mon-Fri, 10am-10pm Sat-Sun; entrées 100-200 CZK

The only café in Prague with exclusively Cubist décor takes its commitment to right angles down to the details. Everything from the coat hooks to the light fixtures is on point. Enjoy a slice of homemade cake, a

CZECH CUISINE

Chlebíčky (open-faced sandwiches) are a perfect picnic treat.

ENTRÉES

- ***Svíčková:*** a local favorite of thinly sliced sirloin beef in vegetable cream sauce with cranberries, cream, and bread dumplings, almost like a Czech take on Thanksgiving flavors. This is what every Czech child writes under "favorite food" in school and continues to love throughout adulthood. Try a classic one at **Café Louvre,** while local vegetarian favorite **Maitrea** (Týnská ulička 6; www.restaurace-maitrea.cz) in Old Town does make a soy-based, meat-free version.
- ***Pražská šunka*** (Prague ham): Head to **Naše Maso** to try *Pražská šunka* (Prague ham), a cured, lightly smoked, boneless ham prepared with traditional butchery techniques recognized by the EU as a regional specialty. Avoid the stands in Old Town Square, known for scamming customers with prices by weight not portion.
- ***Pečená kachní stehna*** (roast duck leg): **U Modré Kachničky** serves delicious duck-based dishes, including *pečená kachní stehna,* which is usually paired with red cabbage and dumplings. This hearty Bohemian-style classic is served on the bone, often in one-quarter or one-half portions.
- ***Pečené vepřové koleno*** (roast pork knuckle): Try the *pečené vepřové koleno* (roast pork knee) at **Lod' Pivovar,** a floating brewery on a boat focused on classic Czech dishes with quality ingredients. The potent flavors of a dark beer sauce, mustard, and horseradish are perfect for refueling on a winter evening.
- ***Guláš*** (goulash): The Czech version of this Hungarian classic involves less (or no) paprika and acts more as a thick sauce than soup. Pork, beef, and venison versions are

breakfast croissant, or a toasted baguette on the second floor of Prague's historic House of the Black Madonna (named for the identifying marker outside) to refuel before climbing the nearby Powder Tower or touring the Municipal House.

NEW TOWN (NOVÉ MĚSTO)

CZECH

✪ Café Louvre

Národní 22; +420 724 054 055 or +420 224 930 949; www.cafelouvre.cz; 8am-11:30pm

available in different venues. Jan Macuch (a former food tour guide with culinary taste I trust) claims that **Czech Slovak Restaurant** makes the best one in Prague.

- ***Smažený sýr*** (fried cheese): Apologies to any vegan readers, but the only traditional vegetarian "meal" is a thick slice of white cheese (often a mild, white Edam) that is breaded, fried, and served with French fries and tartar sauce without a vegetable in sight. The version at Czech pub **Lokál** is a local favorite.

SOUPS

In the same way that many people think of a small salad as a starter to a meal, a Czech lunch always begins with soup:

- ***Česneková polévka*** (garlic soup): Different versions of this fragrant and flavorful dish range from a creamy base to a light broth, often garnished with ham, cheese, potatoes, and croutons. *Česnečka* (the short name) is a fantastic cure for the common cold. Soup menus in Czech pubs often change daily, so keep an eye out for this classic when the weather turns cold.

- ***Kulajda*** (dill and vegetable soup): For a more unusual flavor, watch soup-of-the-day menus for *kulajda,* a blend of dill, mushroom, potato, and egg. You'll find this consistently on the menu at **Staročeská restaurace V Ruthardce** if you take a day trip to Kutna Hora.

SMALL BITES AND PASTRIES

A quick snack in Prague usually centers around bread or a sweet shop:

- ***Chlebíčky*** (open-faced sandwiches): The traditional version of *chlebíčky* would be white bread topped with potato salad and sliced ham, possibly garnished with a radish or carrot. These simple hors d'oeuvres are particularly popular at Czech weddings or New Year's Eve parties at a cabin in the countryside. **Sisters Bistro** makes incredible modern versions with fresh ingredients such as beetroot and goat cheese.

- ***Klobásy*** (sausage): This staple of any pub, beer garden, outdoor market, or food stand is the go-to solution for "we should probably serve some kind of food" at any Czech event. They can be pork or beef, grilled or smoked, and mild or spiced, and are usually served with mustard and a few slices of brown bread.

- ***Medovník*** (honey cake): Czech cakes and pastries offer a wide range of flavors (e.g., gingerbread, poppy seed, forest berries, and cream-filled dough) but one of my personal favorites is *Medovník* or *Medovy Dort,* which translates to "honey cake." Taste this light, flaky delight in Cubist form at Old Town's **Grand Café Orient**.

- Local note: ***trdelník,*** a doughy spiral pastry cooked over coals and dipped in sugar and cinnamon, is a delicious guilty pleasure sold at stands all around Old Town, but it is about as Czech as an "I ♥ NY" t-shirt—its prevalence is a pet peeve of the Honest Prague Guide on YouTube. With claimed roots in Romania, Hungary, Sweden, and Slovakia, it has become a popular tourist attraction across the former Austro-Hungarian Empire. Feel free to indulge, but to maintain your traveler's credibility and avoid dirty looks from locals, skip the Instagram-inspired, sugar-overload trend of filling it with ice cream or hashtagging #traditional.

Mon-Fri, 9am-11:30pm Sat-Sun; entrées 150-300 CZK

Café Louvre has been satisfying local appetites since 1902 and can even claim Albert Einstein and Franz Kafka as former regulars. Enjoy Czech and Austro-Hungarian cuisine in the chandeliered elegance of the First Republic café style established in the early years of Czechoslovakia, located just down the street from the National Theater. This is a great place to try *svíčková,* a Czech favorite of sirloin beef in vegetable cream sauce with cranberries, cream, and bread dumplings, reminiscent of the rich blend of flavors in a Thanksgiving dinner. Select the *kavarna* (café) or *restaurace* (restaurant) when making your online reservation for the most ornately decorated rooms—you can order food in either.

Zvonice

Jindřišská věž; +420 224 220 009; www.restaurantzvonice.cz; 11:30am-midnight; entrées 600-900 CZK

Fine dining and traditional Czech cuisine aren't often synonymous, but this high-end establishment inside the Jindřišská bell tower offers an exception to that rule. Classic takes on Old Bohemian recipes of meat and game come with impressive views and top-notch service. Try the sauerkraut soup (trust me, it's 100 percent better than it sounds) before choosing a main course from veal cheeks, wild boar, or grilled duck breast. Reservations required.

INTERNATIONAL

Pizzeria Kmotra

V Jirchářích 12; +420 224 934 100; www.kmotra.cz; 11am-midnight; entrées 150-200 CZK

The extensive menu of pizza, pasta, and salads at Pizzeria Kmotra caters to a budget-conscious crowd of university students and casual patrons on their way to the bars. Split one of their massive pizzas (ignore any recommendations that these are personal-sized) in an underground, brick-walled cavern setting with cutlery-inspired décor. Reservations recommended.

Lemon Leaf

Myslikova 14; +420 224 919 056; www.lemon.cz; 11am-11pm Mon-Thurs, 11am-midnight Fri, noon-midnight Sat, noon-11pm Sun; entrées 225-275 CZK

Arguably the city's best-loved Thai restaurant sits between Karlovo náměstí and the Vltava River. When your tongue is craving spice beyond the relatively mild palate of Czech cuisine, this menu of soups, spring rolls, and curries will perk up your taste buds, with a few continental options also available. Reservations recommended.

✪ Gran Fierro

Voršilská 14; +420 773 700 377; www.granfierro.cz; 11:30am-midnight Mon-Fri, noon-midnight Sat, 5pm-midnight Sun; entrées 200-500 CZK

The trendy atmosphere at this Argentinian steakhouse and cocktail bar is perfect for a pre-theater meal or post-show drink around a performance at the National Theater or New Stage. Wine fans missing the flavor of rich reds will appreciate a glass of Malbec paired with an order of empanadas. Reservations recommended on weekends, which sometimes include live flamenco music.

Argentinian appetizers at Gran Fierro

BREAKFAST AND BRUNCH

Cacao

V Celnici 4; +420 777 511 677; www.cacaoprague.cz; 8:30am-10:30pm Mon-Thurs, 9:30am-11pm Fri- Sun; entrées 100-200 CZK

Health-conscious travelers and restricted diets are no problem for the staff at Cacao, located right next door to the Museum of Communism. The large, two-story dining room near Náměstí Republiky serves bagels, egg breakfast, smoothies, açai bowls, and delicious espresso to start your day. The menu transitions into fresh soups, salads, and sandwiches for lunch or dinner. Homemade ice cream and a considerable array of cakes will placate the sweet tooth of anyone in your group.

COFFEE, TEA, AND SWEETS

Styl & Interier

Vodičkova 35; +420 222 543 128; www.stylainterier.cz; 8am-10pm Mon-Sat, 8am-8pm Sun; entrées 125-200 CZK

It's easy to miss the entrance to Styl & Interier, tucked into a quiet courtyard just off the bustling streets around Wenceslas Square. This friendly café doubles as an interior-design showroom of wicker home accessories and colorful accent pieces, plus a peaceful summer garden. The seasonal bistro menu of light egg breakfasts and quiches, colorful salads, and homemade desserts is popular with locals and tourists, so reservations are recommended. Try a sparkling, fruit-infused lemonade in the coveted garden seats during summer or some homemade *svařák* (hot spiced wine) and Christmas cookies in winter.

Styl & Interier's patio is a coveted lunch spot.

Oliver's Coffee Cup

Václavské náměstí 58; +420 234 101 138; www.oliverscoffeecup.cz; 8:30am-8:30pm Mon-Fri, 9am-8pm Sat-Sun

For a warm drink and a cozy sofa, take the escalator to the second floor inside one of Wenceslas Square's oldest shopping centers below the National Museum. Oliver's Coffee Cup draws a crowd of young families, friends, and local office workers with a selection of specialty coffee, tea, homemade lemonades, and cakes. Snag a seat beside the picture window for prime people-watching on the square below. Strangely, the only way to exit is an elevator ride one floor down.

Kavarna Slavia

Smetanovo nábřeží 2; +420 224 218 493; www.cafeslavia.cz; 8am-midnight Mon-Fri, 9am-midnight Sat-Sun

The First Republic style of early 20th-century Czechoslovakia is enshrined in Kavarna Slavia. This historic café has stood across from the National Theater since 1884, and is famous for its popularity with politicians and intellectuals. Stop in for coffee and share some sweet crêpes accompanied by live piano soundtrack. Request a seat near the front windows when making an online reservation to enjoy a riverfront view of the Prague Castle.

LESSER TOWN (MALÁ STRANA)

CZECH

✪ Lokál U Bílé Kuželky

Míšeňská 12; +420 257 212 014; www.lokal-ubilekuzelky.ambi.cz; 11:30am-midnight Sun-Thurs, 11:30am-1am Sat-Sun; entrées 100-200 CZK

Lokál's simple, modern take on traditional Czech recipes and pub food is a local favorite. This makes reservations required to join the crowd of travelers and young residents grabbing after-work drinks at the lively tables of this casual beer hall just off the Charles Bridge. Try simple bar snacks like sausages or marinated cheese with a cold glass of Pilsner Urquell on draft.

St. Martin

Vítězná 5; +420 257 219 728; www.stmartin.cz; noon-11pm; entrées 200-300 CZK

The brother-and-sister chef team at St. Martin blends traditional Czech recipes with French and Asian touches discovered through their travels. Mix-and-match from the seasonal menu of soups, salads, grilled meats, vegetarian dishes, and continental sides. The mini turkey burger plus a side dish makes a great light meal, and the wild boar burger is a carnivore favorite. Both the food and the white domed walls of the small dining room embody a classic, modern quality. You'll find a young, trendy crowd on the outdoor patio in the summer.

✪ U Modré Kachničky

Nebovidská 6; +420 602 353 559; www.umodrekachnicky.cz; noon-4pm and 6:30pm-11:30pm daily; entrées 500-600 CZK

The tasting menus of duck or game at U Modré Kachničky are 100 percent worth the splurge. Five or seven courses of decadent flavors can also be paired with local wines and liquors in the most fashionable, old-world living room settings that you can imagine. The staff walk a talented tightrope of friendly professionalism for a clientele of primarily couples sharing romantic meals. Duck and game specials are also available a la carte, and the roast duck with apples, raisins, and honey is a standout. Reservations recommended.

COFFEE, TEA, AND SWEETS

✪ ROESEL—Beer & Cake

Mostecká 20; +420 777 119 368 or +420 212 241 552; roesel-beer-cake.business.site, 10am-10pm daily; entrées 75-200 CZK

The quiet patio and low ceilings of this casual café offer a hidden escape from the crowds surrounding the Lesser Town entrance to the Charles Bridge. In addition to craft beer and homemade sweets, this small, friendly spot with simple wooden furniture serves specialty coffee, seasonal pâtés, and daily lunch and dinner specials. The young, often multilingual staff are patient with an international clientele of locals, foreigners, and families.

a trio of spreads at ROESEL—Beer & Cake

PRAGUE FOOD TOURS

One of the most enjoyable ways to discover Prague's local culture is through your taste buds. These multi-stop adventures usually include small bites at culinary hot spots, with a local guide sharing bits of history and stories about the sights you pass in between restaurants. At the table, guests can chat with each other or ask questions (when their mouths aren't full). A daytime tour often leaves travelers full for hours, so plan on a lighter evening meal if you do add this experience to your itinerary. These tours are generally run by independent teams without an office, so booking is done online.

Eating Prague Tours is the Prague branch of Eating Europe Food Tours (www.eatingeurope.com), with a wide range of daytime and evening options: A four-hour afternoon Prague Food Tour through Old Town and New Town (about 2,300 CZK, Mon-Sat), a four-hour Evening Food Tour though Malá Strana (about 2,500 CZK, Sun-Thurs), and a three-and-a-half-hour afternoon Craft Beer and Food Tour with some incredible skyline views (about 1,600 CZK, Tues-Sat). Most dietary restrictions can be accommodated, but vegan restrictions drastically limit the enjoyment of most tours.

The local Czech couple, Jan and Zuzi, behind **Taste of Prague** (+420 775-577-275; www.tasteofprague.com) are known for having one of the most meticulously updated and beautifully photographed food blogs in town. They offer a Traditional Czech Food Tour (4 hours, 2,500 CZK) beginning from 1pm-3pm that includes 5-6 stops for classic Czech cuisine and beverages. The Prague Foodie Tour (4 hours, 2,700 CZK) includes 5-7 stops beginning from 11am-5pm and including modern takes on Czech food in more local neighborhoods. Some dietary restrictions require an extra charge, and they cannot accommodate vegan diets.

ANDĚL

The Anděl neighborhood, which stretches south of Lesser Town along the riverbank, is a good spot for dining.

CZECH

Kolkovna Olympia

Vítězná 7; +420 251 511 080; www.kolkovna.cz; 11am-midnight; entrées 175-300 CZK

Dark wood details and copper accents set a traditional Czech pub scene in this 222-seat member of the Pilsner Urquell Original Restaurant group, where quality beer is a way of life. Freshly poured pints (or technically, half-liters) complement the menu, from bar snacks of pickled sausage and marinated cheeses to main courses like roast duck and pork knee. The building has been serving customers since 1903, and Kolkovna gave the space a restorative makeover in 2003 without losing any of its historical charm. Grab a hearty meal here after walking (or riding the funicular) down Petřín Hill.

Czech Slovak Restaurant

Újezd 20; +420 257 312 523; www.czechslovak.cz; noon-11pm daily; entrées 250-400 CZK

The jury's still out, but some claim the venison goulash at Czech Slovak Restaurant to be "the best in Prague." The trendy, dimly lit atmosphere surrounds an international crowd enjoying modern twists on traditional dishes. The menu includes Bohemian baked snails, dill and mushroom soup, wild rabbit, and a local-leaning wine list. Reservations recommended.

BREAKFAST AND BRUNCH

Café Savoy

Vlašská 7; +420 731 136 144; www.cafesavoy.ambi.cz; 8am-10:30pm Mon-Fri, 9am-10:30pm Sat-Sun; breakfast 200-400 CZK

The conversations are quiet, chandeliers sparkle overhead, and the patrons practice their best etiquette at this ornate café in the style of the First Czechoslovak Republic. Observe the on-site bakery behind a glass window as the staff prepare the pastries and fresh bread that keeps a large, multi-level dining room smiling. Reservations required.

COFFEE, TEA, AND SWEETS

Kavárna Co Hledá Jméno

Stroupežnického 10; +420 770 165 561; www.kavarnacohledajmeno.cz; noon-10pm Mon, 8am-10pm Tues-Fri, 9am-8pm Sat-Sun

The industrial vibe of Kavárna Co Hledá Jméno ("Café in Search of a Name") is popular with young coffee lovers and remote workers—both the coffee and Wi-Fi are strong. This large, multi-room café is set back from the street, so if you're walking down a driveway it's likely you're in the right place. Brunch is served until noon (or 3pm on weekends) and includes an impossibly fluffy eggs benedict soufflé.

PRAGUE CASTLE DISTRICT (HRADČANY)

CZECH

Kuchyň

Hradčanské nám. 2; +420 736 152 891; www.kuchyn.ambi.cz; 10am-10:30pm; entrées 150-300 CZK

Most restaurants in and around the Prague Castle serve high-priced food that falls short on quality. The 2018 addition of Kuchyň is still a little pricier than your average Czech pub, but the cuisine and experience are worth it. To order, a server guides you into the kitchen and lifts the lids on a stovetop to display your choice of home-cooked meals for the day. Then grab a seat (on the roughly 65-seat terrace if possible) and your food is delivered. Reservations recommended.

VINOHRADY

CZECH

Restaurace U Růžového Sadu

Mánesova 89; +420 222 725 154; www.uruzovehosadu.cz; 10:30am-midnight Mon-Thurs, 10:30am-1am Fri, 11am-1am Sat, 11:30am-10pm Sun; entrées 115-215 CZK; tram and metro stop Jiřího z Poděbrad

Restaurace U Růžového Sadu serves classic, hearty, meat-and-potato meals in a comfortable 90-seat pub with an additional outdoor patio during sunny seasons. Work up an appetite with a walk through nearby Riegrovy sady, then stop in for one of the simple daily lunch specials (think pork schnitzel or grilled chicken with potatoes) served until 3pm at less than 100 CZK for a true taste of Czech-style dining.

INTERNATIONAL

✪ Pho Vietnam Tuan & Lan

Slavíkova 1; 11am-10pm daily; entrées 100-150 CZK; tram and metro stop Jiřího z Poděbrad

The best advertising for the unassuming storefront of Pho Vietnam Tuan & Lan is a regular line out the

classic Czech cuisine at Kuchyň

door. As one of the longest-running Vietnamese establishments in town, this grab-and-go option of pho in a Styrofoam bowl or fresh rolls in rice paper are best enjoyed on a bench across the street at Jiřího z Poděbrad Square (unless you can find space to stand at one of the few tables inside the tiny space). Bring cash and choose your meal before you reach the counter to keep the efficiency moving at its usual fast pace. Vegetarian options are slim to non-existent.

Café Sladkovsky

Sevastopolská 17; +420 776 772 478; www.cafesladkovsky.cz; 11am-1am Tues-Sun, 4pm-1am Mon; entrées 100-200 CZK; tram and bus stop Krymská

Everything about this Vršovice staple is charmingly quirky, from the antique-style furniture to the menu. Mediterranean and Middle Eastern-inspired dishes mingle alongside organic beef or veggie burgers and English breakfasts. The décor channels First Republic cafés style as seen in Café Louvre or Kavarna Slavia but with a more lived-in, vintage vibe (it actually opened in 2011). Service can be on the slower side, but is generally patient and kind with English speakers. Food service finishes at 9:45pm when the bar starts slinging gin cocktails.

VEGETARIAN

Radost Fx

Bělehradská 12; +420 224 254 776; www.radostfx.cz; kitchen open 11am-midnight Tues-Sat, 11am-11pm Sun-Mon; tram stop IP Pavlova or metro stops Náměstí Míru or IP Pavlova

Radost FX has been a dependable vegetarian haven in Prague since 1992. The eclectic menu jumps from nachos to gnocchi, stir-fry to salads (175-215 CZK), with salmon sneaking onto the brunch menu (100-200 CZK). The laid-back vibe extends from a small, quiet café out front to the crowds nursing hangovers and Bloody Marys in the high-backed booths of the windowless restaurant. Some hard-core diners may have not even made it home between breakfast and the all-hours dance party in the downstairs club on Thursday through Saturday nights. Brunch reservations recommended.

Etnosvet

Legerova 40; +420 226 203 880; www.etnosvet.cz/en; lunch 11:30am-4pm Mon-Fri, noon-4pm Sat-Sun, dinner 5pm-11pm Sun-Thurs, 5pm-11:30pm Fri-Sat; entrées 250-400 CZK; tram stops IP Pavlova or Bruselská or metro stop IP Pavlova

For a high-end vegan or vegetarian meal, head to Etnosvet, a short walk from Náměstí Míru. Sample multi-course tasting menus plus wine pairings or choose from the a la carte menu, including tempura vegetables, pesto linguini, or bulgur and cheese salad, at this gastronomic hub of international influences. Reservations recommended.

COFFEE, TEA, AND SWEETS

Monolok

Moravská 18; +420 739 018 195; www.monolok.cz; 8am-10pm Mon-Fri, 9am-7pm Sat-Sun; tram stops Šumavská or Jana Masaryka or metro Náměstí Míru

Friendly service and quality coffee, plus a peaceful courtyard away from the street and surrounded by manmade waterfalls, make Monolok a refreshing place to catch your breath. This multi-room café on a quiet side street in the heart of Vinohrady complements their cakes and light food (think variations on avocado toast or seasonal salads) with a solid wine list and a Wi-Fi signal strong enough to keep digital nomads satisfied.

ŽIŽKOV

CZECH

✪ U Slovanské Lípy

Tachovské náměstí 6; +420 734 743 094; www.uslovanskelipy.cz; 11am-midnight; entrées 175-225 CZK, cash only

This large, casual, traditional Czech pub near the Žižkov Tunnel offers hearty meals with no-nonsense service that keeps the *pivo* (beer) flowing. Slightly off the beaten path below Vítkov Hill and the Žižkov Beer Garden, this local favorite caters to a mixed crowd of residents and visitors (assisted by English-friendly menus). Choose from 10 rotating taps of Czech beers and a main course of flank steak or schnitzel with potato salad. Cash only.

U Sadu

Škroupovo náměstí 5; www.usadu.cz; +420 222 727 072; 8am-2am Sun-Mon, 8am-4am Tues-Sat; entrées 125-250 CZK

With pub food served late every night, this neighborhood watering hole near the base of the Žižkov TV Tower is a last stop for pub-goers on their way home (if they can find a seat among the regulars who have been there since early evening). The large, multi-floor interior has an eclectic, thrift-store style décor of globes, baskets, and random items hanging from the walls and ceilings. Try a Svijany beer with some *smažený sýr* (fried cheese) and tartar sauce, potato pancakes, or a grilled steak to satisfy your late-night cravings.

INTERNATIONAL

✪ Martin's Bistro

Velehradská 4; +420 774 100 378; 11am-10pm Mon-Sat, 10am-4pm Sun; entrées 150-300 CZK

Friendly, multilingual service and seasonal, fresh-from-the-farmers-market ingredients define the vibe at Martin's Bistro. Choose from a weekly revamped menu that might include pasta tossed with fresh veggies and herbs, roast duck or pork entrées, Asian-inspired noodles and curries, or shrimp and cheese appetizers, plus soups, quiches, and desserts. Vegetarian options are almost always available. This local favorite fills up fast, so call for a reservation to ensure an available seat.

meals fresh from the farmers market at Martin's Bistro

BREAKFAST AND BRUNCH

Žižkavárna

Kubelíkova 17; +420 606 281 546; 7:30am-9pm Mon-Fri, 8:30am-9pm Sat-Sun; entrées 50-75 CZK

This quiet neighborhood favorite of international residents and remote workers camped out for hours serves quality coffee and light homemade meals with a friendly, patient approach. The seasonal menu often includes omelets, sandwiches, granola, and a soup of the day, with a slice of carrot or honey cake for dessert. If you can't score one of the 10 tables, take your coffee to go for a short walk to the benches of Jiřího z Poděbrad square.

My Coffee Story

Štítného 8; +420 776 343 008; 8:30am-8pm Mon-Fri, 9am-3pm Sat-Sun; entrées 100-150 CZK

Stop into My Coffee Story for a breakfast of scrambled eggs and waffles or some late-afternoon coffee and homemade cake before heading to the lawn of Riegrovy sady or top of Vítkov Hill to watch the sunset. This cozy, modern café makes a nice pre-theater meeting point before catching a show at The Jára Cimrman Theatre. During the summer months, head to the back of the building to access the rooftop summer terrace.

KARLÍN

CZECH

✪ Eska

Pernerova 49; +420 731 140 884; www.eska.ambi.cz; 8am-11:30pm Mon-Fri, 9am-11:30pm Sat-Sun; entrées 200-600 CZK

Eska is internationally celebrated for serving great food at fair prices. The ground floor of this light, modern warehouse space is dominated by an in-house bakery. Upstairs, the dining room serves simple plates of seasonal vegetables and fresh meats in a laid-back atmosphere of structural support beams softened by hanging plants. Grab an open-faced sandwich for lunch or try the eight-course tasting menu for an indulgent dinner. Reservations recommended.

INTERNATIONAL

Café Frida

Karlínské náměstí 11; +420 728 042 910; www.cafefrida.cz; 9am-midnight Mon-Fri, 4:30pm-midnight Sat-Sun; entrées 125-200 CZK

This casual, colorful, Mexican-inspired restaurant is named for Frida Kahlo. Don't expect too much spice from the burritos, quesadillas, and burgers tailored to a milder local palate. Plenty of vegetarian and meat-lovers' options keep this popular establishment packed with a young, international crowd. Reservations recommended.

BREAKFAST AND BRUNCH

Můj Šálek Kávy

Křižíkova 105; +420 222 310 361; www.mujsalekkavy.cz; 9am-10pm Mon-Sat, 10am-6pm Sun; entrées 150-200 CZK

Make a weekday reservation or show up early on weekends to try one of the most beloved brunches in town. Můj šálek kávy ("My Cup of Coffee") helped to establish a love of high-quality coffee and leisurely weekend meals in the Czech capital. The connoisseurs behind the bar are passionate about their products, catering to the coffee snobs of the Prague community—you may get an eye roll for requesting milk and sugar instead of taking your fair-trade filter coffee black. Choose from a seasonal menu of omelettes and English breakfasts, blueberry pancakes, or light salads and sandwiches as lunchtime hours approach.

LETNÁ AND HOLEŠOVICE

CZECH

Pivovar Marina

Jankovcova 12; +420 220 571 183; www.pivovarmarina.cz; 11am-midnight; entrées 175-350 CZK

This massive riverside venue on the eastern edge of Holešovice houses a brewery serving Czech culinary specialties in one half of the space, and an Italian restaurant in the other. The casual vibe and high, vaulted ceilings of the brewery area is popular with large groups and sports fans during important matches. Try the *svíčková* (roasted sirloin in a sweet vegetable sauce with dumplings) or pork ribs with a local lager.

INTERNATIONAL

Mr. Hot Dog

Kamenická 24; +420 732 732 404; www.mrhotdog.cz; 11:30am-10pm; entrées 50-125 CZK

For a quick bite, grab one of the namesake hot dogs or sliders at this low-key local favorite. The menu of American classics is supplemented with limited-time specials such as lobster rolls, plus a yearly eating contest. Indoor seating is limited, making take-out service before hitting nearby Letná Park a popular option.

Hillbilly Burger

Pplk Sochora 21; +420 774 156 735; www.hillbilly.cz; 4pm-10pm Tues-Fri, noon-10pm Sat, noon-9pm Sun; entrées 150-200 CZK

The guiding principle behind this newcomer to the Prague landscape is simple: Just F*@¢ing Good Burgers. The below-ground dining room is decorated with chalkboard scrawls and exposed brick, with a long backyard patio where smokers congregate. The burgers are hearty, the coleslaw is delicious, and (unlike many local places) the nachos come piled with toppings—meat, beans, corn, sour cream, and guacamole—far beyond the Prague trap of using "nachos" to mean chips, cheese, and salsa.

nachos at Hillbilly Burger in Holešovice

Garuda

Milady Horákové 12; www.garudarestaurant.cz; +420 730 890 424; 10:30am-10pm; entrées 150-275 CZK

The two-story café, restaurant, and "chill out zone" at Garuda blends relaxing elements (think water features and soft lighting) with a trendy, low-key vibe and delicious Indonesian food. This newcomer to the neighborhood is still relatively undiscovered, but an online reservation never hurt anyone. Grab an early meal at a daily happy hour discount from 2:30-5:30pm before watching the sunset at nearby Letná Beer Garden.

SaSaZu

Bubenské nábřeží 306; www.sasazu.com; +420 284 097 455; noon-midnight Mon-Thurs, noon-1am Fri-Sat, noon-11pm Sun; entrées 300-1,000 CZK

High-end dining in Holešovice is rare, but SaSaZu breaks that rule with Southeast Asian-inspired cuisine in a dimly lit nightclub setting inside the Holešovice Market grounds (also referred to as *Pražská tržnice*). Shared plates are served family-style, with starters such as salmon tartar and lobster soup, and flavorful meat-based dishes from a stone oven or grilled in a wok. Glowing red lanterns and sculpted figurines set a vibe that blends elegance and kitsch. Follow up your meal with a performance at nearby circus arts venue Jatka 78, or stick around SaSaZu for that night's dance party or concert in the adjoining club venue. Dinner reservations required.

BREAKFAST AND BRUNCH

✪ The Farm

Korunovacni 17; +420 773 626 177; 8am-10:30pm Mon-Fri, 9am-10:30pm Sat, 9am-8pm Sun; entrées 100-175 CZK

If you're willing to venture a little further for breakfast, join the local crowd of young families and friend groups brunching on fresh eggs, omelets, and avocado-toast variations at The Farm. Add a Bloody Mary or mimosa to start your day in style. These fresh-from-the-farmers-market meals take full advantage of seasonal flavors in a tightly-squeezed dining room and outdoor summer patio. Reservations required.

Kafé Francin

Dukelských Hrdinů 35; +420 778 719 217; www.francin.cz; 7:30am-8pm Mon-Fri, 9am-7pm Sat-Sun; entrées 125-185 CZK

Breakfast at Kafé Francin can fuel a full day of sightseeing. Try the massive sweet or savory crêpes, a hard-to-find bagel sandwich, or an egg and fresh bread breakfast with your morning coffee. Head to the back of the restaurant for plush sofa seating and a browsable bookshelf if space is available, or squeeze into one of the smaller tables in the front of this cozy cafe.

VEGETARIAN

Loving Hut

Dukelských hrdinů 18; www.lovinghut.cz; +420 222 950 768; 11am-9pm Mon-Fri, noon-9pm Sat; entrées 100-150 CZK

The safest bet to ensure you're eating vegan cuisine in Prague is to stick to entirely meat-free establishments. This international chain based around the philosophy of "Be Vegan, Make Peace" offers buffet-style salad bars of vegetable-based options. The simple, cafeteria-style atmosphere inspires a quick meal before hitting the town again.

COFFEE, TEA, AND SWEETS

Café Jedna

Dukelských hrdinů 47; www.cafejedna.cz; +420 778 440 877; 9:30am-11pm; entrées 75-150 CZK

The Veletržní palác ("Trade Fair Palace") branch of Prague's National Gallery also houses a large café lined with sunlit windows and high ceilings. The massive family-friendly seating area is regularly filled with freelance workers, parents with baby strollers, and art fans of all ages. The menu of fresh hummus, soups, sandwiches, and cakes provides a perfect snack or light meal before browsing the multistory art exhibits next door.

Bitcoin Cafe

Dělnická 43; +420 608 088 822; www.paralelnipolis.cz; 8am-8pm Mon-Fri, noon-9pm Sat, noon-8pm Sun, cash or credit not accepted (cryptocurrency only)

As the name would imply, the only way to pay for your coffee in this café is with cryptocurrency (either Bitcoin or Litecoin). Luckily, there is a machine on site and staff on hand to show you how to purchase enough to cover your bill. The gimmick will get you in the door, but the yummy cakes and espresso drinks will keep you in the large, black leather sofas inside this building founded by the Institute for Cryptoanarchy. Observe the tech-focused crowd working to make the internet a place of free information to support a decentralized economy . . . or just enjoy some quality coffee and a comfortable seat.

VYŠEHRAD

CZECH

Hospůdka Na Hradbách

V Pevnosti 2; +420 734 112 214; noon-midnight daily; entrées 50-150 CZK

The best way to enjoy a meal inside the Vyšehrad Complex is outdoors. This locally loved beer garden offers bar snacks like grilled Hermelin cheese or pickled sausages alongside heavier meals of grilled meats, to be eaten under the umbrella-topped picnic benches lining the garden. Imagine a casual, family BBQ setting with the added bonus of a panoramic view from the tables lining the perimeter.

INTERNATIONAL

Yam Yam Vyšehrad

Vyšehrad Metro Station 1670; +420 774 844 443; www.yamyam.cz; 11am-11pm; entrées 150-200 CZK

Yam Yam Vyšehrad's convenient location just outside the Vyšehrad Metro Station makes it an easy stop for simple, quality Thai food. The clean lines, stenciled vines, and splashes of red create a relaxed environment for an international clientele. The extensive, lighthearted menu includes "Ca-la-la-mari" and sections of main courses encouraging visitors to "Eat Some Meat" and "Curry On."

COFFEE, TEA, AND SWEETS

Puro Gelato

Na Hrobci 1; +420 721 438 209; www.purogelato.cz; May-Sept, 10am-9pm Sun-Thurs, 10am-10pm Fri, 9am-10pm Sat; Oct-Apr, 9am-8pm daily; 40-75 CZK

This cozy gelato shop below Vysehrad is a perfect stop before a stroll along the nearby Náplavka embankment beside the Vltava river (where you might have to hide your treat from a few hungry swans). Choose a scoop of your favorite from the daily-made and often unusual flavors (an orange scoop might be mango or carrot) including vegan options, or try the artfully designed cakes and tarts for some warm-weather indulgence.

Kavárna Čekárna

Vratislavova 8; +420 601 593 741; www.kavarnacekarna.cz; 8am-10pm Mon-Fri, 10am-8pm Sat, 1pm-8pm Sun; entrées 50-100 CZK

The unassuming entrance to this casual café extends into long halls of cushions and simple wooden furniture, leading to a massive backyard garden at the base of Vysehrad hill. Patio seating is tucked under brick arches and around patches of grass where the noise of the city disappears. Pair your specialty coffee with homemade cakes, quiches, or the soup of the day.

Accommodations

Prague's accommodation offerings reflect the distinctive personalities of its different neighborhoods. Malá Strana and Old Town are known for historical luxury hotels within steps of major sights. New Town and Vinohrady offer more apartments and trendy, boutique hotels—the Bohemian Hotels and Hostels Group is a local favorite for mid-range, modern style. Vyšehrad, Letná, and Karlín have a more peaceful neighborhood vibe, while Vršovice, Holešovice, and Žižkov tend to draw younger, budget-conscious crowds looking for nightlife and not afraid of public transport.

Some of Prague's older mid-range and budget hotels can feel quite dated, and payment in cash only is not unheard of, so read your booking details carefully when choosing a place. Renovation restrictions in public buildings and a prevalence of stairs also make it a less-accessible landscape for travelers with disabilities. Hotels that do offer specially equipped rooms are noted below when possible, but it's definitely not standard in all accommodation options, so ask about barrier-free travel or accessibility needs before booking.

The Prague landscape offers many alternatives beyond traditional hotel chains. Pensions and aparthotels provide more residential living environments with access to cooking facilities and family-friendly amenities. Design hotels cater to architecture lovers, and the luxury level maintains the outstanding service and modern touches that their clientele expect. If you have any concerns about specifics that might make or break your stay, contact your hosts before booking to confirm your expectations.

OLD TOWN (STARÉ MĚSTO)

UNDER 4,000 CZK

Hostel HOMEr

Melantrichova 11; +420 722 661 922; www.hostelhomer.com; cash only

The 16th-century building of Hostel HOMEr is just steps from Old Town Square and a lively nightlife scene. Choose from 4-bed, female-only spaces (750 CZK) to mixed, 16-bed dorms (600 CZK) plus a few private double and triple rooms (2,500-3,500 CZK), all with shared bathrooms. The domed ceilings, historical décor, friendly 24-hour reception, plus free adapters and Wi-Fi make this a favorite for backpackers of all ages. Payment in cash only.

4,000-7,000 CZK

✪ The Emerald

Žatecká 7; +420 602 666 982; www.the-emerald-prague.com; 3,500 CZK s, 3,000-5,000 CZK d

Every design detail of The Emerald tells a story inside this historic Art Nouveau building in the Josefov neighborhood. Thirteen individual rooms take inspiration from themes including the Orient Express, the Italian region of Tuscany, and Japanese principles of natural harmony. The original architecture is highlighted with copper-chain shower curtains, distressed walls, and natural wood touches. Rooms include a fridge, oven, and private bathroom among the minimal, customized furnishings. There is Wi-Fi but no elevator. These

rooftop terrace and jacuzzi at Emblem Hotel

aparthotels, newly opened in the summer of 2018, cater to independent travelers looking for a familiar, photogenic alternative to hotel life.

OVER 7,000 CZK

Emblem Hotel

Platnéřská 19; +420 226 202 500; www.emblemprague.com; 5,000-10,000 CZK d, 10,000-20,000 CZK suites

The cozy rooms at the family-owned boutique Emblem Hotel make up for their size with comfortable public spaces for socializing. Fifty-nine small rooms (including one accessibility equipped) are decked out in modern style and private bathrooms inside a 1908 building just one street off Old Town Square. A private, 30-minute (1,200 CZK for 2 people) or 60-minute (2,200 CZK for 2 people) reservation of the rooftop Jacuzzi and terrace includes a bottle of prosecco to toast the incredible view. Guests exchange travel tips over complimentary wine in the M Lounge from 6pm-8pm. Splurge on the Library Suite (around 20,000 CZK), with a huge copper bathtub and sliding bookshelf separating the bedroom from a reading lounge.

NEW TOWN (NOVÉ MĚSTO)

UNDER 4,000 CZK

✪ Sophie's Hostel

Melounova 2; +420 246 032 621; www.sophieshostel.com; 400 CZK

Sophie's Hostel is a peaceful alternative to the rowdy, bunk-bed dorm experience with 12 light, clean, private rooms and apartments with en-suite bathrooms, or 17 shared dorm rooms for up to five people (women-only dorms available). This central location near Karlovo náměstí and Náměstí Miru provides an affordable place to lay your head and offers a 10-minute walk from Wenceslas Square without sacrificing a good night's sleep.

Mosaic House

Odborů 4; +420 277 016 880; www.mosaichouse.com; 350-600 CZK dorms, 2,000-4,000 CZK d

This nearly 100-room structure includes both a 38-room hostel ranging from 4-bed to 26-bed shared dorms with bathrooms, plus a 55-room design hotel with one accessibility-equipped private double room. Mosaic House uses energy-efficient appliances, renewable energy sources, and a grey water system to make it Prague's greenest accommodation option. The décor is fun and funky including a Mediterranean-and-Middle-East-inspired restaurant by day and in-house dance party every night on the ground floor. Look for the giant mushroom statues outside the entrance to find your way home to the southern edge of New Town and Vyšehrad. Rooms book out fast so make your reservation early.

Bed & Books Art Hotel

Nekázanka 14; +420 773 317 733; www.hostel-neka-zanka-cz.book.direct/en-gb; 1,250 CZK s, 2,000-5,000 CZK d; cash only

Between a boutique hotel and high-end hostel, Bed & Books offers peaceful comfort in an ethereal palette of distressed wood and pastels. Seven rooms across multiple floors (with no elevator) range from singles up to three-bedroom apartments with shared or en-suite bathrooms and kitchens. The trade offs for a great price, central location, and free Wi-Fi are limited reception hours (check in outside of a 2pm-6pm window costs 250 CZK) and cash-only payments.

MOOo Apartments

Myslikova 22; +420 608 278 422; www.mooo-apartments.com; 2,500-3,500 CZK s, 2,500-10,000 CZK d

Treat yourself to a comfortable home-away-from-home decorated in bovine kitsch at MOOo Apartments. What's with the name? The designers wanted to combine the relaxing feel of the countryside with the urban energy of the city, and many New Town restaurants, bars, and clubs are just stumbling distance down the street. Sixteen one-bedroom apartments (2,500-3,500 CZK) and five two-bedroom apartments (4,500-6,000 CZK) are available, plus two penthouse suites (10,000 CZK) for up to eight people, all with private bathrooms.

4,000-7,000 CZK

Capital Apartments

Václavské náměstí 36; +420 224 240 876; www.capitalapartmentsprague.com; 3,750 CZK studio, 5,000 CZK apartment

Capital Apartments caters to families, large groups, and young travelers looking for a front-row seat to the action around Wenceslas Square. With 23 apartments spread across three central buildings, options range from studios to 4-bedroom suites accepting up to 12 guests. The décor is modern, minimal, and comfortable with basic kitchen amenities and private bathrooms. Request a Wenceslas Square location for balcony views, or just around the corner on Vodičkova Street for a (slightly) quieter experience.

Miss Sophie's

Melounova 3; +420 210 011 200; www.miss-sophies.com; 4,000 CZK s, 4,500 CZK d

The convenient location and casual chic of Miss Sophie's 16-room boutique hotel with en-suite bathrooms makes this an elegant favorite just one metro stop or a 10-minute walk off of Wenceslas Square. A newly added private Jacuzzi and sauna (normally 1,500 CZK for 90 minutes, 750 CZK with direct booking) are waiting to pamper tired travelers after a long day of crisscrossing cobblestoned streets. A simple buffet breakfast or hot brunch is served across the street at Sophie's Kitchen for an extra 150-200 CZK.

✪ Dancing House Hotel

Jiraskovo Namesti 6; +420 720 983 172; www.dancinghousehotel.com; 3,000-8,000 CZK d

There is no comparison for sleeping inside one of the city's most famous sights, the Dancing House. Request a riverside room with floor-to-ceiling windows and wake up to a view of the Prague Castle. You set the mood inside these 31 spacious, modern rooms with en-suite bathrooms and a choice of multi-colored LED lights. A welcome drink and buffet breakfast served under a sparkling chandelier are included from the Fred and Ginger restaurant on the top floor.

LESSER TOWN (MALÁ STRANA)

UNDER 4,000 CZK

✪ The Nicholas Hotel Residence

Malostranske namesti 5; +420 210 011 500; www.thenicholashotel.com; 2,000 CZK d, 3,500-5,000 CZK suites

The charming nine-room Nicholas Hotel Residence offers one of the most centrally located home bases in Malá Strana, just next door to the Church of St. Nicholas and the busy square of Malostranské náměstí. The expansive, comfortable furnishings include living-room spaces, well-equipped kitchen facilities, washer-dryer, and free Wi-Fi, great for families and couples of all ages. Toss on your robe for the continental breakfast buffet served in the hallways, where you can load up your plate and say "*Dobré ráno*" (good morning) to your neighbors before taking breakfast back to your room to enjoy. Twenty-four-hour reception is friendly and helpful, even if you've got an odd-hour arrival.

private spa and jacuzzi at Miss Sophie's Prague

Old Crooked Beams

Malostranské náměstí; +420 604 212 613; www.oldcrookedbeams.com; around 3,000 CZK d

For a truly personal experience, try the privately owned apartment at Old Crooked Beams. This comfortable apartment with one queen-sized bed plus a kitchen and private bathroom is perfect for couples and includes customized restaurant advice from the English owner and a convenient location beside St. Nicholas Church. Get the experience of visiting a local friend even if you don't know anyone in town.

Friday Songs Apartments

Nerudova 10; +420 733 301 766; www.fridaysongs.cz; 1,200 CZK s, 2,500-3,500 CZK d

Imagine living just steps from the Prague Castle. This boutique residential option run by a super-friendly Czech-Australian couple truly feels like home. Choose from a single loft (1,200 CZK), one-bedroom (2,000 CZK), two-bedroom (2,500 CZK), or three-bedroom residence (5,000 CZK), all with en-suite bathrooms, comfortable living areas, and well-stocked kitchens. Expect a warm welcome and answers to any possible questions at check in. Two-night minimum stay required.

4,000-7,000 CZK

EA Residence U Bílé kuželky

Malostranske namesti 5; +420 271 090 832; www.ubilekuzelky.cz; 3,500-5,000 CZK d

In true tavern style, you can sleep above the Czech pub Lokál U Bílé kuželky in this boutique, 14-room hotel. Simple, clean lines and en-suite bathrooms housed under exposed wooden beams offer modern comfort with the added ability to stumble upstairs after your last beer from the popular pub below. This is also a great location for photographers hoping for a sunrise session on the Charles Bridge, just steps away.

OVER 7,000 CZK

Aria Hotel

Trziste 9; +420 225 334 111; www.ariahotel.net; 6,000 CZK d, 7,000-25,000 CZK suites

Aria Hotel's roughly 50 music-themed rooms with en-suite bathrooms are dedicated to the greats of contemporary, classical, opera, and jazz music, ranging from Beethoven to the Beatles. Elegant touches include a rooftop terrace, fireplace lounge, small fitness center, free access to the neighboring Vrtba Gardens, and a music concierge offering personal recommendations for local concerts. Buffet breakfast and Wi-Fi are complimentary.

✪ Golden Well Hotel

U Zlaté studně 4; +420 257 011 213; www.goldenwell.cz; 6,500-8,000 CZK d

The boutique Golden Well Hotel, known as U Zlaté Studné in Czech, is as well known for its impressive rooftop restaurant as the decadence of its 17 en-suite rooms and two luxurious suites (around 15,000 CZK). This peaceful property tucked between the Prague Castle's lower gardens and Wallenstein Gardens, just slightly off the main tourist track through Malá Strana, was originally owned by Roman Emperor and Bohemian King Rudolf II and refurbished after decades of neglect to reopen in the new millennium. This splurge-worthy destination is perfect for a romantic weekend.

The Alchymist Grand Hotel and Spa

Trziste 19; +420 257 286 011; www.alchymisthotel.com; 8,000 CZK d, 9,000-25,000 CZK suites

The Alchymist Grand Hotel and Spa goes all-in on the historic charm of its 16th-century Baroque surroundings. Rich hues, ornate headboards, private bathrooms, and decorative details in every room and suite set a truly regal tone. The underground Ecsotica Spa includes a plunge pool, saunas, Indonesian-inspired massage and aromatherapy treatments, and a small, stone-walled fitness center. A buffet breakfast is included and can also be delivered to your room.

Augustine Hotel

Letenská 33; +420 266 112 233; www.augustinehotel.com; 10,000 CZK d, 15,000-40,000 CZK suites

The luxurious Augustine Hotel spreads 101 en-suite rooms of historical ambience (with one equipped for accessibility) across seven historic buildings, including a 13th-century former monastery. The Cubist details and a subtle color palette create a sense of regal calm just off the bustling square and transport hub of Malostranské náměstí, with individual suites offering tower views, historic frescoes, or custom glass designs. A 24-hour fitness center plus a wellness center of spa treatments and a Turkish hammam round out the menu of indulgent experiences.

Mandarin Oriental

Nebovidska 1; +420 233 088 888; www.mandarinoriental.com; 10,000-20,000 CZK d, 20,000-40,000 CZK suites

Attentive service, Spices Asian Restaurant, and a spa housed inside a Renaissance chapel keep the guests of Mandarin Oriental in a state of bliss. The quiet location, with 79 en-suite guest rooms (one accessibility equipped) plus 20 suites is tucked between the green lawns of Park Kampa and Petřín Hill. Guests are encouraged to relax and unplug, and Wi-Fi comes at a premium. Start your day with morning yoga in the chapel instead of checking your email, and end with tikka masala on the terrace dining room.

PRAGUE CASTLE DISTRICT

(HRADČANY)

UNDER 4,000 CZK

Romantik Hotel U Raka

Černínská 10; +420 220 511 100; www.hoteluraka.cz; 2,500-7,000 CZK d

To mix a peaceful, residential vibe with the convenience of walking to the Prague Castle, book early for a spot in the six-room Romantik Hotel U Raka. This tiny, family owned cottage at the top of hilly Hradčany is as cute as they come. Comfortable apartments with en-suite bathrooms are decorated in deep reds and exposed brick, accented with the artistic family's own paintings and sculptures. Private residences surround a quiet cobblestoned courtyard. Enjoy a light snack in the warm breakfast nook or outdoors on the terrace in summer months.

VINOHRADY

UNDER 4,000 CZK

Czech Inn

Francouzská 76; +420 210 011 100; www.czech-inn.com; 125 CZK dorm, 1,500 CZK studio

For lively budget accommodation in Vršovice, steps away from the trendy bistros and adult beverages of Krymská Street, check into the pun-intended Czech Inn. This massive, modern staple of the Bohemian Hostels group offers stylish rooms from private studios (1,500 CZK) to 36-bed mixed dorms and shared bathrooms (125 CZK) with free Wi-Fi throughout the building. There is a seven-night maximum stay.

the massive Czech Inn Hotel

Aparthotel Lublaňka

Lublanska 59; +420 222 539 539; www.lublanka.hotel.cz; around 2,500 CZK d

This side street between Náměstí Miru and Karlovo náměstí makes Aparthotel Lublaňka a comfortable home with basic furnishings to lay your head. Thirteen en-suite rooms are kitchen-equipped and breakfast is included. Just below the hotel, the newly opened SUN.DAY Terrace serves all-day brunch in the courtyard. Cocktails and karaoke at onsite BER.LIN Bar (6pm-2am) liven up the nights.

Pure White

Koubkova 12; +420 220 992 569; www.purewhitehotelprague.com; 2,500 CZK s, 3,500 CZK d

Pure White boutique hotel offers 37 en-suite rooms of modern comfort on a quiet side street in Vinohrady. Reception is open 24 hours with a menu of pillow preferences, in-room Wi-Fi, and breakfast included. Business travelers and sophisticated sightseers can decompress in the lobby bar.

✪ Royal Court Apartments

Legerova 48; +420 725 702 326; www.royalcourthotel.cz; 3,000 CZK studio, 3,500 CZK suite

The boutique selection of 17 studios and family apartments at Royal Court Apartments comes decorated with brightly colored details, ranging from purple roses to American flags, that give each room a playful personality. With full kitchen amenities and private bedrooms and bathrooms, these spacious temporary residences are great for couples, small friend groups, and families traveling with teens. The lively surrounding area just off the IP Pavlova metro stop is flush with restaurants and public transport connections, with a tourist information center on the ground floor to answer any questions.

ŽIŽKOV

UNDER 4,000 CZK

Hotel Amadeus

Dalimilova 10; +420 210 011 400; www.amadeushotel.cz; 1,200 CZK s, 1,500 CZK d

Hotel Amadeus is slowly transforming from an older Czech hotel to a trendy Žižkov branch of Miss Sophie's Hotel under new management by the Bohemian Hostels Group. This live-like-a-local environment of 28 en-suite rooms is located on a quiet square near the Jára Cimrman Theater, far from the crowds of the city center. No matter the hotel name on the door upon your arrival, you can expect clean lines, vintage design touches, and friendly service in this boutique multi-story location with a tranquil courtyard.

Hotel Theatrino

Borivojova 53; +420-227 031 894; www.hoteltheatrino.cz; 1,750 CZK s, 3,000 CZK d

Hotel Theatrino sits in the heart of this pub-heavy residential neighborhood popular with international students, young professionals, and long-term local residents who remember its working-class roots. Far from the crowds of the city center, this large, five-story collection of simple rooms with rich red accents and a large, ornate conference hall caters to groups and business travelers. Free Wi-Fi, 24-hour reception, and a private sauna for rent round out the offerings.

OVER 7,000 CZK

One Room Hotel

Mahlerovy Sady 1; +420 210 320 081; www.towerpark.cz; 15,000-20,000 CZK d

The level of exclusivity is right there in the name. One Room Hotel describes the single luxury suite available at the top of the Žižkov TV Tower. Wake up to a panoramic view, set your musical mood with the in-room computer and Bose sound system, and enjoy complimentary L'Occitane cosmetics in the en-suite bathroom. With breakfast included and Oblaca restaurant and bar occupying the floors below, you may struggle to find reasons to leave your sky-high perch over Prague.

KARLÍN

UNDER 4,000 CZK

Pentahotel Prague

Sokolovská 112; +420 222 332 800; www.pentahotels.com; 2,500 CZK s, 3,000-5,000 CZK d

The neon lighting and modern design of the seven-story Pentahotel Prague demonstrate the growing (and grown-up) nightlife scene. The 227 en-suite rooms are a bit outside the center, but right on a public transportation line in this largely residential neighborhood packed with restaurants and wine bars. Free Wi-Fi is natural for the young, trendy clientele, and the bar staff of the lobby's Penta Lounge perform double duty as the reception desk.

LETNÁ AND HOLEŠOVICE

UNDER 4,000 CZK

Sir Toby's

Dělnická 24; +420 210 011 610; www.sirtobys.com; 250-750 CZK dorms

Sir Toby's has been a favorite of the backpacking community and anyone looking to escape the traditional tourist track since its humble beginnings in 1999. Vintage-style, 4-bed, or 12-bed dorm rooms with shared bathrooms are restricted to travelers ages 18-39, while the all-ages, private en-suite rooms (1,500-3,500 CZK) upstairs are impressively insulated from noise. The Wi-Fi is strong, the staff are friendly, and your bunkmates are likely to stumble home at all hours. Buffet breakfast in the downstairs bar includes fruit, cereal, and a make-it-yourself pancake station.

Residence Milada

Milady Horákové 12; +420 775 888 830; www.residencemilada.com; 2,500 CZK s, 3,500 d

Rich red tones and eight multi-bed, en-suite apartments in the boutique Residence Milada cater to families and close friends comfortable with shared sleeping areas. Deluxe and Family Apartments (5,000-9,000 CZK) with soundproof rooms can sleep up to five guests, and include a washing machine, modern bathroom facilities, and fully equipped kitchen and dining-room spaces. If you don't feel like cooking, grab breakfast nearby at Café Letka, or try a film brunch at independent cinema Bio Oko.

VYŠEHRAD

4,000-7,000 CZK

Corinthia Hotel

Kongresová 1; +420 261 191 111; www.corinthia.com; around 3,500-5,000 CZK d

You don't have to stay in the tourist center to enjoy five-star elegance in Prague. The towering Corinthia Hotel offers more than 500 rooms with private bathrooms and modern amenities, five of which are equipped for accessibility, and incredible views of the city skyline. Situated just off the Vyšehrad metro stop, this location is perfect for relaxing evening walks around the Vyšehrad Complex or exploring more of Prague's neighborhoods. The hotel itself houses four restaurants for breakfast, grilled meats and pizzas, Asian cuisine, and a cocktail lounge as well as a full swimming pool, top-floor spa, and gym facilities.

Information and Services

TOURIST INFORMATION

If you're looking for brochures of entertainment options and day trips, answers to lingering questions about transportation, or really just anything you want to ask in English, Prague's Tourist Information Centers are there to help. You'll find offices in some of the most popular tourist areas. The **Old Town Square location** (Staroměstské Náměstí 1, 9am-7pm) is at the Old Town Hall, next to the Astronomical Clock, while **Wenceslas Square's closest base** (Rytířská 12, 9am-7pm) is on the main street connecting it to Old Town—walk past the large New Yorker store at the base of the square and keep an eye out on your left-hand side. You'll also find a tourist-friendly base beside the **Charles Bridge Tower** (Mostecká 4, 9am-8pm) on the Malá Strana side of the Vltava River.

BUSINESS HOURS

While office workers may get an early start and fill public transport from 6am-9am, many independent shops don't open until 10am (although supermarkets and shopping malls tend to open earlier, at 8am or 9am). Shops start to close down between 5pm-7pm. Most weekend hours are limited, but shops are not closed entirely.

Lunch hour is early during weekdays, and pubs may fill up as early as 11am. You can usually expect dinner service to last until at least 10pm. Many independent coffee shops don't cater to the pre-work crowd and instead open around 10am on weekdays and possibly even later on weekends.

EMERGENCY NUMBERS

The universal emergency number across Europe is **112**, and operators can direct you toward any specific emergency needs if you are unable to reach a police station. Additional numbers are available for fire (**150**) and ambulance (**155**), but these services are not guaranteed to speak English, so 112 is your safest bet to be redirected.

In case of emergency (e.g., lost or stolen possessions, criminal encounters) you'll want to file a police report for official documentation. English fluency among Prague police officers on the street is not guaranteed, but the following stations are intended to have an interpreter on site at all times for concerns in multiple languages.

- **New Town** (Jungmannovo námesti. 9, +420 974 851 750)
- **New Town** (Krakovská 11, +420 974 851 720)
- **Old Town** (Benediktská 1, +420 974 889 210)
- **Malá Strana** (Vlašská 3, +420 974 851 730)

CRIME

The Czech Republic was ranked 10th in the world in the 2019 Global Peace Index. Crime is low, water is safe to drink, threat of terror attacks is minimal, and solo travelers can walk almost all streets safely at any hour. However, travelers from some ethnic or religious backgrounds, particularly those with darker skin or wearing head coverings, may experience xenophobic attitudes and unwanted attention. Anti-immigrant or anti-Muslim marches are usually met with an equal or larger march in support of diverse societies, but this is a divisive political issue in the country.

HOSPITALS AND PHARMACIES

If you're in need of emergency medical attention, **Motol Hospital** (V Úvalu 84; www.fnmotol.cz; metro stop Nemocnice Motol) has a specific, English-speaking reception area for foreigners. Depending on the type of insurance you have, visitors may have to pay a deposit on arrival before seeing a doctor and then settle the bill after receiving treatment. **Na Homolce Hospital** (Roentgenova 2; +420 257 273 289; www.homolka.cz; bus stop Nemocnice Na Homolce) also offers English-speaking reception and quality medical care.

You can spot pharmacies (*lekarna* in Czech) by looking for a green cross outside the buildings. **Lékárna U svaté Ludmily** (Belgická 37; www.lekbelgicka.cz; +420 222 513 396) is located next to Náměstí Miru and open 24 hours a day.

MENTAL HEALTH SERVICES AND EMERGENCY SUPPORT

Local expat Gail Whitmore (+420 775 248 363, www.counselinginprague.com) offers crisis support specializing in depression, sexual violence, domestic violence, and LGBTQI+ support to English speakers in Prague. Confidentiality is ensured and help is available at any hour of day or night.

FOREIGN CONSULATES

- **Embassy of the United States** (Tržiště 15, www.cz.usembassy.gov, +420 257 022 000)
- **Canadian Embassy** (Ve Struhách 95/2, www.canadainternational.gc.ca, +420 272 101 800)
- **British Embassy** (Thunovská 14, www.gov.uk, +420 257 402 111)
- **Irish Embassy** (Tržiště 13, www.dfa.ie, +420 257 011 280)
- **Embassy of South Africa** (Ruská 65, www.mzv.cz, +420 267 311 114)
- **Australian Consulate** (Klimentska 10, 6th Floor, www.dfat.gov.au, +420 221 729 260)
- **Consulate of New Zealand** (Václavské náměstí 9, www.mfat.govt.nz, +420 234 784 777)

CURRENCY EXCHANGE

Many of the city's currency exchange offices advertise zero-percent commission in large letters, but offer abysmal rates in small print when you actually hand over your cash. Two trusted offices to change money are **Visitor Change** (Na Můstku 2, 9am-7pm) at the information center or **eXchange** (Kaprova 14) just off Old Town Square past St. Nicholas Church. ATMs generally offer a fair rate, but check with your bank about any fees for withdrawing money abroad.

DID YOU KNOW . . . ?

Every city has its fun facts and local secrets that define its personality. Here are a few nuggets of knowledge you should know about Prague and the Czech Republic:

- There are more than 10 million people in the Czech Republic, and about **1.3 million** of them live in Prague. Roughly 10 million tourists join them on the streets and beds of the city each year.
- The Czech Republic's second-largest city is **Brno,** in the southeast region of Moravia, and the third-largest is **Ostrava,** a former mining town located in the northeast near the borders of Poland and Slovakia.
- Prague has a number of **nicknames** including the Golden City, the Heart of Europe, and the City of a Hundred (or a Thousand) Spires.
- Despite all those spires, a large portion of the population identify as **atheist or agnostic,** followed by **Catholics** as the largest organized religion. There is also a sci-fi streak, with more than 15,000 Czechs identifying as **"Jedi Knights"** as their religious affiliation on the last census.
- The Czech Republic is the official name of the country, and **Czechia** was approved in 2016 as an official short version accepted on paperwork and uniforms for the national sports teams. The controversial decision is divisive among the locals, who either love it or hate it and refuse to use it.
- Decisions in Prague have had a galactic impact. The 2006 meeting of the International Astronomical Union that decided to demote **Pluto** was held in Prague.
- The US and the Czech Republic have been connected since the formation of Czechoslovakia in 1918. **Thomas Garrigue Masaryk,** the first Czechoslovak president, married an American woman and took her maiden name as his middle name—how's that for avant-garde feminism?

Transportation

GETTING THERE

AIR

International flights will most likely arrive at **Vaclav Havel International Airport (PRG)** (Aviatická, www.prg.aero). There are two terminals, with Terminal 1 serving flights from outside the Schengen area (e.g., North America, the UK, Asia, Africa, and the Middle East) and Terminal 2 serving flights from within Europe's Schengen countries. The airport is small and reasonably easy to navigate, with hit-or-miss public Wi-Fi available.

Airport Transportation

The airport is 17 kilometers (about 10.5 miles) east of the city center, and transportation from the airport to the city center is not always straightforward. There is no direct public transportation link, but you can catch **buses** from Terminal 1 or Terminal 2 (routes 100 or 119, 32 CZK transport ticket), which run frequently from about 4:45am until around 11pm. After about a 15-20-minute ride, transfer to the green metro line at the last bus stop, Nádraží Veleslavín.

The trip between the airport and the city center takes roughly 35-55 minutes total.

For an easier (and usually slightly cheaper) ride into the city, try local ride-sharing providers **Liftago** (www.liftago.cz) or international operators **Bolt** (www.bolt.eu) and **Uber** (www.uber.com). These do require setting up a profile, so it's best to download and enter information before your trip. Rideshares pick up passengers along the strip of pavement in the short-term parking lot that sits in front of Terminal 1 and Terminal 2 (not at the sidewalk in front of arrivals). The ride into the city takes roughly 20-30 minutes and costs 350-700 CZK.

There are no taxi stands at the Prague Airport, so if you want to take a taxi, ask one of the airport information desks (Fix Taxi or Taxi Praha) to arrange one for you or negotiate your fare in advance—Prague taxis have a reputation for overcharging foreigners. The ride into the city takes roughly 20-30 minutes and costs around 500-800 CZK in a taxi.

TRAIN

The national rail company is called **České dráhy** (www.cd.cz), with unpredictable service varying between older models with minimal amenities and newer trains with Wi-Fi and electrical outlets. When booking a ticket in person or online, make sure to specify that you want a seat reservation unless you're okay standing in the train-car halls during peak seasons. Two private carriers, **Regiojet** (www.regiojet.com) and **Leo Express** (www.leoexpress.com), also run on the same lines with more consistently modern service and guaranteed seating at varying prices. Trains arrive and depart efficiently and reliably, so be sure to find your platform with plenty of time to spare.

There are three train stations serving Prague. The Main Railway Station is called **Praha—Hlavní nádraží** (Wilsonova 8), and is often written as *Praha hl. n* in Czech. This station is located in the center of New Town and connects directly to the red Metro line C. This station serves both domestic and international destinations and is filled with restaurants, shopping, and even a supermarket. This is the most common station that international tourists will arrive or depart from.

simple comfort on Czech National Railways

Two smaller stations also offer connections to destinations abroad and within the Czech Republic: **Praha—Masarykovo nádraží** (Havlíčkova 2) is in New Town not far from Náměstí Republiky and next to tram stop Masarykovo nádraží. Indirect trains requiring transfers to other European destinations may depart from or arrive at this station.

Train station **Praha—Holešovice** (Partyzánská 26) is located along the red Metro line C at the metro stop with the same name. Some indirect trains to domestic or international destinations may stop at this local station, one stop outside of Prague's main central train station (Hlavní nádraží). This may be a more convenient place for travelers staying in Letná or Holešovice to board or depart these trains.

BUS

Prague's main **Florenc Bus Station** (Křižíkova 6, www.florenc.cz) can be tricky to find. It is connected to the Florenc Metro station along the red Metro line C and yellow metro line B, but you have to follow signs for the specific exit to "Autobusové nádraží" or you may find yourself a few streets away. Multiple bus companies arrive and depart from Florenc at all hours, but the terminal building of fast food, indoor seating, carrier information counters, and luggage storage is only open between 6am and 10pm. Travelers may have to wait outside for late-night connections and overnight buses.

Some buses may stop on the street above the Main Railway Station of **Praha—Hlavní nádraží** (Wilsonova 8). There are staircases and elevators to reach the station from the parking area. This stop is most common for international routes on private companies such as Flixbus or Eurolines.

The **Na Knížecí Bus Station** (Na Knížecí) in the Smichov neighborhood serves domestic routes to places such as Český Krumlov or Karovy Vary. The outdoor platforms do not offer much customer service or shelter, so double-check your departure information and bundle up in winter if departing from this station. Na Knížecí is easily accessible on the yellow metro line—just follow the signs with a picture of a bus for the correct exit out of the large, underground Anděl metro stop. Na Knížecí is also accessible via tram 20 from Malá Strana (10-15 minutes) or tram 5 from Wenceslas Square (15-20 minutes). A taxi from Wenceslas Square takes 10-20 minutes, depending on traffic, and should cost 150-250 CZK.

The **Černý Most** bus station lies at the end of the yellow Metro line B. The bus stops are located downstairs from the subway platforms. Day trips to Liberec depart hourly from this outdoor station for most of the day, and there are a few fast-food options and a RegioJet information center on the lower level.

GETTING AROUND

Prague's public transportation system, **Dopravní podnik hlavního města Prahy** (www.dpp.cz), is one of the best in the world, with easy access to almost every part of the city via metro and tram for most neighborhoods, or by bus for a few of the more residential areas or the outskirts.

TRANSIT PASSES

Public transport tickets are sold in chunks of time, not single rides. They are valid from the moment they are validated, *not* when they are bought, so don't forget to stamp your ticket when you're ready to use it. Individual tickets are available for 30 minutes (24 CZK) or 90 minutes (32 CZK), as well as 24-hour passes (110 CZK) or 72-hour passes (310 CZK). There are no week passes, but a monthly unlimited pass is only 670 CZK. Prague transport tickets can be used on all metro, tram, and bus lines, and also include use of the funicular on Petřín Hill and the ferries crossing the Vltava River during warmer months. Tickets are valid for unlimited rides during the allotted time, including transfers between the various modes.

Paper tickets are available to purchase from yellow automated machines inside Metro stations and near some major tram stops, or in person at limited information desks (see www.dpp.cz for locations). A few updated machines accept credit cards, but many require cash in coins (not bills), so a multi-day pass can save the hassle of finding a machine plus the right change for every individual ride, especially if searching late at night. Some modern trams allow you to pay with a credit card onboard, but you'll need a contactless credit card and if anything goes wrong then you're stuck without a ticket. You can also use the PID Lítačka smartphone app to purchase tickets on Wi-Fi or data. Some corner stores around town also sell transport tickets, but availability is inconsistent. It is not possible to buy a ticket onboard most public transport in Prague.

Tickets work on an honor system. You validate your ticket before entering and then keep the ticket with you as proof of payment. Inspectors can do random checks at any time, and anyone caught without a ticket will be removed and required to pay a hefty 1,500 CZK fine on the spot—inspectors will accompany you to an ATM if you don't have cash on hand. Excuses such as ignorance or simply forgetting to stamp your ticket are not accepted, so be sure to validate every time and keep your ticket in a safe, accessible place.

METRO

Prague's underground subway system consists of three lines: the green **Metro line A** running from Dejvice through the Old Town and into Vinohrady and Žižkov, the yellow **Metro line B** running from Anděl across Old Town and New Town and into Karlín, and the red **Metro line C** connecting Holešovice with the city center and Vyšehrad. Most stations have a single platform with service in both directions (Vyšehrad, Hlavní Nádraží, and Černý Most are exceptions).

The metro runs from 5am to midnight daily, with trains arriving every two to three minutes in peak hours and 5-10 minutes in off-peak hours. Many stations have a digital display counting down until the arrival. Validate your ticket in the yellow boxes located at the entrance to the stations, usually at the top of stairs or escalators before you reach the platform.

Not all metro stations are accessible via elevator (see www.dpp.cz for barrier-free travel) and most stations combine escalators and stairs, so be prepared to lift any luggage that you're traveling with. Many of the escalators are quite steep and faster than travelers may be used to. The deepest station at Náměstí Miru takes over two minutes to travel 53 meters (almost 175 feet) down one of the longest escalators in all of Europe.

TRAM

The tram system runs 24 hours a day, switching to limited night-tram schedules at midnight. **Tram 22** is particularly popular among tourists,

Prague's newer trams

TRANSIT ETIQUETTE

color-coded signs in Prague's Metro stations

- **Noise:** The atmosphere on Prague's public transport is generally quiet, and loud conversations or phone calls will be met with dirty looks from the residents.
- **Seating:** There is a line of succession when it comes to seating—riders are expected to stand up and offer their spots at any stop to elderly people, injured individuals with crutches or a cane, pregnant women, and young children.
- **Boarding:** Always let the departing passengers exit before attempting to board. During rush hours, passengers near the doors often step off the train and stand near the doors to let passengers off before re-entering, so maintain an awareness of anyone needing to squeeze past, especially when traveling with luggage or a backpack.
- **Escalators:** When riding the escalator in metro stations, passengers who want to walk use the left side and those who want to stand stay to the right—the locals take this seriously, so don't block the path with luggage or a group of side-by-side riders.

connecting the Prague Castle to Malá Strana, Vinohrady, and New Town. Night trams generally begin with the number nine (e.g., 92, 97). If you have a single-ride paper ticket, be sure to validate it onboard in small yellow boxes near some of the doors. Tram rides can be a bit jerky, so be sure to hold on when the train starts to move to avoid tumbling down the aisles.

Construction and maintenance on the tram lines are prevalent during the summer months, so many tram routes may be interrupted. Information is often posted at the stop, but not always in English, so having a map or data-enabled phone can be useful to tackle surprise route changes. The transit authority website (www.dpp.en) usually provides updates in English.

BUS

Prague's city buses connect to some of the more remote neighborhoods and trips to the Prague airport. Validate your ticket on board in small yellow boxes near some of the doors. Like trams, buses run at all hours, and night buses also begin with the number nine (e.g., 92, 97).

TAXI AND RIDE-SHARING

Taxi service in Prague is notorious for taking indirect routes and overcharging foreigners, particularly if flagged down off the street near touristy areas. You may ask your hotel or restaurant to call a cab for you to be on the safe side. Smartphone travelers can also use local ride-sharing providers **Liftago** (www.liftago.cz) or international operators **Bolt** (www.bolt.eu) and **Uber** (www.uber.com) for a safe ride that is tracked on a map and doesn't require having the local currency on hand.

Public transport can generally take you anywhere that taxis could during the day, but a taxi can be helpful if you're out on the town after midnight, when the metro stops running and trams and buses switch to limited night routes.

CAR

Driving in Prague is more trouble than it's worth: lots of one-way streets, confusing parking zones, and restrictions (see www.parkujvklidu.cz for details). Cars stick to the right side of the road in the Czech capital, so look right first at any intersections.

However, a car can be useful for day trips and seeing some of the countryside. You can find many international rental car companies, including **Avis** (www.avis.cz; +420 221 851 225; 7:30am-6pm Mon-Fri, 8am-noon Sat-Sun) or **Budget** (www.budget.cz; +420 602 165 108; 8am-8pm daily), at the Prague Airport.

KUTNÁ HORA

Kutná Hora is a quieter comple- ment to the cosmopolitan experience of Prague and remains accessible for travelers on a tight schedule. Less than an hour to the east, this city of historical importance contains fascinating architecture and contemporary touches. Symbols of its silver mines, which established the city's royal status in the 14th century, are etched in the medieval monuments, while its "bone church" at the Sedlec Ossuary remains the most famous draw for tourists. The historic city center, St. Barbara's Cathedral, and Cathedral of the

HIGHLIGHTS

- ✪ **SEDLEC OSSUARY:** Kutná Hora's famed "bone church" contains thousands of artfully arranged human skeletons. It's surprisingly peaceful (page 166).
- ✪ **ST. BARBARA'S CATHEDRAL:** Soak up the traditional Gothic beauty of this Roman Catholic cathedral from both the interior pews and the surrounding green grass (page 168).
- ✪ **GASK GALLERY OF THE CENTRAL BOHEMIAN REGION:** Catch a glimpse of contemporary Czech art with a creative approach to curation (page 168).

Assumption at Sedlec have all earned their places on the UNESCO World Heritage List.

ORIENTATION

A visit to the fairly small town of Kutná Hora centers around three main areas: the **historical town center**, the churches around the **Sedlec suburb** to the northeast, and three separate **train stations** lining the eastern edge of town. The cobblestoned center is easily walkable, while taxis or a local tourist shuttle service save time and add convenience for reaching Sedlec or transporting luggage to and from the train stations.

PLANNING YOUR TIME

Kutná Hora is easily doable as a **day trip** from Prague without accommodation. **Spending the night** before a day of sightseeing can offer an early start or a more leisurely pace to explore the lesser-known sights without the worry of missing the semi-frequent train service.

SIGHTSEEING PASSES

If you plan to visit multiple sights, the **combined ticket** to the Ossuary, Church of the Assumption, and St. Barbara's Cathedral (220 CZK) is a good value. Buy it in cash at your first stop.

St. Barbara's Cathedral after dark

Itinerary Idea

The majority of Kutná Hora sights open around 8am or 9am and close around 5pm or 6pm, so catching an early train can help you make the most of your time. This will be a day spent largely on your feet, so choose your footwear accordingly. Make sure you have some local currency in your pocket, as ATMs in Kutná Hora are less prevalent than in Prague, and make reservations for lunch at **Staročeská restaurace V Ruthardce** and dinner at **Čtyři sestry** before you set out. This itinerary won't work on Mondays, when GASK is closed.

ESSENTIAL KUTNÁ HORA

1 Arrive at the main train station of **Kutná Hora hl. n.**

2 Check the signage (or follow the crowds) to the **Church of the Assumption of Our Lady and Saint John the Baptist.** Buy your combined church ticket and borrow a printed text in English to spend roughly half an hour admiring the bright, sunny interior.

3 Present your combined ticket to enter the **Sedlec Ossuary** and its famous "bone church." Give yourself at least an hour to explore the underground ossuary, the surrounding cemetery, and the chapel that sits above the bones.

4 When you're ready to leave, check in with the cash desk to join a tourist shuttle bus to the city center. Request a drop-off at **Staročeská restaurace V Ruthardce** for a hearty lunch of Czech cuisine.

5 After lunch, stop into the tiny **Chocolate Museum & Chocolaterie.** Spend 10 minutes browsing the nostalgic artifacts and indulging in some specialty coffee or hot chocolate.

6 Walk down Barborska street, admiring the statues and city views along the cobblestoned walkway, to reach **GASK Gallery of the Central Bohemian Region.** Depending on your interest or stamina, you could spend anywhere from an hour to more than two hours taking in the exhibits of Czech artists from the 20th and 21st centuries.

7 Next door to GASK, use your final stop of the combination church ticket for **St. Barbara's Cathedral.** Spend about half an hour gazing up at the ceilings and snap a photo of the exterior silhouette from the stairs behind the cathedral. Then kick back and relax your feet for a break in the grassy courtyard around the building.

8 Take a 20-minute stroll to reach the **Italian Court.** Ambitious travelers could head inside to catch one of the final tours, make your own silver

Kutná Hora

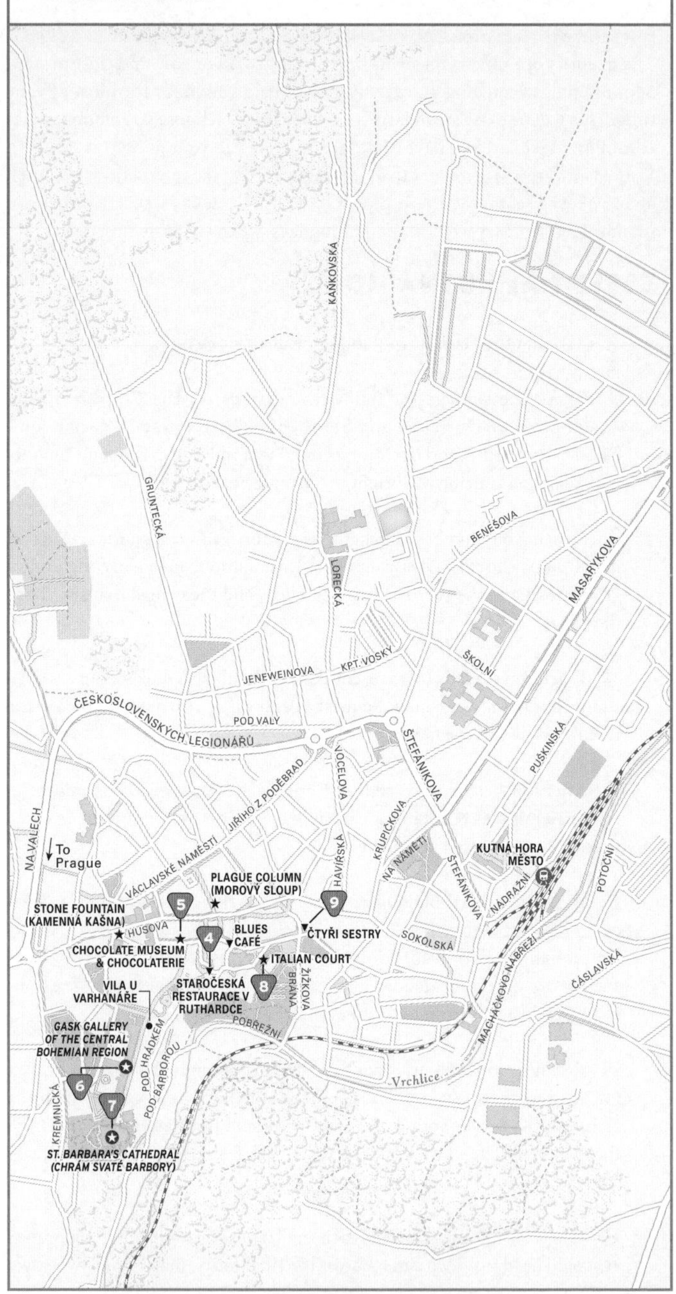
KAŇKOVSKÁ
GRUNTECKÁ
LORECKÁ
BENEŠOVA
MASARYKOVA
ŠKOLNÍ
JENEWEINOVA
KPT. VOSKY
ČESKOSLOVENSKÝCH LEGIONÁŘŮ
POD VALY
ŠTEFÁNIKOVA
PUŠKINSKÁ
JIŘÍHO Z PODĚBRAD
VOCELOVA
NA VALECH
To Prague
VÁCLAVSKÉ NÁMĚSTÍ
KRUPIČKOVA
NA NÁMĚSTÍ
HAVÍŘSKÁ
KUTNÁ HORA MĚSTO
POTOČNÍ
NÁDRAŽNÍ
PLAGUE COLUMN (MOROVÝ SLOUP)
STONE FOUNTAIN (KAMENNÁ KAŠNA)
HUSOVA
BLUES CAFÉ
ČTYŘI SESTRY
SOKOLSKÁ
CHOCOLATE MUSEUM & CHOCOLATERIE
ITALIAN COURT
ČÁSLAVSKÁ
MACHÁČKOVO NÁBŘEŽÍ
VILA U VARHANÁŘE
STAROČESKÁ RESTAURACE V RUTHARDCE
ŽIŽKOVA BRÁNA
POBŘEŽNÍ
GASK GALLERY OF THE CENTRAL BOHEMIAN REGION
POD HRÁDKEM
POD BARBOROU
Vrchlice
KREMNICKÁ
ST. BARBARA'S CATHEDRAL (CHRÁM SVATÉ BARBORY)
4
5
6
7
8
9

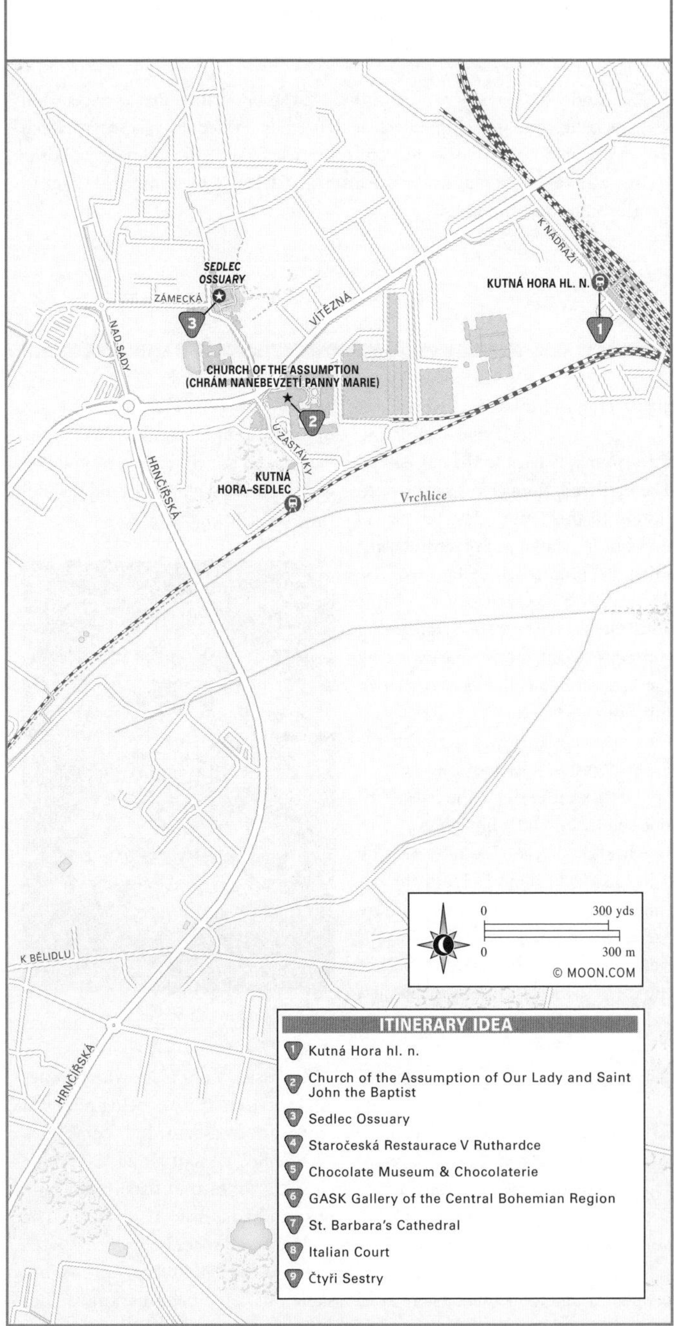
SEDLEC OSSUARY
ZÁMECKÁ
3
NAD SADY
VÍTĚZNÁ
K NÁDRAŽÍ
KUTNÁ HORA HL. N.
1
CHURCH OF THE ASSUMPTION (CHRÁM NANEBEVZETÍ PANNY MARIE)
2
U ZASTÁVKY
KUTNÁ HORA–SEDLEC
HRNČÍŘSKÁ
Vrchlice
K BĚLIDLU
HRNČÍŘSKÁ
0
300 yds
0
300 m
© MOON.COM
ITINERARY IDEA
1 Kutná Hora hl. n.
2 Church of the Assumption of Our Lady and Saint John the Baptist
3 Sedlec Ossuary
4 Staročeská Restaurace V Ruthardce
5 Chocolate Museum & Chocolaterie
6 GASK Gallery of the Central Bohemian Region
7 St. Barbara's Cathedral
8 Italian Court
9 Čtyři Sestry

coin, or just grab an outdoor courtyard bench to enjoy an evening view of terraced gardens and city skyline.

9 End your evening with a dinner of seafood, grilled meats, vegetarian specialties, and fresh ingredients with friendly service at **Čtyři sestry.** Keep an eye on both the clock and your train ticket. Give yourself plenty of time to call a taxi (that may not arrive immediately) for a 10-minute ride back to the main train station.

Sights

Sightseeing in Kutná Hora works best if you start with the farthest sights and work your way back to the city center. The walk from Kutná Hora's main train station to the Sedlec Ossuary passes by a lesser-known architectural sight worth stepping into, the **Church of the Assumption of Our Lady and Saint John the Baptist.** A good sightseeing strategy is to take your time exploring the artistic detail in every corner of this church while the first wave of train travelers makes their way straight to the **Sedlec Ossuary.** By the time you walk up the street after them, the crowds inside should be a little bit lighter.

An eight-person Tourist Shuttle Van (35 CZK) departs from the ossuary whenever three people or more are ready to go. This is the best option to reach the historical center of the town, which is otherwise about a half-hour walk.

TOP EXPERIENCE

✪ SEDLEC OSSUARY

U Zastávky; +420 326 551 049; www.sedlec.info; Nov-Feb 9am-4pm daily; March and Oct, 9am-5pm daily; April-Sept, 8am-6pm Mon-Sat, 9am-6pm Sun; 50 CZK

According to legend, hundreds of people wanted to be buried here after holy soil was sprinkled on these lands in the 13th century. Add a dash of the Plague and the Hussite wars, and you get the crowded burial ground that defines this site's name.

Coat of Arms at the Sedlec Ossuary

An ossuary is a place where bones are kept, usually after being removed from an overcrowded cemetery. The Sedlec Ossuary, aka the "bone church," takes that functional purpose and adds an artistic twist. The underground space holds the remains of more than 40,000 people whose skeletons have been arranged into various configurations and decorations. The most eye-catching structures are a skeletal chandelier in the center of the room that contains every bone in the human body and a coat of arms of the Schwarzenberg family, who funded the creation of the space in the late 1800s. Look for the name "F. Rint" beside the stairs, a signature of František Rint, the designer who shaped the space into its current form.

While a room full of bones may sound creepy, the towers, pyramids, and columns actually provide an air of peace and wonder. Note that as of 2020, photography rules at this sacred site will change. Visitors hoping to take pictures will need to apply for permission at least three days in advance (see website for further details, unclear at the time of writing). The rule comes in response to a rise in the number of tourists and their inappropriate behavior, such as touching the bones or adding accessories to skeletons in order to take selfies. The organizers hope to restore a level of reverence and respect to the final resting place of those whose remains compose the décor.

Take some time to explore the interior of the Church of All Saints, located directly on top of the ossuary. The upstairs chapel holds interesting biblical artwork, and the ornate graves surrounding the grounds are worth perusing.

CHURCH OF THE ASSUMPTION OF OUR LADY AND SAINT JOHN THE BAPTIST (CHRÁM NANEBEVZETÍ PANNY MARIE)

Zámecká 279; +420 326 551 049; www.sedlec.info; 50 CZK

The excessively named and inconsistently translated Church of the Assumption of Our Lady and Saint John the Baptist is the oldest Cistercian cathedral in Bohemia, built at the end of the 12th century. Tall, pale yellow walls curve into thin white beams lining the muraled ceiling. A spiral staircase on the left-hand side leads to a behind-the-scenes tour of the wooden attic. The church opens at 9am Mon-Sat and 11am on Sundays all year long, closing at 4pm from Nov-Feb, 5pm in March and Oct, and 6pm April-Sept. Note that photography restrictions at the Sedlec Ossuary, scheduled to begin in 2020, will also apply to the Church of the Assumption. At the time of writing, this included requesting photo permission at least three days in advance, but check the website for updated rules and restrictions.

Kutná Hora's Plague Column

PLAGUE COLUMN (MOROVÝ SLOUP)

Šultysova; destinace.kutnahora.cz; free

The early 18th-century Plague Column is a memorial to the thousand or more people who lost their lives to the Plague of 1713. The Virgin

Mary looks over the city from atop a base held by symbolic miners from this treasury town, which was historically known for its silver reserves. Photography fans may spend some time finding their favorite angle of this 16-meter (roughly 50-foot) decorative feature with various pastel-colored buildings in the background.

STONE FOUNTAIN (KAMENNÁ KAŠNA)

Husová; destinace.kutnahora.cz; free

This 15th-century Gothic stone fountain, located just a few streets from the Plague Column, served as a reservoir for drinking water when the silver mining trade interfered with the natural flow of groundwater, making fresh water harder to come by. The ornate, 12-sided design was filled by a system of wooden pipes that functioned until 1890. Today, the ornate stonework of the exterior against an open cobblestoned square makes for a particularly photogenic moment. Look through a small diamond in the door on the west side of the fountain for a peek into the interior structure.

the Stone Fountain

✪ ST. BARBARA'S CATHEDRAL (CHRÁM SVATÉ BARBORY)

Barborská; +420 327 512 115; destinace.kutnahora.cz; Jan-Feb 10am-4pm; Mar, Nov, and Dec 10am-5pm; Apr-Oct 9am-6pm; combined ticket 220 CZK

The crown jewel of Kutná Hora and symbol of the city is the Gothic St. Barbara's Cathedral. St. Barbara's is named after the patron saint of the miners who defined this town. A walk toward the cathedral along Barborska Street, a cement walkway lined with stone statues, whets the visual appetite. Admiring every detail of the tall sloping curves of the exterior, combined with the frescoed ceilings inside, will give your neck a workout. The grass courtyard around the church provides a peaceful place to relax after a day of sightseeing.

The church is about half an hour to an hour's walk from either Kutná Hora město or Kutná Hora hl. n, so you may want to take a taxi.

✪ GASK GALLERY OF THE CENTRAL BOHEMIAN REGION

Barborská 51-53; +420 725 377 433; www.gask.cz; 10am-6pm Tues-Sun; 80-200 CZK

The multi-story GASK contemporary art gallery takes a creative approach to curating paintings, sculpture, and multimedia pieces from Czech artists of the 20th and 21st centuries. I recommend a solid 90 minutes to take in the permanent exhibition of "States of Mind—Beyond the Image" (80 CZK), spread across two floors and organized into 21 pairs of opposing themes or emotions. Connected rooms and hallways each house 5-10 pieces from different artists on opposing themes, such as solitude and friendship, fear and courage, gentleness and cruelty, and prejudice and understanding. Czech perspectives in the third floor's "confinement and freedom" room offer particularly striking connections to world history, and the multimedia

the Gothic beauty of St. Barbara's Cathedral

interpretation of "Enjoyment" on the second floor caught my eye.

Other sections of the gallery hold rotating exhibitions of individually ticketed artists (80 CZK each), while an all-access gallery pass (200 CZK) is also available. Audio guides are only available in Czech, but the captions and walls around the art are adorned with quotes in English and Czech by international artists, writers, and pop culture figures, from Czech cartoonists to Marcus Aurelius and John Lennon. Kindly docents with varying levels of English are stationed on each floor to check tickets and direct visitors. The ground-floor cashiers are usually multilingual and able to offer advice about ticket options, the onsite bookstore and local design shop, and the coin-operated locker and cloakroom.

the gardens at GASK

ITALIAN COURT

Havlíčkovo náměstí 1; +420 327 512 873; www.pskh.cz; Nov-Feb 10am-4pm; Mar and Oct 10am-5pm; April-Sept 9am-6pm

If you step inside the fortified walls of the Italian Court, you'll be following in the footsteps of kings and silversmiths from as early as the 13th century. King Wenceslas IV took a liking to the site and added royal residences and an ornate chapel to the medieval royal mint and treasury. This early financial center of the Czech lands produced a silver coin called the *Prague groschen*. The currency began with a strict ratio of 90 percent silver and 10 percent copper, but was reduced over the centuries into more diluted forms by subsequent kings over the centuries. Visitors can recreate a kitschy version of the experience (149 CZK), complete with a photograph in a coin maker's robe and handheld tools to make their own silver coin souvenir, but advance reservations must be made online.

stained glass at the Italian Court

You may also cross paths with Mina, the one-eyed black cat that roams the premises, adding an air of mystery to the vast collection of tourist experiences now housed here, including a museum of local legends and ghosts (85 CZK). For more historical and educational explorations of the premises, submit an online reservation request for an English guided tour of the Royal Mint (85 CZK), Royal Palace (85 CZK), or a combination ticket of both (115 CZK). Even if you never step foot inside the building, the courtyard views and terraced gardens surrounding the Italian Court, with unobstructed views to St. Barbara's Cathedral and a charming stone frog decorating a small pond, are worth a visit.

CHOCOLATE MUSEUM & CHOCOLATERIE

Komenského náměstí 18; +420 603 184 037; www.chocomuseum.cz; 10am-noon and 1pm-5pm daily

The tiny two-room chocolate shop in Kutná Hora's historic center is one part paradise for anyone with a sweet tooth, one part nostalgia for a golden era of chocolate production, and one part vintage advertising. The rear section of the shop tells the forgotten story of Lidka, an internationally recognized brand of Czech chocolate. Two passionate Kutná Hora businessmen, Zdeněk Koukol and Eduard Michera, founded Lidka in the early 20th century. Their factories were nationalized under Communism, but the founders never shared their recipes for the beloved brand.

This small but proud chocolate museum now holds an endearing collection of newspaper articles, metal chocolate molds, labels, and posters from bygone eras. If the shop isn't too busy, the staff are happy to share personal memories while offering samples to taste. The shop currently carries the 2018 reincarnation of the Lidka brand alongside other Czech and international labels. Their wall of assorted bite-sized chocolate pieces, made with ingredients like sheep or goat's cheese, black tea, or a touch of chili, makes for affordable (12 CZK) and easily transportable souvenirs.

Food

Blues Café

Jakubská 562; +420 602 438 634; www.blues-caffe.cz; 9am-7pm Tues-Thurs, noon-8pm Fri-Sat, noon-6pm Sun; entrées 50-100 CZK

Baguettes, quiches, soups, and sweets satisfy a crowd of silver-haired ponytails, tattooed teenagers, and budget travelers at this music-themed café and bar. Gruff but efficient service includes multilingual menus and staff, and local cash is required to pay your bill. The dining room of mismatched wooden furniture surrounded by concert fliers and classic rock posters doubles as a live music venue on infrequent weekends. The building's entryway also serves as a vintage music shop of classic records and CDs.

✪ Staročeská Restaurace V Ruthardce

Dačického náměstí 10; +420 607 286 298; www.v-ruthardce.cz; noon-11pm Sun-Thurs, noon-1am Fri-Sat; entrées 150-300 CZK

No matter which chair or wooden bench you claim in the dimly lit dining room, glass-enclosed winter garden, or casual courtyard of this massive, multi-room Czech restaurant, you can expect hearty meals and efficient service. Try the *kulajda* soup of dill, cream, potatoes, and a poached egg as a starter, or pair it with a beetroot and goat cheese salad for a lighter meal. Hungrier visitors should stick to one of the many grilled chicken or steak dishes. Reservations recommended.

kulajda soup at Staročeská restaurace V Ruthardce

Čtyři Sestry

Havlíčkovo náměstí 16; +420 327 512 749 or +420 722 019 546; www.ctyrisestry.cz; 11am-10pm Mon-Sat, 11am-4pm Sun; entrées 150-300 CZK

Pale pastels and light wood set the tone at the "Four Sisters" restaurant near the Italian Court. The décor feels sophisticated enough for date night, but solo travelers and families are welcomed just as warmly. The seasonal menu covers an array of seafood, steaks, soups, salads, and Czech specialties with sections for vegans, vegetarians, and children. Prices run a little higher than a typical Czech pub for filling portions of fresh ingredients and a refreshing amount of vegetables in carnivore country. Reservations recommended.

Čtyři sestry (Four Sisters) restaurant

Accommodations

Vila U Varhanáře

Barborská 11; +420 327 536 900; www.uvarhanare.cz; around 1,500 CZK d

Location is everything for this boutique hotel of 10 en-suite rooms at the end of St. Barbara's statue-lined stone walkway, next to the GASK gallery in the historical town center. The simply furnished and slightly dated décor has a homey feel, but fades into the background against views of historical monuments and solidly modern Wi-Fi speeds. Booking includes a decent hot-and-cold breakfast buffet including eggs, sausages, baked beans, fruit, and gluten-free cereal (but no dairy-free milk options) from 7-10am on weekdays and 8am-1:30pm on weekends.

Transportation

GETTING THERE

TRAIN

You can reach Kutná Hora in about an hour on the national rail service, **České dráhy** (www.cd.cz; 200-250 CZK round trip), leaving from Prague's main train station (Praha hl. n.) about once an hour from 4:30am, with the last trains departing to Prague around 10:15pm. Some trains are direct while others require a transfer in Kolín. There are three stops: Kutná Hora město is closest to the center of town, Kutná Hora–Sedlec is closest to two major sights, and Kutná Hora hl. n. is the third stop, requiring the fewest transfers but a short walk.

Before purchasing your ticket, you have a decision to make: buy a direct ticket to Kutná Hora hl.n. and walk for 10-15 minutes to the Sedlec Ossuary, or purchase your ticket to Kutná Hora-Sedlec, which means going to Kutná Hora hl.n. and transferring to a small local train that drops you off steps away from the Church of the Assumption and Sedlec Ossuary. Either way, you are likely to return to Prague from the Kutná Hora město station, closest to the center of town, which is included in a return ticket to either station.

CAR

Kutná Hora is just over an hour east of Prague (roughly 80km/50mi) on highway **D11**, **Route 2**, or **D1/E65.** There is some free street **parking** around the Sedlec Ossuary and Cathedral of the Assumption at Sedlec, and you can find a list of parking places in town at destinace.kutnahora.cz/d/parking.

GETTING AROUND

Because Kutná Hora's sights and train stations are spread across town, they are more easily reached with a little help from local transport options. The **Tourist Bus** (+420 733 551 011) provides rides for 3-8 people from the Sedlec Ossuary to the city center, to St. Barbara's Cathedral, or to the main train station when time allows (at driver's discretion). For traditional taxi service, call **Taxi Kutna Hora** (+420 800 100 512, +420 777 239 909, or +420 327 512 618).

LEAVING KUTNÁ HORA

The majority of travelers do this day trip as a Prague-Kutná Hora-Prague loop. The last two trains from Kutná Hora to Prague on the state railway depart around 9pm and 10:30pm. Kutná Hora could potentially provide drivers, or those okay with indirect trains on the state rail service, an eastern head-start on the way to **Olomouc** (175 km/110 mi, 2.5-3.5 hours by car) or **Brno** (150 km/93 mi, 2-3 hours by car).

LIBEREC

Liberec, located an hour's bus or car ride to the north of Prague, falls halfway between cosmopolitan and country life. This university town near the German border is filled with interesting architectural sights and a diverse selection of international restaurants, and is a popular summertime base for sunbathing and beach volleyball. The pace of life is laid-back, with events on the main square (such as an Easter market, Christmas-tree lighting, or a big win by a local sports team) drawing most area residents and families to gather and celebrate.

HIGHLIGHTS

- **JEŠTĚD HOTEL AND TV TOWER:** Catch a view of three countries from this architectural-award-winning tower on top of a mountain range (page 178).
- **TOWN HALL:** Reminiscent of the elegance of Vienna, Liberec's Town Hall is particularly beautiful at Christmas, when lights twinkle on the square below (page 179).
- **LIBEREC RESERVOIR:** Join locals to sunbathe in the grass, walk laps around the water, and kick back with beer and snacks at the outdoor pub on a sunny day (page 182).

Liberec is a coveted place to live for its easy access to Prague, where some residents commute for work, and proximity to the natural beauty of nearby forests and mountains. This was my first Czech home and charmed me into staying far longer than I expected. Get a peek at local life with some tourist-friendly attractions thrown in.

ORIENTATION

Liberec is the fifth-largest city in the Czech Republic, with a population around 100,000 people. The majority of your time will be spent in an easy-to-navigate **city center** that makes an L shape from the **Fügnerova bus station**, uphill to the **Town Hall** and **main square**, and then east to the **reservoir.** One set of tram tracks runs through the center of town, and most sights are within a 20-minute walk. The one sight requiring public transport, **Ještěd Hotel and TV Tower,** sits on the mountain range above the town and is accessible by tram and cable car, by taxi, or a multi-hour walk for those with time and energy to spare.

PLANNING YOUR TIME

One day in Liberec is plenty of time to get a taste of life outside of Prague, and regular bus service connects the two cities all day long. An **overnight trip** offers a more relaxing getaway, with plenty of nearby nature to explore and a chance to experience the nightlife. Liberec also makes a good jumping-off point for a hike in **Bohemian Paradise** (known locally as Česky Ráj) with closer train connections than Prague to the protected nature area.

view from Ještěd TV Tower

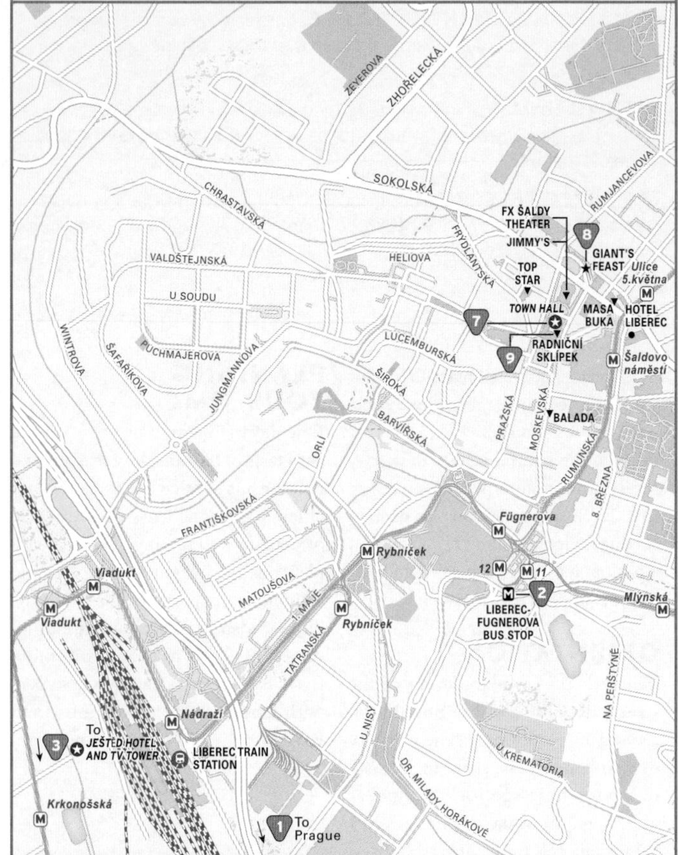

Itinerary Idea

Before leaving your Prague home base, book your Regiojet bus tickets online (www.regiojet.com) and make reservations for dinner at **Radniční Sklípek.**

ESSENTIAL LIBEREC

1 Grab a hotel breakfast or a quick bite in **Prague,** then jump on the yellow metro line to the final Černý Most stop. Go downstairs to the bus platforms for a one-hour Regiojet ride to Liberec.

2 Get off at the first **Fügnerova bus stop** (not the final bus station) in

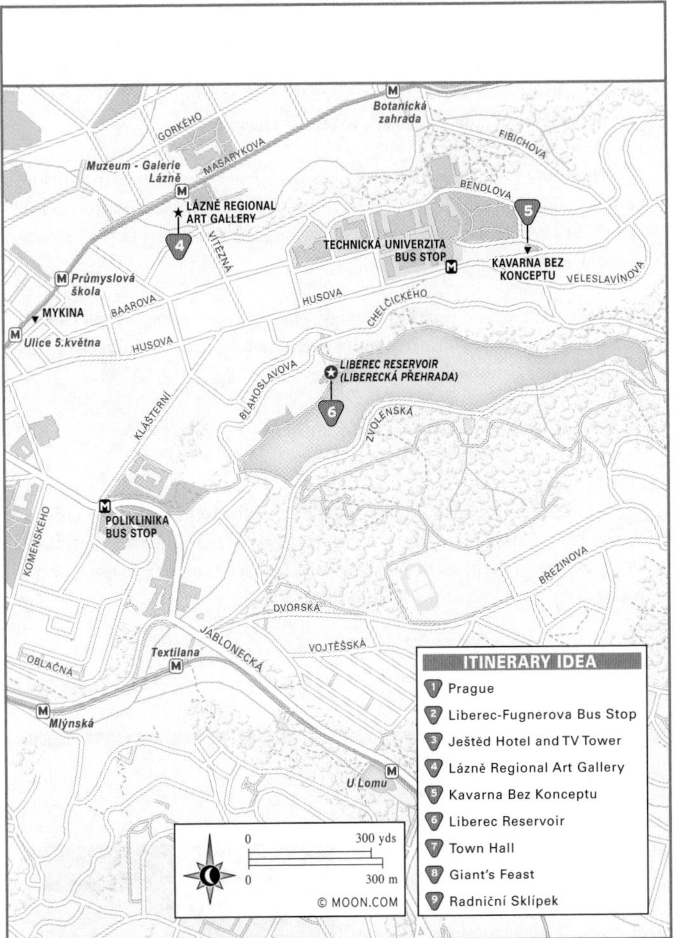

the center of Liberec. Buy a 24-hour tourist tram ticket (50 CZK) from the counter at Fügnerova and hop on the #2 or #3 tram (across the street from the Forum Liberec mall) for a 15-minute ride. Don't forget to stamp your ticket onboard to validate it.

3 From the final Horní Hanychov tram stop, follow the signs to catch a scenic cable car ride up to **Ještěd Hotel and TV Tower.** Give yourself a solid 90 minutes to admire the mountaintop views and grab lunch or a drink inside the retro-futuristic café.

4 Take the cable car down again and jump back on tram #2 or #3 for a 20-minute ride to the Muzeum-Výstaviště stop. Pop into **Lázně Regional Art Gallery** and spend 30 minutes browsing the latest exhibition.

5 From the art gallery, turn right to follow Masarykova street, admiring the historical homes for five minutes along this tree-lined block. Continue walking to arrive at **Kavarna Bez Konceptu.** Grab some specialty coffee or homemade lemonade, or a snack to take to the reservoir.

6 Turn right out of the café and cross the street to enter the winding forest paths down to the **Liberec Reservoir.** Grab a Svijany beer or soft drink from the outdoor pub and find a spot on the grass near the volleyball courts to soak up the outdoor vibe.

7 When afternoon turns to evening, exit the reservoir and walk over to Liberec **Town Hall.** Pause to admire and snap a few exterior photos of this architectural landmark.

8 Swing by David Černý's sculptural **Giant's Feast** bus stop, located just behind the town hall and FX Šaldy Theater.

9 Find the entrance to **Radniční Sklípek** on the right side of the Liberec Town Hall. Indulge in a hearty, traditional Czech meal and fresh draft beer. Keep an eye on the clock to avoid missing the last bus back to Prague, which pulls away from Fügnerova at 8pm sharp.

Sights

TOP EXPERIENCE

✪ JEŠTĚD HOTEL AND TV TOWER

Horní Hanychov 153; hotel +420 485 104 291 or +420 605 292 563; restaurant +420 731 658 045; www.jested.cz/en; free

Liberec's most distinctive building overlooks the city from a perch on top of the surrounding mountain range. The slender point of the Ještěd Hotel and TV Tower has earned international architectural acclaim for its ability to blend seamlessly into the natural silhouette.

Dine in the sky at Ještěd's retro-futuristic restaurant.

On a clear day, visitors can see beyond the borders of Germany and Poland from the surrounding courtyard. The bronze "Little Martian" statue by sculptor Jaroslav Róna, which

Ještěd Tower defines the Liberec skyline.

spends a lifetime crying at the base of the tower, plays off comparisons of the structure to a spaceship in the sky. On the opposite side of the tower, a plaque embedded in bricks marks the location of the last free radio broadcast made in 1968 by Vaclav Havel and Jan Tříska before the next few decades of Russian occupation.

The hotel and restaurant housed inside the curved walls maintain a charmingly nostalgic imagination of futuristic design from a 1970s perspective. Rounded chandelier light fixtures hang overhead as visitors gaze out of the floor-to-ceiling windows of the 120-seat restaurant and 50-seat café. A spontaneous snack or afternoon drink is usually available, but reservations are recommended to enjoy dinner with a panoramic view among the stars.

The easiest way to reach the tower is a cable car ride (150 CZK round-trip), departing from the base of the hill, a short walk from the Horní Hanychov tram stop. The cable car runs from 8am-7pm most days, with a late start of 2pm-7pm on Mondays and finishing an hour earlier at 6pm from November through March. In winter, the ride includes a view overlooking the small Ještěd ski slope, which reverts to green grass in the warmer months.

✪ TOWN HALL

Náměstí Dr. E. Beneše 1; +420 485 101 709; www.visitliberec.eu; June-Sept 9am-3pm weekdays, 9am-11am Sat (9am-3pm on Thursdays only from Oct-May); English tour 170 CZK, tower access 30 CZK; tram stop Šaldovo Náměstí

The Liberec Town Hall draws the eye of anyone setting foot on the main square. Designed by Austrian architect Franz von Neumann, the building draws comparisons to another Central European masterpiece—the Vienna Town Hall. The intricate Neo-Renaissance façade and turquoise-topped spires are a testament to the Austro-Hungarian rule of the 19th century. Balcony access is fun for a bird's-eye view of the area. Otherwise, set up shop across the square next to the statue of Neptune and his trident, which used to provide drinking water to local residents, and find the best angle to fit the entire building inside your camera lens. Around the holidays, the town hall overlooks Christmas and Easter markets on the main square with homemade crafts, hot wine (*svařák*), and fresh pastries, while summer months bring food, beer, and music festivals. The lively, central location means easy access to lots of pubs and restaurants, including **Radniční sklípek** in the town hall basement.

GIANT'S FEAST

Nám. Dr. E. Beneše 27; free

One of Liberec's bus stops is topped with a fairy tale scene, created by sculptor David Černý in his signature controversial style. The bus stop entitled "Giant's Feast" is shaped like a table and topped with two beer mugs in Czech and German style on either side of a severed head on a plate. The head is rumored to symbolize Konrad Henlein, a German politician from the Sudetenland and member of the Nazi party. A menorah on its side refers to a local synagogue that was burned down in 1938. The vase and Venus flytrap are thought to symbolize the Liberec museum and botanical gardens along Masarykova street. A pair of Czech sausages sit beside a trash can on the sidewalk next to the stop. This quirky artistic statement is located just beyond F. X. Šaldy Theatre and the Liberec Town Hall.

sculptural bus stop "Giant's Feast"

Lázně Regional Art Gallery

LÁZNĚ REGIONAL ART GALLERY

Masarykova 14; +420 485 106 325; www.ogl.cz; 10am-5pm Tues-Wed and Fri-Sun, 10am-7pm Thurs; 80 CZK; tram stop Muzeum-Výstaviště

A blend of historic roots and modern innovation are embodied in the walls of the Lázně Regional Art Gallery. This former spa and swimming pool, built in the early 1900s, underwent extensive interior renovations to create the clean lines and bright archways that have welcomed visitors since its reopening in 2013. Grab coffee in the café and a quick peek at the current art exhibit along a walk from the town hall to the reservoir.

Nightlife and Entertainment

Liberec nightlife is a delightfully odd experience that blends nostalgia with youthful energy. Two of the largest clubs just off the main square draw a mix of young professionals, university students, and international (particularly German) tourists. The age range is an eclectic blend, reminiscent of wedding receptions where aunts and uncles feel comfortable letting loose alongside younger cousins or friends of the newlyweds. Drinks flow until the early morning, with a line of taxis outside to offer a safe ride home if needed.

CLUBS

Jimmy's

Náměstí Dr. E. Beneše 22; +420 720 187 399; www.jimmys.cz; 5:30pm-4am Fri-Sat

The dance club underneath FX Šaldy Theater is an all-ages, retro music dance party topped off with a sparkling disco ball. University students and older generations mix on the dance floor, bouncing to pop hits and sing-along classics from *Dirty Dancing* or *Grease*. Bars are stocked with draft beer and cocktail favorites, and the dress code is one step above the casual attire in most pubs.

F. X. Šaldy Theater

Top Star

Mariánská 587; topstarclub.cz; 8pm-5am Fri-Sat

After a week of university or work life, a young crowd likes to unwind across the three stories of Top Star dance club. Electronic music pumps through the dim lighting and go-go platforms in the basement, while retro tunes keep the third floor spinning. The middle floor offers a bar, coat check, and café tables for a break with current hits as a soundtrack. While they open at 8pm, the party generally starts closer to midnight.

THEATER

F. X. Šaldy Theater

Náměstí Dr. E. Beneše 22; +420 485 101 523; www.saldovo-divadlo.cz/en; tram stop Šaldovo Náměstí

The sculpture-topped, Neo-Renaissance F. X. Šaldy Theater hosts opera, ballet, and theater—largely in Czech but sometimes with subtitles—directly behind the Liberec Town Hall. The elegant interior décor includes a main curtain designed by Austrian painter Gustav Klimt.

laid-back life at the Liberec reservoir

Recreation

✪ Liberec Reservoir (Liberecká Přehrada)

Liberecká Přehrada; www.liberecky-kraj.cz; enter near bus stops Poliklinika or Technická Univerzita

Students and young families sprawl across blankets on a grassy hill beside the Liberec Reservoir on any sunny day—fair warning that swimsuits are somewhat optional for the under-six or 60+ crowds. Sausages, cold beer, and soft drinks from the onsite snack bar keep the crowds in good spirits. Park bench seating is available under the shade of a wooden roof. For healthier picnic fare, stop into nearby **Kavarna Bez Konceptu** in advance for homemade sandwiches, pastries, and specialty coffee. The just-over-a-mile pathway around the reservoir offers a peaceful walk—particularly around sunset—surrounded by a lush ring of evergreen trees and alongside runners, a few cyclists, and parents pushing baby strollers. The footpath draws consistent traffic through all seasons, circling around ice skaters and hockey players if the reservoir freezes over in winter. The stone dam flanked with turrets on the west adds the requisite fairy-tale backdrop to the photogenic scene.

Food

CZECH

Radniční Sklípek

Náměstí Dr. E. Beneše 1; +420 602 602 260; www.sklipekliberec.cz/en; 11am-11pm Mon-Thurs, 11am-midnight Fri-Sat; entrées 125-300 CZK; tram stop Šaldovo Náměstí

The translation of Radniční Sklípek—"Town Hall Cellar"—tells you exactly where to find this 250-seat, traditional Czech beer hall. Try the pork schnitzel (known locally as *řízek*) with a foam-topped glass of locally brewed Svijany beer, and glance up between bites to admire the stained-glass windows and dark wooden details. Despite the massive dining room size, reservations are recommended, particularly on weekends.

Balada

Moskevská 13; +420 485 110 109; www.balada-liberec.cz; 10:30am-midnight Mon-Sat, noon-10pm Sun; entrées 125-300 CZK; tram stop Šaldovo Náměstí

For a cozier setting, head down Moskevská Street to Balada. Exposed-brick walls and eclectic wooden furniture set a warm, comfortable vibe across three small rooms. The garlic soup (*česneková*) is a perfect starter before a hearty Czech meal on a cold day.

INTERNATIONAL

Masa Buka

Sokolská 168; +420 723 153 523; www.masabuka.cz; 11am-10:30pm Tues-Thurs, 11am-midnight Fri, 11:30am-midnight Sat; entrées 125-300 CZK; tram stop Šaldovo Náměstí

Fans of Greek cuisine encircle the dining room floor and indoor balcony of family-owned Masa Buka. The bright, blue-and-white design and fresh ingredients set the Mediterranean scene at this popular restaurant, just a two-minute walk from the Liberec Town Hall. Make a reservation, and note that the kitchen closes roughly two hours before the restaurant, to ensure a leisurely meal.

COFFEE, TEA, AND SWEETS

A growing interest in specialty coffee has created a turbulent landscape of aspiring cafés opening (and closing) around Liberec. That said, there are two established favorites serving delicious lattes and lemonade alongside homemade cakes and open-faced sandwiches.

Kavarna Bez Konceptu

Husova 87; +420 485 111 947; www.bezkonceptu.cz; 8am-8pm Mon-Fri, 9am-8pm Sat-Sun; bus stop Technická Univerzita; 50-100 CZK brunch

Kavarna Bez Konceptu offers a bright, relaxed atmosphere decorated with local artwork near the Liberec Reservoir.

Stop by Bez Konceptu for reservoir snacks.

Mykina

5. května 62; +420 482 710 746; www.mikynapoint.cz/en; 8am-7pm Mon-Fri, 9am-7pm Sat, 10am-6pm Sun; tram stops Průmyslová Škola or Ulice 5. Května; 85-150 CZK brunch

Between the Lázně Regional Art Gallery and Town Hall, Mykina's friendly baristas keep the brunch crowds satisfied.

Accommodations

Hotel Liberec

Šaldovo Square 6; +420 482 710 028; hotel-liberec.eu; 1,000 CZK s, 1,500-1,750 CZK d

Convenience is the key selling point for this smack-in-the-center, 80-room hotel popular with business travelers and German families popping across the border. En-suite singles, doubles, triples, and a few family apartments offer your basic coffee, tea, and solid Wi-Fi. Some remodeled rooms are decked out in pops of colors and scenic murals. Skip the hotel bar and restaurant for the variety of options within steps of the front door. A brightly lit entryway on a main intersection will guide you home after dark.

Ještěd Hotel

Horní Hanychov 153; +420 485 104 291 or +420 605 292 563; www.jested.cz/en; 2,000 CZK s, 2,000-3,500 CZK d

While Ještěd Hotel is not the most convenient option, waking up in the clouds is an experience in itself. The en-suite or shared rooms are decorated in retro chic, as if someone in the 1970s imagined a futuristic rocket, with floor-to-ceiling windows of breathtaking sunrise views. A high-end restaurant offers updates on Czech classics for dinner (200-450 CZK) until midnight, and a buffet breakfast is included. Plan on a 30-minute taxi ride (about 400 CZK) from the center of town if your luggage is larger than a backpack.

Transportation

GETTING THERE

BUS

Regiojet (www.regiojet.com) offers hourly service to Liberec from Černý Most bus station, located at the end of Prague's Yellow metro line B (1 hour, 100 CZK). Download the **Regiojet app** for impressive flexibility—cancelling and rebooking is available online up to 30 minutes before departure for most tickets. Ride in comfortable style with reasonably reliable Wi-Fi, leather seats, and some buses with seat-back entertainment. Take note that buses run from Prague-Liberec from 7am-11pm, but the last Liberec-Prague bus departs at 8pm. Book your trip to Liberec-Fügnerova (instead of Liberec-AN) to be dropped off at the first stop in the center of town instead of the main bus terminal—the **Fügnerova bus stop** is smack in the middle of town.

Fügnerova bus stop

CAR

Liberec is located about 70 miles (110 kilometers) northeast of Prague on **Route D10/E65.** Two large **parking garages** for both the Forum and Plaza shopping malls in the city center offer free parking on weekends (20-30 CZK/hour on weekdays). Otherwise, paid street parking requires a semi-complicated system of registration with the city and a working smartphone (see www.parking.liberec.cz/en).

GETTING AROUND

You can walk about 1 kilometer (a little over half a mile) to the city center, or get **tram No 3.** From there, almost every sight can be reached **on foot.** The city transport consists of buses and a tram line. The central terminal is **Fügnerova stop** (see www.dpmlj.cz). You could also try **City Taxi Liberec Ltd** (+420 800 501 501).

LEAVING LIBEREC

Consider **8pm** a hard deadline for both the last Regiojet bus leaving Fügnerova and the last train to Prague from the main train station. Trains start again at 4am and Regiojet buses run every 30-60 minutes from 5:30am to 8pm.

While Regiojet is the simplest connection from Prague, some travelers may want to use the Liberec Train Station for connections to Turnov to explore nearby Česky Ráj ("Bohemian Paradise"). The main **Liberec train station** is located at Žitavská 2 near the Nádraží tram stop, about a 15-20 minute walk uphill or a three-minute #3 tram ride from the Fügnerova bus stop in the center of town. Direct train service from Liberec to **Turnov** on the national railway (www.cd.cz) takes around 40-45 minutes (64 CZK) and runs about every two hours from 4:30am-10:30pm.

BOHEMIAN PARADISE (ČESKÝ RÁJ)

For Czechs, spending time outdoors (or "in the nature" as Czechs like to say) is a national pastime. One of the most accessible places to explore on a day trip from Prague is the protected landscape area of **Český ráj,** known as either "Bohemian Paradise" or "Czech Paradise." The main draw to this UNESCO-protected, 181-square-kilometer (roughly 70-square-mile) area is the vast landscape of geographic beauty. A walk from the train station through the small town of Turnov leads to the vast forest, dirt paths,

HIGHLIGHTS

- **HLAVATICE LOOKOUT TOWER:** Climb an iron staircase built into sandstone rock to see for miles in every direction (page 192).
- **VALDŠTEJN CASTLE:** Cross a statue-lined bridge for a peek inside the gates of a former aristocratic palace (page 192).
- **JAN'S VIEWPOINT:** Enjoy the natural beauty of sandstone rock formations in quiet solitude from a platform tucked between the trees (page 192).

and sandstone rock formations—not to mention a few castle ruins for ambitious hikers.

ORIENTATION

Český ráj (+420 481 540 253, www.cesky-raj.info/en), aka Bohemian Paradise, is a massive nature preserve that stretches across roughly 181 square kilometers (70 square miles) of hiking paths, castle ruins, and sandstone rock formations. The small, quiet town of **Turnov,** intersected by the **Jizera River,** sits at its edge. It's a quiet town, with most travelers passing through to get into the hills of Bohemian Paradise.

Travelers by train will arrive at the **station** in the center of Turnov. From the station, a steady flow of hikers depart and follow the **marked paths** through the town, which lead to the adjacent protected nature area of Bohemian Paradise. A large **map** just outside the train station, as well as colored **stripes** throughout Turnov on lampposts and the trees of Bohemian Paradise, provide evidence of the popularity of this hiking route through town to the great outdoors.

Also take note that while this area draws many hikers, the level of signage and the amount of English spoken in shops and restaurants in Turnov is far more limited than the capital city, so consider navigating the **language barrier** a part of your adventure.

the many paths of Bohemian Paradise

PLANNING YOUR TIME

Bohemian Paradise works best as a **day trip** from Prague for most travelers, although staying **overnight** in the nearby city of **Liberec** could give you an earlier head start on hiking. The Turnov train station does not offer **luggage storage,** so it's best to travel with a backpack or have a home base in either Prague or Liberec. The train ride from Prague with local stops takes about two hours, and the ride from Liberec is about 45 minutes.

Itinerary Idea

A day in Bohemian Paradise will most likely begin at the Turnov train station. Dress for the journey and pack light so that you can set off as soon as your train pulls into the station. Hiking boots aren't required for the route described below, but **comfortable shoes** that you don't mind getting a little dirty are definitely recommended. Keep an eye out for **brown street signs** in Turnov pointing toward popular tourist sights, along with **color-coded stripes** along the streets and hiking paths to ensure that you're going the right way. Before leaving Prague, grab a hearty breakfast and pack a backpack with a water bottle, sunscreen, and snacks. Double-check your **train times** to ensure you can get back to Prague at the end of the day.

ESSENTIAL BOHEMIAN PARADISE

The moderate, 10-kilometer (6-mile) round-trip to Jan's Viewpoint (Janova vyhlídka) includes the rock formations that the area is known for, multiple viewpoints of both civilization and natural landscapes, and one historic chateau, with no guide or overnight camping required. Be aware that this route is not terribly well signed, so a **paper map** or **phone with GPS** can be handy, or keep your eyes out for the **colored stripes** on light posts and gates along the way. The last stop in this itinerary, Janova vyhlídka (or "Jan's Viewpoint"), roughly 3 kilometers (3 miles) from the train station, is a good place to turn back if you're on a tight schedule. Otherwise, you can continue on to **Marian's Lookout** and the **Trosky Castle ruins** to extend the hike.

1 Arrive at **Turnov Train Station.**

2 Turn right out of the main train station and follow the yellow path for about 10-15 minutes, crossing a flower-lined bridge over the Jizera River. After the bridge, continue straight on Paleckeho to reach Sobotecká Street. Continue along Sobotecká Street for five minutes to reach the small **Turnov město train station.**

3 From Turnov město train station, turn left onto a cement road and watch for red stripes marking the trail through a residential area for about 25 minutes. Keep an eye out for a clearing of wooden sculptures on your left about 10 minutes after entering the woodsy area and continue uphill to reach the **Hlavatice Lookout Tower.** Spend 15 minutes relaxing on the benches and admiring the panoramic view of the town and surrounding mountains.

4 Keep walking along the red line for another 20 minutes to reach **Hospůdka U Hradu,** next to Valdštejn Castle. Refuel on Czech hot dogs (*párek*) or fried cheese (*smažený sýr*) with French fries, or grab a bench seat and dig into your own snacks.

Bohemian Paradise

5 Enjoy the characters along the statue-lined bridge to **Valdštejn Castle** and peek your head into the courtyard, but skip the self-guided tour unless you're a major historical-architecture fan.

6 Behind the pub, follow the red path for about 15 minutes, keeping an eye to your left for signs to **Jan's Viewpoint (Janova vyhlídka)** along a blue path. This is one of your last moments before turning back, so soak up the view of the sandstone rocks and look for a Czech flag flying on top or tiny rock climbers scaling the sides.

7 From Jan's viewpoint, backtrack the way you came to reach the rest area in front of Valdštejn Castle and get ready for a 90-minute walk back into town. Head down a path to the right of the castle and follow the green path to a parking lot. Then continue through residential streets along the red path to take you back to Turnov město train station. This time continue straight, following the train tracks over another bridge and past a soccer field. Turn right onto Koškova and left up one set of stairs to reach Nádražní Street, which should start to look familiar. Continue 5-10 minutes up the road to the main **Turnov Train Station** for a two-hour ride back to Prague.

Jizera River in Turnov

Sights

OLD JEWISH CEMETERY

Sobotecká; www.synagoga-turnov.cz

A small section of Turnov's 16th-century Jewish Cemetery lies underneath a highway overpass along the road toward Bohemian Paradise. The granite headstones seem to arise out of nowhere, on a grassy hill that was located on the outskirts of town until the highway was added in the late 1980s. Only 19 Jewish citizens returned to Turnov after World War II, and the local congregation ceased to exist in the 1960s. Today, the local synagogue is owned and run by the city and is kept open largely for tourism purposes. It's worth pausing alongside these headstones to remember a community that was forced out of their homes, leaving behind evidence of centuries of existence along the German border.

the Old Jewish Cemetery under a Turnov highway

To get to the Jewish Cemetery, turn right out of the main train station and follow the yellow path down Nádražní Street and onto Paleckeho Street for about 10-15 minutes, crossing a beautiful flower-lined bridge over the Jizera River. After the bridge, ignore the yellow path and continue straight on Paleckeho to reach Sobotecká Street. Turn right, walking another 5-10 minutes along the green line to find Turnov's Old Jewish Cemetery tucked under an overpass on your left.

Hiking

You could return to Bohemian Paradise multiple times, taking multiple paths (over multiple days, even), and stumble upon something new on every visit.

TRAIN STATION TO TROSKY CASTLE

This route encompasses all three sights in the itinerary section above, plus a couple of sights farther along for ambitious hikers. A rigorous 18-kilometer (11-mile) round trip from Turnov to Mariánská vyhlídka (Marian's Lookout) would require an early-morning start and a decent pace to ensure enough daylight hours and to avoid missing the last trains from the main Turnov train station. A 36-kilometer (22-mile) hike from Turnov to Trosky Castle should include an overnight stay within Bohemian Paradise to break up the hike into enough daylight hours to see it all.

✪ Hlavatice Lookout Tower (Skalní Vyhlídka Hlavatice)

www.cesky-raj.info/en; free

After about a 30-minute stroll heading south through the streets of Turnov from the main train station, you'll finally hit the edge of what feels like a forest. Follow the red path uphill into the forest, past the wooden sculptures marking the Gate to Bohemian Paradise and up to Hlavatice Lookout Tower. A 36-step iron staircase spirals around the outside of this small sandstone rock serving as a viewpoint over the surrounding towns. A plaque at the top points out the skyline highlights, including the Jizera River and the Ještěd Tower over the city of Liberec.

view from Hlavatice Lookout Tower

✪ Valdštejn Castle (Hrad Valdštejn)

+420 739 014 104 or +420 733 565 254; www.hrad-valdstejn.cz; April and Oct, weekends only, 10am-5pm; May and Sept, 9:30am-5pm Tues-Sun; June-Aug, 9am-6pm daily; admission ticket 70 CZK (cash only)

Follow the red path on an easy incline from Hlavatice Lookout Tower to Valdštejn Castle. The royal residence was established in the 13th century and—when it wasn't under attack—was owned by the Valdštejn (or Wallenstein) family, whose name you may recognize from the peaceful senate gardens below the Prague Castle. All visitors are free to admire the expressive stone sculptures of patron saints that line the cement bridge leading to the entrance.

bridge to Valdštejn Castle

If you like, you can buy a ticket to head inside. The interior of the castle showcases its centuries of renovations and additions with a variety of architectural styles. Exhibits range from a classicist palace decorated in simple elegance and family portraits to the more historic feel of the mid-1800s Romantic Palace, now devoted to local plant life and former hunting lifestyles. A chapel to St. John of Nepomuk, seen on the cement bridge with his golden crown of five stars, helped to establish this site as a pilgrimage from the surrounding areas. Guided tours in English (40 CZK per person, cash only) must be arranged in advance.

✪ Jan's Viewpoint (Janova Vyhlídka)

www.cesky-raj.info/en; free

Follow the red path for about 15 minutes beyond Valdštejn Castle, keeping an eye out for a blue trail on the left-hand side and a small sign marked with the name *Janova vyhlídka* in Czech, which means "Jan's Viewpoint." Turning left onto this blue path leads to a railing-lined corner of the forest overlooking sandstone rock formations. If you look closely, you might spot a few climbers ascending or descending. This is also a good point to evaluate how much farther you want to continue—it's another hour to the Marian Lookout (Mariánská vyhlídka), and at least another two hours to the twin peaks of Trosky Castle.

Marian's Lookout (Mariánská Vyhlídka)

www.cesky-raj.info/en; free

Continuing south from Janova vyhlídka, the blue trail will run into the yellow trail, where you'll want to turn right to reach Mariánská vyhlídka or "Marian's Lookout." While Janova vyhlídka (Jan's viewpoint) focuses on the natural beauty of the sandstone rocks, Mariánská vyhlídka adds the pointed towers of the Renaissance Hrubá Skála Chateau to the panoramic skyline, alongside the distant silhouette of the Trosky Castle ruins.

Trosky Castle (Státní Hrad Trosky)

www.hrad-trosky.eu; April and Oct., weekends only, 9am-4pm; May and Sept, 9am-4pm Tues-Sun; May and June, 9am-5:30pm Tues-Sun; June-Aug, 9am-5:30pm daily; 90 CZK (cash only)

Before you venture any further from Mariánská vyhlídka, consider that going on to Trosky Castle will leave you more than 13 kilometers (over 8 miles) from the Turnov train station, and there are no public transport options from Trosky back to Prague. That

Trosky Castle

said, if you've got the daylight hours and the energy to spare, continue along the yellow trail until it intersects with the red trail. This will lead you to the twin towers of the Trosky Castle ruins, each of which has its own name: the old woman or crone (*Baba*) tower is shorter and wider, while the young lady, maiden, or virgin (*Panna*) is the taller and thinner of the two. This 14th-century fortress on top of volcanic rocks stood strong throughout the Hussite Wars but was eventually abandoned, leaving the remains with an air of mystery—plus some modern touch-ups—that you can visit today. The two-towered silhouette is a defining symbol of Bohemian Paradise and a regular source of inspiration for Czech poets and painters.

Food

Many hikers prefer to pack a bag with snacks to eat along the hike. The walk through Turnov also offers plenty of small shops to grab a pre-made sandwich, pretzels, or a cold drink to toss into your backpack for a picnic later on.

Hospůdka U Hradu

Turnov 24; +420 773 686 064; www.hrad-valdstejn.cz; April and Oct, weekends only, 10am-5pm; May-Sept, 10am-5pm daily; entrées 100-200 CZK

If you prefer to pack light and don't mind a slightly touristy vibe, try the Hospůdka U Hradu or "Pub at the Castle" outside Valdštejn Castle. The hearty menu of traditional Czech cuisine, from fried cheese to grilled sausages, is best enjoyed outdoors on the surrounding picnic benches.

Pizzerie Restaurant Plaudit

Bezručova 698; +420 481 311 288; www.plaudit.eu; 11am-11pm Sun-Thurs, 11am-midnight Fri-Sat; pizzas 150-200 CZK

For a slightly more formal bite in town (but no need to change out of your hiking clothes before catching the train back to Prague), head to Pizzerie Restaurant Plaudit. This North Bohemian chain offers a wide selection of thin-crust pizzas with interesting toppings (think corn or a fried egg) alongside a full menu of chicken, steak, and pasta dishes. The 10-minute walk from the station allows for a leisurely meal to refuel after a day on your feet.

refreshment at Hospůdka U Hradu

Accommodations

There are a few accommodation options within a 30-60-minute walk of Marian's lookout for travelers planning a multi-day hike.

Hrubá Skála Chateau and Wellness Center

Hrubá Skála 1; +420 271 090 832; www.hrubaskala.cz; 1,800-2,500 CZK d

To add a touch of luxury to a hiking trip, consider spending the night inside the protected area of Český ráj at the Hrubá Skála Chateau and Wellness Center. The Renaissance-style chateau includes six simple, dorm-style rooms sleeping 3, 4, 5, or 6 guests (1,250-1,700 CZK) plus double, triple, and family rooms with en-suite bathrooms. Revitalizing massages, full body wraps, and Turkish baths at the onsite spa are available to pamper your body after hours on your feet.

Transportation

GETTING THERE

The easiest way to explore Český Ráj without a car is by train to the small town of Turnov. Traveling by car could also provide some flexibility to the start and end times of your hike.

TRAIN

Trains depart from either Prague's main train station (Praha hl. n.) or the centrally located Praha Masarykovo nádraží roughly every two hours, via the national rail service **České dráhy** (www.cd.cz, 250-300 CZK round trip). The direct journey with local stops takes just under two hours, while some routes require transfers of two and a half hours or more, so check the online schedule carefully. Service to Turnov begins just before 6am. Service from Liberec begins around 4am, departing roughly every two hours until around 10pm (www.cd.cz, 125 CZK round trip).

Turnov's main **train station** is about a 30-minute walk from the edge of Bohemian Paradise.

CAR

Český Ráj is roughly 89 kilometers (55 miles) northeast of Prague on **highway E65.** The drive takes about an hour. **Parking lots** are available near some popular areas (e.g., Turnov or Trosky Castle), usually for a fee, around 50-100 CZK.

LEAVING BOHEMIAN PARADISE

The last train from Turnov back to Prague departs shortly after **9pm.** The last train to Liberec departs Turnov just after **11pm.**

KARLOVY VARY

An aura of relaxation surrounds this peaceful valley town of pastel buildings and natural springs beside the Ohře River. The main attractions of Karlovy Vary (also known as Carlsbad in English) are the fifteen thermal springs of drinking water, tapped and free-flowing for all pedestrians to taste. Tiny, decorative "spa cups" with a helpful spout are sold every few steps in shops and stands. The various temperatures and mineral contents give each spring a distinctive flavor and are believed by many to have healing powers. Join the ranks of King Charles

HIGHLIGHTS

- ✪ **MILL COLONNADE:** Sample the natural spring waters tapped for generations of royals and visitors in this columned riverside monument (page 201).
- ✪ **ELISABETH SPA:** Release the stress of daily life with a mineral bath, massage, or deep breaths in a relaxing salt cave (page 202).
- ✪ **DIANA OBSERVATION TOWER:** Take a funicular ride or a 45-minute hike to get a hillside view over the town (page 203).
- ✪ **GRANDHOTEL PUPP:** Have a drink in a Hollywood-favorite hotel before browsing the celebrity names engraved in the courtyard bricks (page 203).
- ✪ **BECHEROVKA MUSEUM & FACTORY:** Discover the history of a Czech liquor that's said to have curative properties (page 204).

IV, who founded the town in the 14th century, along with Russia's Peter the Great, Mozart, Beethoven, Franz Kafka, and many modern Hollywood stars who have come to "take the waters" over the centuries.

ORIENTATION

Navigating the riverside town **on foot** is a major part of the health-focused Karlovy Vary experience. Most sights and activities lie within a 30-minute walk along the **Teplá River**, which is a small branch off the larger Ohře River stretching into Germany to the west. The river valley is largely flat, with options for **hillside hikes** above the streets of the quiet spa town.

PLANNING YOUR TIME

Karlovy Vary is a little more than two hours from Prague, making it a reasonable **single-day** destination or a relaxing place to take a **weekend** break from city life (though you could also opt for the traditional **three-week spa visit** recommended by Czech physicians in order to experience significant health benefits). It's pretty quiet after dark, so arrive early if you want to squeeze in sights and a quick spa treatment without staying overnight. For a peaceful, crowd-free experience, try an **off-season** visit when the spas, hotel pools, restaurants, and city streets are blissfully quiet.

Park Colonnade in Dvořák's Park

Karlovy Vary

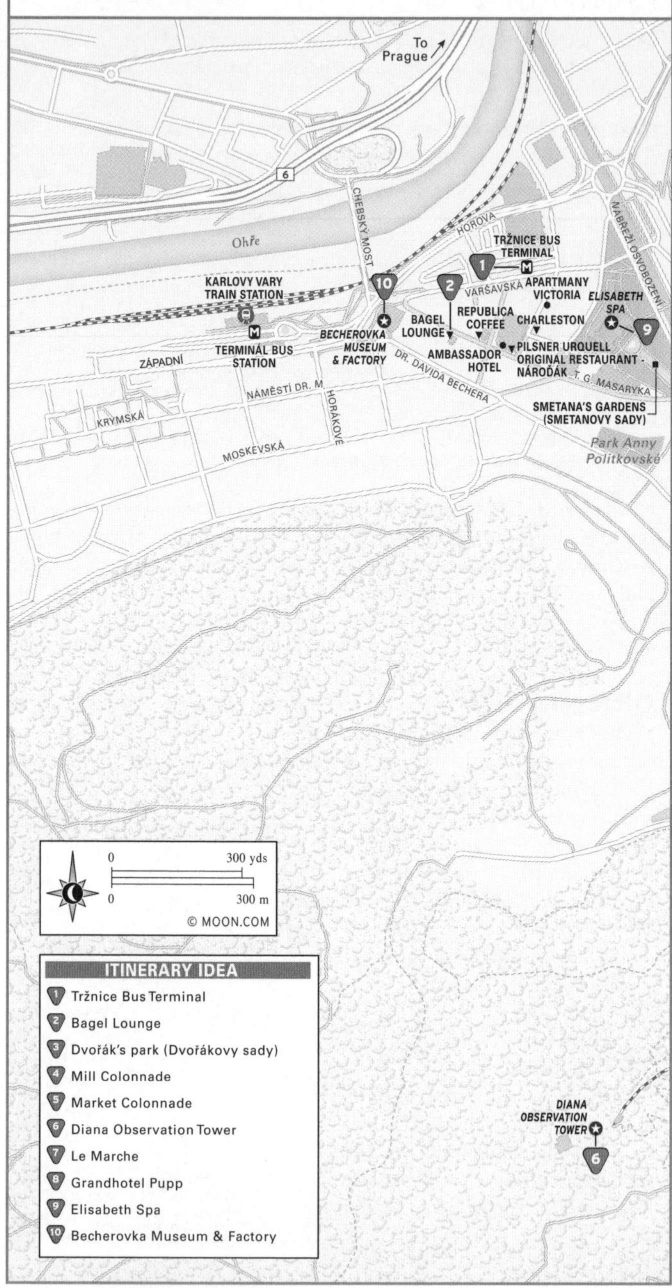

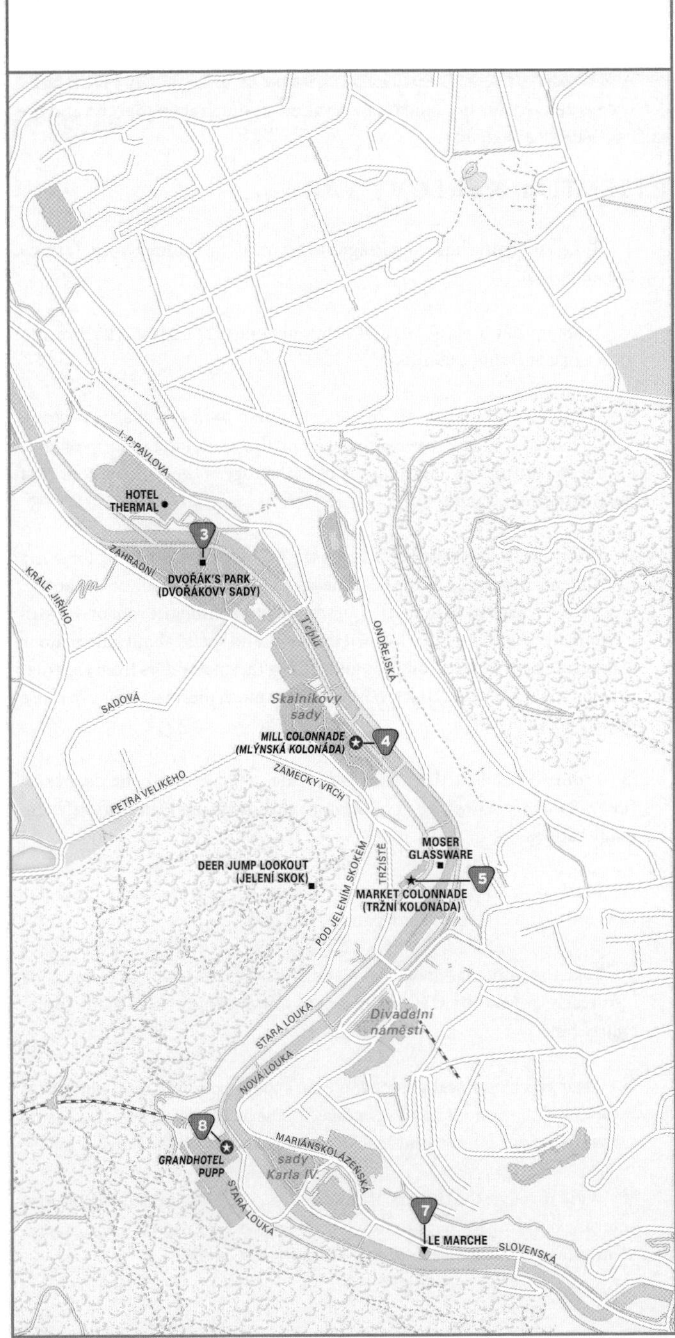
I. P. PAVLOVA
HOTEL THERMAL
3
ZAHRADNÍ
KRÁLE JIŘÍHO
DVOŘÁK'S PARK (DVOŘÁKOVY SADY)
Teplá
ONDŘEJSKÁ
SADOVÁ
Skalníkovy sady
MILL COLONNADE (MLÝNSKÁ KOLONÁDA)
4
ZÁMECKÝ VRCH
PETRA VELIKÉHO
MOSER GLASSWARE
TRŽIŠTĚ
DEER JUMP LOOKOUT (JELENÍ SKOK)
POD JELENÍM SKOKEM
5
MARKET COLONNADE (TRŽNÍ KOLONÁDA)
Divadelní náměstí
STARÁ LOUKA
NOVÁ LOUKA
8
GRANDHOTEL PUPP
MARIÁNSKOLÁZEŇSKÁ
sady Karla IV.
STARÁ LOUKA
7
LE MARCHE
SLOVENSKÁ

Itinerary Idea

A few days before your trip, make a reservation for lunch at **Le Marche** and the salt caves at **Elisabeth Spa.**

ESSENTIAL KARLOVY VARY

1 Take a morning bus from Prague to arrive at the Karlovy Vary, **Tržnice bus terminal.**

2 Walk up Zeyerova Street and turn right onto T. G. Masaryka Street to grab a bite at **Bagel Lounge.**

3 Cross the river and walk over to **Dvořák's park (Dvořákovy sady).** Keep your eyes on the street vendors along this walk for a spa cup of your liking. Step inside the Park Colonnade at the edge of the park for your first taste of thermal waters.

4 Continue beside the river to reach the **Mill Colonnade.** Look for stairs near the northern side of the colonnade next to a large Becherovka bottle, and climb five minutes to reach a viewpoint just behind the roof of the Mill Colonnade. Then climb back down the stairs and spend about half an hour wandering between the columns and tasting thermal waters from the free-flowing spouts. (Don't drink too heavily—too much thermal water can cause digestive discomfort.)

5 From the end of the Mill Colonnade, head around the corner to the **Market Colonnade.** Try 1-2 more sips of spring water of differing temperatures.

6 Make your way over to **Diana Observation Tower.** Take a funicular ride and climb 150 stairs for a panoramic view.

7 Take the funicular down again and cross the river, following alongside it to reach **Le Marche** restaurant, where you can enjoy a luxurious three-course lunch.

8 After lunch, follow the same route back to the courtyard at **Grandhotel Pupp.** Find the famous names engraved in the bricks before heading inside for a coffee or cocktail at the Malá Dvorana bar, just off the hotel lobby.

9 Walk through the flowers of Smetanovy sady (Smetana's Gardens) and enter the building to check in for your reservation at **Elisabeth Spa.** Spend 45 minutes relaxing on a lounge chair in the salt caves.

10 If you have time, stop by **Becherovka Museum & Factory** gift shop on your way to Karlovy Vary, Terminál, to catch a bus back to Prague.

Thermal Springs and Spas

THERMAL SPRINGS

To experience the most popular activity in Karlovy Vary, all you have to do is take a walk. The mineral springs that flow underground have been organized into a system of fountains housed inside gazebos and stone temples alongside the river. Many of these open-air structures are named "colonnade" for the rows of columns that define their architectural style.

Visitors are free to walk the city streets and sample most of the waters at all hours of the day. You can fill any container you like, although plastic bottles are not the best choice for the hottest of the springs. For the best experience, grab a porcelain spa cup (prices vary wildly depending on size and decoration, but expect between 100-1,000 CZK) from any of the vendors along the colonnades.

✪ MILL COLONNADE (MLÝNSKÁ KOLONÁDA)

Mlýnské nábř; www.karlovyvary.cz

The 19th-century stone design of the Mill Colonnade embodies the royal atmosphere of Karlovy Vary's history. This temple of health is the largest and most popular in town, housing five separate springs between its

view from the rooftop of the Mill Colonnade

THE SPA EXPERIENCE

Spa towns in the Czech Republic focus less on indulgence in white fluffy robes and more on natural treatments to improve your health. It's not unusual for local physicians to prescribe an extended stay for locals suffering from various illnesses and conditions. Services like mineral baths, salt caves, aromatherapy, and massages are usually accessible to travelers with a reservation in advance, but other services may require a physician's consultation, so read the fine print when booking online. The overall environment of these spas may also have a more clinical vibe than travelers are used to, but don't let that deter you from indulging in the local approach to wellness.

symmetrical, arched halls. Some of the waters flow from taps emerging from the floor or walls, while others pool into shallow basins around the fountains. The triangle-topped entrances to this open-air structure are embellished with twelve sandstone statues representing the calendar months. A staircase just beside the northern entrance, next to a large Becherovka bottle, leads to a grassy viewpoint at a rooftop level behind the colonnade that is perfect for photography.

thermal springs in the Mill Colonnade

MARKET COLONNADE (TRŽNÍ KOLONÁDA)

Tržiště; www.karlovyvary.cz

The white-latticed exterior of the Market Colonnade sets a more natural, delicate tone around the spring named for Charles IV as well as the Market Spring and Lower Castle Spring. The building was designed in the late 1800s in a Swiss-inspired style, and sits near the Moser glassware store (Tržiště 7) of equally delicate souvenirs.

As you continue along the river, keep an eye out for a musical patch of sidewalk, where stepping on the metal plates creates different tones. Take a moment to dance out a tune in front of Hotel Jessenius, about halfway between the Market Colonnade and the Grandhotel Pupp.

SPA

TOP EXPERIENCE

✪ ELISABETH SPA

Mírové náměstí 2; +420 353 222 536; www.spa5.cz; 8am-7pm Mon-Fri, 9am-7pm Sat, 10am-6pm Sun; treatments 120-800 CZK

The manicured courtyard of the Elisabeth Spa, named for Austro-Hungarian Empress Sisi, sets a decadent atmosphere as you enter the massive, early-1900s building. Inside, the individual treatment rooms feel more like doctor's offices that offer mineral baths, aromatherapy, hot stone massages, heat-, hydro- and electro-therapy treatments, and a swimming pool. Splurge on a relaxation package or spend an affordable 45 minutes wrapped in a blanket and breathing deeply in the salt caves to feel your stress melt away. The salt cave experience (a personal favorite) is often recommended to open up the

Elisabeth Spa: elegance outside, health inside

lungs and treat conditions such as bronchitis or asthma in a landlocked country far from any sea air. Imagine a cave-like setting with walls and a sand-like floor of salt, reclining chairs, soft lighting, and relaxing music to set the mood. Elisabeth Spa is a long-running local favorite that combines relaxation with the historic ambiance that defines this town for a memorable wellness experience. Most spa treatments require advance booking.

Other Sights

✪ DIANA OBSERVATION TOWER

Vrch přátelství 1; www.dianakv.cz; Nov-Mar, 9am-4:45pm; April and Oct, 9am-5:45pm; May-Sept, 9am-6:45pm; free

Avid hikers can climb the hill to the Diana Observation Tower, but many travelers opt for an easy three-minute ride from the funicular beside the Grandhotel Pupp (90 CZK return), saving their strength for the 150-step climb to the top of the tower, although elevator access is also available. The roughly 130-foot (40-meter) structure offers sweeping views of the city center and the surrounding forests in a remote area on the edge of town.

To hike to the tower, follow a path winding off Pod Jelením skokem street through the forest for about one and a half miles (2.2 km) to the west.

✪ GRANDHOTEL PUPP

Mírové náměstí 2; +420 353 109 111; www.pupp.cz

This stately building at the southern end of Karlovy Vary's spa center is as much a tourist destination as it is an accommodation option. Built in 1701, the glowing white palace wrapped around the bend of the Teplá River has hosted its fair share of both actual royalty (Empress Marie Therese, Napoleon Bonaparte) and Hollywood royalty (John Travolta, Scarlett Johansson, Sean Bean). The hotel itself has held a cinematic spotlight as well, acting as backdrop for Queen Latifah's romantic comedy *Last Holiday*, impersonating a Montenegrin hotel in the James Bond film *Casino Royale*, and appearing in the opening scene of the Edith Piaf biopic *La Vie En Rose*.

Stop by the outer courtyard to read some of the names and years etched in brick, offering a mini-Walk of Fame of the centuries of celebrities and historical figures who have stayed here. For a taste of the interior elegance without the hefty luxury hotel price tag, try an afternoon drink at **Malá Dvorana** just off the lobby, where a portrait of Morgan Freeman keeps watch over the white tablecloths and French doors, or splurge on dinner at **Becher's Bar**, decorated in deep red, green, and bronze tones.

✪ BECHEROVKA MUSEUM & FACTORY

T. G. Masaryka 57; +420 359 578 142; www.becherovka.com; 9am-5pm Tues-Sun; 150 CZK

Legend has it that the only two people in possession of the herbal recipe to make the Czech digestif *Becherovka* refuse to fly together in order to ensure its safety. The quintessentially Czech drink was created in 1807 and is best described as "tasting like Christmas." A one-hour self-guided

Grandhotel Pupp, a Hollywood hotel

Becherovka, Karlovy Vary's unofficial 13th spring

tour of the recently renovated Jan Becher Museum holds more fun facts about the eventful history of this local cure-all liquor, plus interactive exhibits that include vintage advertisements, a chance to smell the ingredients before and after fermentation, a virtual-reality look at the bottling process, and a taste of specialty flavors only available onsite. Reserve a place online in advance to ensure the intro film is available in English.

Festivals and Events

SPRING

Most facilities are open year-round, but **spa season** officially kicks off the first weekend of May, when a costumed King Charles IV rides a white horse through town and the mineral spas receive an annual blessing. Runners should mark their calendars for the **Mattoni half-marathon** (www.runczech.cz), which also falls in early May.

King Charles IV kicks off spa season in May

SUMMER

The **Karlovy Vary International Film Festival** (www.kviff.com) takes over the town in late June and early July.

FALL

The **Vary Září Festival** (varyzari.karlovyvary.cz) brings light shows and video mapping to the city's historic buildings in September.

THE KARLOVY VARY INTERNATIONAL FILM FESTIVAL

Cannes, Venice and . . . Karlovy Vary, Czech Republic? That's right: since 1946, Karlovy Vary has hosted the Karlovy Vary International Film Festival (www.kviff.com), an annual gathering of the international cinematic community. The film festival (one of the oldest in the world, even operating for 40 years under Communist occupation) screens around 200 feature-length and short films from around the world in venues across town over eight days in late June or early July. Awards are given for the Official Selection (a Best Picture equivalent), "East of the West" (for films from Central and Eastern Europe, the Balkans, Greece, the former Soviet Union, and the Middle East), and Best Documentary.

The Crystal Globe for Outstanding Artistic Contribution to World Cinema is known to bring Hollywood actors and filmmakers to the festival. Past recipients include Morgan Freeman, Judi Dench, and Susan Sarandon.

The **Grandhotel Pupp** serves as both a screening location and popular accommodation choice among the celeb set. The etched names in the brick courtyard of the hotel act as a mini-Walk of Fame or a guestbook of the hotel's esteemed visitors from centuries before the film festival began. These famous names range from Empress Maria Theresa in 1732 to Leonardo DiCaprio in 1994. Daniel Craig's brick (2006) is a testament to the hotel's starring role in the James Bond film *Casino Royale*.

If you want to join the film-loving fun of the festival, book your lodging (and your spa treatments) well in advance, as this quiet town comes alive.

Parks

Stretches of landscaped lawns and sprawling parks are woven throughout the riverside valley, with hillside hiking paths lining the slopes behind the buildings. You won't need to go out of your way to reach these parks, and will likely pass through them on a walk through the town.

Smetana's Gardens (Smetanovy Sady)

Colorful blooming flowers are shaped daily to display the date at the entrance to these pristinely manicured gardens in front of the Elisabeth Spa, providing a fantastic photo-opp in spring and summer. Lime trees and benches line the long paths, offering a quick taste of nature at the busier northern edge of town, or a calming walk to your spa appointment.

Dvořák's Park (Dvořákovy Sady)

The grassy area connecting the cement courtyard of Hotel Thermal to the grand Mill Colonnade marks the beginning of spa central. Dirt paths lined with benches curve around a peaceful pond, past a statue of the park's namesake composer, and leading to the small Park Spring housed at the end of a cream-colored gazebo with a long, arched hallway. Most visitors

peaceful Dvořák's Park

bypass the park to head straight to the springs, but a leisurely fifteen-minute detour acknowledges Karlovy Vary's stress-reducing approach to a slower pace of life.

Deer Jump Lookout (Jelení Skok)

Deer Jump Lookout

The tree-lined hills behind the Mill and Market Colonnades hide a small bit of history between their branches. A statue of a deer (actually a chamois, for any picky zoologists) symbolizes the 14th-century legend of the town's founding. Emperor Charles IV was supposedly hunting in the area when one of his dogs chased a deer off a cliff and fell into one of the thermal pools below. Charles was impressed that the waters cured his dog's injuries and dipped his own limbs into the pools with similar results. Thus, the healing powers of the spa town were born. To reach the hillside lookout, look for a yellow-marked path off Pod Jelením skokem street, or take the funicular to Diana's Tower and follow a ten-minute path through the woods.

Food

CZECH

Pilsner Urquell Original Restaurant—Národňák

T. G. Masaryka 24; +420 353 408 523; www.narodak.eu; 11am-11pm daily; entrées 185-300 CZK

Pilsner Urquell Original Restaurant - Národňák

The Pilsner Urquell pub stamp of approval means the beer is fresh, the taps are sparkling clean, and the menu is mostly fried. Visitors mix with locals on their lunch break in the mid-sized dining area, lined with wooden bar stools, green banquettes, and the signature copper tanks and light fixtures. For the best value, come early and stick to the daily lunch menu (100-150 CZK) of Czech specialties at this slightly touristy pub connected to the Ambassador Hotel.

INTERNATIONAL

Bagel Lounge

T. G. Masaryka 45; +420 720 022 123; kv.bagellounge.cz; 8am-8pm Mon-Thurs, 8am-10pm Fri-Sat, 8am-7pm Sun; entrées 100-150 CZK

A large map asking customers "Where Are You From?" welcomes international visitors to this small, fast-casual café, where cushioned bucket seats create a modern-meets-retro vibe. Bagel sandwiches include inventive flavor combinations like duck with orange and hoisin sauce or hummus, zucchini and sun-dried tomato, and plenty of vegan and vegetarian options. Breakfast is served until 11am, with espresso drinks or tea included in simple meals of croissants or scrambled eggs (99 CZK) or the more elaborate breakfast sandwiches, avocado-and-egg meals, or English breakfasts (129 CZK).

Charleston

Bulharská 1; +420 353 230 797; www.charleston-kv.cz; 2pm-11pm; entrées 200-500 CZK

Refuel after a day of walking with a hearty meal of steak, poultry, or seafood at Charleston. This English-style pub tucked below street level is decorated in dark wood and warm reds, serving a late-night crowd of international diners and drinkers.

✪ Le Marche

Mariánskolázěnská 4; +420 730 133 695; www.le-marche.cz; noon-10pm Mon-Sat

The mood at Le Marche is pure elegance in pale blue and white tones, with watercolor paintings and a sparkling chandelier decorating the dining room of roughly twenty-five seats. Three-course lunches (490 CZK) and multi-course dinner options (790-1,290 CZK) change daily and are based on seasonal flavors, often with a French twist. Reservations are essential for a luxurious lunch (noon-3pm) or an indulgent dinner (6pm-10pm).

French-inspired meals at Le Marche

BREAKFAST AND BRUNCH

Republica Coffee

T. G. Masaryka 28; +420 720 347 166; 7am-7pm Mon-Fri, 8am-7pm Sat-Sun; entrées 100-150 CZK

Karlovy Vary's coffee snobs congregate at Republica Coffee for flat whites and breakfast pastries. The efficient baristas don't skimp on quality to increase efficiency, so there may be a short wait at peak times. Grab a table in the pop-art balcony area or one of the candy-colored chairs on the outdoor terraces.

Accommodations

Apartmany Victoria

Jugoslávská 10; +420 222 532 547; www.apartments-victoria.penzion.cz; 1,500 CZK d (cash only)

Apartmany Victoria provides a comfortable home base and a helpful staff full of personal recommendations. These kitchen-equipped apartments with one-, two-, or three-bedroom options are decked out in clean, light-wood details. The convenient location is just around the corner from the Tržnice bus terminal, a 15-minute walk from the Mill Colonnade, and is surrounded by casual dining options. The one quirk of this quiet, mid-sized option with on-site massage services is the cash-only payment upon arrival.

✪ Hotel Thermal

I. P. Pavlova 11; +420 359 002 201; www.thermal.cz; 2,000-3,000 CZK s, 2,500-3,500 CZK d

This massive cement building of 273 rooms (three accessible) offers river and forest views in the center of town. The beautifully renovated wellness area includes a mid-sized swimming pool, jacuzzi, and multiple saunas. English-speaking staff on the second floor schedule spa treatments, including salt chambers (165 CZK), whirlpool baths (450 CZK), and massages (500-1,300 CZK). Hotel décor centers around historical photos of the annual international film festival, and a health-conscious buffet breakfast is included.

the serene spa environment hidden inside Hotel Thermal

Ambassador Hotel

T. G. Masaryka 24; +420 353 408 100; www.grandhotel-ambassador.cz; 2,000 CZK s, 2,500-3,500 CZK d

This 1900s cultural-center-turned-hotel mixes simple muted pastels with modern metallic bathrooms across 83 en-suite rooms. Access to a small lap pool and multiple saunas are included, and wellness treatments from hot stone massages (1,650 CZK) to wine, beer, or chocolate baths (700 CZK) provide fun add-ons. The two-minute walk to the Tržnice bus stop, an on-site pub and nightclub, and multiple restaurants on your doorstep make this a convenient option that attracts families, couples, and groups.

Ambassador Hotel

Grandhotel Pupp

Mírové náměstí 2; +420 353 109 111; www.pupp.cz; 8,000 CZK s, 10,000-20,000 CZK d

There is no comparison to the luxury of sleeping in a landmark at the Grandhotel Pupp. The 228-room selection ranges from basic singles to premier suites and apartments with balcony views stretching over the river. Décor goes from simple, modern design in forest-facing rooms to the jewel-toned, 18th-century elegance of the riverside suites. Facilities include an on-site spa and wellness center, relaxation pool and sauna, a salt cave, and a fitness center. Breakfast and room service tack on additional costs, and accessible rooms are available. This special-occasion splurge raises the aristocratic feel of a royal spa weekend.

Transportation

GETTING THERE

Buses are a better option than the train for getting to Karlovy Vary. Trains take longer, cost twice as much, and drop you off at a less convenient station.

TRAIN

State-run **České dráhy** trains (www.cd.cz) depart from Prague's main train station (Praha hlavní nádraží) roughly every two hours from about 5am to 7pm (3 hours, 300-350 CZK round trip). The **train station** is across the Ohře River from the center of town, requiring a 15-minute walk to hotels on the northern side of town and about half an hour's walk from the Grandhotel Pupp at the opposite end.

BUS

Comfortable coach service, from **Regiojet** (www.regiojet.com, 300-350 CZK round trip) or **Flixbus** (www.flixbus.com, 250-315 CZK), departs from Prague's Florenc bus station almost every hour between 6am and 10pm. The journey takes just over two hours, finishing at two stops, both of which are on the northern end of town. The first bus stop, **Karlovy Vary's Tržnice**, will be more convenient for the majority of visitors walking 10 minutes into town, while the **main bus station** just five minutes further down the river can be an easier place to find a taxi if you have large luggage or would like a ride to accommodation near the Grandhotel Pupp at the opposite end of town.

CAR

Karlovy Vary is located about two hours (roughly 80 miles/129 kilometers) west of Prague on **Route 6**. For updated information and pricing on parking garages around town, check www.karlovyvary.cz. Hotel Thermal's 320-space secure **parking garage** in the center of town costs 40 CZK per hour or 250 CZK per day. You might also find space at smaller, unmonitored, outdoor **parking lots** near the Tržnice bus stop (40 CZK per hour or 300 CZK for 5-24 hours) or main Terminál bus station (20 CZK per hour, 60 CZK for 24 hours).

GETTING AROUND

With a compact city center that lines the river, most of Karlovy Vary is designed to be **walkable**. If you need a taxi, try **KV Taxi** (+420 777 141 413, www.kv-taxi.cz).

LEAVING KARLOVY VARY

Buses depart for Prague from the **Karlovy Vary, Terminál station** roughly every hour between 5am-8pm on **Regiojet**, and around 7am-6pm on **Flixbus**. Note that outgoing buses do not stop to pick up passengers at the Tržnice stop, where most passengers likely got off when they arrived. Tržnice is about five minutes closer to town than Terminál, so give yourself a few extra minutes to walk to the main station.

PILSEN

Pilsen (or Plzeň in Czech) is best known for its namesake brewery, Pilsner Urquell, and the beer scene is definitely a major draw. The fourth-largest city in the Czech Republic also caters to some niche interests, including larger-than-average architecture, family travel, and military history. Pilsen offers chances to climb the highest church spire in the country, tour the underground tunnels of the city, and discover local connections to puppets, planets, and US Army General George S. Patton. Many of the sights showcase a strong sense of respect

HIGHLIGHTS

- **CATHEDRAL OF ST. BARTHOLOMEW:** Climb the tallest church spire in the country for views of Pilsen's city center (page 219).
- **PILSNER URQUELL BREWERY:** Taste more than 175 years of beer expertise with a tour of the country's largest and most popular Czech brewery (page 219).
- **GREAT SYNAGOGUE:** One of the largest houses of Jewish worship in the world is filled with architectural beauty and art exhibits (page 223).
- **PURKMISTR BEER SPA AND MICROBREWERY:** Relax in a bathtub full of beer ingredients, with a free-flowing tap of lager within arm's reach (page 226).
- **BREWERIES AND BREW PUBS:** Compare the internationally known Pilsner Urquell brand with local microbrews in more modern pubs (page 227).

for tradition and historical anniversaries, while the growing hospitality scene filled with modern, independent businesses adds character to an already lively landscape.

ORIENTATION

Pilsen centers around the main square, **Náměstí Republiky,** and most sights lie within a 15-20 minute walk. The historical city center is surrounded by a ring of **parks** that line the south and east sides, with busy motorways to the north and west. Travelers will likely spend most of their time inside this loop. The **Radbuza River** and its many bridges curve along the southeast side of Pilsen, separating the Pilsner Urquell Brewery grounds from the city center. Public transportation (buses or trams) can be helpful to reach outlying sights like the Pilsner Brewery or the Purkmistr Beer Spa and Microbrewery. Find current transport schedules and info at www.pmdp.eu.

The **tourist information center** is located next to the Renaissance Town Hall in Republic Square (Náměstí Republiky).

PLANNING YOUR TIME

It is possible to pop into Pilsen, located roughly one hour southwest of Prague, for **a day** and knock out a few major sights (along with a few beers) between morning and evening. That said, trying to cram the selection of worthwhile sights, guided tours, and pubs into just one day could be exhausting. Pilsen has plenty to see and do over **2-3 days,** if you've got the time. Some of the main attractions only run English tours at specific times of day, so spending at least one night gives you some flexibility to plan around these restrictions. A hotel room also gives you the chance to enjoy the local **nightlife** that hits its stride after the last buses and trains depart for Prague.

Pilsen

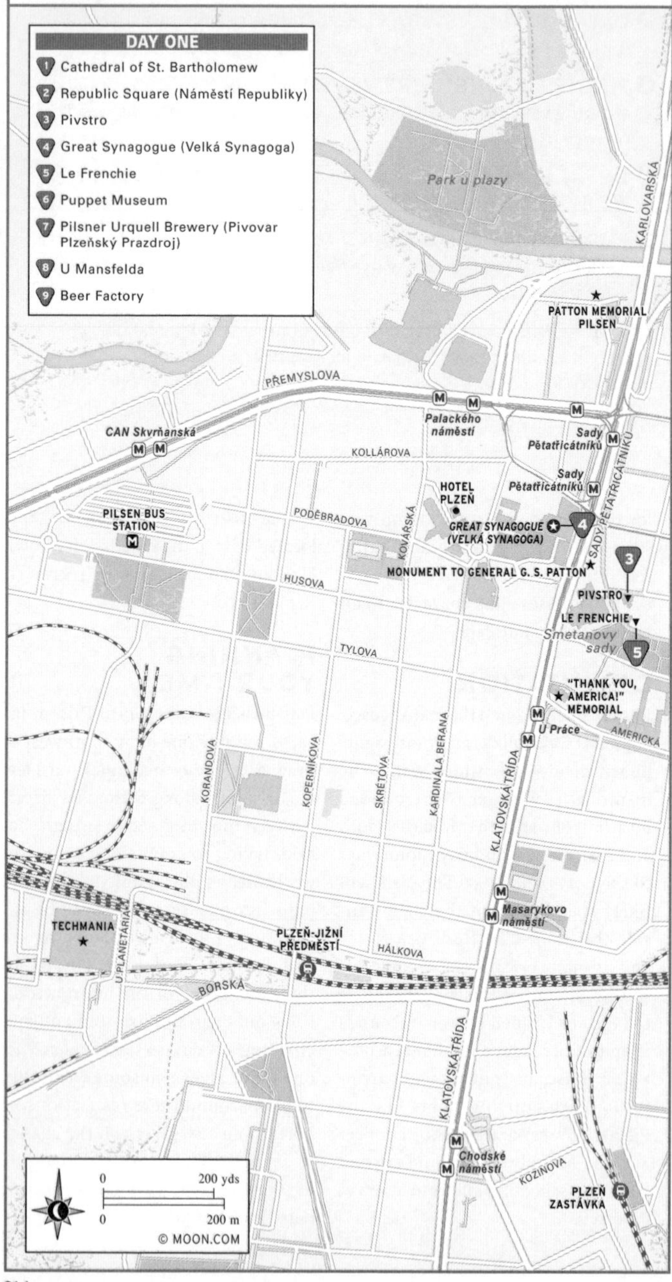

PILSEN

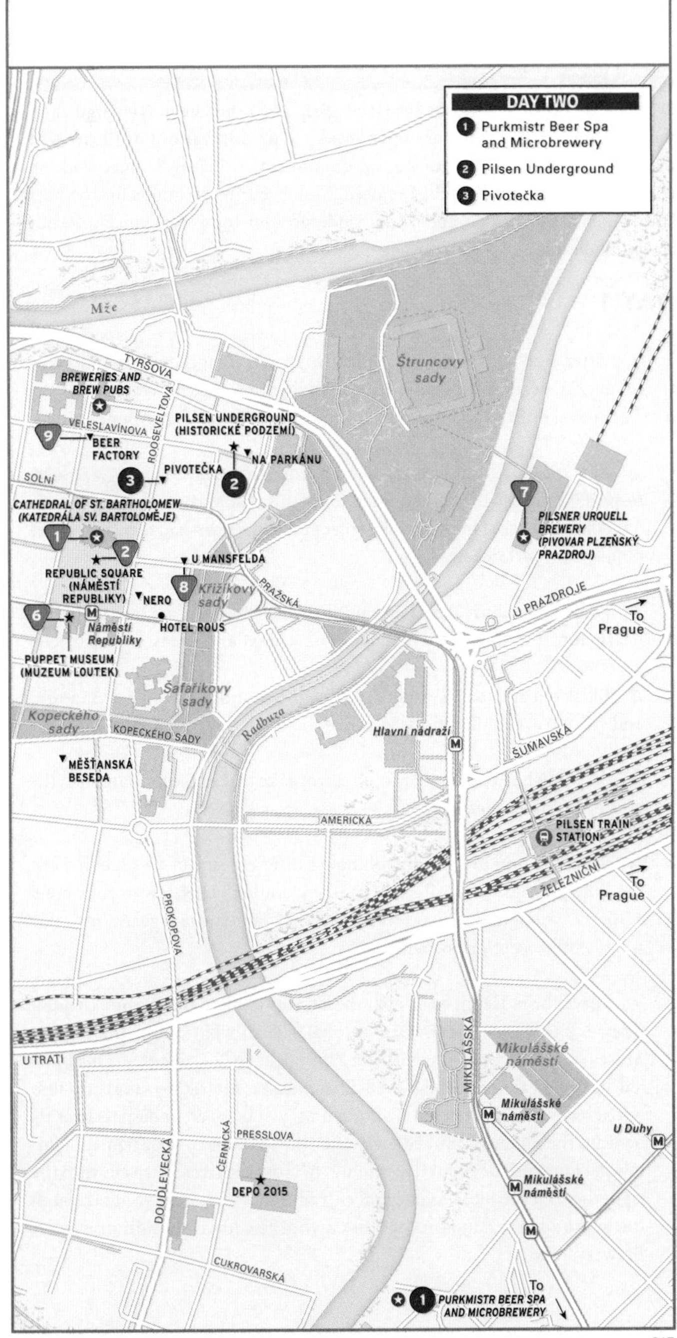
DAY TWO
1 Purkmistr Beer Spa and Microbrewery
2 Pilsen Underground
3 Pivotečka
Mže
TYRŠOVA
BREWERIES AND BREW PUBS
VELESLAVÍNOVA
ROOSEVELTOVA
9 BEER FACTORY
PILSEN UNDERGROUND (HISTORICKÉ PODZEMÍ)
NA PARKÁNU
3 PIVOTEČKA
2
SOLNÍ
CATHEDRAL OF ST. BARTHOLOMEW (KATEDRÁLA SV. BARTOLOMĚJE)
1
2
REPUBLIC SQUARE (NÁMĚSTÍ REPUBLIKY)
U MANSFELDA
8 Křižíkovy sady
PRAŽSKÁ
NERO
6
Náměstí Republiky
HOTEL ROUS
PUPPET MUSEUM (MUZEUM LOUTEK)
Šafaříkovy sady
Kopeckého sady
KOPECKÉHO SADY
Radbuza
MĚŠŤANSKÁ BESEDA
Štruncovy sady
7 PILSNER URQUELL BREWERY (PIVOVAR PLZEŇSKÝ PRAZDROJ)
U PRAZDROJE
To Prague
Hlavní nádraží
ŠUMAVSKÁ
AMERICKÁ
PILSEN TRAIN STATION
ŽELEZNIČNÍ
To Prague
PROKOPOVA
U TRATI
MIKULÁŠSKÁ
Mikulášské náměstí
Mikulášské náměstí
U Duhy
Mikulášské náměstí
PRESSLOVA
ČERNICKÁ
DOUDLEVECKÁ
DEPO 2015
CUKROVARSKÁ
To Prague
1 PURKMISTR BEER SPA AND MICROBREWERY

Itinerary Ideas

Day 1 of this itinerary works best Tues-Fri, when the Great Synagogue and recommended restaurants are open. Make your reservations at **Pivstro, U Mansfelda**, and **Beer Factory** a few days in advance. Day 2 won't work on Sunday, when one of the pubs is closed. Make your reservations for the beer bath, lunch at **Purkmistr**, and Pilsen Underground Tour when you book your accommodation.

DAY 1

1 After arriving from Prague and dropping off luggage at your accommodation, head to the center of town and climb the church tower of the **Cathedral of St. Bartholomew** to admire the view and get your bearings.

2 Exit the cathedral and wander around **Republic Square (Náměstí Republiky)** to see the three golden fountains and Marion plague column. Stop into the tourist information center beside the town hall to pick up three public transport tickets.

3 Fuel up for a busy day ahead at **Pivstro**, a "brewhemian bistro," with a hearty lunch accompanied by a microbrew for your first taste of local beer.

4 Block out an hour to explore the **Great Synagogue (Velká synagoga)** and current art exhibit inside.

5 Stop into **Le Frenchie** for some carrot cake and coffee to counteract the effects of a lunchtime beer.

6 Spend 30 minutes getting to know a different side of Czech culture at the **Puppet Museum.** Alternately, if you couldn't check in to your hotel earlier, now might be a good time to get keys and move luggage into your room while reception is open.

7 Leave the museum by 4pm at the latest to walk to the **Pilsner Urquell Brewery (Pivovar Plzeňský Prazdroj).** Turn right out of the Puppet Museum and continue downhill on Zbrojnická for 2-3 minutes. Then turn left and follow the park's edge for 8-10 minutes, as Šafaříkovy sady turns into Křižíkovy sady and then into Pallova, until you reach an underpass to cross beneath the highway. Immediately after the underpass, turn right and follow the footpath for about five minutes to cross the river. Then curve to the right to reach the Jubilee Gate and entrance to the brewery. Walk through the gate and check in at reception on your left for a 100-minute Pilsner Brewery Tour.

8 The main highway intersection, just outside the brewery, is not well designed for pedestrian crossing. After your tour, look for a spiral metal staircase and overpass just beyond the Jubilee Gate. Cross the overpass and head to the Hlavní nádraží tram stop. Use your first transport ticket and take the #1 or #2 tram one stop across the river to Anglické nábřeží, then walk to **U Mansfelda** for a well-earned dinner.

9 If you've got the energy for one more post-dinner drink, sample another local microbrew at **Beer Factory** before heading to bed.

DAY 2

Check www.pmdp.eu to confirm bus times around your beer bath appointment, and don't forget your transport tickets when you leave in the morning. This is a fairly beer-heavy day, so feel free to adjust this itinerary to your own habits and tolerance levels, or add a riverside walk to DEPO 2015 instead of a pub. Many places also serve mild or non-alcoholic beer options.

1 After enjoying a hotel breakfast, check out and store your luggage. Then, roughly 40-45 minutes before your appointment at **Purkmistr Beer Spa,** head to either the Muzeum bus stop or the Anglické nábřeží bus stop. Use your second transport ticket to take the #13 bus to Generála Lišky (30 minutes), then walk over to the Purkmistr grounds. Head inside and check in at reception for your 40-minute beer-bath experience to recharge from a long first day. Stay on the grounds for lunch and a beer flight at the onsite restaurant **Purkmistr Microbrewery.**

2 Leave the Purkmistr grounds shortly after 1pm and walk back the way you came. The Generála Lišky bus stop, for the #13 back into town, is located on the opposite side of the street about one minute north of where you got off. Doze for 25-30 minutes on the bus and get off next to the river at Anglické nábřeží. Walk over to the **Pilsen Underground** for a one-hour English tour at 2:20pm. Afterward, use your post-tour voucher for a free small beer and reasonably priced bowl of goulash or garlic soup at the adjoining Na Parkánu pub and restaurant.

3 Sample one last microbrew at **Pivotečka** as a farewell to Pilsen before catching an evening bus or train back to Prague.

Sights

REPUBLIC SQUARE (NÁMĚSTÍ REPUBLIKY)

nám. Republiky; www.pilsen.eu

Pilsen's main square is the center of city life and full of iconic symbols, old and new. In the center, the **Cathedral of St. Bartholomew** stands tall, with artistic monuments marking the four corners of the square. The **Marion plague column** stands in the northwest corner, with the Pilsen Madonna on top and saints lining the base. This column was built in 1681 to show appreciation for Pilsen having remained relatively unscathed by Central Europe's late-17th-century plague outbreak. Also in the northwest corner is the 16th-century **Renaissance Town Hall**, with designs etched into the exterior (a style called *sgraffito*) and topped off by a golden clock.

The abstract **golden fountains** in the remaining corners of the square represent three elements of Pilsen's coat of arms—an angel, a greyhound, and a camel—each with connections to the city's Catholic history. The angel is . . . an angel, the greyhound represents loyalty to the Holy Roman Empire, and the camel comes from local legend. While under attack in the 15th century from Hussite rebellions, Pilsen soldiers supposedly stole a camel from the Protestants' camp, refusing to return or sell the creature back. The story made its way onto the coat of arms as a source of pride. If you're having trouble determining which fountain is which, look for

golden camel fountain in Náměstí Republiky

angel wings, a sitting dog, and two tiny humps on the camel's back. The statues were installed in 2010 (eliciting mixed reactions from locals) in preparation for Pilsen's year as the European Capital of Culture in 2015. Twilight is an excellent time to photograph these glittering gold fountains against a dramatic cathedral silhouette.

Náměstí Republiky plays host to regular events and festivals throughout the year, particularly during the **Pilsen Liberation Festival** at the end of May or the **Gambrinus Day** beer festival in June. Stop by the **farmers market** on Saturday mornings from March onward to grab a breakfast pastry alongside the regular shoppers.

✪ CATHEDRAL OF ST. BARTHOLOMEW (KATEDRÁLA SV. BARTOLOMĚJE)

nám. Republiky; nove.katedralaplzen.org; tower 10am-6pm; 50 CZK

Like many massive buildings conceived in medieval times, construction of St. Bartholomew's Cathedral lasted for centuries, beginning in 1295; it was finally completed in the 16th century. The 103-meter (roughly 335-foot) church spire is the tallest in the Czech Republic, which makes the 301-step climb, to take in the skyline and life on the square below, totally worth it. Note that the interior of the church is closed for renovations through 2020.

You may notice a steady stream of people photographing or touching one of the angels along the bars outside the back of the church. The habit comes from an urban legend of forbidden love. I've heard variations on the story: an executioner in love with a wealthy woman was crying on this spot when his love either (a) married another man, or (b) had a friend stand in the ceremony for him, since his profession excluded him from entering the church. Overcome with grief, he had trouble standing and grabbed onto the angel to steady himself. The bourgoise ladies watching the scene decided that the angel must have miraculous powers. Word spread quickly, and to this day, superstitious visitors arrive to touch the tiny winged symbol and wish for good luck.

Cathedral of St. Bartholomew and angel fountain

TOP EXPERIENCE

✪ PILSNER URQUELL BREWERY (PIVOVAR PLZEŇSKÝ PRAZDROJ)

U Prazdroje 7; +420 377 062 888; www.prazdrojvisit.cz/en; 10am-7pm daily; 250 CZK

While Pilsner Urquell may not be the country's oldest brewery—that title belongs to the 10th-century Břevnov Monastery on the outskirts of Prague—it's definitely the most famous. King Wenceslas II bestowed brewing rights on the townspeople of Pilsen in the 13th century, which satisfied local beer drinkers for a few centuries. By 1838, however, people were fed up with the price and quality of the beverage, and 36 barrels were dumped in front of the town hall. This revolt sparked the creation of a municipal brewery (today's Pilsner Urquell Brewery), completed in 1842 and still producing the country's most beloved brand. (**Tip:** For a deep dive from a resident journalist and beer geek into the historical documentation around the foundation, check out www.beerculture.org.)

Pilsner Urquell Brewery tour

A 100-minute brewery tour covers history and the brewing process while guiding visitors through the bottling factory, brewhouse, and naturally temperature-controlled cellars. The tour is lighthearted and informative, appropriate for beginners and beer-lovers alike, ending with a taste of delicious unfiltered lager straight from the underground barrels. English tours run daily at 1pm, 2:45pm, and 4:30pm, with the addition of 10:45am, 3:45pm, and 5:30pm options in summer months. Confirm exact times for your visit on the website and make an online reservation to ensure you get a coveted spot on these popular tours. Previous visitors include royal names, including Austro-Hungarian royalty Franz Joseph I and his wife Elisabeth (nicknamed Empress Sisi) in 1885.

Even if you don't partake in the full tour, the brewery's surrounding grounds just outside the city center are worth a tram ride or short walk across a bridge to visit. The iconic arches of the **Jubilee Gate** at the entrance to the grounds were built to celebrate the 50th anniversary in 1892 (and also featured on the Pilsner Urquell label). The massive, 500-seat, onsite **Na Spilce restaurant** (entrées 180-300 CZK) draws regular crowds for post-tour *pivo* and Czech food in traditional (while admittedly touristy) pub style. Summer concerts (usually 50 CZK) are often held in the courtyard on Thursdays; check the website to confirm schedules when visiting. The **gift shop** stocks beer-themed souvenirs for every budget, size, and baggage limitation, including an extensive selection of glassware, keychains, and clothing, or a bottle of unpasteurized Pilsner poured and capped straight from the tap.

Note that the Pilsner Brewery entrance is near a busy intersection without crosswalks. Ignore any GPS directions that instruct you to walk on the main road to get there. See the Itinerary Ideas section for how to reach the grounds safely on foot or from the nearest tram stop of Hlavní nádraží.

PILSEN UNDERGROUND (HISTORICKÉ PODZEMÍ)

Veleslavínova 6; +420 377 062 888; www.plzenskepodzemi.cz/en; April-Sept, 10am-6pm; Oct-Mar, 10am-5pm; 120 CZK

A network of tunnels from the 14th

to 18th centuries crisscrosses the city underneath the streets of Pilsen. The 50-minute **Pilsen Underground Tour** provides an entertaining mini-history lesson in this underground labyrinth, previously used to store food and beer, hide from attacks, or send secret messages during times of war. You'll want warm layers—the temperature is around 6°C (40°F)—to go with the hard hat that is provided for safety. An English-speaking guide walks groups of 3-20 people past small exhibits covering medieval times, attempted sieges on the city, everyday family life and cooking tools, and the weaponry of various wars.

Tours run from April to August, with one English tour scheduled daily at 2:20pm and additional options on weekends or peak months (July and August) at 11:20am or 3:20pm. Confirm times during your visit and make your online reservation before arrival to guarantee a spot. The Pilsen Underground Tour also comes with a voucher for a small beer at one of four Pilsner-branded restaurants. Redeem yours at the adjoining **Na Parkánu restaurant,** where the service can be traditionally gruff, or save it for the 500-seat Na Spilce beer hall on the Pilsner Brewery grounds.

The Pilsen Underground shares an entrance and a cash desk with the **Pilsner Brewery Museum** (90 CZK), a kitschy look at brewing history and artifacts—think coasters, beer posters, and scenes of mannequins in vintage bartending getups. Self-proclaimed beer geeks might enjoy a 30-45 minute self-guided wander if you arrive early for an underground tour, but I'd recommend a quick beer at nearby brew pub Pivotečka instead.

PATTON MEMORIAL PILSEN

Pobřežní 10; +420 378 037 956; www.patton-memorial.cz; 9am-4pm Wed-Sun; 70 CZK (cash only)

The collector and memorabilia enthusiast behind this small military history museum has curated a touching personal tribute to the US military's involvement in Pilsen's liberation near the end of Wold War II in 1945. Unlike the rest of the Czech Republic, where the Soviet Army played a primary role in driving Nazi soldiers out, the southwest sliver of the Czech Republic got support from troops led by US General George S. Patton. A recent 2019 remodel of the memorial gives the place a modern look, with text-based displays in Czech and English along the walls detailing the major battles and dates. Glass cases hold authentic artifacts including uniforms, weapons, magazine covers, communication devices, canned foods, cola bottles, bits of shrapnel, and maps with hand-drawn notes of planned routes. Contributions by the French, Belgian, and Luxembourg armies also receive recognition. A quick glimpse of the artifacts could take 30 minutes, but allow at least an hour to properly read through the descriptions on a self-guided tour.

Anyone with a familial connection to World War II will appreciate the diligent inclusion of the names and ranks of soldiers and their divisions whenever possible. Supporters of the museum include General Patton's family, whose contributions include a signed cap from Patton's uniform donated by his grandson. A video installation at the end of the tour displays scenes from the Liberation Festival in 2015, showing the many US veterans who returned to take part in the parades and celebrations, many of whom also

THE AMERICAN-PILSEN CONNECTION

"Thank You, America!" Memorial

As the only major Czech city to be liberated during World War II by US instead of Soviet military support, the city of Pilsen has a unique connection to the United States. You can find monuments across the city cementing this historical sentiment. The event is also celebrated with the annual Pilsen Liberation Festival, held in May.

The **"Thank You, America!" Memorial** is appropriately located at the end of America Street (*Americká ulice*), just up the road from the Great Synagogue. Two rectangular towers inscribed with "Thank you, America!" in both English and Czech are flanked by Czech and American flags. Many local residents remember discussion of the US involvement in the fight for freedom being outright denied or taboo while under Communist rule, so the monument wasn't installed until 1995, and was given a structural touch-up in 2018. These days it's often used as a meeting point for friends, or as a seat to devour a kebab from a nearby shop. You will likely find flowers and commemorative events around the area during the Liberation Festival.

Continuing one-and-a-half streets north along the main road of sady Pětatřicátníků will bring you to a patch of grass beside the J. K. Tyl Theater, across from the Great Synagogue. The tall sculptural **Monument to General G. S. Patton** doesn't exactly scream "America" at first glance. However, if you take a few steps back and look at the empty space created by the curves, you'll see a profile of the general in a military cap. The rust-colored metal is meant to evoke images of the tanks that rolled into the city to help bring freedom to the people of Pilsen. The monument was erected on May 1, 2015, to commemorate the 70th anniversary of the end of the war.

The place to find the full story on the US military involvment in the end of WWII is the **Patton Memorial Pilsen,** located a 10-minute walk north of the metal monument. The small warehouse building houses a collection of artifacts chronologically arranged to remember important battles and turning points, up to Pilsen's liberation and relevant events of subsequent years.

continue to visit every year. Slow down when exiting to avoid missing two touching documents lining the walls, with signatures of visiting veterans surrounding a promise from Pilsen that "We Will Always Remember" opposite a plaque from the US replying "Thank you for honoring and remembering America."

✪ GREAT SYNAGOGUE (VELKÁ SYNAGOGA)

sady Petatricatniku 11; +420 377 235 749; www.zoplzen.cz; April-Oct, 10am-6pm; 70 CZK

Pilsen's visually stunning house of Jewish worship from the late 19th century is one of the largest in the world. The massive synagogue served the local Jewish community from 1893-1942, before Nazi rule invaded Pilsen and sent members of the local Jewish community to concentration camps. The building was then used for storage and the production of German military uniforms, and suffered damage from fighting in the streets because of its prominent location on a main road. Ever since that time, Pilsen's (significantly smaller) Jewish community has been raising money for its maintenance and repair.

the Great Synagogue

These days, with a congregation of roughly 100 people, the synagogue is mainly focused on cultural events and tourism. The interior hallways are lined with exhibitions from photographers and artists, with recent shows including documentary photographs from military events and social life in the early 20th century. Head to the back of the building and take the staircases to the balcony for an up-close look at the brightly colored stained-glass windows. The names incorporated into the designs (e.g., Hoffman, Leou, Popper) acknowledge families who have made significant contributions to the building's construction and renovation. Then grab a seat on the cushioned pews to admire the painted arches of the ceilings and the column-lined aisles from above.

Plan on 30 minutes for a quick glance at just the architectural beauty, or at least an hour to take in the current art exhibit, which extends from the ground floor into the second-story balconies.

PUPPET MUSEUM (MUZEUM LOUTEK)

nám. Republiky 23; +420 378 370 801; www.muzeum-loutek.cz/en; 10am-6pm Tues-Sun; 60 CZK

One of Pilsen's quirkier characteristics is its connection with puppet theater, an essential element of any Czech child's upbringing. Traveling puppet theaters were a popular element of the 18th and 19th centuries, traveling from region to region and performing in Czech (as opposed to German). This exposure to Czech language and folk art was arguably connected to the growing Czech National Revival movement, which later helped to establish Czechoslovakia's independence from the Austro-Hungarian Empire.

Three floors of exhibits in this museum on Pilsen's main square cover the history of puppet theater from the 1800s to today, with signage in Czech, German, and English. Explanations may be fairly detailed for your average visitor, so feel free to breeze through the ground floor to get to the more interactive elements above. For a glimpse of the best-known figures of Czech pop culture, look for father-and-son duo Spejbl and Hurvínek, created in the early 20th century, or the Good Soldier Švejk, based on a legendary figure from Czech literature. Interactive videos near the stairwells are worth watching, and the second floor holds a functioning puppet performance set to music, with marionettes up to 100 years old. Head to the third floor to play with some of the puppets yourself.

The museum is an interesting cultural education for adult travelers as well as families; however, be forewarned that many of the historical puppets present stereotypical and potentially offensive caricatures of non-white races and ethnic backgrounds. Give yourself 30-60 minutes to explore the whole museum.

DEPO 2015

Presslova 14; +420 702 019 508; www.depo2015.cz; 8am-10pm Mon-Fri, 10am-10pm Sat, 10am-6pm Sun

For a glimpse at the more modern, experimental side of Pilsen and a break from guided tours, take a 10-15 minute walk along the rainbow-painted riverfront path of Anglické nábřeží to DEPO 2015. This industrial arts, events, co-working, and makers' space came to life in a former transport depository as part of Pilsen's year as the European Capital of Culture in 2015 (hence the "Depo" in the center's

DEPO 2015's artist and maker space

name). The concrete grounds include a public garden of flower boxes lined with refurbished sculptures, a shared warehouse space for pursuits like metal or woodworking, and an indoor collection of independent shops and exhibition spaces. The peaceful indoor café is popular with students and the digital nomad set.

To get an overview of the grounds and the surrounding neighborhood, climb roughly 65 steps to the top of the metal observation tower in the center of the courtyard for a great view before taking in the aroma of the herbs growing in the community garden. Head inside to find a classic car defying gravity by hanging sideways off a wall. Then browse through the rotating market stalls for items like specialty food products or knitted accessories, all in the shadow of an alien spaceship-like sculpture hanging over pallet furniture. The café's plant-covered walls, succulent centerpieces, and metal sting-ray lights create a peaceful, nature-inspired vibe. Enjoy specialty coffee, a microbrew, or a daily lunch special (around 100 CZK) along the lines of goulash, grilled pork, or pasta, served from 11am-2pm. A range of special events held onsite range from swing-dance evenings to street food and classic car festivals, with details on their website or Facebook page.

TECHMANIA

U Planetária 1; +420 737 247 585 or +420 737 247 581; techmania.cz/en; 10am-6pm daily; 240 CZK

Three reasons to visit Pilsen's science center and planetarium: (1) you're an adult who loves space and natural sciences; (2) you're traveling with children; or (3) you're looking for a rainy-day activity. The gigantic playground of STEM subjects spreads across two warehouses with tons of interactive exhibits, including a human gyroscope (often used in astronaut training), weights comparing the gravitational pull on different planets, and a detailed history of Czech industry and transportation, complete with vintage vehicles. The celestial exhibits in the planetarium chronicle Czech participation in various international space missions. Adults may want to see sculptor David Černý's controversial Entropa piece, a collection of stereotypes representing 27 EU nations, which hangs from the ceiling of the science center.

Techmania Science Center and Planetarium

All exhibits, including interactive touchscreens, are available in Czech, English, and German. Commentary for planetarium shows and 3-D films is also available in English and German via headphones.

To get to Techmania, take a 15-minute bus ride on the #15 bus from the U Práce bus stop (near the "Thank You, America" Memorial) to the Techmania bus stop, which puts you just across the street from the exhibition grounds.

✪ PURKMISTR BEER SPA AND MICROBREWERY (PIVNÍ LÁZNĚ PURKMISTR)

Selská náves 2; +420 377 994 366; www.purkmistr.cz/en/spa; 10am-10pm daily; 900 CZK single beer bath; 1780 CZK double

Think of the 25-30 minute bus ride from Pilsen's city center to the Purkmistr Beer Spa as your first step in relaxing and detaching from modern life. The enclosed grounds in a quiet residential neighborhood include a hotel, restaurant, microbrewery, and spa to treat all five senses to beer-inspired experiences.

The Purkmistr experience comes enthusiastically recommended. The patient staff can easily answer questions in English and guide visitors through the process of stashing belongings in a locker room, finding your private room, and climbing into a wooden tub of water, barley, and hops mixed to soothe the skin and hair. A calming waterfall runs down one wall and a free-flowing tap of Purkmistr's delicious house lager is within reach to quench your thirst. The 20-minute soak is counted down on a digital wall clock so you know when to get out. A post-bath wrap in a dimly lit relaxation room afterward allows the ingredients to soak in—ideally they shouldn't be washed off for hours to get the full cosmetic benefit. A beer bath is intended to reduce stress, open pores, and add a glow to your skin and hair (so feel free to dunk your head). Beer baths are available in partitioned rooms with single tubs or two individual tubs for couples or friends. Reservations for spa treatments are recommended.

bathe in *pivo* at Purkmistr Beer Spa

Before heading back to the bus, stop by the onsite **Purkmistr Microbrewery** (entrées 175-300 CZK) for some classic Czech cuisine and a flight of the inventive range of beers produced here. The Purkmistr grounds also host the Slunce Ve Skle ("Sun in a Glass") Beer Festival in September, with live music and a variety of Czech microbrew stands to sample.

To get to Purkmistr, take the #13 bus from the Muzeum bus stop for about 30 minutes, getting off at Generála Lišky. Then follow Štefánikova street, sloping down to your right, for about five minutes to reach the Purkmistr grounds. To catch the #13 bus back into town, the Generála Lišky stop is located about one minute north of where you got off on the opposite side of the street, and runs roughly every 20 minutes from 8am to 11pm (see www.pmdp.eu to confirm schedules).

Bars and Nightlife

Pilsen's city center is surrounded by pubs, drawing crowds of all ages to sample their selections. More traditional pubs—usually identifiable by their wood furniture, red and green accents, and exclusively Pilsner Urquell on tap—share the scene with newer microbrew pubs. The younger generation includes more industrial styles or eclectic atmospheres (think clever signage and kitschy details) with taps that pour more than a classically perfected lager, expanding to IPAs, red ales, wheat beers, or porters. International and domestic beer fans tend to center around Náměstí Republiky, where plenty of pubs fall within a few streets of the main square. With lots of pubs closing around 11pm or midnight, it's not a super late-night scene, so let your dinner reservations transition into drinks and savor every sip at your leisure.

TOP EXPERIENCE

✪ BREWERIES AND BREW PUBS

✪ Beer Factory

Dominikánská 8; +420 379 422 526; beerfactoryplzen.cz; 11am-11pm Sun-Thurs, 11am-midnight Fri-Sat; entrées 150-300 CZK, beer 40-60 CZK

An all-ages crowd, from families with children to groups of beer-drinking friends, fills the ground floor, balcony, and 60-seat outdoor patio at Beer Factory. The onsite microbrewery embraces its industrial atmosphere of brick walls and copper tanks. Wake your taste buds up from lager overload with a crisp, citrusy Nevada Ale or the not-too-heavy Porter Robust-a with a subtle coffee finish. Reservations recommended.

Pivotečka

Rooseveltova 4; +420 722 282 671; noon-11pm Mon-Sat; 40-60 CZK beer

A quirky blend of vintage vibes and kitschy Tiki-bar décor somehow works for this cozy brew pub, with half-beer-bottle light fixtures putting a creative twist on the mason-jar or exposed-lightbulb trend. The rotating selection of local and international options are scrawled in chalk over the bar. Follow your mood to a shadowy corner table on the ground floor or settle into a wicker chair on the rope-lined, sunlit balcony and enjoy the sweet indulgence of day drinking.

Na Parkánu

Veleslavínova 4; +420 724 618 037; www.naparkanu.com/en; 11am-11pm Mon-Wed, 11am-midnight Thurs, 11am-1am Fri-Sat, 11am-10pm Sun; 40-60 CZK beer

For the traditional, nostalgic Czech pub experience, where the staff may not always smile but the Pilsner will always be fresh, grab a bench at Na Parkánu behind the Pilsen Underground. The building has a storied history as a malt house, former prison, locksmith, hospital building, and workshop. It officially housed a pub beginning in 1966 and was renovated to the current timeless look in 2004. The pints (sorry, half-liters) come with a perfect foam head, and the garlic soup is delicious. Reservations recommended.

Festivals and Events

SPRING

Pilsen's city center fills with parades, ceremonies, and US army veterans in early May for the **Pilsen Liberation Festival** (slavnostisvobody.cz/en).

SUMMER AND FALL

Beer festivals spread from summer into autumn with **Gambrinus Day** (www.gambrinus.cz/gambrinusden) on Náměstí Republiky in June, the **Slunce Ve Skle ("Sun in a Glass") Microbrew Festival** at the Purmistr Brewery and Spa in September, and **Pilsner Fest** (www.pilsnerfest.cz) at the Pilsner Brewery in early October.

WINTER

Add a touch of brightness to a winter trip with the **BLIK BLIK light festival** (www.depo2015.cz/blik-blik-ag105/blik-blik-a1423) in March, organized by DEPO 2015, when the streets glow with artistic installations and video-mapping projections on buildings across town.

Food

CZECH

U Mansfelda

Dřevěná 9; +420 377 333 844; www.umansfelda.cz; 11am-11pm Mon-Thurs, 11am-midnight Fri-Sat, 11am-10pm Sun; entrées 150-300 CZK

Classic Czech recipes, reasonable prices, and English-friendly menus make this restaurant and pub just off the main square a popular choice for travelers and workers on their lunch break. The shaded balcony fills up in the summer, and the indoor pub and dining areas are loud and lively on Friday nights. For a traditional taste of rich flavors, go for the roast duck, boar goulash, or *svíčková* (a sirloin dish in a vegetable cream sauce) with a side of dumplings. Reservations recommended.

INTERNATIONAL

✪ Pivstro

Bezručova 31; +420 725 886 889; brewhemian.eu/cs/pivstro; 11am-11pm Tues-Sat; entrées 150-200 CZK

Menu variety and service with a smile keep the small indoor dining room and patio seats filled at this casual "brewhemian bistro" near the Great Synagogue. International food options range from nachos and burritos to bagels, pulled pork sandwiches, and veggie burgers, with lots of vegan and vegetarian options. The beer menu always includes Belgium's renowned Delirium Brewery, Pilsner Urquell, and a crisp house ale alongside rotating taps with more adventurous options like sour beers, fruit-infused creations, or hoppy IPAs.

Nero

nám. Republiky 14; +420 604 574 434; nero-plzen.business.site; 11am-11pm Tues-Sat; entrées 200-300 CZK

The prices, meals, and décor are one step above a casual pub, with plush purple booths, candlelit tables, and a view of Náměstí Republiky. Seasonal, Italian-inspired menus use fresh ingredients to create dishes like prawn and parmesan pasta, gnocchi with goat cheese and fresh tomatoes, and a yummy selection of bruschetta. Nero attracts a young, trendy clientele, but there's no need to dress up for dinner unless desired. Reservations recommended.

CAFÉS

Le Frenchie

Smetanovy Sady 6; +420 777 943 410; www.lefrenchie.cz; 8:30am-8pm Mon-Fri, 9:30am-8pm Sat, 9:30am-7pm Sun; 50-75 CZK coffee; cash only

Bring your sweet tooth and cash to enjoy this mellow café located on the edge of the park that wraps around the city center. Warm up with hot teas and espresso drinks, or cool down with iced coffee or homemade lemonade. An eclectic mix of furniture, pop art, and a cozy book nook decorate the L-shaped seating area. Try some carrot cake or an open-faced sandwich, or take your drink for a walk in the park just outside.

classic Czech cuisine at U Mansfelda

Měšťanská Beseda

Kopeckého sady 13; +420 378 037 916; 11am-11pm daily; beer 40-60 CZK

Go back to the early 20th century and the birth of then-Czechoslovakia's First Republic in this gorgeously restored historical café. Eye-catching detail draws attention in every direction, from decorative wooden ceilings and golden chandeliers to a mural of the aristocratic class enjoying salon-style gatherings. Go local and traditional with your drinks, a Pilsner Urquell beer or glass of *Bohemia sekt* bubbles, to complete the elegant experience.

Accommodations

Hotel Plzeň

Budilova 15; +420 377 224 034; en.hotelplzen.cz; 1,500-2,000 CZK d

Expect a young-to-middle-aged crowd in this option behind the Great Synagogue. Thirty-eight en-suite rooms range from doubles to quadruples with black, white, and glass design elements getting a touch of color from fashion paintings and classic Hollywood portraits. Wi-Fi and buffet breakfast are included, and you'll find a pizzeria and a Czech restaurant on site. A wizened regular or two may be smoking outside while you redeem your welcome drink in the hotel bar, and the staff might throw in a wink and joke at their colleagues' expense during check-in.

✪ Hotel Rous

Zbrojnická 7; +420 725 072 052; www.hotelrous.cz; 1,900 CZK s, 2,200 CZK d

Plenty of historical charm is spread across 18 en-suite rooms on three floors (with an elevator) in this super-convenient location one street off the main square of Náměstí Republiky. The maroon and gold palette gives the whole place a warm, regal feel. Amenities include free Wi-Fi, a leisurely noon checkout, decent hot-and-cold breakfast included, and incredibly kind staff with varying levels of English always willing to help. Don't miss the mural of famous Czechs throughout history painted on the back side of the building.

mural of famous Czechs at Hotel Rous

Transportation

GETTING THERE

Pilsen is located roughly one hour southwest of Prague by train, bus, or car. Pilsen's main bus and train stations both offer a fairly easy walk to the city center, roughly 10-20 minutes from either one to the main town square.

TRAIN

The Czech national rail service (www.cd.cz, 95-110 CZK one-way) runs one or two direct trains every hour between 5:45am to 11:30pm, departing from Prague's main train station (Praha hlavní nádraží).

BUS

Regiojet (www.regiojet.com, 90-100 CZK one way) offers hourly service between 9am and 11pm departing from Prague's Zličín bus station. Flixbus (www.flixbus.com, 50-130 CZK one-way) runs at least once an hour between 8am and midnight, and Leo Express (www.leoexpress.com, 75-85 CZK one-way) coaches leave every 1-2 hours between 8am and 7:30pm. Both Flixbus and Leo Express routes depart from Prague's Zličín, Florenc, or Praha hlavní nádraží bus stations, so check your tickets carefully.

Most bus routes stop first at the residential Plzeň, Divadlo Alfa stop on the outskirts of town before continuing onward to Pilsen's main bus station (written on most tickets as "Plzeň, CAN"), so don't hop off too early.

CAR

Pilsen is located about one hour's drive (roughly 100 kilometers/60 miles) southwest of Prague on the D5/E50 highway. Visit www.pilsen.eu for updated information on parking rates and locations. For parking, the City of Pilsen recommends that visitors use the 24-hour, multi-story Rychtářka parking garage, about three streets away from Náměstí Republiky (5-10 CZK per hour). You can check the up-to-the-minute capacity of the 377-space structure at www.parkingplzen.cz.

LEAVING PILSEN

Return train service runs later in the evening than most buses, which translates to more time in Pilsen for anyone squeezing in a day trip.

Regiojet buses back to Prague run every 1-2 hours between 5am and at least 6pm (sometimes later on weekends or summer months). Flixbus routes depart for Prague around 4:30am to 7pm, and LeoExpress buses run Prague-bound service from about 8am to 3pm. The Czech national rail service offers direct train service from Pilsen to Prague between 6am and 9pm, departing once or twice every hour.

There are a couple of options for further connections from Pilsen. The Czech national rail service (www.cd.cz) runs one 8am train daily from Pilsen to Český Krumlov, transferring in the town of České Budějovice (3 hours, 200-220 CZK). Karlovy Vary is also just over an hour's drive north. Most other destinations, particularly those to the north or east, require a transfer in Prague.

ČESKÝ KRUMLOV

In many towns, the term "fairy-tale atmosphere" can feel clichéd, but the pastel colors, red-orange rooftops, and medieval atmosphere of Český Krumlov deserve to retain full rights to the phrase. The main draws to this carefully preserved 13th-century city are the Český Krumlov Castle, encircled by the curves of the Vltava River, and the chance for summer river-rafting fun. Creative spaces devoted to local artists also provide evidence that South Bohemia's natural beauty has been inspiring painters and photographers for centuries.

HIGHLIGHTS

- ✪ **CASTLE TOWER:** The panoramic views available year-round over the river and surrounding city are equally gorgeous in glistening sun or blanketed in snow (page 239).
- ✪ **BAROQUE THEATER:** This ornate Baroque playhouse inside Český Krumlov Castle has been meticulously restored, down to the wooden nails and hand-cranked noise machine. Accessible only on tour (Tues-Sun May-Oct) (page 241).
- ✪ **FOTOATELIER SEIDEL:** The 19th-century home and studio of photographer Josef Seidel intertwines photography and family life into a beautifully curated walk through history (page 242).
- ✪ **RAFTING THE VLTAVA RIVER:** Take a paddle down the Vltava River, stopping at riverside pubs and floating mojito stands along the way (page 243).

Expect heavy tourist traffic during summer months, and be aware that there may be some anti-tourist sentiment around town. (A local artist even hired people to live "normal" lives in the summer of 2018 to draw attention to tourism pushing the locals out of town.) Use the local language whenever possible, and consider visiting during one of the shoulder seasons. Late spring and early autumn are equally beautiful and half as crowded, and most castle sights are still open. A peaceful day in winter, when fewer castle tours are available, could also make up for it with the magic of city streets dusted in snow.

ORIENTATION

The Vltava River curves in an S-shape through the medieval city of roughly 13,000 residents, creating an **island-like landscape** connected by **pedestrian bridges** and centered around the large **castle complex.** Český Krumlov is a mainly flat, walkable city covered in cobblestones (so wear comfortable shoes or sandals to prevent twisted ankles). The two bus stops, **Český Krumlov, Špičák** or **Český Krumlov, AN,** are both around a 15-minute walk or a short taxi ride from the historical center of town. **Český Krumlov train station,** not recommended, is at least a 20-minute walk outside of town. Other than resident vehicles or taxis, Český Krumlov's protected center is a pedestrian-only zone.

UNESCO-protected medieval streets

PLANNING YOUR TIME

While Český Krumlov is often called a "day trip" from Prague, the city is much better enjoyed with an overnight stay of **2-3 days.** A three-hour bus, car, or train journey each way means that single-day tourists and bus tours swarm the most popular sights in the late morning, lunchtime, and afternoon. Spending at least one night gives you a head-start on sights in the morning, quiet nights, and the chance to enjoy a full day on the water, rafting the Vltava River, and another seeing the sights on land. Reserve your hotels and tours in early spring for a summertime trip because many hotels (especially the more affordable ones) in this popular vacation destination are booked months in advance.

Consider the season when planning your visit. While the Castle Tower and expansive Museum are open year round, access to the castle gardens and tours of some royal residences run only from **April** to **October.** Baroque Theater tours are offered only between **May** and **October. Shoulder seasons** and **winter** visits are perfect for seeing the peaceful, artistic side of Český Krumlov, when both the city streets and places like the Egon Schiele Gallery and Fotoatelier Seidel will be less crowded. Visitors interested in river rafting should watch the forecasts between **May** and **September** when boat rentals are available. Choosing your Český Krumlov time

try Český Krumlov in winter

is a tradeoff between summer months (June-August) that are full of fun but bordering on over-tourism, and off-seasons with more breathing room and less stress on the city, but limited access to some of the sights that draw the crowds.

Český Krumlov's location on the southern border of Bohemia is most common as a one-off trip from Prague, but could also be a jumping-off point as part of an eastern path to **Brno** or **Mikulov** in South Moravia, or northwest to **Pilsen.**

SIGHTSEEING PASSES

Invest in a **Český Krumlov Card** (www.ckrumlov.info, 300 CZK) for combined access to five museums, including the Castle Museum and Tower, the Museum Fotoatelier Seidel, and the Egon Schiele Art Gallery. The card can be purchased in person at the included sights or the Tourist Information Center (Náměstí Svornosti 2; +420 380 704 622; www.ckrumlov.info).

Itinerary Ideas

At least a week before your arrival, make your lunch reservations at **U dwau Maryí**, dinner reservations at **Nonna Gina**, and rafting reservations at **Maleček Rafting and Canoe.** This itinerary works from May to September, when river rafting is available and the Castle Gardens are open.

DAY 1

1. Start the day with a hotel breakfast or a 6am bus from Prague, and head straight to the Castle Tower before the steady stream of day trip tour groups descend on the city. Climb the stairs and photograph the skyline before descending to the self-guided tour of the **Castle Tower Museum** in the base of the building. Grab coffee at the onsite Cafe Hrádek.

2. Enjoy a leisurely walk through the free open **courtyards** of the castle.

3. Continue beyond the courtyards and into the hedge-lined **Castle Gardens.** Wander through the manicured flower beds and stone staircases.

4. Have lunch on the riverside at **U dwau Maryí,** about a 15-minute walk away from the Castle Gardens. Treat yourself to an Old Bohemian Feast as a reward for a full morning of sightseeing.

5. After lunch, visit the photography museum of **Fotoatelier Seidel.** Spend roughly one hour touring the family home and studio of a local photographer housed in an Art Nouveau building.

6. With your camera eye ready, enter the small public park of **Seminární zahrada** and turn your camera lens (or your gaze) toward capturing the city skyline from this unobstructed viewpoint.

7. If you're up for one more cultural stop, make it the **Egon Schiele Gallery.** Grab a quick coffee in the ground floor café and explore three floors of classic and contemporary arts inspired by a local protégé of Austrian painter Gustav Klimt.

8. For dinner, indulge in Italian food at **Nonna Gina** and get a good night's sleep for a day on the river tomorrow.

DAY 2

Secure any valuables in your hotel room before leaving for the day, and double-check the time of your rafting reservation.

1. Feel free to sleep in a little before enjoying a hearty breakfast of eggs

Český Krumlov

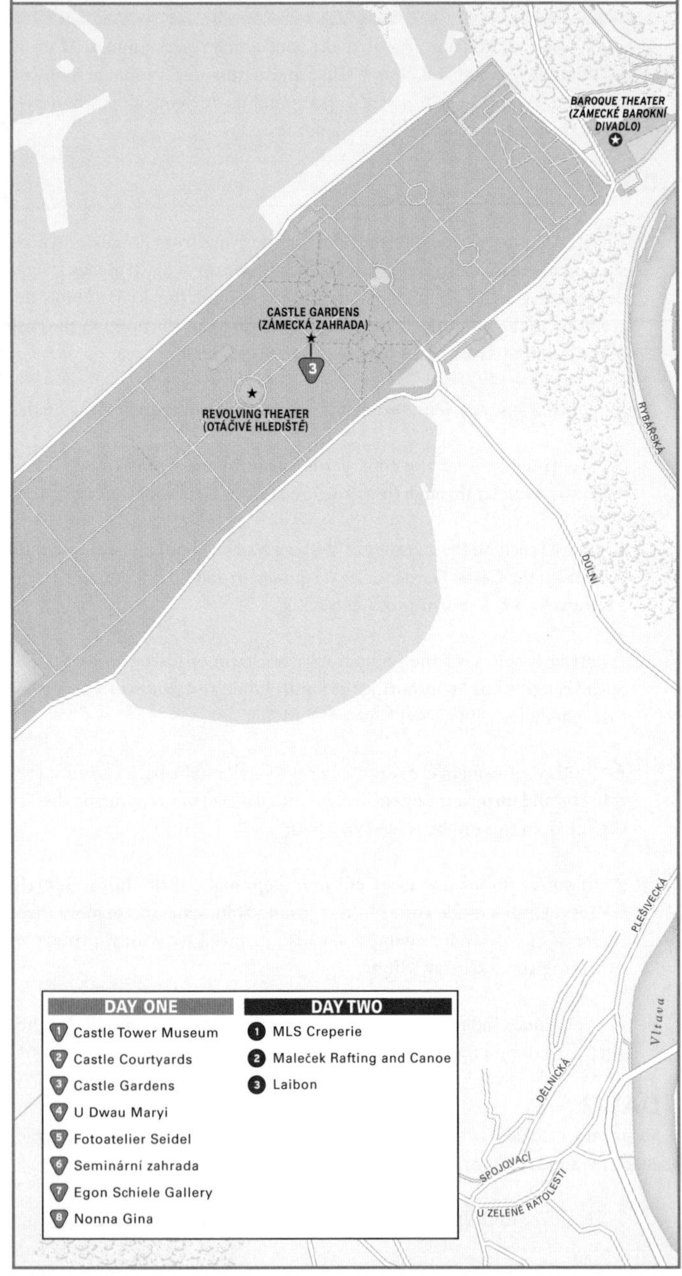

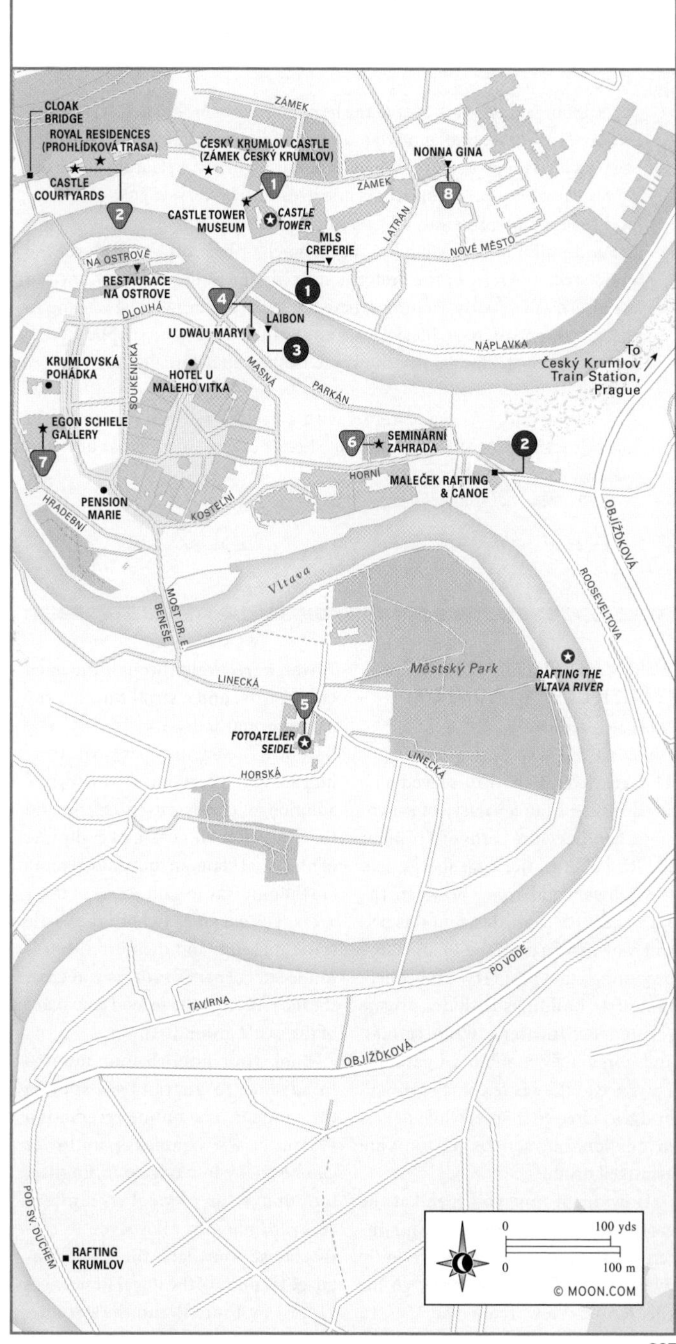

ČESKÝ KRUMLOV ITINERARY IDEAS

and crêpes at **MLS Creperie.** You'll need the energy for an active day of paddling.

2 After breakfast, walk over to the headquarters of **Maleček Rafting and Canoe.** From here, slather on the sunscreen, secure your valuables in a dry bag provided for protection, and join the parade of boats floating down the Vltava River. Pop-up cocktail bars midstream and riverside pubs offer fast-food snacks along the way, all generally of equal quality. Hop out of your raft and pull it onto dry land to take a lunch or beer break whenever the mood strikes. Arrive at the designated finish line in the center of town in late afternoon or early evening, where the Maleček staff will be waiting to pick up your boats, oars, lifejackets, and any other borrowed supplies. Walk back to your hotel for a quick shower to freshen up before dinner.

3 Meet up at **Laibon** and refuel with a healthy portion of *Bryndzové halušky,* a traditional Slovak meal of sheep's cheese and a cross between macaroni and gnocchi.

Sights

ČESKÝ KRUMLOV CASTLE (ZÁMEK ČESKÝ KRUMLOV)

Zámek 59; +420 380 704 721; www.zamek-ceskykrumlov.cz

This castle and château served as a royal residence to a variety of aristocratic families—the Lords of Krumlov, the Rosenbergs, the Eggenbergs, and the Schwartzenbergs—between the 13th and 19th centuries, and was privately owned up until the 1940s before becoming state property. The collection of 41 buildings includes private residences, theaters, wine cellars, and gorgeously manicured gardens. Entrance to the castle courtyards and bridges is free of charge, while tickets to individual attractions and tours are arranged onsite.

How much time you spend at the castle depends entirely on your interests. For a simple, budget-friendly overview of the atmosphere, go for the iconic view from the **Castle Tower,** a free walk through the open **courtyards,** and a stroll through the massive manicured **gardens.** The **Baroque Theater** (my personal favorite part of the castle) is a worthwhile addition for performing arts fans, and the **Royal Residences** add a glimpse of historical glamour, but guided tours are the only way to gain access to these areas. The entrance to both the castle tower museum and the tower itself is in the left corner as soon as you cross the moat to enter the second courtyard of the castle grounds.

Book your English tour months in advance to guarantee a spot in the summer. The online reservation system at www.zamek-krumlov.cz can be tricky to navigate in English, but npuvstupenky.colosseum.eu/ceskykrumlov/list allows you to easily choose your date, time, and language for tours of the Royal Residences (Tour I or Tour II) and the Baroque

Theater. The ticket counter in the second courtyard of the castle also offers in-person sales for that day only. The busy staff can be a bit surly if you hold up the line, so stop by the tourist information center and gift shop just inside the castle gates on the right for friendly, patient answers to any questions first.

TOP EXPERIENCE

✪ CASTLE TOWER

Nov-March, 9am-3:15pm; April-May and Sept-Oct, 9am-4:15pm; June-Aug, 9am-5:15pm; 150 CZK (with Castle Museum admission)

The Castle Tower dominates the silhouette of the hilltop fortress and symbolizes the city itself. A climb up 162 stairs rewards visitors with impossibly wide panoramic views of the city. Arrive early or toward the end of the day to avoid the maximum limit of 50 people on the snug balcony.

CASTLE TOWER MUSEUM

Zamek 59; www.zamek-ceskykrumlov.cz; 150 CZK (with Castle Tower admission)

Many visitors head straight to the top of the tower for a photo of its iconic city views, but the 14-room museum at the base of the building is absolutely worth browsing. Laminated texts in multiple languages are available to read in front of each exhibit, but a free audioguide offers a more enjoyable experience. Wander through a collection of portrait halls, former administrative offices, and glass cases full of 19th-century artifacts including board games, glasses, and porcelain dining sets. Continue through a treasury of sacred art, an armory of weapons and soldiers' uniforms, and a collection of family photos from former castle residents, the Schwarzenburg family. One

Český Krumlov Castle

hour is plenty of time to complete the self-guided tour.

This attraction also comes with the added bonus of being open year-round, with no reservations required. The lobby of the tower includes a reasonably priced gift shop and coin-operated lockers for a deposit of 10 CZK. The cozy onsite **Café Hrádek** offers a handful of wooden tables for a quick beer, wine, coffee, and cake before continuing further into the castle grounds.

CASTLE GARDENS (ZÁMECKÁ ZAHRADA)

Zámecká zahrada, +420 380 704 721, www.zamek-ceskykrumlov.cz, April-Oct, 8am-5pm; May-Sept, 8am-7pm

One place to experience free, peaceful entertainment at the Český Krumlov Castle is a leisurely stroll through the colorful Castle Gardens at the back of the complex. The upper garden of rectangular edges was formerly used for horseback riding, while the lower area has a more ornate, decorative feel. The 17th-century landscape of geometric hedges, swirling flowers, and stair-lined fountains stretches far enough to feel secluded even in the busiest months.

REVOLVING THEATER (OTÁČIVÉ HLEDIŠTĚ)

Zámecká zahrada; +420 386 711 222; www.revolvingtheatre.com

In addition to the Baroque Theater inside the castle walls, a modern, metallic Revolving Auditorium and Open-Air Theater sits at the back of the Castle Gardens. Performances range from ballet and opera to drama and puppet theater, and generally run June-September with ticket prices ranging 500-1,500 CZK, depending on the show. Even a simple afternoon walk around this theater can be fun, to admire the lighting arrangements and imagine the scenes that could pop up in several open plots of grass around the rotating seats. These de facto garden stages are just waiting for the audience to swing in their direction.

Revolving Theater in Český Krumlov Gardens

CASTLE COURTYARDS

One way to enjoy the Český Krumlov Castle without reservations year-round is a leisurely walk through its five connected courtyards, which act as a long line of outdoor hallways running through the grounds. The first fairly non-descript courtyard lies before the moat and holds the tourist information center as well as close-up exterior views of the Castle Tower. Entering the large second courtyard brings you officially inside the grounds, where you'll find the entrance to the Castle Tower and Museum on your immediate left and ticket offices in the far left corner. This second courtyard is another gorgeous viewpoint to photograph the Castle Tower, and a popular meeting place for tour groups.

The smaller third and fourth courtyards are visual sights in their own right, with *sgraffito* designs sketched on the tall surrounding walls of the Royal Residences. Look for the stairs around the fourth courtyard on your right to duck underground and explore the free sculpture exhibit of "The Czech-Krumlov Surreality" in the cellars.

After the enclosed third and fourth courtyards, you will cross the sculpture-lined **Cloak Bridge** (a favorite spot for selfies and skyline views) to reach the fifth outdoor courtyard, which acts as a pathway to the Castle Gardens. The fifth courtyard also holds the entrance to the Baroque Castle Tour in the right corner and a pricey outdoor café on the left. Look up to your right to find a decorative sundial clock on the wall. Further ahead on the left, 26 stone windows lining the edge of the fifth courtyard make popular frames for photographs of the city. This path through the five courtyards acts as a sort of self-guided tour of the grounds, giving some sense of the aristocratic atmosphere and beauty of the place without stepping foot inside any of the buildings.

ROYAL RESIDENCES (PROHLÍDKOVÁ TRASA)

Zámek 59; +420 380 704 721; www.zamek-ceskykrumlov.cz

Guided tours of the Royal Residences are the only way to get access into the personal lives of some of the famous families that called this castle home.

Tour Route I (320 CZK, in English) lasts one hour and is available from April through October, with English tours usually around 10:30am and 2:30pm. This route covers older sections of the castle, decorated in elegant Renaissance and Baroque styles from the 16th-18th centuries. Highlights include the golden altar of St. George's chapel, paneled ceilings over the bedrooms and dining areas used by the Rosenberg family, and the cartoon-like paintings lining the Masquerade Hall.

Tour Route II (240 CZK, in English) concentrates on the 19th- and 20th-century influence of the Schwarzenberg family, and is available from June through August and on weekends in September. One-hour tours run from 9am until 4pm or 5pm, except Mondays. Highlights include an extensive collection of large-scale portraits, multiple bedroom suites used by both the aristocratic residents and chambermaids, and leisure areas like the Smoking Salon, Music Room, and Reference Library.

Purchase your tickets for specific dates, times, and languages in advance at npuvstupenky.colosseum.eu/ceskykrumlov/list, or stop by the ticket counter in the second courtyard first thing in the morning to confirm the time of any English tours available that day and secure a spot.

✪ BAROQUE THEATER (ZÁMECKÉ BAROKNÍ DIVADLO)

Zámek 59; +420 380 704 721; www.zamek-ceskykrumlov.cz

The meticulously restored Baroque Theater inside the castle is renowned across Europe for its attention to historic detail. Dramatic performances were a part of castle life as early as the 1500s, but a 17th-century remodel created the appearance that has been maintained to this day. This theater and the **Drottningholms Slottsteater** in Sweden are the only two preserved Baroque theaters in existence in the world. The guided, 45-minute tour (350 CZK) is the only way to see the hand-painted scenery, stark audience divisions between the aristocracy and the commoners, the wood-and-rope mechanics used to change sets, and the inventive machines used to create sound effects like wind and rain—raise your hand fast when the guide asks for volunteers to demonstrate the sounds.

English tours usually run at 10am from Tues-Sun from May through October. Purchase your tickets at npuvstupenky.colosseum.eu/ceskykrumlov/list, or hit the box office early in the morning to reserve a space in person on the day you want to see it.

EGON SCHIELE GALLERY

Široká 71; +420 380 704 011; www.schieleartcentrum.cz; 10am-6pm daily; 180 CZK

One of the most interesting sights outside the castle grounds is the three-story Egon Schiele Gallery. Schiele was an Austrian contemporary of Gustav Klimt in the early 1900s, and was known for his nude figures and provocative style. A permanent exhibit chronicles his life, including his adopted home of Český Krumlov and his success in Vienna, while the gallery rotates contemporary modern artists through the space.

✪ FOTOATELIER SEIDEL

Linecká 272; +420 736 503 871; www.seidel.cz; 100 CZK

Take a walk through early 20th-century life through the eyes of local photographer Josef Seidel in this restored Art Nouveau home and studio. Admission begins with a six-minute video detailing the life of the family with individual audio-guided commentary in your chosen language before the self-guided tour continues through the home at your own pace (usually under an hour). The Seidel family's collection of 10,000 carefully labeled photos and negatives, documenting local life and the natural beauty of the forests and hills of the Šumava area, were confiscated under Communist rule, but luckily were recovered intact and are now displayed throughout the residence. Photography fans will love the cases filled with classic camera equipment and accessories.

Fotoatelier Seidel, a photographer's home turned museum

The museum is open from 9am-noon and 1pm-5pm year round (last entry at 4pm), but closes on Mondays during the off-season (from October to March). Make an online reservation in advance to arrange a souvenir photo shoot with a selection of period costumes (500-2,500 CZK depending on number of poses) in the light-filled portrait studio on the top floor.

SEMINÁRNÍ ZAHRADA

Horní Street; free

This small public garden directly opposite the Hotel Ruze on Horní Street

postcard views from Seminární zahrada

offers uninterrupted views of the skyline, including the Český Krumlov Castle and Tower over the red-orange roofs and cobblestoned streets below. Compare camera angles from opposite ends of the low brick wall lining the edge of the grassy park, or grab a seat on one of the benches and enjoy the view with your own eyes. Be prepared for a steady stream of fellow travelers and possible selfie sticks in high season. Early morning hours before bus tours arrive, or sunsets in spring and autumn, are ideal for a little more breathing room.

Recreation

✪ RAFTING THE VLTAVA RIVER

The winding curves of the Vltava River through Český Krumlov can be as much a draw as the man-made attractions on dry land. Largely during the summer months of July and August (but possible from May-September, if weather permits), groups of Czechs and international travelers pile into rented boats (sometimes decked out in themed costumes) to spend the day floating and paddling downstream. This is one of the few times that the informal version of "*ahoj*" (meaning "hi") gets tossed at everyone you see.

Multiple boat-rental companies cater to this hobby, with trips ranging from a short cruise through town (about 300-350 CZK per person) to an all-day journey from neighboring towns like Rožmberk or Vyšší Brod (about 600-750 CZK per person) on a large inflatable raft or canoe. The river is lined with pubs and restaurants for breaks and the occasional cocktail stand popping up in the middle of the water. Conditions are generally mild, but the weirs—sort of mini-waterfalls along the sides of the river that all

rafters on the river

boats slide down at various points—can provide some excitement.

Storage is usually available at the rental office, where drivers shuttle groups to their starting points, and dry bags are provided—but to be on the safe side, you should leave electronics and sentimental valuables behind. You can spot the true pros with plastic bottles of beer, attached with rope to the back of the boats, dragging behind in the water to stay cool.

Maleček Rafting and Canoe

Kaplická 27; +420 380 712 508; www.malecek.cz

The laid-back staff at Maleček offer short boat trips through the city center or longer day trips from the surrounding areas. Rental prices include the use of inflatable rafts or canoes, paddles, life-jackets, and a sealable bag for valuables. The staff will drive you to your starting point and collect the equipment at the end point of your trip. Plan to spend 15-20 minutes learning the safety regulations and signing paperwork to complete your rental. You can also stock up on beverages here (beer, soft drinks, and water) to have in the raft.

For a full-day trip, Maleček will drive your group to a starting point in Rožmberk or Vyšší Brod for ambitious athletes (6-10 hours) or to Pískárna for a half-day trip at a more leisurely pace of drifting and paddling (3-4 hours).

Rafting Krumlov

Pod Svatým Duchem 135; +420 777 066 999 or +420 777 629 316; www.rafting-krumlov.cz

Rafting Krumlov offers similar services to Maleček: inflatable rafts and canoes with equipment and transport included for one-day excursions, plus the option to rent inner-tubes and paddleboards.

Food

CZECH

Restaurace na Ostrove

Na Ostrově 171; +420 608 731 606 or +420 606 698 382; www.naostroveck.cz; 10am-10pm daily; entrées 100-150 CZK

Restaurace na Ostrove is tucked onto a small pseudo-island just across the river from the Castle Tower. This casual, friendly pub setting can hold 30 guests inside and another 60 outdoors. Mixed salads, soups, baguettes, and bar snacks offer lighter alternatives, with full meals of mostly grilled meats also available. The laid-back staff may take some time to get to each table, but they generally do so with a smile.

balcony seating by the river at Restaurace na Ostrově

✪ U Dwau Maryi

Parkán 104; +420 380 717 228; www.2marie.cz; 11am-10pm daily; entrées 125-200 CZK

The riverside location of U Dwau Maryi is as much a draw as the fantastic Old Bohemian meals. On a warm day, the wooden tables along the grass-and-stone patio are filled with families and friends discussing the day's events. During cooler months, the stone walls and cozy nooks indoors keep diners warm and dry. Try the Old Bohemian Feast of smoked meat and vegetables alongside your choice of chicken, rabbit, or pheasant.

Old Bohemian Feast from U Dwau Maryi

VEGETARIAN

Laibon

Parkán 105; +420 728 676 654; www.laibon.cz; 11am-midnight daily; entrées 125-200 CZK

Laibon offers an extensive vegetarian menu, ranging from guacamole and hummus to Indian-style dishes and soy or tempeh-based meals. The earthy tones and stone walls set a calm vibe inside, with popular riverside picnic benches during warmer months.

INTERNATIONAL

Nonna Gina

Klášterní 52; +420 380 717 187; 11am-11pm daily; entrées 150-250 CZK (cash only)

Choose from more than 35 different pizzas served alongside soups, salads, pastas, and risotto at this casual, two-story Italian restaurant, complete with red checkered tablecloths upstairs. The attention to culinary detail, with spiced olive oils for dipping pizza crusts and sparkling lemonades infused with fresh fruit, brings a mixed crowd of solo travelers, locals on their lunch break, and international friend groups down this quieter side street below the castle gates. Save room for a slice of tiramisu. Reservations recommended.

BREAKFAST AND BRUNCH

Mls Creperie

Latrán 12; +420 608 982 665; www.mls-bistros.cz; 10am-6pm daily; entrées 150-250 CZK

Start your morning with sweet or savory crêpes at MLS Creperie, or go for an egg breakfast and see if you can resist the smell of *trdelník*, a sweet doughy treat and popular guilty pleasure in touristy areas, on your way out the door. Of the multiple locations around town, the Latrán street dining room of white walls and colorful chairs is reasonably spacious.

Accommodations

Hotel U Maleho Vitka

Radniční 27; +420 380 711 925; www.hotelvitek.cz; 1,100-1,350 CZK s, 1,700-2,040 CZK d

If you prefer a slightly livelier environment, Hotel U Maleho Vitka attracts a younger crowd to their 20 rooms of simple wood furnishings and exposed beams. The historic atmosphere comes with free Wi-Fi and a central location just off the town square. Each room of these three former residences combined into one large location has a slightly different character; you can browse them online before booking.

Pension Marie

Kájovská 67; +420 222 539 539; www.pension-marie.hotel.cz; 2,000-2,500 CZK d

Pension Marie is a cozy, home-like setting for small groups and families. The 15th-century town house is decorated with simple, modern furnishings and brightly colored walls in a relatively quiet area just down the street from the Egon Schiele Gallery. Free Wi-Fi and breakfast in the on-site Italian restaurant are included.

cozy comfort at Pension Marie

Stay at Krumlovská Pohádka for a "Krumlov fairy tale."

✪ Krumlovská Pohádka

Široká 74; +420 777 127 982; www.krumlovskapohadka.cz; 3,500-4,500 CZK d

This family-owned boutique hotel seamlessly mixes centuries of design elements. The 19th-century façade and preserved 16th-century ceiling murals set a medieval tone, complemented by modern in-room amenities (think rainforest showers and Netflix-equipped televisions). The nine individually designed rooms range from a simple, functional single to a deluxe, three-room family suite. Breakfast in the onsite café is included.

Transportation

GETTING THERE

Regular bus service from Prague is the simplest, most affordable method to reach Český Krumlov. Trains run less frequently and drop you farther from town, and cars are forbidden from the city center so they require offsite parking for the length of your stay.

TRAIN

The national rail service **České dráhy** (www.cd.cz, 200-350 CZK) runs one direct, three-hour train service from Prague daily around 8am. The main **train station** of Český Krumlov is a 30-minute downhill walk from the center of town, with local taxi service available.

BUS

Locally owned **Regiojet** (www.regiojet.com, 125-200 CZK) coaches depart from Prague's Na Knížecí station in the Smichov neighborhood to Český Krumlov roughly every hour from 6am to 9pm. The three-hour journey includes complimentary hot drinks and seat-back screens with English movies. Wi-Fi is solid near major cities, but less reliable in the countryside. Regiojet stops at both the **Český Krumlov, Špičák** and **Český Krumlov, AN** bus stations on opposite sides of the city center. Both options are potentially convenient for a walk into town depending on the location of your accommodation.

Flixbus (www.flixbus.com, 200-385 CZK) also runs direct buses from multiple locations in Prague, so check your departure station carefully.

The main **bus station** (Český Krumlov, AN) is about a 10-15 minute walk from the center of town. The smaller **Český Krumlov, Špičák** bus stop may also be convenient for some travelers.

CAR

Český Krumlov is a two-to-three-hour drive, about 160 kilometers (just over 100 miles) south of Prague on **highway D3** and **Route 3** or taking **Route 4** and **Route 20/E49.** The historic center is a pedestrian area, meaning car access is restricted and tightly monitored. Some hotels may be able to request parking permits (100 CZK per day) with a single entry during specific hours for their guests, if arranged in advance. Four paid parking lots (P1, P2, P3, and P5) scattered around the city center range from 40-50 CZK per hour to 360-450 CZK per day. See www.ckrumlov.info for full details.

GETTING AROUND

The historic center of Český Krumlov is a compact, **walkable** area and a **car-free** zone. If you need a registered taxi to transport luggage from the bus or train stations to your accommodation, try **Green Taxi** (+420 800 712 712, www.green-taxi.cz).

LEAVING ČESKÝ KRUMLOV

Regiojet runs hourly bus service between Prague and Český Krumlov beginning around 6am, with the last bus to Prague departing Český Krumlov at **8pm** daily. **Flixbus** service is a little less frequent, but includes a last departure from Český Krumlov to Prague at **9pm** on weekends and **7pm**

on weekdays. The national rail service runs one direct **train** from Český Krumlov to Prague around 2pm daily.

Public transportation connections without connecting through Prague are somewhat limited, but the national rail service does run once-daily trains in the afternoon either east to **Brno** (about 6 hours, 250 CZK) or northwest to **Pilsen** (4.5 hours, 200-220 CZK), both requiring a transfer in the town of České Budějovice.

BRNO

The Czech Republic's second-largest city, Brno is regularly referred to as the "capital of Moravia" for both its historical and modern importance. The town has a subtle sense of humor, with light-hearted legends hidden in the details of its historical sights. Modern architecture is treated with a sense of pride usually reserved for the towering Gothic spires of the Brno skyline. The "Moravian capital" went from official governmental distinction to a proud nickname in 1949, when then-Czechoslovakia was reorganized into 13 smaller administrative

HIGHLIGHTS

- **OSSUARY AT ST. JAMES CHURCH:** Brno's ossuary—the second largest in Europe—isn't as famous as the one in Kutná Hora, but the local sculptures and classical music composed specifically for its halls make it special in its own right (page 255).
- **OLD TOWN HALL:** Admire the symbolic representations of local legends, then climb the tower for panoramic city views (page 257).
- **10-Z BUNKER:** Explore a former nuclear fallout shelter—recently declassified, historically curated, and open to the public (page 258).
- **BARS AND PUBS:** Sample craft cocktails in inventive atmospheres or join the beer-lovers in a pub to experience the upbeat vibe of local nightlife (page 260).

regions called *kraje*. The continued use of the name symbolizes a friendly rivalry with Prague, the western capital of Bohemia. These days, Brno's buzzing nightlife, international and vegetarian dining options, and tourist attractions (both above and below ground) draw visitors to the vibrant university town.

ORIENTATION

Brno's cobblestoned streets are incredibly walkable. City life centers around **Náměstí Svobody (Freedom Square)** and most tourist destinations, as well as the main **train** and **bus stations**, are reachable within a 15-minute walk. The urban city center is framed by the hillside silhouettes of **Špilberk Castle** to the west and **Peter and Paul's Cathedral** on Petrov Hill to the south. The green parks around **Masaryk University** and **Brno's National Theater** form another informal border on the northeast corner. Most visitors will spend a majority of time within this central area, unless you choose to visit **Villa Tugendhat**. The popular architectural landmark is in a residential neighborhood to the north, about a 30-minute walk or a 15-minute tram ride from the city center.

PLANNING YOUR TIME

Trying to see all of Brno's sights in one day could cause your legs to give out after racing between hilltop landmarks, or your eyes to gloss over from architectural overload. Roughly **two days** in Brno gives you a more relaxed pace, with the opportunity to enjoy the city's renowned nightlife. Regular trains (about 2.5 hours from Prague) and bus connections (roughly 3.5 hours from Prague) provide flexible options for arrival and departure times. Additional destinations nearby include the Baroque beauty of **Olomouc**, about an hour northeast, or the châteaux and vineyards surrounding **Mikulov**, roughly an hour to the south.

Do you remember why the Town Hall spire is twisted?

SIGHTSEEING PASSES

A **Brnopas** (290 CZK for two days, 390 CZK for three days, www.gotobrno.cz) could be worth the money depending on your itinerary. It includes free entry to the Old Town Hall Tower, the Ossuary at St. James Church, the Tower at St. James Church, the Tower at Saints Peter and Paul's Cathedral, and the gardens at Villa Tugendhat, plus free public transport. There are also discounts at Špilberk Castle, 10-Z Bunker, and a 100-CZK discount on performances at Janaček Theater. You can buy it online at www.gotobrno.cz, or stop by the **Tourist Information Center** in the Brno Town Hall to pick one up in person.

Itinerary Ideas

Browse the program of Brno's Janáček Theatre while planning your trip to find a performance that suits your style. A few days before arrival, make reservations for lunch at **4pokoje**, dinner at **Soul Bistro**, and drinks at **Bar Který Neexistuje**. Modern architecture fans should book roughly six months in advance to add an interior tour of **Villa Tugendhat** to this itinerary.

DAY 1

1 After an early-morning train ride from Prague, drop off any luggage at your accommodation and refuel with a light breakfast and specialty coffee at **SKOG**.

2 Walk toward the spires of **Cathedral of Saints Peter and Paul** on Petrov Hill. Admire the stained-glass interior before climbing the church tower for a southern perspective over the city. If you arrive around 11am, you'll hear the church bell chime as if it's actually noon.

3 Stroll through the former market square of Zelný trh (Cabbage Market) and turn left onto Radnická Street to reach the **Old Town Hall**. Look for the twisted spire, the "dragon" of Brno, and an infamous wagon wheel around the entrance. Then take 30 minutes to climb the tower for a city-center perspective of the surrounding silhouettes. On your way out, stop by the ground-floor tourist information center to buy two tram tickets (and maybe a few postcards).

Brno

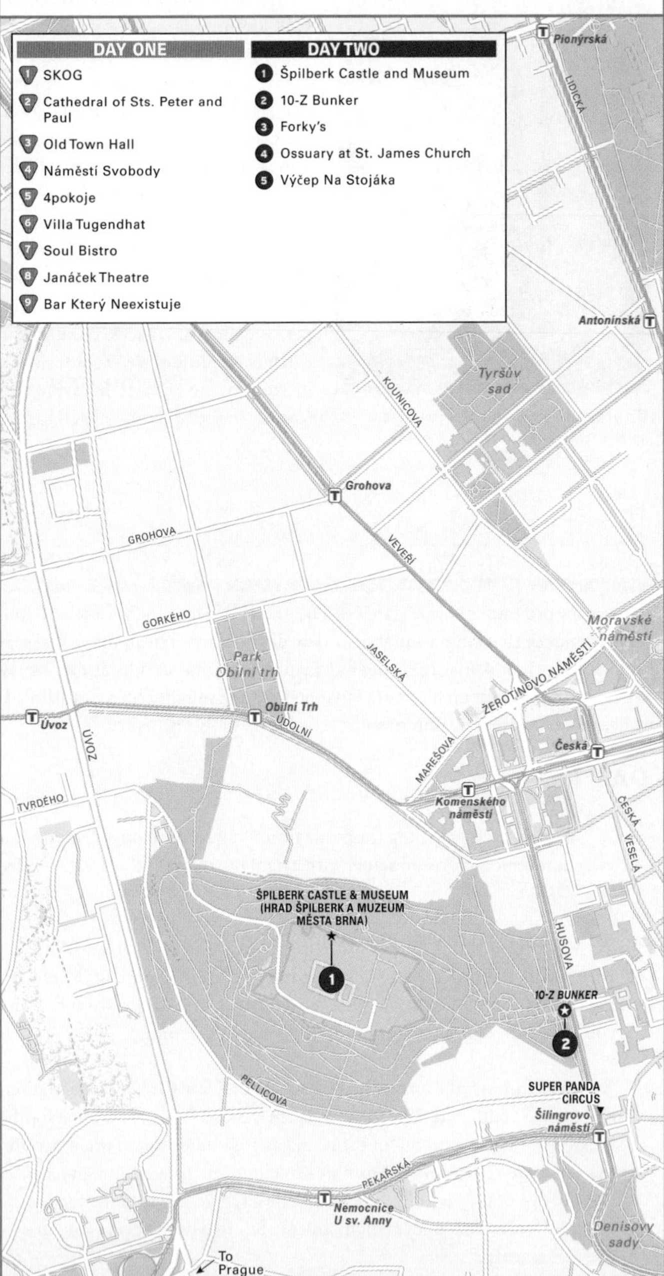
DAY ONE
1 SKOG
2 Cathedral of Sts. Peter and Paul
3 Old Town Hall
4 Náměstí Svobody
5 4pokoje
6 Villa Tugendhat
7 Soul Bistro
8 Janáček Theatre
9 Bar Který Neexistuje
DAY TWO
1 Špilberk Castle and Museum
2 10-Z Bunker
3 Forky's
4 Ossuary at St. James Church
5 Výčep Na Stojáka
Pionýrská
LIDICKÁ
Antonínská
Tyršův sad
KOUNICOVA
Grohova
GROHOVA
VEVEŘÍ
GORKÉHO
Moravské náměstí
ŽEROTÍNOVO NÁMĚSTÍ
JASELSKÁ
Park Obilní trh
Obilní Trh
ÚDOLNÍ
Úvoz
ÚVOZ
MAREŠOVA
Česká
Komenského náměstí
TVRDÉHO
ČESKÁ
VESELÁ
ŠPILBERK CASTLE & MUSEUM (HRAD ŠPILBERK A MUZEUM MĚSTA BRNA)
HUSOVA
10-Z BUNKER
PELLICOVA
SUPER PANDA CIRCUS
Šilingrovo náměstí
PEKAŘSKÁ
Nemocnice U sv. Anny
Denisovy sady
To Prague

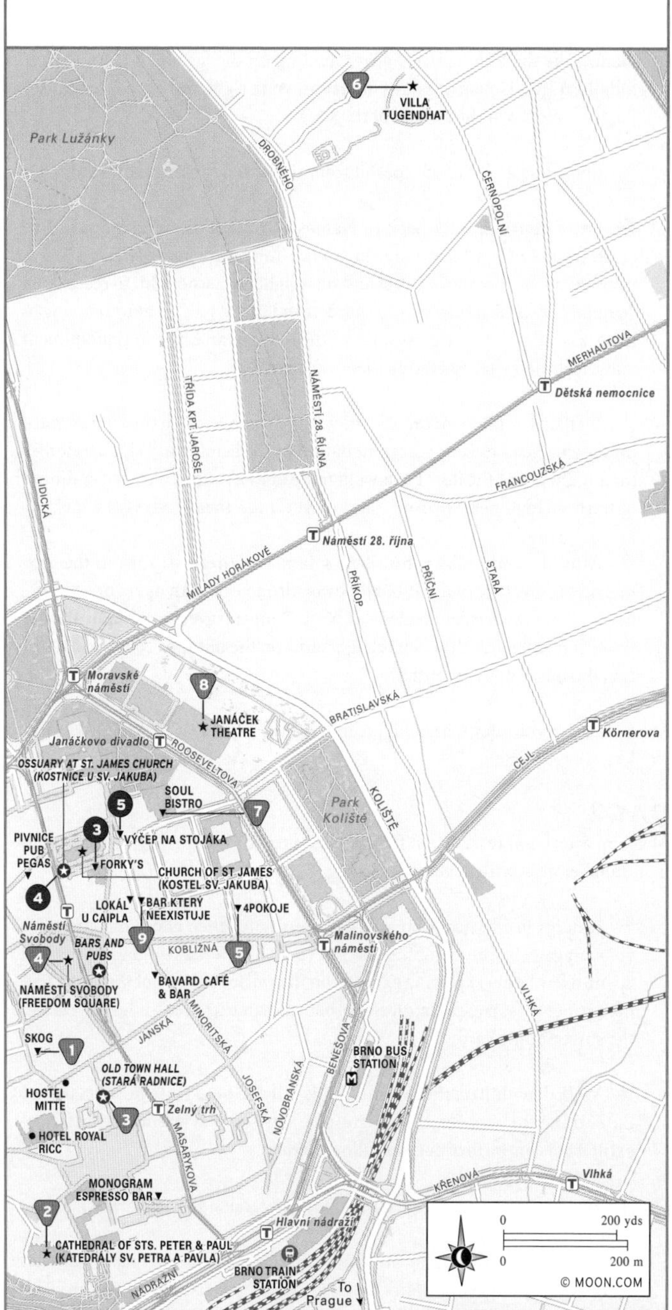

VILLA TUGENDHAT
Park Lužánky
DROBNÉHO
ČERNOPOLNÍ
MERHAUTOVA
Dětská nemocnice
TŘÍDA KPT. JAROŠE
NÁMĚSTÍ 28. ŘÍJNA
FRANCOUZSKÁ
LIDICKÁ
Náměstí 28. října
MILADY HORÁKOVÉ
PŘÍKOP
PŘÍČNÍ
STARÁ
Moravské náměstí
JANÁČEK THEATRE
BRATISLAVSKÁ
Körnerova
Janáčkovo divadlo
ROOSEVELTOVA
OSSUARY AT ST. JAMES CHURCH (KOSTNICE U SV. JAKUBA)
CEJL
SOUL BISTRO
Park Koliště
KOLIŠTĚ
VÝČEP NA STOJÁKA
PIVNICE PUB PEGAS
FORKY'S
CHURCH OF ST JAMES (KOSTEL SV. JAKUBA)
LOKÁL U CAIPLA
BAR KTERÝ NEEXISTUJE
4POKOJE
Náměstí Svobody
BARS AND PUBS
KOBLIŽNÁ
Malinovského náměstí
NÁMĚSTÍ SVOBODY (FREEDOM SQUARE)
BAVARD CAFÉ & BAR
JANSKÁ
MINORITSKÁ
VLHKÁ
SKOG
BENEŠOVA
BRNO BUS STATION
OLD TOWN HALL (STARÁ RADNICE)
HOSTEL MITTE
JOSEFSKÁ
NOVOBRANSKÁ
Zelný trh
HOTEL ROYAL RICC
MASARYKOVA
MONOGRAM ESPRESSO BAR
KŘENOVÁ
Vlhká
Hlavní nádraží
CATHEDRAL OF STS. PETER & PAUL (KATEDRÁLY SV. PETRA A PAVLA)
BRNO TRAIN STATION
NÁDRAŽNÍ
To Prague
0
200 yds
0
200 m
© MOON.COM

4 Head next to Náměstí Svobody (Freedom Square). Ignore the crowds posing in front of the Astronomical Clock and find the more artistic monuments, like the four carved figures holding up the façade of Dům U Čtyř mamlasů (the House of Four Giants) on your right and the 17th-century Plague Column at the far end of the square.

5 Enjoy a seasonal lunch special from the afternoon menu at 4pokoje.

6 From 4pokoje, walk back to Náměstí Svobody (Freedom Square) to catch tram #9 for a 10-minute ride to the Tomanova stop. Then walk five minutes down Tomanova Street and turn right on Černopolní to reach Villa Tugendhat. Grab a ticket for the garden and spend half an hour relaxing in the grass, admiring the glass walls of the modern architectural monument and a hillside view over the city from the north.

7 Walk five minutes to the Tomanova stop again to catch the #9 tram back into town. Head to your accommodation to freshen up and change clothes for a night at the theater. Then walk to Soul Bistro for an early-ish dinner of fresh salad or hearty risotto (and maybe a pre-theater glass of wine).

8 After dinner, walk over to Brno's Janáček Theatre. Take in the geometric architecture of the 1960s lobby before enjoying an opera or a performance from the resident ballet company. Budget travelers and non-theater types can still enjoy the colorful lightshow on the outdoor courtyard fountain during summer months.

9 Finish your day with a nightcap from the extensive cocktail list at Bar Který Neexistuje.

DAY 2

Make an afternoon reservation for the Ossuary at St. James Church around 2 or 3pm before starting your sightseeing.

1 Indulge in a leisurely breakfast at your hotel, then check out and store your luggage before climbing the hill to Špilberk Castle and Museum. Spend a few hours exploring exhibits on the storied history of the castle and the former prison area. In nice weather, add an extra half-hour to relax in the surrounding gardens.

2 Walk downhill on the east side of the hill and onto Husova Street to find the entrance to 10-Z Bunker. Spend about an hour navigating the historical exhibits of this former nuclear fallout shelter.

3 Head over to Forky's for a delicious cafeteria-style vegetarian lunch.

4 After lunch, walk along St. James Church to the large cement slab that marks the underground stairs to the Ossuary at St. James Church. Pick

up a laminated English description from the ticket counter and spend 30-45 minutes exploring the artfully arranged bones with a classical music soundtrack. On your way out of the Ossuary, look up and take a moment to giggle at the tiny sculpture of a man exposing his rear end on the window of Church of St. James. Then head inside the cathedral and enjoy a 20-minute wander through the light-filled interior.

5 It's never too early for a beer in the Czech Republic. Walk around the rear of St. James Church to find **Výčep Na stojáka,** a standing-room-only pub, and indulge in a late-afternoon or early-evening beer before heading back to Prague (or onward to the nearby towns of Mikulov or Olomouc).

Sights

✪ OSSUARY AT ST. JAMES CHURCH (KOSTNICE U SV. JAKUBA)

Jakubské náměstí; +420 515 919 793; www.ticbrno.cz; 9:30am-6pm Tues-Sun; 140 CZK; tram stops Náměstí Svobody or Česká

Kutna Hora is probably the most well-known Czech town for skeletal sightseeing, but a discovery beneath Jakubské náměstí may be changing that status. Overcrowded cemeteries in the 18th century often led to remains being excavated every 10 to 12 years, when skeletal remains would be moved to underground ossuaries. The Ossuary at the Church of St. James, discovered in 2001, is estimated to hold around 50,000 skeletal remains from residents lost to cholera, plague, the Thirty Years' War, and the Swedish siege of 1645. This makes it Europe's second-largest ossuary, behind the catacombs in Paris.

The underground space is organized into columns and pyramids built from bones, with paths for visitors to observe and pay their respects. A curated selection of contemporary sculptures adds to the display and a soundtrack composed specifically for the experience completes the serene scene, which has been open to the public since 2012. No more than 20 visitors are allowed to enter at one time, so reservations are recommended.

CHURCH OF ST. JAMES (KOSTEL SV. JAKUBA)

Jakubské náměstí 2; +420 542 212 039; www.svatyjakubbrno.wz.cz; 9am-6:30pm daily; free; tram stops Náměstí Svobody or Česká

One of Brno's (literally) cheeky monuments adorns the exterior walls

interior of St. James's Church

of the Church of St. James. A small stone man called *Nehaňba* (meaning "Unashamed" or "Shameless") can be seen gripping the top of one of the exterior windows and exposing his bottom in the direction of Petrov Hill. One theory is that architect Anton Pilgram (mentioned again in an Old Town Hall legend) was poking fun at the slow construction work on the Cathedral of Saints Peter and Paul.

The interior of this bright 13th-century church, renovated from Romanesque to Gothic to Baroque and to Gothic again over the centuries, is unusual for its three aisles of the same height. The décor is simpler than Brno's Cathedral of Saints Peter and Paul, with tall arched windows and intricate patterns of wooden beams lining the vaulted ceilings, creating an aesthetic more serene than ostentatious.

the central St. James Church

NÁMĚSTÍ SVOBODY (FREEDOM SQUARE)

free; tram stop Náměstí Svobody

Business and trade have filled this market "square" (actually a triangle) since at least the 13th century, when it was known as *Dolní trh* (Lower Market). Christmas and Easter markets cover the cobblestones in colder months, and summertime events bring lounge chairs and sidewalk seating ideal for people-watching into the open space. Visitors to Brno are likely to criss-cross this square a few times while navigating the city, making it easy to enjoy as part of a walk to your next destination.

In contrast to Prague's ornate, historical Astronomical Clock, the city of Brno installed a large, black granite timepiece on the southern end of the square in 2010. This structure is often referred to as Brno's "Astronomical Clock," although it doesn't exactly display the positions of the sun, moon, and stars—or the time, for that matter. I'll leave the shape open to the viewer's interpretation (the design was inspired by a bullet, but is most often compared to male genitalia). Crowds start to gather around the sculpture as 11am approaches, and early birds arrive hours in advance to stick their arms inside four holes around the sculpture. When the church bells of the Cathedral of Saints Peter and Paul chime twelve times at 11am to commemorate the defeat of the Swedish Army, a small glass marble drops from inside the clock. People hold their spots for up to an hour, hoping for a chance to catch the once-a-day souvenir.

The rest of the square holds architectural monuments with more traditional, postcard-style beauty. If you look closely at **Dům U Čtyř mamlasů** (the House of Four Giants), just behind the Astronomical Clock, you'll spot four carved figures holding the façade of the building on their shoulders. A Baroque **Plague Column** from the late 17th century stands tall in the northwest corner of the square. In summer months, **Česká Street** behind the column is often shaded by a canopy of colorful umbrellas, auctioned off each year to support various charities.

✪ OLD TOWN HALL (STARÁ RADNICE)

Radnická 2; +420 542 427 150; www.ticbrno.cz; May, 10am-8pm daily; June-Aug, 10am-10pm daily; Sept-Oct, 10am-6pm daily; Nov, 10am-6pm Fri-Sun; entrance 70 CZK; tram stop Zelný trh

The Old Town Hall holds more of the city's fantastical tales. The Brno Dragon (okay, so it's actually a taxidermied crocodile) hangs from the ceiling just inside the entrance. One theory posits that the exotic beast was imported by a wealthy resident in the city's early days, meaning the creature could easily have been mistaken for a monster by locals who had never seen one. Anyway, the crocodile terrorized the town until a visiting butcher came up with a plan. He wrapped limes in an ox fur (or squeezed them onto it, depending on who tells the tale) and left it for the dragon to eat. The crocodile then drank from the river, and his stomach expanded and burst, slaying the dragon that now decorates the municipal building.

The wagon wheel on the wall beside him has a less incredible origin story. Georg Birck from the town of Lednice bet a group of his friends (likely over many beers) that he could cut down a tree, carve it into a wagon wheel, and roll it to Brno in less than a day. His skeptical friends accepted, and were shocked when he pulled off the task. Spoiler alert: this wheel on the wall didn't actually come from a single tree, but the legend did inspire an annual event of rolling wooden wheels between the two towns each October.

The final fantastical tale of the Old Town Hall explains the front of the building. If you look closely at the sculpted turrets over the entrance, you'll find that one appears to twist off track. This is supposedly because architect Anton Pilgram was unhappy about not being paid. Of course, the other side counters that it was actually a result of the architect drinking too much. Either way, don't let structural concerns stop you from climbing the tower for a panoramic view from the city center.

These days, the Town Hall functions largely as a draw for visitors, with an information center and a panoramic view of the city center rewarding visitors who climb the stairs of its 200-foot (63-meter) tower.

Climb Brno's Town Hall Tower for great views.

CATHEDRAL OF SAINTS PETER AND PAUL (KATEDRÁLA SV. PETRA A PAVLA)

Petrov 9; +420 543 235 031; 8:15am-6:30pm Mon-Sat, 7am-6:30pm Sun; free (tower entrance 40 CZK); tram stop Zelný trh

The towering shape of the Cathedral of Saints Peter and Paul, also called *Petrov* for the hill it sits on, might look familiar to any visitors who have looked at their Czech currency. The neo-Gothic cathedral graces the face of the 10-CZK coin and is an icon of the Brno skyline. Renovations expanded the 13th-century Romanesque Basilica that previously stood on this site. The unusual central location of the towers, crowd-funded and added to the building in the early 1900s, are the result of limited space on the top of Petrov Hill. Highlights of the ornate Baroque interior include stained-glass windows that depict the life of Jesus. Climbing 30 steps to the top of the tower gives you an incredible vantage point to admire the city.

When you leave the cathedral, keep your eyes peeled for another pair of saints, Cyril and Methodius, carved in minimalist, post-modern style: two faceless bodies marked with crosses. This statue, on a small platform just downhill from the entrance of the cathedral, was unveiled in 2013, marking the 1,150th anniversary of the pair's arrival in Moravia. Cyril and Methodius are credited with bringing Christianity in a Slavic language to the region.

Don't be confused if you hear the cathedral's clock chime 12 times on the 11:00 hour. Legend has it that in 1645, during the Thirty Years' War, the Swedish army was frustrated after months of unsuccessful attacks. The general declared that if they didn't take the city by noon, they would turn around and go home. An enterprising local decided to reset the bells to one hour earlier, and the Swedish army stuck to their word and retreated.

✪ 10-Z BUNKER

Husova ulice; +420 542 210 622; www.10-z.cz; 11:30am-6:45pm Tues-Sun; tram stop Šilingrovo náměstí

The purpose of this underground shelter has varied from wartime protection to recreation and education over the last century. Neighborhood residents raced inside to hide from World War II bombings in November of 1944. Then the bunker enjoyed a brief stint as a wholesale wine shop in the mid-1940s before being seized by Communists in 1948. Its subsequent conversion to a 500-person nuclear fallout shelter cloaked the space in confidentiality for decades until its declassification in 1993. The title "10-Z" is a holdover from its top-secret code name.

Explore a former bomb shelter at 10-Z Bunker.

Today, neon orange signs welcome visitors inside. Historian and academic Pavel Paleček has worked to create an educational space that defies its oppressive past. The resulting museum and hostel opened in 2016, decorated with multimedia exhibits, artifacts donated by local residents, and Wi-Fi—powered by the only functioning wires of an original switchboard. A 40-60 minute guided tour in English (240 CZK per person) can be booked online in advance and customized to guests' interests, offering a bit more context and technical insight than wandering the maze of hallways on your own (150 CZK), which is also enjoyable.

Špilberk Castle and Museum

ŠPILBERK CASTLE AND MUSEUM (HRAD ŠPILBERK A MUZEUM MĚSTA BRNA)

Špilberk 1; +420 542 123 611; www.spilberk.cz; April-Sept, 10am-6pm; Oct-Mar, 9am-5pm; 150 CZK; tram stop Komenského náměstí

Just outside the city center, on a hill beside Petrov, sits the Špilberk Castle and Museum of the City of Brno. Czech King Přemysl Otakar II established the fortified castle in the 13th century to give Moravian rulers a residence that commanded respect. The building changed hands throughout the centuries. It was owned by the city of Brno in the 16th century, confiscated by the Habsburg empire in the 17th century, and converted to a prison in the 17th and 18th centuries, later to be used by the Nazis. Today the building is back in the hands of the city and houses the Museum of the City of Brno, with the surrounding grounds offering yet another perspective to view the city from above. The permanent exhibits of the former prison grounds and historical photographs charting the city's architectural development make the castle interior a worthy draw, alongside the hilltop views.

VILLA TUGENDHAT

Černopolní 45; +420 515 511 015; www.tugendhat.eu; Mar-Dec, 10am-6pm Tues-Sun; Jan-Feb, 9am-5pm Wed-Sun; tram stops Tomanova or Dětská nemocnice

The Functionalist style of Villa Tugendhat was overseen by German-American architect Ludwig Mies van der Rohe around 1930 at the request of Greta and Fritz Tugendhat, a wealthy Jewish family. The modern family home included rooms for their children and nannies, as well as areas to entertain. The Tugenhadt family was forced to flee in 1938, and the carefully restored furniture and grounds maintain the historical appearance designed by its innovative creator.

A tour of Villa Tugendhat, which requires around six months of advance notice, allows you to experience Brno's UNESCO-protected jewel of modern architecture. The early-20th-century geometric design is unique in a country famous for spire-filled skylines. Entrance is possible only in the presence of a licensed guide. The 60-minute tour (300 CZK) points out decorative details and the history of the architect's and residents' families, while a 90-minute tour (350 CZK) tacks on technical elements like the engine rooms, laundry, and storage spaces. Access to the garden, included in the guided tours, is also available on its own (50 CZK) for those who just want to admire the building's exterior and hillside view of the city.

Villa Tugendhat sits on the outskirts of the city and is accessible via tram #9 from the city center or by taxi. Walking from the city center takes roughly 30 minutes, uphill.

Bars and Nightlife

✪ BARS AND PUBS

Thanks to its population of university students and young residents who stick around after graduation, Brno's landscape of laid-back pubs and craft cocktail bars is rarely short of customers. The streets around Jakubské náměstí in particular are lined in almost every direction with restaurants and bars (and is continuously expanding).

Bar Který Neexistuje

Dvořákova 1; +420 734 878 602; www.barkteryneexistuje.cz; 5pm-2am Sun-Tues, 5pm-3am Wed-Thurs, 5pm-4am Fri-Sat; cocktails 100-150 CZK

Despite its name, Bar který neexistuje (or "The Bar That Doesn't Exist") is absolutely real. Passionate mixologists serve craft cocktails on two floors. Choose from a specialty cocktail list, an extensive-is-an-understatement list of spirits, or just describe your mood to the staff for a custom-made order. Reservations are recommended to snag a seat in this busy, sophisticated space, where brightly lit liquor bottles serve as the backdrop.

Super Panda Circus

Šilingrovo náměstí 3; +420 734 878 603; www.superpandacircus.cz; 6pm-2am Mon-Sat; cocktails 125-150 CZK

In the words of Super Panda Circus, this is "a completely different world where nothing makes sense." The cocktail experience involves surprise flavors and unusual containers in a speakeasy-style environment, where patrons have to ring a doorbell and wait for an available seat. Join an upbeat, international crowd, preferably at the bar, where you can watch the staff show off their flair for flipping bottles and passion for the craft.

Výčep Na Stojáka

Běhounská 16; +420 702 202 048; www.vycepnastojaka.cz; noon-midnight Mon-Fri, 2pm-midnight Sat-Sun; beer 45-65 CZK

The local beer-drinking crowd spills out of Výčep Na Stojáka and onto the surrounding streets of Jakubské náměstí. The name roughly translates to "A Place for Standing," with a minimally decorated interior of tall tables and no stools in sight. The selection of rotating microbrews brings a steady stream of the local university student crowds and young professionals meeting after work.

Performing Arts

THEATER

Janáček Theatre

Rooseveltova 1-7; +420 542 158 111; www.ndbrno.cz; tram stop Janáčkovo divadlo

Much like Prague's National Museum, Brno's Janáček Theatre was a cultural idea that was decades in the making. The 1880s proposal faced decades of planning, crowd-funding, design competitions, world wars, and changes in government, delaying the actual construction until the 1960s.

Janáček Theatre

This historical shift meant that, in contrast to the golden glamour of Prague's old-world concert halls, Brno's resident opera and ballet companies are housed in the clean, minimalist lines of modern architecture, including an open foyer of white marble walls and a comfortable 1,100-seat auditorium. For a performance with a local connection, try an opera by the namesake Czech composer Leoš Janáček with English surtitles or a ballet performance of *Romeo and Juliet,* which made its world premiere in Brno in 1938.

The cement courtyard in front of the theater offers its own free entertainment for non-ticket holders, with a geometric fountain and colorful projected lightshow surrounded by lines of benches and greenery. The water feature is particularly beautiful in the evenings with the glowing lights of the theater as a backdrop.

Festivals and Events

SUMMER

The **Ignis Brunensis fireworks festival** (www.ignisbrunensis.cz) lights up the sky in late May and June each summer, while the **Marathon of Music festival** (www.maratonhudby.cz) brightens August with multi-genre concerts and buskers performing across the city.

pop-up circus at Brno's Marathon of Music

WINTER

Christmas markets twinkle in city squares in December, and a **Queer Ball** (www.queerball.cz/en) celebrates the LGBTQ community in February or March.

Food

This cosmopolitan dining destination caters to a variety of tastes, including an exceptional array of vegetarian-friendly options and a specialty coffee scene so good that it inspired the creation of the **European Coffee Trip** blog (www.europeancoffeetrip.com).

CZECH

Pivnice Pub Pegas

Jakubská 4; +420 542 210 104 or +420 542 211 232; brnopivovar.hotelpegas.com; 10am-midnight Mon-Thurs and Sat, 10am-1am, Fri, 11am-11pm Sun; entrées 175-350 CZK

Pivnice Pub Pegas, located inside the hotel of the same name, is a tourist-friendly environment with the accessibility of English menus and vegetarian options (try the risotto). The staff are friendly and multi-lingual, and the décor of dark wooden tables and arched doorways sets a traditional Czech pub vibe. Try a Pegas beer from the first on-site microbrewery to open in Moravia (in 1989).

Lokál U Caipla

Kozí 3; +420 731 594 671; lokal-ucaipla.ambi.cz; 11am-midnight Mon-Thurs, 11am-1am Fri-Sat, 11am-10pm Sun; entrées 115-400 CZK

If you're looking for a modern Czech pub experience, the trusted Ambiente Restaurant Group has a presence in Brno as well. Lokál U Caipla serves high-quality meat-and-cheese-based meals alongside light Pilsner and dark Kozel beers at long wooden tables that wrap around the restaurant. Bright silver tanks keeping the *pivo* cold add a modern, industrial element to the décor.

INTERNATIONAL

Soul Bistro

Jezuitská 7; +420 773 179 212; 8am-10pm Mon-Thurs, 8am-11pm Fri, 10am-11pm Sat; entrées 100-200 CZK; tram stops Janáčkovo divadlo or Náměstí Svobody

Stop by the casually cool Soul Bistro for a breakfast bagel in the morning or a selection of seasonal lunch specials ranging from fish & chips to stir-fried rice. The dining room is divided into intimate spaces with minimalist, Scandinavian-inspired design. Soul Bistro is just off the busy square around St. Jacob's church, pairing nicely with a visit to the Ossuary or a beer at Výčep Na Stojáka.

sophisticated style at Soul Bistro

✪ 4pokoje

Vachova 6; +420 770 122 102; www.miluju4pokoje.cz; 7am-3am Sun-Tues, 7am-4am Wed-Thurs, 7am-5am Fri-Sat; entrées 150-250 CZK

The atmosphere, menu, soundtrack, and prices at 4pokoje change nine times throughout the day. In other words, every visit in the 22 hours the venue is open is a different experience. The name, meaning "four rooms," describes the café, bistro, bar, and nightclub spread across multiple floors, each with distinct, brightly colored and neon-lit personalities. The rotating menu has plenty of international and vegetarian options, like pancakes and breakfast sandwiches, hot dogs, and specialty cocktails. You'll get hearty comfort food in winter and refreshing fare on a hot day.

VEGETARIAN

Forky's

Jakubské Náměstí 1; +420 515 908 665; www.forkys.eu; 8am-9pm Mon-Thurs, 8am-10pm Fri, 9am-10pm Sat, 9am-6pm Sun; entrées 75-150 CZK

Forky's is an entirely plant-based, vegan concept. Their 2018 move into a large, multi-story space on Jakubské náměstí pays tribute to the growing demand for ethical, health-conscious cuisine among a younger generation of Czechs and international residents, including no plastic packaging. Try one of the Asian-inspired noodle dishes or veggie burgers for a hearty meal, or build your own Superbowl of fresh vegetables.

BREAKFAST AND BRUNCH

Bavard Café & Bar

Poštovská 4; +420 734 142 108; 7am-5pm Tues-Fri, 9am-5pm Sat-Sun; entrées 125-175 CZK

You'll spot Bavard Café & Bar's unassuming location from the glowing coffee pot over the entrance. Young couples and crowds of friends at outdoor tables devour benedicts with various toppings over fluffy bread soaked in hollandaise sauce during the warmer months. This popular brunch spot may require a short wait, but the staff will keep you in coffee when the kitchen gets backed up.

COFFEE, TEA, AND SWEETS

SKOG

Dominikánské náměstí 5; +420 607 098 557; www.skog.cz; 8am-1am Mon-Thurs, 8am-2am Fri, 10am-2am Sat, 12pm-10pm Sun; entrées 50-150 CZK

SKOG is the embodiment of modern coffee culture: pallet-based furniture and wooden spool tables, minimalist touches of fresh flowers and exposed lightbulbs, solid Wi-Fi for the freelance crowd, and a purist approach to specialty coffee. The two-story space just around the corner from the Town Hall offers plenty of seating spread across creaky wood floors. Seasonal food options are strictly vegan and vegetarian.

SKOG is a staple of Brno's specialty coffee scene.

Monogram Espresso Bar

Kapucínské náměstí 12; +420 603 282 866; www.monogramespressobar.cz; 8:30am-6:30pm Mon-Fri, 10am-5pm Sat

Monogram Espresso Bar earns a discerning stamp of approval from the European Coffee Trip blog, run by two Brno-based caffeine connoisseurs. The intimate space draws an informed

Forky's is a vegan and vegetarian favorite.

crowd able to discuss the quality of beans, preferred preparation method, and favorite flavors from around the globe. The passionate staff are usually happy to share their expertise in English.

Accommodations

✪ Hostel Mitte

Panská 11; +420 734 622 340; www.hostelmitte.com; 450-1,000 CZK rooms, 1,350-2,000 CZK private apartments

Both the ground floor café and the individual rooms of Hostel Mitte manage to squeeze quality and personality into every bit of available space. The hostel rooms are decorated around historic trivia connected to the city (The Battle of Austerlitz or Vila Tugenhadt), while private apartments focus on famous names like Alfons Mucha or Mozart. Details in each room give travelers information on where to explore the legacies of their namesakes. Cozy rooms and curtains around the bunks provide an air of peace and privacy.

Hostel Mitte and Café in one

10-Z Bunker

Husova ulice; +420 542 210 622; www.10-z.cz; around 625 CZK dorm beds, 850 CZK s, 1,800-2,200 CZK private rooms, 1,250 CZK d

Spending the night inside 10-Z Bunker's former nuclear fallout shelter is an extraordinary historical experience. Rooms range from 30-bed dorms to 4-to-5-person private rooms, 2-person quarters, or a single officer's quarters, all with shared bathrooms. Pack warm PJs for a night in a sleeping bag on military-grade bunks, with décor of desks, lockers, and artifacts. A modest but yummy breakfast from the cafeteria is included.

Hotel Royal Ricc

Starobrněnská 10; +420 542 219 262; www.royalricc.cz; 2,000-2,500 CZK d

The family-run Hotel Royal Ricc combines old-world charm and a convenient location just off Brno's cabbage market square. Exposed beams, rich dark wood furnishing, and muraled staircases add an air of elegance to a comfortable atmosphere, with 24-hour reception available to answer questions. Don't skip the beautifully presented breakfast buffet before heading uphill to the Cathedral of Saints Peter and Paul or down a few streets to the town hall.

Transportation

GETTING THERE

A train ride from Prague to Brno offers the most comfortable ride for a reasonable price.

FROM PRAGUE

TRAIN

The national rail service **České dráhy** (www.cd.cz, 125-350 CZK) takes about two-and-a-half hours from Prague's main train station (Praha hl. n.) to Brno's main train station **(Brno hl. n.)**, leaving roughly twice an hour from 4:45am until almost midnight.

Local providers **Regiojet** (www.regiojet.com) run direct two-and-a-half hour trains (100-175 CZK) roughly every two hours from around 5:30am until roughly 8:30pm. Splurge on business class (250-450 CZK) for a reserved leather seat in a four-seat compartment, free sparkling wine and coffee on departure, food available for purchase, and solid Wi-Fi.

The main Brno train station is located just off the center of town, with an easy walk to most accommodation options.

BUS

Czech company **Regiojet** (www.regiojet.com) runs three-and-a-half-hour coach service (150-200 CZK) from Prague's Florenc Bus Station to **Brno's Grand Hotel**, located directly in front of the main train station. Service often includes an attendant offering complimentary hot drinks, plus in-ride entertainment with movies in English on seat-back TV screens. Wi-Fi is solid near major cities, but less reliable in the countryside.

Leo Express (www.leoexpress.com) and **Flixbus** (www.flixbus.com) also offer regular bus connections (150-375 CZK) from Florenc.

Brno's main **bus stops** are both located in the city center, offering an easy walk to most accommodation options.

CAR

Brno is located about 210 kilometers (130 miles) and between two and three hours (depending on traffic) southeast of Prague on **highway D1/E65.** As of new 2018 rules, visitors to Brno are only allowed to drive or use street parking in limited areas outside the center, with fees of 20-40 CZK per hour (see www.parkovanivbrne.cz for details). Many parking garages have limited daytime hours or a 24-hour limit, but **Pinki Park** (www.bkom.cz) offers 88 spaces of multi-day parking for around 300 CZK per day.

FROM MIKULOV

Regional bus 105, run by the **South Moravian Integrated Public Transport System** (locally known as *Integrovaný Dopravní Systém Jihomoravského Kraje,* www.idsjmk.cz, 60 CZK, just over an hour's journey) departs from the main train station around once an hour, and stops at Mikulov's u parku bus stop in the south and the Brněnská stop on the northwestern side of town before continuing to Brno. This option is only appropriate for travelers with small hand luggage.

GETTING AROUND

Brno's city center is fairly flat and **walkable,** with easy public transport options (www.dpmb.cz, 16 CZK) that include a **tram** line running through the center of town. Local rideshare app **Liftago** offers local service around Brno, or you can use the **City Taxi** service (+420 777 014 004, www.citytaxibrno.cz).

LEAVING BRNO

Buses and trains to Prague run consistently from around 2am to midnight via **Regiojet** (2.5 to 3 hours, buses 200-250 CZK, trains 100-400 CZK), and every 1-2 hours from about 7:30am to 5:40pm on **LeoExpress** (buses, 2.5 to 3 hours, 100-150 CZK). The Czech national rail service runs hourly direct service from around 4:30am to 9:30pm (trains, 2.5 to 3 hours, 200-300 CZK).

Direct buses to Olomouc leave Brno with morning, afternoon, and evening service finishing around 6:30pm on **Regiojet** (1 hour, 89 CZK), or one daily route from **LeoExpress** at 9:30pm (325 CZK). Czech national rail service to Olomouc, with transfers, is also available until around 9:30pm (1.5 to 2 hours, 100-150 CZK).

Travelers with luggage should use the Czech national rail service with indirect service to Mikulov from around 4am to 8:30pm (1.5 hours, 100-125 CZK trains), changing in Břeclav. Local regional buses from the South Moravian Integrated Public Transport System run every 1-2 hours from around 5am to 10:30pm (1 hour, 60 CZK), for travelers with light hand luggage only.

LEDNICE AND VALTICE CHÂTEAUX

Think of Mikulov, Lednice, and Valtice as a sort of tri-city area, often referred to as the Lednice-Valtice Area or Complex. The strategic location of this trio on the southern border of the Czech Republic and Austria, roughly halfway between Vienna and Brno, made it an important center of historic trade routes and observation. Today the area is best known for the majestic châteaux that once housed the aristocracy of the Austro-Hungarian Empire.

The most recognizable residents of these summer homes and royal residences were the

HIGHLIGHTS

- ✪ **HOLY HILL:** A perfect sunset view over the town of Mikulov is your reward for a 30-minute hike (page 277).
- ✪ **VALTICE CHÂTEAU:** Slide through 25 rooms in protective slippers on a tour of this 14th-century royal residence (page 281).
- ✪ **CZECH NATIONAL WINE CELLAR:** Pay by the hour (or more) to taste 100 of the country's best wines (page 282).
- ✪ **LEDNICE CHÂTEAU:** The expansive gardens and greenhouse of this postcard-worthy palace were designed to impress (page 283).

Liechtensteins. (Yep, you can thank the same family that now has a small European country named after them while you tour the beauty of their elaborate home renovations.) The distinctive grounds and gardens surrounding all three of these châteaux are open to anyone, but guided tours are usually required to see the interiors.

The region of South Moravia is also prime location for some of the country's best vineyards. Moravia embraces wine in the way that Bohemians love their beer. You'll find the country's 100 best local wines of each year in the cellar of Valtice Château at the Wine Salon of the Czech Republic. In the evenings, wine fans savor their favorites in the more intimate wine bars around the town of Mikulov.

ORIENTATION

Mikulov is a small town of just over 7,000 people, smack in the middle of Czech wine country. The South Moravian location near the **Austrian border** is surrounded by hills, making this former defensive stronghold a secluded home base to explore the larger Lednice-Valtice area. Both **Valtice** and **Lednice** Châteaux require a public bus ride from **Mikulov** (20 or 60 minutes, respectively), so it's easier to visit these sights on separate days, or you can choose just one of the royal residences for your itinerary. Mikulov is easily navigated **on foot,** with **bus stops** scattered around the town to reach nearby sights.

PLANNING YOUR TIME

If you're going to travel four hours from Prague to Mikulov, it's worth spending **2-3 days** soaking up the views, wine, and stately homes of South Moravia. Give yourself time to enjoy the small-town charm, surrounding hikes, and a leisurely evening of *vino* without rushing through it all.

Brno is roughly an hour's drive, train, or bus ride from Mikulov, so you could compare the historical capital of Bohemia (**Prague**), the modern capital of Moravia (**Brno**), and a quieter glimpse of life in the countryside (Mikulov) in about a week.

Lednice and Valtice Châteaux

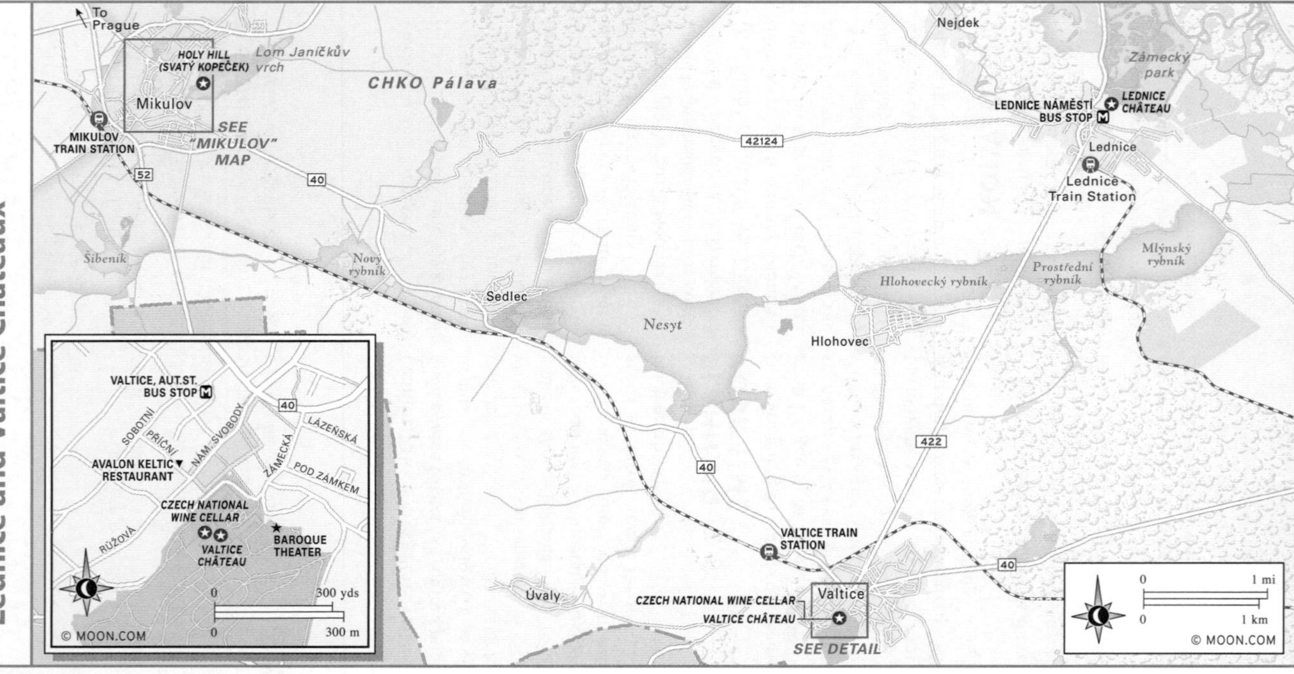

Itinerary Ideas

During summer months, book online tour tickets for Valtice Château weeks in advance, along with reservations for Day 1 lunch at **Restaurace Marcela Ihnačáka** and Day 2 dinner at **Restaurace Templ.** Pack some comfortable walking shoes that can get a little dirty and make sure you have cash for dinner for Day 1, plus coins for two city bus rides on Day 2. Book a hotel in Mikulov for two nights as a home base.

DAY 1: MIKULOV

1 After a late morning arriving from Prague or Brno and stashing luggage at your hotel, grab lunch on the terrace of **Restaurace Marcela Ihnačáka.**

2 Spend 30-60 minutes wandering between headstones on the paths of the **Jewish Cemetery,** set on a hillside landscape.

3 Exit the cemetery where you entered and follow a small hiking path 10 minutes uphill to approach **Goat Tower** from behind. Take in the surrounding view with the keen eye of a soldier defending their territory.

4 Head next to **Mikulov Château.** Give yourself an hour to explore the gardens and get lost in the paths between the château buildings.

5 Exit the château gates and turn left twice to find the entrance to the **Church Tower of St. Wenceslas.** Climb the clock tower, browse the mini-art gallery, and enjoy a panoramic view from the center of town. (If you weren't able to properly check into your hotel room on arrival, this would be a good time to do so.)

6 Have a leisurely Italian dinner at **Amici Miei,** where you can rest your feet before one more evening climb.

7 Hike along the Way of the Cross, following the blue trail 15-20 minutes to the top of **Holy Hill.** Explore the grounds, relax, and stay to watch the sun set over the Mikulov skyline before following the same path downhill again.

8 Treat yourself to a few glasses of wine at **Vinotéka Volařík** to celebrate a full day on your feet.

DAY 2: VALTICE

1 Start with a light hotel breakfast in Mikulov, then walk over to the "Mikulov, Pod Kozím hrádkem" bus stop. Catch bus 585 around 8:30am (confirm the day's schedule at www.idsjmk.cz), and make sure to have 25

Itinerary Ideas

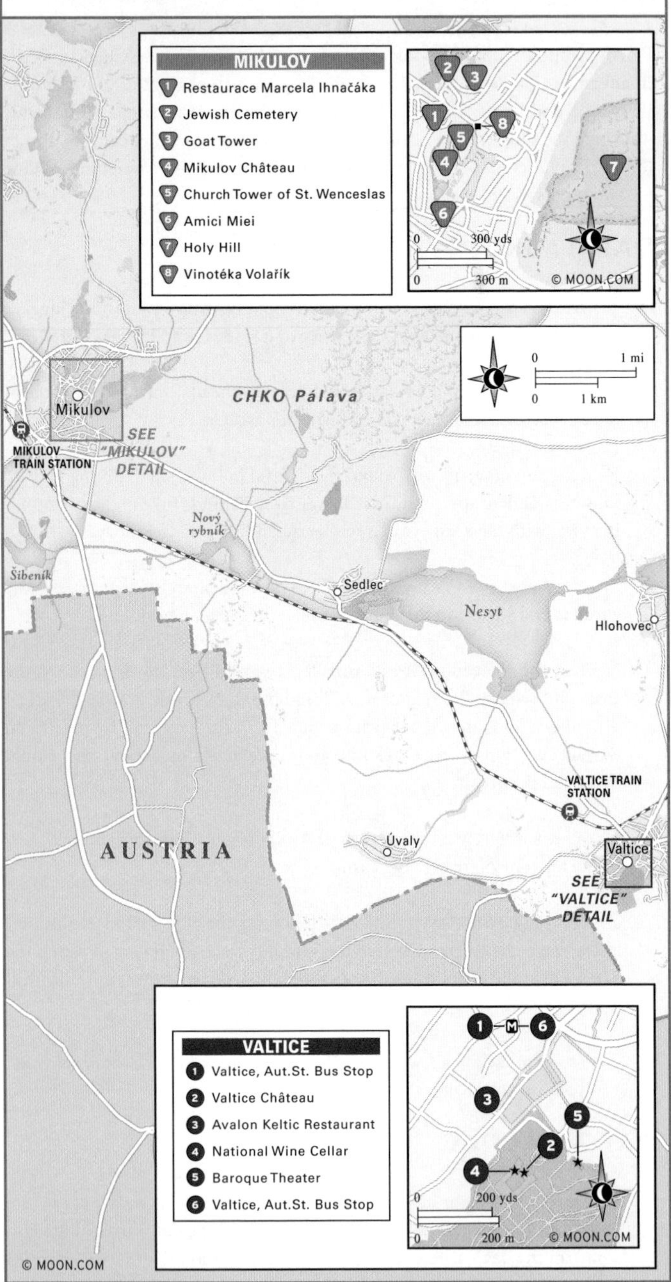

CZK in cash for the driver to take a 20-minute ride to the **"Valtice, aut. st." bus stop.**

2 Exit the bus and follow the signs directing you to the entrance and cash desk of the **Valtice Château.** Check in at the gift shop/cash desk for your one-hour Château Tour in English at 10am. Before the tour begins, spend any free time photographing the statue-lined courtyard from the base of the staircase.

3 Now that you've worked up an appetite, exit the château and have a proper lunch at **Avalon Keltic Restaurant** to prepare for some afternoon wine tasting.

4 Retrace your steps to the gift shop/cash desk of the Valtice Château to find the entrance to the **National Wine Cellar.** Purchase a 90-minute ticket to taste the best Czech wines and choose a few favorites to take as souvenirs.

5 Return to the grounds of Valtice Château and find the meeting point down and to the right of the courtyard stairs for a 45-minute tour of the **Baroque Theater** at 3pm (make sure to reserve your spot in advance).

6 You can race to catch a 4:07pm bus back to Mikulov, or browse the gift shop and take your time until the 5:20pm bus leaves (confirm the daily schedule at www.idsjmk.cz). To get there, exit the château grounds and reverse your original route up Poštovní and Za Radnicí Streets to the **"Valtice, aut. st." bus stop.** Enter bus 585 and pay the driver 25 CZK to reach the "Mikulov, u parku" bus stop.

Mikulov

Czech poet Jan Skácel famously compared the town of Mikulov to a piece of Italy that God moved to Moravia, making it a beautiful home base for day trips to the surrounding area. The center of this small town is easily walkable, with regular public transport connections to the neighboring châteaux.

SIGHTS

MIKULOV CHÂTEAU (ZÁMEK MIKULOV)

Zámek 1; +420 519 309 014; www.rmm.cz; May-June and Sept, 9am-5pm Tues-Sun; July-Aug, 9am-6pm daily; April and Oct-Nov, 9am-4pm Fri-Sun; tickets 30-60 CZK

When approaching the town from the train station, the red rooftops and single tower of the Mikulov Château may not exactly stun observers. However, this gift from Otakar II of the royal Přemysl dynasty to the Liechtenstein family in the 13th century was an influential move. The Liechtensteins completed construction and used Mikulov as a home base to spread

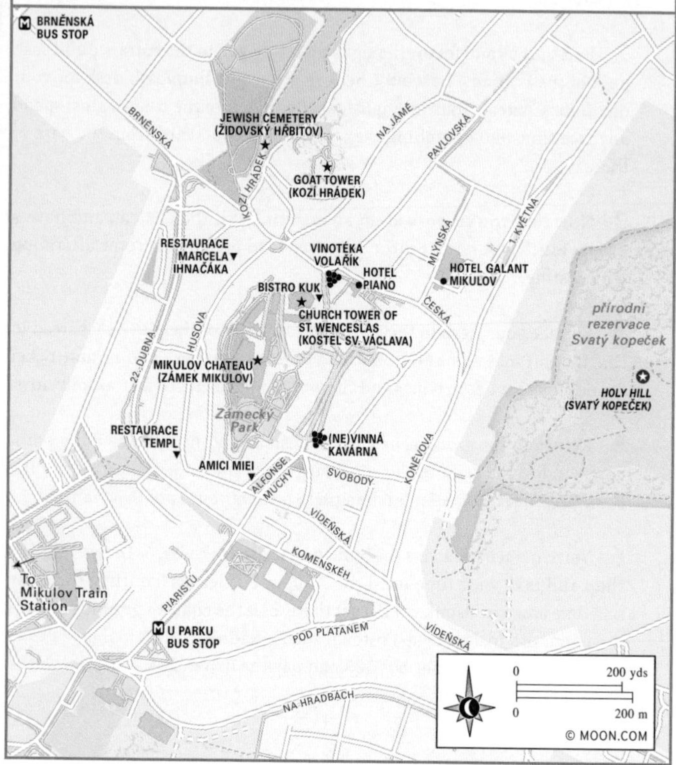

their influence across South Moravia, including the area's other, more famous (and arguably more impressive) châteaux.

Entering through the main gate from the center of town opens up views of manicured gardens, curved archways, detailed sculptures, and a lookout point from the edge of the gardens over the city that will take your breath away. The interior is semi-accessible, through a mix-and-match package of guided tours through various exhibits located inside the château. The indoor exhibitions, including an 18th-century library (60 CZK), an octagonal chapel (30 CZK), and an enormous barrel from 1643 in the wine cellar (60 CZK) are more appropriate for curious history buffs than the general public, and a stroll through the courtyard may be enough for visitors on a tight schedule or saving their château enthusiasm for Lednice and Valtice.

CHURCH TOWER OF ST. WENCESLAS (KOSTEL SV. VÁCLAVA)

Kostelní náměstí 4; www.farnostimikulovska.cz; 50 CZK

At first glance, it would be easy to assume that the tower of this Roman Catholic church was part of the neighboring Mikulov Château. Its

the historic town of Mikulov in Moravia

cream-colored walls extending skyward toward a balcony of curved arches definitely give off a regal vibe, but the religious roots of this location run deep. A 12th-century Romanesque church previously hosted visitors on the grounds that now hold the Church of St. Wenceslas. A fire in the 1500s destroyed the previous Gothic-style tower and grounds. This led to renovations in the Mannerism era of architecture, an inventive trend away from the symmetry of Rennaissance buildings. The following era of Baroque architecture also added some influence in 1768 with the curved dome on top of the clock tower.

Similar to the Town Belfry by St. Nicholas in Prague, this tower historically played a role in town safety. The fourth-floor balcony level used to house an apartment for the tower keeper, and its 360-degree views allowed them to survey the skyline for any signs of fire or impending attacks. Today's visitors are more likely to admire Holy Hill or take an overhead look at the Mikulov Château grounds after the 135-step climb. The lower landings are also worth a browse. Read the history of the building on the first level, see the bells on the second, and spend some time in a small art gallery that extends across the third and fourth landings.

Mikulov Château and gardens

HIKING IN MIKULOV

The town of Mikulov lies within the **Pálava Nature Reserve,** a protected area known for the diverse flora and fauna that decorate the hilly landscapes in between vineyards. Hiking paths here are lined with lush trees, delicate flowers, and views for days from springtime through autumn.

GOAT HILL

The slow incline and 10-minute hike to Goat Hill is an easily accessible route for almost any traveler in sensible footwear. The viewpoint around the former observation tower to the north is dotted with rich green branches and rock clusters that add texture to the hillside landscape.

HOLY HILL

Holy Hill takes the nature game up a notch. Wildflowers and feather grass add wispy detail and pops of color to the sprinkling of stones along dirt pathways that wind along the southeast edge of town. A moderate 15- to 20-minute hike along the blue trail takes hikers to a sunset vantage point and historic chapels, but the nature preserve extends much further behind the religious monuments, with longer hiking paths (www.mikulov.cz) for outdoor enthusiasts to explore.

In this largely wine-tourism-fueled town, summer and autumn opening hours are the most consistent. The tower is open daily at 10am from June-October, closing at 6pm in October, 7pm in September, 8pm in August and June, and 9pm in July. You can also visit on April weekends (Fri-Sun) from 10am-6pm and May weekends (Fri-Sun) from 10am-7pm.

slightly hidden entrance to the Church Tower of St. Wenceslas

JEWISH CEMETERY (ŽIDOVSKÝ HŘBITOV)

Kozí hrádek 11; +420 519 512 368 or +420 731 484 500; www.zidovskyhrbitovmikulov.cz; May-June, 10am-5pm daily; July-Sept, 10am-6pm daily; April-Oct, 10am-4pm Tues-Sun; Oct, 11am-4pm Tues-Sun; 30 CZK

Mikulov's Jewish Cemetery, the largest in the Czech Republic, stands in sharp contrast to the cramped headstones of Prague's Old Jewish Cemetery. This quiet hillside resting place has easy paths that wind between more than 4,000 graves.

In previous centuries, Mikulov provided sanctuary to Jews who were fleeing from religious persecution in Austria. Rabbi Loew, the infamous creator of the Golem hiding in Prague's Old-New Synagogue, served the area in the mid-16th century, bringing even more importance to the town. The Jewish population grew to nearly half of the town in the 1800s, with Jews and Christians co-existing in peace and tolerance. Tragically, a combination of emigration and the horrors of World War II left no Jewish residents in the area today.

GOAT TOWER (KOZÍ HRÁDEK)

Na Jámě; +420 608 002 976; www.mikulov.cz; free

The easy incline of a 10-minute walk from the town center or a five-minute journey from the Jewish Cemetery to the "Goat Tower" of Kozí hrádek makes a hilltop vantage point accessible to even the most novice hikers. This 15th-century structure served as strategic defensive surveillance of the surrounding trade routes leading to Vienna, Brno, and Prague. The inconsistent opening hours are signaled manually when the flag is flying, but entrance to the small building is secondary to the panoramic views of the city from its base.

TOP EXPERIENCE

✪ HOLY HILL (SVATÝ KOPEČEK)

Svatý kopeček; www.mikulov.cz; free

You may sometimes read or hear Mikulov's Holy Hill referred to as *Tanzberg* or *Taneční hora* (meaning "Dancing Mountain"), named for the mystical pagan ceremonies held here in pre-Christian times. The hill became a pilgrimage site in the 17th century, when Cardinal Franz von Dietrichstein built a chapel named after St. Sebastian to promote the spread of Catholicism and express his appreciation for making it through the plague of 1622. Sebastian, the patron saint often associated with survival, is usually depicted as defiantly living through a barrage of arrow-inflicted wounds.

Follow the blue hiking path at the base of Holy Hill from Novokopečná Street for about 15-20 minutes to pass 14 small chapels representing the

St. Sebastian's Chapel and Bell Tower on Holy Hill

Stations of the Cross. Seven of these (numbers 1, 8, 10, 11, 12, 13, and 14) originally sat on the top of Holy Hill, with the remaining seven added between 1750-1776, when the religious community came to an eventual consensus that 14 was the appropriate number. If you peek through the metal bars lining their gates, you can get a shadowy glimpse of the religious statues inside these small Baroque structures. Two dominant buildings stand on top of Holy Hill: the Greek-style domed roof of **St. Sebastian's Chapel,** and the freestanding 17th-century **Bell Tower** beside it. Visitors can enter St. Sebastian's Chapel and the Bell Tower on summer weekends from July to mid-September, 10am-4pm on Saturdays and 10am-2pm on Sundays.

The 30-minute hike from the center of town to the peak of Holy Hill is a moderate path lined with benches and rest areas. Many visitors miss the quieter plateau behind the religious monuments, where swirling rocks line the grounds and the skylines offer a more natural landscape of vineyards and countryside. Keep an eye out for small purple irises on the hillside, one of the rare plant species that helped to classify this area as a protected nature reserve. The grassy area in front of St. Sebastian's is a popular viewpoint for photographers and couples, especially around sunset, with unobstructed views over the entire town of Mikulov.

WINE

Vinotéka Volařík

Kostelní náměstí 9; +420 519 512 076; www.mhmikulov.cz; noon-midnight Mon-Sat, 10am-10pm Sun; 45-75 CZK per glass

The lantern-lit, covered terrace of Vinotéka Volařík (along with a few indoor tables) seats wine connoisseurs comfortably, even during the occasional summer storm. This intimate wine shop next door to Hotel Piano also serves as a tasting room, with a mid-sized wine list of local varietals available by the glass. The relaxed, award-winning wine bar is a great place to enjoy an evening al fresco. Smoking is permitted on the outdoor terrace.

Mikulov's Vinotéka Volařík

(Ne)Vinná Kavárna

Náměstí 18; +420 776 257 829; www.nevinnakavarna.cz; 9am-6pm Sun-Thurs, 9am-11pm Fri-Sat; 50-100 CZK per glass

Despite its name, (Ne)Vinná Kavárna (meaning "(No) Wine Café") actually has plenty of *vino* to offer, alongside specialty coffee and sweet homemade treats. The walls are lined with wooden china cabinets, typewriters, a piano, and other home-style touches to create a comfortable, casual vibe. Twenty-five wooden terrace seats outdoors make for great people-watching while sampling a glass of the local Riesling.

FOOD

Bistro Kuk

Kostelní náměstí 4; +420 728 332 485; 8am-10pm Sun-Thurs; snacks 50-100CZK

The bright, geometric design and upbeat soundtrack at Bistro KUK sets a modern vibe for the young crowd of coffee lovers and fans of fresh-baked goods. This is one of the few places in town that you'll find any non-dairy milk options. Menus are available in Czech and English.

Amici Miei

Alfonse Muchy 10; +420 608 822 348; www.amici-miei.eu; 9am-11pm Sun-Thurs, 9am-midnight Fri-Sat; entrées 150-200 CZK; cash only

Italian flags and red and green décor set the bright, kitschy scene at Amici Miei, which is Italian for "my friends." This small restaurant and wine bar, just downhill from the main restaurant row of Náměstí street, draws Czechs as well as international travelers. Choose from a small selection of pasta dishes and bruschetta with seasonal toppings. In the summer, grab an outdoor table in front of the restaurant or across the street on the covered patio. This is a great place to pair your meal with a local glass of sweet white Pálava wine, indigenous to this region. Cash only. Some staff speak English.

✪ Restaurace Marcela Ihnačáka

Husova 8; +420 519 510 692; www.hotel-tanzberg.cz; 11am-11pm; entrées 150-350 CZK

No matter where you stay in Mikulov, stop into Boutique Hotel Tanzberg for a meal at the 45-seat Restaurace Marcela Ihnačáka. If the weather allows, request one of the additional 25 coveted spots on the quiet outdoor terrace. Named for the famed local chef, this upscale yet casual choice serves fresh, seasonal salads, pastas, and meat dishes alongside a full menu of Jewish specialties (not guaranteed to be kosher) in tribute to the restaurant's location in the historical Jewish Quarter. Reservations are essential, but the same menu is also available in the casual pub setting of **Pivnice Golem**, also on the ground floor of the hotel.

Restaurace Templ

Husova 50; +420 606 368 319; www.templ.cz; 11am-10pm Mon-Thurs, 11:30am-11:30pm Fri-Sat, 11:30am-10pm Sun; 200-400 CZK

Restaurace Templ, inside the hotel of the same name, blends regional Czech flavors with modern style in a variety of indoor and outdoor spaces—a 20-seat, Renaissance-style restaurant, a bright 22-person bistro, and a relaxing outdoor patio in the summer. The seasonal menu skews toward meats like pork loin or wild boar, hearty pastas and risottos, and occasionally adventurous vegetarian options. Check the website for an idea of the latest creations. Reservations recommended.

Restaurace Templ's peaceful terrace

ACCOMMODATIONS

✪ Hotel Piano

Česká 2; +420 519 512 076; www.mhmikulov.cz; 1,300 CZK d

Whoever trains the staff at Hotel Piano should teach a worldwide master class on cultivating friendly service. This smack-in-the-center boutique hotel of 13 double rooms plus family suites (1,800 CZK) makes full use of the available space. Super-comfy beds, free Wi-Fi, and hints of subtle elegance, like mini-chandeliers or framed fine-art prints, enhance the modest appeal, along with bonus views of the small chapels sitting on top of the grass-covered Holy Hill to the east or the Mikulov Château to the southwest. The impressive breakfast buffet includes eggs, sausage, and bacon alongside cereal, fresh bread, fruit, tea, and coffee, to be enjoyed in the jazz-themed dining room or on the quiet terrace. Stays beyond two nights are treated to a complimentary bottle from neighboring wine bar Vinotéka Volařík.

Hotel Galant Mikulov

Mlýnská 2; +420 519 323 353 or +420 725 422 219; www.mikulov.galant.cz/en; 2,500-3,000 CZK d

Families and groups fill these 125 en-suite rooms, with free Wi-Fi, a buffet breakfast, onsite winery and micro-brewery, 24-hour reception, and one multi-floor family suite (3,500 CZK). Use of the glass-enclosed lap pool and rooftop jacuzzis requires a surcharge, but the views are worth the splurge. Take a post-breakfast, all-ages soak at 150 CZK for two hours between 9am-3pm, or 300 CZK between 4pm-10pm (for adults only). Additional spa services are available by appointment. This eco-friendly hotel is also committed to energy-efficient design and sustainable practices. Free onsite parking for guests.

rooftop jacuzzi at Hotel Galant Mikulov

GETTING THERE

If you're driving, note that some hotels, such as Hotel Galant, offer free onsite **parking** for guests. There are a few parking garages just outside the town center, with the closest, **Parkoviště** (A. Muchy 7), open 9am-5pm at 40-50 CZK per hour.

FROM PRAGUE

The easiest way to get from Prague to Mikulov is by **train.** The national rail service, **České dráhy** (www.cd.cz, 450-500 CZK), runs hourly, transferring at Břeclav for the four-hour journey. Trains depart from just before 6am until around 6pm, with a few late-night options requiring multiple transfers. **Regiojet** (www.regiojet.com, 150-550 CZK) also runs between Prague and Břeclav every two hours from about 5:30am-5:30pm, but this requires a transfer to České dráhy to reach Mikulov. The main train station of **Mikulov na Moravě** is a 15-20 minute walk from the center of town, with local taxi service available.

There is no direct bus connection from Prague to Mikulov.

If you're driving, Mikulov is roughly three or four hours (about 240 km/150 mi) southeast of Prague on **highway D1/E65.**

FROM BRNO

Regional bus 105, run by the **South Moravian Integrated Public Transport System** (locally known as Integrovaný Dopravní Systém Jihomoravského Kraje, www.idsjmk.cz, 60 CZK, just over an hour's journey), departs around once an hour from Brno's ÚAN Zvonařka stop, just south of the main train station. Local service in Mikulov stops at the **Brněnská bus stop** on the northwestern side of town before continuing to the **u parku bus stop** to the south. This option is appropriate for travelers with hand luggage only.

Travelers with luggage should use the **Czech national rail service** with indirect service to Mikulov, from around 4am to 8:30pm (1.5 hours, 100-125 CZK), changing trains in Břeclav.

If you're driving, Mikulov is located about 55 kilometers (roughly 35 miles) south of Brno, which takes about an hour on **Routes 52/E65.**

GETTING AROUND

The compact center of Mikulov is entirely **walkable**, with multiple **bus stops** connecting Mikulov to the surrounding châteaux in Lednice and Valtice. For taxi service, try **Nejlevnější Taxi Mikulov** (+420 607 856 205, www.nejlevnejsi-taxi-mikulov.cz) or **Taxi Mikulov** (+420 606 707 770, www.taxi-mikulov.cz).

Valtice and Lednice

✪ VALTICE CHÂTEAU

Zámek 1; +420 778 743 754; www.zamek-valtice.cz

The Liechtenstein family helped to establish the splendid, 100-room Valtice Château in the 14th century. In 1945, it was confiscated to be used for various labor camps under Communist rule. Ongoing renovations since the 1970s have maintained the beauty of the building, which is only accessible through a one-hour basic guided tour (320 CZK) that runs every 1-2 hours, either in English (usually 10am and 2pm) or with printed English text provided. Small groups don slippers over their shoes to protect the floors, and swish through approximately 25 staged rooms and halls of royal portraits, muraled ceilings, and canopy beds. The château opens at 9am from late March until the end of October, closing at 3pm in October, 4pm in March and April, and 5pm from May

the aristocratic beauty of Valtice Château

to September. Monday entry is only available during the months of July and August.

Beyond the basic château, theater fans will enjoy a behind-the-scenes tour of the newly reconstructed **Baroque Theater** (90 CZK), modeled after the historically preserved Baroque Theater in Český Krumlov. The 45-minute theater tour runs every 1-2 hours, mainly on weekends from April-June or Wed-Sun in July and August, either in English (reservations required) or with printed English text provided. Be sure to save time to visit the National Wine Cellar in the basement of the château, where you can enjoy a taste of the country's 100 most prized wines.

WINE

TOP EXPERIENCE

✪ Czech National Wine Cellar

Zamek 1–Valtice Château; +420 519 352 744; www.vinarskecentrum.cz; Feb-Dec, 9:30am-5pm Tues-Thurs, 10:30am-6pm Fri-Sat; June-Sept, Sundays only, 10:30am-5pm; tastings 100-500 CZK

For an overview of the best Czech wines available, add a trip to the National Wine Cellar, located in the basement of Valtice Château. Every August, a professional panel selects the 100 best wines in the country. The winners are available to taste in this cellar, arranged by varietal along the long brick halls. Tasting packages are based on time: Taste as many wines as you like in 90 minutes (399 CZK) or 150 minutes (499 CZK), or choose 16 pre-paid pours on a shorter time limit (a hearty lunch before visiting is a good idea to avoid getting overly tipsy). Descriptive charts in multiple languages offer detailed information, including the varietal, winemaker, region, alcohol and sugar contents, and the number of bottles produced. Grab a bottle for purchase from below these posters.

Czech National Wine Cellar

Look for the ivy to find Avalon Keltic Restaurant.

FOOD

Avalon Keltic Restaurant

Příční 46; +420 721 384 290; www.avalonvaltice.com; 11am-11pm Tues-Sun; 125-250 CZK

Budget time for a quick lunch at Avalon Keltic Restaurant as part of your day trip to the Valtice Château. The light-hearted, medieval hunting-lodge décor indoors is accented by patches of exposed brick and swords fastened to the walls. The summer garden is cloaked in ivy around a serene waterfall and a fish pond dotted with water lilies, with Celtic music

the palace Lednice in the Lednice-Valtice complex

keeping the mood light and fun. This is a popular stop for cyclists in spandex crisscrossing the Moravian wine trails. The menu items resemble Czech specialties, but with a lighter twist—grilled chicken and cranberry sauce, or duck confit with beet root and potato dumplings—and vegetarian options are available. Try a cold Svijany (my personal favorite Czech beer) with your meal before walking around the corner to the château gates.

GETTING THERE

Bus route 585 (20 CZK) on the **South Moravian Integrated Public Transport System,** locally known as Integrovaný Dopravní Systém Jihomoravského Kraje (www.idsjmk.cz), departs at least once every hour between 5:30am-3pm from Mikulov to Valtice. The ride takes about 20 minutes, with multiple stops in Mikulov, terminating at **bus stop Valtice, aut. st.,** just a few streets away from the château entrance. Return service on Route 585 to Mikulov from the Valtice, aut. st stop runs about once an hour until around 7pm. Bus route x58 runs more often, but with fewer stops in Mikulov, so it may require a longer walk.

✪ LEDNICE CHÂTEAU

Zámek 1; +420 519 340 128; www.zamek-lednice.com; tours 80-300 CZK

Lednice Château provides the most striking exterior silhouette of the three stately homes in this region. The Lichtenstein family, who dominated the area from the 13th century onward, renovated the existing structure into a bright, Neo-Gothic summer palace in the mid-1800s, smaller in size than Valtice but with much more expansive gardens and equally ornate interiors. A stroll through the swirling floral patterns takes visitors to the Minaret (80 CZK), also called the Turkish Tower, which gives you an aerial viewpoint of the entire grounds.

Different guided tours are the only opportunity for visitors to explore the château's interior and surrounding buildings. Highlights worth the price include the one-hour Representative Rooms tour (330 CZK), which explores the ground floor's distinctively color-coded décor, including the Blue Room, Turquoise Hall, and Red Smoking Hall. Gardening fans will want unlimited, non-guided access to the greenhouse (80 CZK) to see the plant life housed in a steel, iron, and glass design that was ahead of its time in 1842. Additional tour options focus on Princely apartments (300 CZK) and marionettes (300 CZK). The Lednice Château opens on weekends from 10am-4pm in February, November, and December, or 9am-4pm in April and October. Weekday access is added from May to September, with hours from 9am to 5pm. Monday entry is only available during the months of July and August.

GETTING THERE

Bus number 570 (25 CZK) on the **South Moravian Integrated Public Transport System,** locally known as Integrovaný Dopravní Systém Jihomoravského Kraje (www.idsjmk.cz), takes just under an hour to get to, from multiple stops around Mikulov (see www.idsjmk.idos.cz for route details) to the **Lednice náměstí bus stop** just outside the château. Route 570 runs every 1-2 hours from around 6:30am-7:30pm.

OLOMOUC

Olomouc is often described as having "all the charm of Prague without the crowds," but the city is slowly gaining international name recognition in its own right. Olomouc retains a sense of pride in its historical importance, claiming the country's second-oldest university and previously serving as the capital of Moravia during the Renaissance period of the 17th century. The Thirty Year's War (1618-48) hit the city hard and political power migrated south to Brno.

HIGHLIGHTS

✪ **ASTRONOMICAL CLOCK:** Get a glimpse of Socialist Realism style in this artistic time-capsule of the Communist era (page 294).

✪ **ARCHDIOCESAN MUSEUM:** Admire the opulence of religious art housed in the spiritual capital of Moravia (page 295).

✪ **BAROQUE FOUNTAINS:** Go on a sightseeing scavenger hunt to discover six water features inspired by Roman mythology (page 296).

Today, the pastel colors of the UNESCO-listed Old Town create a postcard-worthy backdrop against a landscape of religious monuments. This spiritual capital of Moravia is roughly two and a half hours east of Prague. The population seems to fluctuate with the seasons or even the weekends. The university town gets significantly quieter during weekends and summer months, when many Czech students return to their surrounding hometowns. Summertime brings a Baroque opera and theater festival and a popular half-marathon to town, and Christmas markets sparkle in both squares in December.

ORIENTATION

Picturing a long triangle that points northeast can help you navigate the center of Olomouc. **Horní náměstí** (the Upper Square) marks the historical center of town. Walking southeast from Horní náměstí takes you to **Dolní náměstí** (the Lower Square), which may feel counterintuitive since you walk uphill from the "Upper Square" to get to the "Lower Square." Connecting these two squares draws the short base of the triangle.

Walking northeast from either Horní náměstí or Dolní náměstí will take you toward the **university area,** where you'll find the Museum of Modern Art and more boutique-style hotels and restaurants. The Archdiocesan Museum and Wenceslas Cathedral sit in the farthest northeast corner, the point of our imagined triangle, on the religious square of **Václavské náměstí.** Tram tracks line the main road sloping gently uphill in this direction, whose street name changes from "**Denisova**" to "**Náměstí Republiky**" around the Triton Fountain, and then into "**1. máje**" as it continues toward the spires of Wenceslas Cathedral.

You may notice some unusual street names around Olomouc, such as "8. května," "1. máje," or "28. října." These streets are named after significant dates (the 8th of May in modern Czech, the 1st of May in a more poetic form, and the 28th of October). The numbers are part of the street name, so an address of "8. května 15" refers to house number 15 on 8. května Street.

For a physical overview of the city, take a look at the miniature model of the center found on the northern half of Horní náměstí. The city center is incredibly **walkable,** with Dolní náměstí only about 15 minutes on foot from the Archdiocesan Museum in the northeast corner. The main **bus and train stations** are slightly outside of town, about 20 minutes on foot from Václavské náměstí and half an hour's walk from the town center. I recommend a **taxi** if you've got any luggage.

PLANNING YOUR TIME

The journey to Olomouc is doable as a **day trip** from Prague, particularly by train, but the city is best taken at a slow pace to soak in all the beauty and history. Many of the historical monuments are outdoors, so **good weather** helps, but their beauty can still brighten up a crisp February afternoon.

Note that the Museum of Modern Art and the Archdiocesan Museum are free on **Sundays** and closed on **Mondays,** while the organ at Wenceslas Cathedral puts on a show every **Monday** and **Wednesday.** The historical figures of Olomouc's Astronomical Clock make a slow-moving, hand-cranked parade daily at **noon**; however, you may want to be there at a different time for a better view. **Prague, Olomouc,** and **Brno** make a great three-stop itinerary, exploring three distinctive regions of the Czech Republic; all are easily accessible, with regular train connections.

Upper Square at Christmas

INFORMATION AND TOURS

The Olomouc Town Hall houses the town's **Tourist Information Center.** A one-hour "Olomouc in a Nutshell" guided tour (50 CZK) runs daily from mid-June through the end of September at 9:30am, 11am, 12:30pm, 2pm, 3:30pm, and 5pm. (Tours previously included access to the Town Hall Tower, but at the time of writing the tower was closed for renovation until at least 2020.) The info center also offers a self-directed audio guide to rent from two hours (100 CZK + 300 CZK deposit) up to six hours (250 CZK + 300 CZK deposit), giving basic commentary at your own pace.

SIGHTSEEING PASSES

An **Olomouc Region Card** (240 CZK for 48 hours, +420 722 706 505, www.olomoucregioncard.cz/en/) is worth the price for the ability to visit the Archdiocesan Museum and the Museum of Modern Art over two days—plus it includes an Information Center tour, free public transportation, and discounts to select restaurants. Pick one up at the main train station in Olomouc or the Tourist Information Center inside the Town Hall.

Alternatively, a **combined ticket** to the Museum of Modern Art and the Archdiocesan Museum (150 CZK) comes at a discount, but requires you to visit both places on the same day. To avoid museum overload, I recommend utilizing the Olomouc Region Card instead, as the Archdiocesan Museum is an impressive but intensive sightseeing experience.

Olomouc

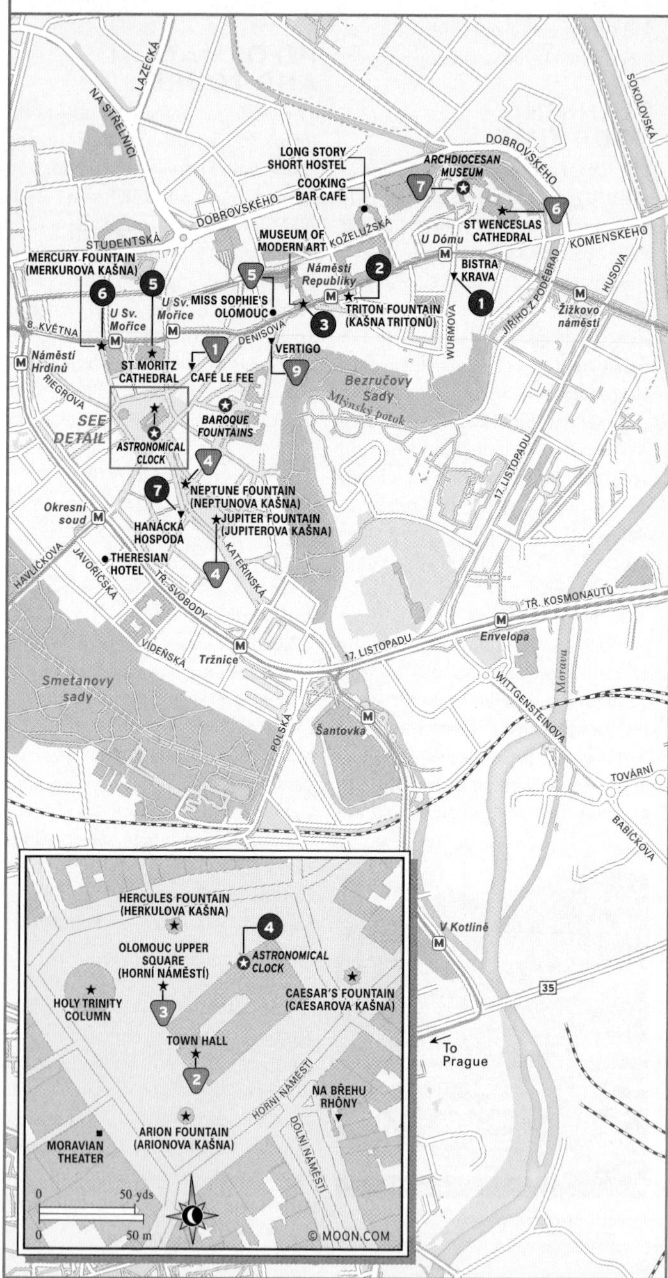

LONG STORY SHORT HOSTEL
COOKING BAR CAFE
ARCHDIOCESAN MUSEUM
ST WENCESLAS CATHEDRAL
MUSEUM OF MODERN ART
BISTRA KRAVA
MERCURY FOUNTAIN (MERKUROVA KAŠNA)
MISS SOPHIE'S OLOMOUC
TRITON FOUNTAIN (KAŠNA TRITONŮ)
VERTIGO
ST MORITZ CATHEDRAL
CAFÉ LE FEE
BAROQUE FOUNTAINS
SEE DETAIL
ASTRONOMICAL CLOCK
NEPTUNE FOUNTAIN (NEPTUNOVA KAŠNA)
JUPITER FOUNTAIN (JUPITEROVA KAŠNA)
HANÁCKÁ HOSPODA
THERESIAN HOTEL
Bezručovy Sady
Mlýnský potok
Smetanovy sady
Šantovka
Morava
To Prague
HERCULES FOUNTAIN (HERKULOVA KAŠNA)
OLOMOUC UPPER SQUARE (HORNÍ NÁMĚSTÍ)
HOLY TRINITY COLUMN
CAESAR'S FOUNTAIN (CAESAROVA KAŠNA)
TOWN HALL
NA BŘEHU RHÔNY
ARION FOUNTAIN (ARIONOVA KAŠNA)
MORAVIAN THEATER
© MOON.COM

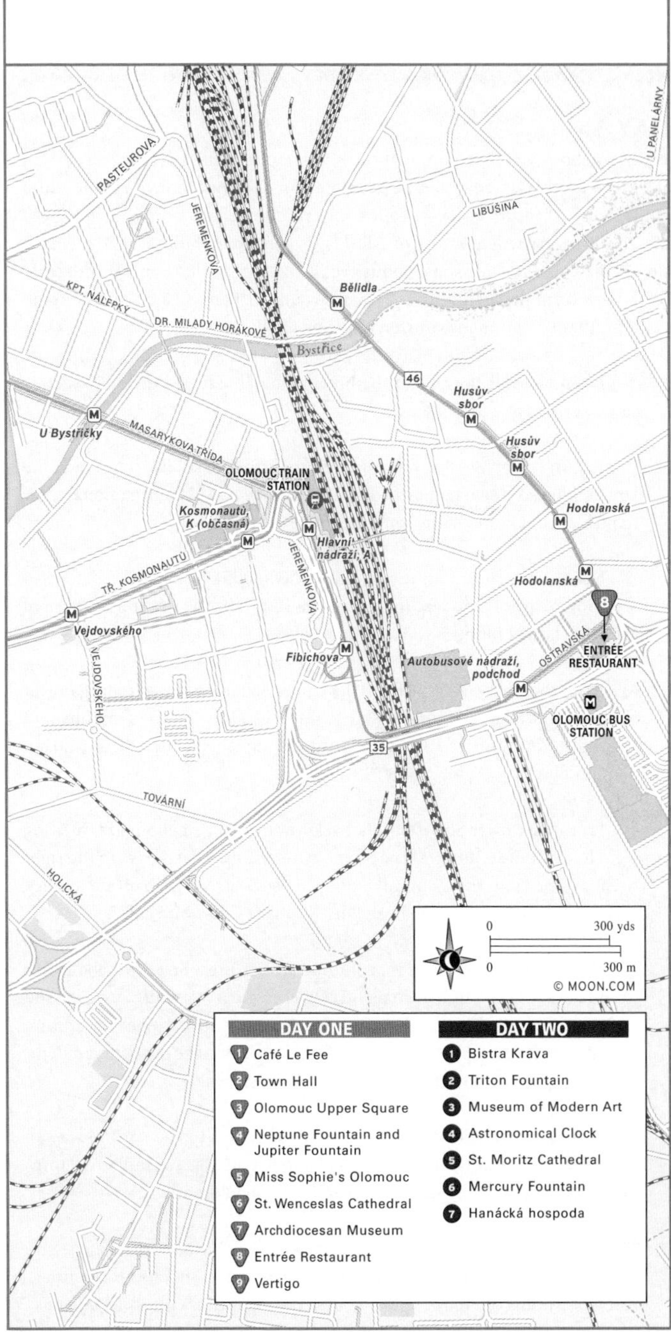
PASTEUROVA
JEREMENKOVA
LIBUŠINA
U PANELÁRNY
KPT. NÁLEPKY
DR. MILADY HORÁKOVÉ
Bělidla
Bystřice
46
Husův sbor
Husův sbor
U Bystřičky
MASARYKOVA TŘÍDA
OLOMOUC TRAIN STATION
Kosmonautů, K (občasná)
Hlavní nádraží, A
Hodolanská
Hodolanská
TŘ. KOSMONAUTŮ
JEREMENKOVA
Vejdovského
VEJDOVSKÉHO
Fibichova
Autobusové nádraží, podchod
OSTRAVSKÁ
ENTRÉE RESTAURANT
OLOMOUC BUS STATION
35
TOVÁRNÍ
HOLICKÁ
0
300 yds
0
300 m
© MOON.COM
DAY ONE
1 Café Le Fee
2 Town Hall
3 Olomouc Upper Square
4 Neptune Fountain and Jupiter Fountain
5 Miss Sophie's Olomouc
6 St. Wenceslas Cathedral
7 Archdiocesan Museum
8 Entrée Restaurant
9 Vertigo
DAY TWO
1 Bistra Krava
2 Triton Fountain
3 Museum of Modern Art
4 Astronomical Clock
5 St. Moritz Cathedral
6 Mercury Fountain
7 Hanácká hospoda

Itinerary Ideas

DAY 1

When you book your accommodation for Olomouc, make a dinner reservation at **Entrée** for this first day. Before departing for Olomouc, download the audio guide to the **Archdiocesan Museum** onto your preferred mobile device. Note that this itinerary will not work on Monday, when the Archdiocesan Museum is closed, but could include some bonus organ music if you start on a Wednesday. Book your train departing from Prague around 7:30am-8:30am and arriving between 10am-11am to maximize your time in Olomouc.

1 Drop off your luggage at the hotel and grab a light lunch of sweet or savory crêpes at **Café Le Fee.**

2 Around noon, walk a few minutes up Ostružnická Street to reach the Upper Square (Horní náměstí). Stop into the **Town Hall** Information Center to pick up an Olomouc Region Card.

3 Use your card to join the one-hour "Olomouc in a Nutshell" tour of **Olomouc Upper Square,** including the Holy Trinity Tower and three of the city's famed fountains.

4 After the tour, continue from the Upper Square to the adjoining Lower Square (Dolní náměstí) and spend 15 minutes admiring the symbolism of **Neptune Fountain** and **Jupiter Fountain,** along with the nearby Marian plague column.

5 From the Lower Square, walk back toward the Upper Square, turning right to continue onto Ztracená Street. After 4-5 minutes, curve to the right to follow the tram tracks uphill along Denisova Street. Stop off for a quick coffee and a sightseeing break at **Miss Sophie's Olomouc** café.

6 Once the caffeine kicks in, continue up Denisova Street for about five minutes as it turns into 1. máje Street. Then turn left onto Dómská and right onto Václavské nám. Pop into **St. Wenceslas Cathedral** to admire the interior for 15 minutes. Bonus points if you catch the quick organ demonstration, on the hour from 1-4pm on Wednesdays.

7 Walk next door from St. Wenceslas Cathedral to the **Archdiocesan Museum.** Use your Olomouc Region Card to enter and spend 60-90 minutes exploring the religious and royal history of Olomouc.

8 Head back to your hotel if you want to upgrade your outfit before taking a 10- to 15-minute taxi to **Entrée Restaurant** (reservations essential). Allow 2-3 hours to enjoy a multi-course tasting menu with wine pairings.

9 Hop in a taxi back into town. If you're not too exhausted, stop into **Vertigo** for a nightcap and a look at the rowdier side of nightlife in a university town.

DAY 2

Before leaving your accommodation, download the audio guide to the **Museum of Modern Art** onto your preferred mobile device and don't forget your Olomouc Region Card. Note that this itinerary will not work on Monday, when the museum is closed.

1 Start with hotel breakfast or grab some eggs or pancakes at **Bistra Krava.** Check out of your accommodation and store your luggage before leaving.

2 Turn right out of Bistra Krava onto Wurmova and a quick left onto 1. máje Street. After about five minutes, pause to admire the **Triton Fountain** at nám. Republiky.

3 Continue another few minutes downhill along the tram tracks to reach the **Museum of Modern Art.** Take a two-minute loop through the graffiti-lined pedestrian tunnel across the street before using your Olomouc Region card to enter. Allow at least an hour to explore two floors of exhibits and an observation deck.

4 If you can make it out of the museum around 11:45am, follow Denisova Street to Ostružnická Street for about five minutes to reach the Upper Square just before noon, when the **Astronomical Clock** puts on its once-a-day performance of historical moving parts.

5 From the Astronomical Clock, turn around and walk two minutes up Opletalova Street and turn left on 8. května Street to reach **St. Moritz Cathedral.** Step inside for 20 minutes to admire the organ and ornate interior.

6 Turn left out of St. Moritz Church and walk about a minute down 8. května Street to find the **Mercury Fountain,** the last Baroque fountain of the collection.

7 Follow 28. října Street toward the Upper Square and continue into the Lower Square to find **Hanácká hospoda** on your right. Enjoy a late lunch with a taste of Olomouc cheese before leaving the city.

Sights

Contrasting Olomouc's **Upper Square (Horní náměstí)**, where the Holy Trinity Column and Town Hall are located, with the Old Town Square in Prague can offer an interesting perspective, demonstrating what these cities have in common while drawing attention to their subtle differences.

HOLY TRINITY COLUMN

Horní náměstí–radnice; tourism.olomouc.eu

It takes big dreams to create majestic monuments. In a proposal to the Olomouc city council, builder Wenzel Reinder wrote, "I am going to build a column to the honor and glory of the Almighty God, the Virgin Mary, and saints that will have no equal in any other town with its height and splendor." Construction of the column, which started in 1717 and was completed in 1754, means it outlasted Reinder's lifetime but arguably fulfilled his goals.

The symbolic Baroque beauty now standing 35 meters (roughly 115 feet) tall in Horní náměstí's western corner is not your typical plague column (a type of monument scattered across Central Europe, usually built in thanks for surviving 17th- and 18th-century outbreaks of disease). The exceptionally large and ornate structure in Olomouc towers over Vienna's column (21 meters/69 feet) from 1693, or even smaller Czech versions found in Kutná Hora or Prague's Malá Strana neighborhood.

The top of the column displays a sculpture of the Holy Trinity and Archangel Michael, stars of the sacred show. As your eyes scan downward, the Assumption of Mary is

Olomouc Holy Trinity Column

next, followed by three tiers of saints, then apostles, and finally torchbearers circling the base. The column's golden cannonball, visible just above the Assumption of Mary, has an interesting backstory: In 1754, the Holy Trinity Column of Olomouc was finished and consecrated in the presence of devout Hapsburg royal couple Marie Theresa and Holy Roman Emperor Francis I. Four years later, in 1758, cannonballs threatened to destroy the beloved monument during a Prussian attack. The townspeople of Olomouc reportedly asked the army commander to spare the sacred sculpture and he surprisingly agreed. The cannonball honors the brave request to protect the monument that still stands today.

For a handheld guide to the meaning of each of the column's features, download the free "Olomouc UNESCO" mobile app before you arrive. The interior of the column even houses a tiny chapel, accessible from 9am-2pm between April and September. Stop by the Information Center inside the town hall, where they hold the key to the chapel, if you want to arrange access outside these hours.

So how does this compare to Prague? Olomouc's most famous structure pays tribute to the Catholic faith of the 1800s, while noted 15th-century religious reformer Jan Hus dominates the central square in the Bohemian capital. These days, the base around the Holy Trinity Column provides a local meeting place, a seat for children to enjoy some ice cream, and a place for visitors to pause and admire the pastel backdrop of the surrounding buildings.

TOWN HALL

Horní náměstí–radnice; +420 585 513 385; tourism.olomouc.eu; 9am-7pm daily

The Gothic Town Hall in the center of Horní náměstí has stood through six centuries of conflicts and everyday life since 1378. (By comparison, only a sliver of Prague's original town hall survived the Prague Uprising of 1945.) This staying power has led to a collection of architectural periods preserved in the building's exterior details. Check out the ornate Italian Renaissance staircase on the west side of the building, for example, or the copper gargoyle dragons extending from the four corners of the rooftop.

A few of the exterior details hold darker symbolism as well. The four turrets around the tower may not appear threatening, but they actually signify that the town of Olomouc had its own executioner. On the back side of the building, you'll find plenty of gargoyle faces twisted into grotesque expressions. Look below the windows for a bearded man with one hand outstretched, supposedly representing an unpaid stoneworker.

Olomouc's Town Hall in the Upper Square

In addition to the architectural interest it offers, the Olomouc Town Hall holds the Tourist Information Center. It was once possible to access the Town Hall Tower via tour; however, at the time of writing, the tower was closed for renovation.

✪ ASTRONOMICAL CLOCK

Horní náměstí-radnice; tourism.olomouc.eu

Like Prague's Town Hall, Olomouc's Town Hall features an Astronomical Clock on its face. Both clocks originally date back to the 15th century, but the Olomouc version now represents a distinctly different period of history. The Olomouc clockface went through a variety of styles during various building renovations, from Gothic to Renaissance to Baroque. In 1945, at the end of World War II, retreating Nazi soldiers opened fire on the clock, badly damaging the historical façade.

Under the new era of Communist rule in the mid-1950s, the clock was renovated to reflect the official ideological style of Socialist Realism. Types of traditional work associated with each month of the year, such as digging fields or harvesting crops, are portrayed in mosaics lining the curves around the clock, where you might typically expect to find religious symbolism. The top of the archway depicts a distinctly Moravian springtime festival called the Ride of the Kings. The mechanic and scientist figures at the base on either side of the clock faces reinforce the importance of work over worship under socialist rule.

The clock still runs on its 1898 machinery, the only piece rescued and restored from its 1945 destruction. Similarly to Prague, the Olomouc clock also puts on a mechanical parade of figures—this time with the proletariat instead of apostles. The five-minute performance of tiny workers slowly circling and hammering bells is hand-cranked by one man every day at noon. (Fair warning: the performance is interesting but underwhelming overall, and you may want to get an up-close look at the clockfaces at another hour without any crowds.)

Astronomical Clock in Socialist Realism style

ST. MORITZ CATHEDRAL

8. května 15; +420 585 223 179; tourism.olomouc.eu; April-Jun and Sept-Oct, 7am-6pm; July-Aug, 7am-7pm; Nov-Mar, 7am-4:30pm; free

Step inside St. Moritz for a glimpse of the largest organ in Central Europe, made in 1745, tucked underneath the pale pink ribbons lining the vaulted ceilings. Plan your visit around the **International Organ Festival** in September (www.mfo.cz) to hear it in all its glory. This late-Gothic church also holds an intact 15th-century sculpture of Christ on the Mount of Olives sitting below the organ. The church tower with city views was previously a popular highlight, but at the time of writing the tower was under renovations planned to continue through 2021. The interior beauty of the church is still worth a look around, taking care not to disturb the religious services held Mon-Sat at 8:00am, Sun at 7:30am, 9am, and 10:30am, and Fri from 9am-noon.

MUSEUM OF MODERN ART

Denisova 47; +420 585 514 111; www.muo.cz; 10am-6pm Tues-Sun; 100 CZK / 150 CZK with Archdiocesan Museum; free Sun

Three of the artistic attractions around this museum don't even require entrance. A giant mural entitled "Selfie Made King" covers the brick wall of the building beside the museum. One of Czech sculptor David Černý's pieces, called "The Robber," hangs from the outer ledge of the building, and occasionally moves from side to side when the machinery is working (which can be inconsistent). Graffiti artists also decorate the small pedestrian tunnel known as Lomená Galerie, directly across the street from the museum.

"Robber" hanging outside the Museum of Modern Art

After admiring the artistic exterior, the actual museum collection is absolutely worth heading inside. Download a 35-minute audio guide (www.muo.cz) to your phone in advance; headphones are available for rent (20 CZK) from the cash desk. You may want to check any heavy clothing layers in the free cloakroom; it can be warm inside. Head upstairs to start with distant views of Wenceslas Cathedral and the Town Hall spires from the glass-enclosed observation deck. Then start your self-guided walk through 16 artistic styles from the 1900s-1990s on the top floor, wandering among Cubist paintings and Surrealist sculptures. Continue downward to find more geometric movements and early expressions of political freedom from the late 20th century. Give yourself an hour in total to pause the audio guide, and enjoy a few extra minutes in front of your favorite pieces.

✪ ARCHDIOCESAN MUSEUM

Václavské náměstí 3; +420 585 514 111; www.muo.cz; 10am-6pm Tues-Sun; 100 CZK / 150 CZK with Modern Art Museum; free Sun

The opulence and extravagance often inspired by the Catholic Church is on full display throughout the Archdiocesan Museum, embodied by the giant gilded carriage from 1746 that begins the self-guided tour of the building. The museum route winds through 16 halls and cellars holding an array of Madonna statues, jewelry, and ornate ceilings inspired by the four elements. An impressive collection of paintings comes later in the tour, so don't be afraid to breeze through any early rooms. Similarly to the Museum of Modern Art, visitors should download the free, 45-minute audio guide (www.muo.cz) in advance. A detailed viewing of each exhibit, pausing the audio guide between its 36 installments, could easily run over 90 minutes.

The latter half of the museum covers two infamous events that took place on this site, one tragic and one triumphant. Sixteen-year-old King Vaclav III ("Wenceslas" in English), the last member of the royal bloodline, was murdered in 1306. He suffered three stabs to the chest in the Přemyslid Castle that stood in this location centuries before it was a museum. The Bloody Gallery, a balcony marking a loose approximation of where the event took place, now offers a peaceful view of the surrounding grounds. In a lighter tale of famous young men, an 11-year-old Mozart also lived in Olomouc with his family, detailed in a small exhibit toward the end of the self-guided tour. He composed his Symphony No. 6 in F Major here in 1767.

ST. WENCESLAS CATHEDRAL

Václavské náměstí; +420 731 402 036; tourism.olomouc.eu; 6:30am-6pm Mon-Tues and Thurs-Sat, 6:30am-4pm Wed, 7:30am-6pm Sun; free

The Romanesque-style Basilica from the 12th century that stood on this site got a Gothic makeover from 13th-century renovations resulting from fire. The three defining spires of St. Wenceslas Cathedral, a symbolic element of the Olomouc skyline, came much later, when the front two towers were added during neo-Gothic renovations in the 1800s. The cathedral is worth a quick peek inside before or after a visit to the Archdiocesan Museum. Visitors with a strong interest in religious history can arrange a one-hour guided tour (90 CZK per person) in advance through www.psmorpheus.com for a closer inspection of the cathedral's history and functionality of its organ. For a less-intensive taste of organ music, time your visit around public musical demonstrations held on Mondays (when the Archdiocesan Museum is closed) at 2pm, 3pm, 4pm and 5pm, and Wednesdays on the hour between 9am-4pm except noon.

St. Wenceslas Cathedral

TOP EXPERIENCE

✪ BAROQUE FOUNTAINS

Olomouc reportedly had plans to create three Holy Trinity Columns and seven Baroque stone fountains around the city. They came close, with two columns (now standing in Horní náměstí and Dolní náměstí) and six historical fountains scattered throughout town, along with the addition of modern stone fountains. These decorative water features, built between the late 17th and early 18th centuries, symbolize a cultural and artistic revival of Olomouc after surviving the Thirty Year's War in the mid-17th century. This collection of monuments makes for a fun sightseeing scavenger hunt as you explore the rest of the city.

Hercules Fountain (Herkulova Kašna)

Horní náměstí

The famously strong son of Jupiter (or Zeus in Greek mythology) is surrounded by benches around the middle of the Upper Square. Hercules is depicted protecting the town of Olomouc, symbolized by the checkered eagle on his arm, from the seven-headed hydra threatening to attack at his feet. The snake also bears the name of Mandík, the artist who created the fountain in 1687-88, making it the second oldest of the original six. This fountain previously stood where the Holy Trinity Column now resides, but was shuffled east in 1716 to make room for the tribute to Catholicism. Don't skip the bronze mini-architectural model providing an overview of Olomouc's center, just a few steps further to the east.

Caesar's Fountain and Town Hall

Caesar's Fountain (Caesarova Kašna)

Horní náměstí

The largest Baroque stone fountain in town, completed in 1725, holds Gaius Julius Caesar (grandson of Augustus) on horseback in the southeast corner of the Upper Square behind the Town Hall. Local legend credits the original founding of Olomouc to the Roman Emperor. Two men at the base of the stone symbolize the Danube and Morava Rivers, seen holding shields from the Austrian and Moravian coats of arms. The dog seated underneath the horse's tail may be seen as a sign of loyalty to the ruling Hapsburg empire at the time of construction.

Arion Fountain (Arionova Kašna)

Horní náměstí

The third fountain in the southwest corner of the Upper Square is the newest in town (and thus is not a member of the original Baroque six). It was added to the landscape in 2002. The playful scene sticks to the trend of mythological symbolism, with the Greek poet and musician Arion embracing the dolphin that rescued him (according to legend). A turtle with a plant-like obelisk on his back and a sculpted pair of children share the pool, often accompanied by actual human children taking a dip in warmer months. If you need a water break, a small marble-and-bronze drinking fountain topped with tiny

Arion drinking fountain in Upper Square

dolphins sits beside the popular family hangout.

Mercury Fountain (Merkurova Kašna)

8. května

The Roman god associated with travel, commerce, and relaying messages (known as Hermes in Greek) seems appropriately placed between a bank and a shopping center, just down the street from St. Moritz Church. The 1727 fountain is often praised for its artistic merit among the bunch, with flowing folds of fabric draped around Mercury as he lifts his caduceus (a winged staff encircled by two serpents) into the air. The caduceus may appear to be a symbol of medicine to many US travelers—thanks to its adoption by the US Army Medical Corps, the Public Health Service, and the Marine Hospital—but this is a case of mistaken iconography. The confusion likely stems from the caduceus's similarity to the Rod of Asclepius (a non-winged staff encircled by a single serpent, carried by the god of healing and medicine), used by the World Health Organization and medical institutions around the globe.

Neptune Fountain (Neptunova Kašna)

Dolní náměstí

The Roman god of the sea (Poseidon in Greek) was the first completed figure, added to the Lower Square in 1683. Neptune stands atop a rock on the backs of four "sea horses"—equines submerged in water, not the spiral-tailed marine animal. He holds a trident pointed down toward the tumultuous waters in yet another protective stance, which symbolizes the gods ensuring the safety and welfare of the city. Neptune also provides a protective bit of light to travelers finding their home at night, as the fountain is illuminated from below in the evenings. A second, smaller plague column, built in the early 1700s and dedicated to the Virgin Mary, stands in the center of the Lower Square. The Marian Column stands between the Neptune Fountain at the top and Jupiter Fountain at the far end, and is perfectly parallel to Hanácká hospoda, if you're looking for a place to taste Olomouc cheese.

Jupiter Fountain (Jupiterova Kašna)

Dolní náměstí

The king of the gods (Zeus in Greek mythology) holds court in the Lower Square. The fountain base from 1707 originally held a statue of St. Florian, but the Christian saint of firefighters and the Austrian town of Linz didn't exactly vibe with the mythology theme. St. Florian was replaced with the imposing figure of Jupiter, battling enemies of Olomouc with lightning in his right hand and a trusted eagle at his feet. Added in 1735, the king of the gods was the last of the six original statues, arriving fashionably (or one could say powerfully) late to his defensive position at the far end of Dolní náměstí.

Triton Fountain (Kašna Tritonů)

Náměstí Republiky

It makes sense for a fountain depicting the mischievous offspring of Neptune to sit in the university area, slightly outside the town center near the Museum of Modern Art. A playful young deity with his chin raised holds two dogs on chains while standing inside a half-seashell on the backs of men. The fountain's composition was likely inspired by the Fontana del Tritone in Rome. The 1709 structure originally stood further downhill, at the busy intersection of Denisova, Ztracená, Ostružnická, and Pekařská streets, but was moved to its current location in 1890 as a result of city planning to make way for traffic.

Bars and Nightlife

Olomouc nightlife changes character from street to street. A concentration of pubs along the southern side of Dolní náměstí tends to be large and traditionally Czech (or they appear so for the benefit of visitors), with wooden benches and Czech lager on draft. Independent cafés closer to Horní náměstí cater toward theater goers and a slightly more sophisticated scene. The student crowd congregates around the university for dive bars and affordable drinks served late.

PUBS

✪ Vertigo

Univerzitní 6; +420 777 059 150; 6pm-2am daily

Party animals of all ages (but primarily university students) keep the drinks flowing in this dark, grungy underground pub with neon lights popping up in various corners. If you're feeling adventurous, request your favorite song on YouTube from the bartenders while placing your order. Residents tell me that dancing on the tables is not unheard of after midnight.

WINE BAR

Na Břehu Rhôny

Dolní náměstí 2; +420 775 321 500; www.nabrehurhony.cz; 3pm-11pm Sun-Thurs, 3pm-midnight Fri-Sat; 300-1,000 CZK per bottle

Grab a patio table and watch the foot traffic between Dolní náměstí and Horní náměstí while you sip a selection of French wines, including vegan options. Arched ceilings and a scattering of small tables provide indoor seating with hands-off service that allows each to enjoy their own company and conversation in this sophisticated setting.

Performing Arts

THEATER

Moravian Theater

Horní náměstí 22; +420 585 500 500; www.moravskedivadlo.cz; box office 9am-6pm Mon-Fri; tickets 200-350 CZK

Olomouc's resident home of opera, ballet, and theater on the Upper Square celebrates its 100th Czech anniversary in 2020, but has consistently given a home to previous empire ensembles since 1830. Renovations in 2018 ensured that the plush red seats lining the floor and balconies are up to modern standards of comfort. Browse the program of dance performances from Sept-June to avoid a language barrier, and make sure to pack a semi-formal outfit to enjoy an artistic night out.

Festivals and Events

SPRING

Folk dancing and smelly cheese fill the Upper and Lower squares in late April for the **Olomouc Cheese Festival** (tvaruzkovyfestival.olomouc.eu). Classical music fans should make note of the annual **Dvořák's Olomouc Festival** (www.mfo.cz) celebrating the Czech composer in May.

SUMMER

Runners fill the streets for the **Mattoni Half-Marathon** (www.runczech.cz) in June. The elaborate costumes, wigs, makeup, and drama of the **Baroque Opera Festival** (baroko.olomouc.eu) in July are thoroughly entertaining even if you don't understand a single word of the lyrics. (Trust me.)

FALL AND WINTER

Classical music fans can hear the St. Moritz organ at the **International Organ Festival** (www.mfo.cz) in September. The spiritual capital of Moravia comes alive during Advent season in the weeks leading up to Christmas, with ice skating and **Christmas markets** (www.vanocnitrhy.eu) filling the Upper and Lower Squares.

Olomouc hosts a summer Baroque Opera Festival.

Food

INTERNATIONAL

Café Le Fee

Ostružnická 13; +420 737 147 006; 8am-9pm Mon-Thurs, 8am-10pm Fri, 9am-9pm Sat, 9am-8pm Sun; entrées 80-100 CZK

The service is casual and the décor is shabby living-room chic in this mellow, salon-style café just a few steps off Horní náměstí. Grab a chair near the front window to people-watch through plants while you sample a French-inspired menu of sweet crêpes and savory gallettes. Take your espresso, prosecco, or homemade lemonade into the interior garden for a more peaceful setting. Breakfast options of eggs, bagels, and croissants are served until 11am on weekdays and 1pm on weekends.

Cooking Bar Café

Koželužská 31; +420 606 090 469 or +420 588 008 278; www.longstoryshort.cz; 7am-9pm daily; entrées 150-300 CZK

The expansive outdoor patio of Long Story Short Hostel turns into a lively barbecue scene whenever the weather allows. A young crowd of hostel guests and neighborhood folks sprawls across wooden benches for a seasonal menu that could include beef, lamb, or goat-cheese burgers grilled within sniffing distance, or a vegan paté made from white beans, sun-dried tomatoes, and pickled zucchini. Soups, sandwiches, and homemade cakes are also available in a small indoor dining room year round, and vegan, vegetarian, and gluten-free options are always available. Reservations recommended.

✪ Entrée Restaurant

Ostravská 1; +420 585 312 440; www.entree-restaurant.cz; 11am-2pm and 5pm-midnight daily; entrées 300-500 CZK

A 10-15 minute taxi ride to Entrée, named Best Restaurant in the Czech Republic in 2018, offers a treat for culinary tourists. Entrée's open kitchen showcases the choreographed dance of chefs preparing artistic plates of seafood, meats, and veggies drizzled in inventive sauces. Questions and dietary restrictions are handled with refreshing ease by an educated staff. Add a wine pairing (625-800 CZK) to a tasting menu (1150-1350 CZK) for a taste of Czech culinary excellence. Reservations essential.

VEGETARIAN

Bistra Krava

Wurmova 5; +420 775 115 779; bistrakrava.blogspot.com; 8am-7pm Mon-Fri, 9am-7pm Sat; entrées 100-150 CZK

Origami cranes and bright white walls cast a sense of calm over this cute second-story café near the Ardiocesan Museum and Wenceslas Cathedral. Grab a light breakfast of eggs, ham, or pancakes until 11am, with coffee from a local independent roaster. The daily lunch menu, served from 11am-2pm, includes two types of soup alongside chicken curries, pastas, and fresh salads, most with vegan and vegetarian modifications available. Homemade sandwiches, quiches, and cakes fill in the gaps for lighter snacks throughout the day.

OLOMOUC CHEESE

Tasting Olomouc cheese, known as *tvarůžky*, is a love-it-or-hate-it experience. The local delicacy, protected by UNESCO as a regional specialty dating back to the 1500s, is often referred to as "stinky cheese" for its pungent aroma. Local producers start with a base of skimmed cows' milk, mix in some salt, and air-dry at controlled temperatures to a rich golden color. The resulting thick, sticky substance with a hardened rind can be spread on bread (best washed down with a cold pilsner) or used in sweet pastry recipes. Olomouc cheese resembles the bright orange hue of cheddar cheese, but with a softer consistency. It has a much sharper, concentrated, pungent flavor, that is not for the faint of heart.

Olomouc Cheese at Hanácká hospoda

The name "tvarůžky" comes from the Czech *tvaroh*, which many locals translate as "cottage cheese" but which is actually closer to the more obscure dairy product called "quark" in English. The Olomouc region is the only area to produce this uniquely Czech cheese, and even celebrates the divisive delicacy with a yearly festival in late April, the **Olomouc Cheese Festival** (tvaruzkovyfestival.olomouc.eu), complete with folk dancing and microbrew tents on the Upper and Lower Squares.

Taste *tvarůžky* for yourself at **Hanácká hospoda** (Dolní náměstí 38; +420 774 033 045; www.hanackahospoda.com; 11am-midnight daily; entrées 150-250 CZK), a traditional Czech pub lined with wooden benches on the edge of the Lower Square. Split a platter of Olomouc cheese and fresh bread (90 CZK) served with a selection of pickled vegetables, or make it a meal deep-fried in beer batter (145 CZK).

Accommodations

✪ Miss Sophie's Olomouc

Denisova 33; +420 587 203 509 or +420 587 203 500; miss-sophies.com/olomouc; 1,700-2,000 CZK d

The charm is in the details—think preserved medieval wall tiles, or a pulley to lift luggage in a building whose 8th-century foundations won't allow for an elevator. Wooden beams, pastel touches, and elegant simplicity set a peaceful tone across the eight-room boutique hotel with a leisurely noon checkout. Enjoy a complimentary buffet breakfast and specialty coffee in Miss Sophie's Café or upgrade to omelets or waffles (50 CZK). Both

Miss Sophie's Hostel Olomouc, peaceful simplicity

the 50-seat dining room and outdoor garden attract local couples alongside hotel guests.

Long Story Short Hostel

Koželužská 31; +420 588 008 278 or +420 606 090 469; www.longstoryshort.cz; 400-600 CZK dorm, 1,500-3,000 CZK d

Cool kids pack the bunk-bed dorms with private or shared bathrooms, plus four private en-suite rooms decked out in minimalist black-and-white. Fresh flowers and window-lined hallways lighten the vibe of these converted army barracks. The amenities go way beyond hostel standards, with rainforest showerheads and heated bathroom floors, 24-hour laundry service (200 CZK for 10kg/22lbs), and an exceptional breakfast buffet (150 CZK) of fresh seasonal vegetables, bread and spreads, eggs, pastries, cereal, and alternative milk options.

dinner on the terrace at Long Story Short Hostel

Theresian Hotel

Javořičská 5; +420 581 113 113; www.theresian.cz; 2,500-3,000 CZK d

Every amenity is sleek, modern, and luxurious in this splurge-worthy spa hotel five minutes from the Lower Square. Thirty-three rooms in minimalist neutral colors, including wheelchair-accessible options and three spacious suites with A/C, are designed to strip away the stress of any day. Spa entry (350 CZK for guests) buys access to a jacuzzi, saunas, fitness center, and additional massage services (200-1,000 CZK). Buffet breakfast and free Wi-Fi are included.

Transportation

GETTING THERE

Olomouc is located east of Prague in the northern half of Moravia. The journey takes just over two hours by train, three by car, and four by bus.

TRAIN

Train service from **Regiojet** (www.regiojet.com, 150-300 CZK one-way) is a comfortable, affordable option running every 1-2 hours between 5:45am and 9:45pm from Prague's main train station (Praha hlavní nádraží). A small splurge for business class (300-500 CZK one-way) is worth it for the privacy, solid Wi-Fi, and steward service, including a free cookie, water, coffee drinks, and a welcome glass of sparkling wine or juice. **Leo Express** (www.leoexpress.com, 300-750 CZK one-way) also offers direct trains from Praha hlavní nádraží every 1-2 hours from 8am to 8pm, and the **Czech national rail service** (www.cd.cz, 220-300 CZK one-way) runs hourly direct service from around 5:30am to 11:45pm.

BUS

Flixbus (www.flixbus.com, 150-350 CZK one-way) offers a few direct bus-service routes between 2:25am and 11:45pm, departing from either Prague's Zličín, Florenc, or Praha hlavní nádraží bus stations, so check your ticket carefully.

CAR

Olomouc is located about three hours (roughly 240-280 kilometers/150-175 miles) east of Prague on either the **D1** or **D11** highway. **Central Parking Olomouc** (Koželužská 29, +420 585 229 958), a secure parking garage near the university area, costs 20 CZK per hour or 250 CZK per day. Paid street parking is available through automated machines for 30 CZK per hour (see tourism.olomouc.eu for information on zones).

GETTING AROUND

TAXI

Try **S taxi** (+420 704 048 484) for help with heavy luggage between transport stations or a ride to Entrée restaurant.

LEAVING OLOMOUC

Buses and trains from Olomouc to Prague run consistently from around 6am to 8pm via **Regiojet**, every 1-2 hours between 5am and 5pm on **LeoExpress**, and from 6am to 11pm with direct and indirect routes from **Flixbus**. The Czech national rail service runs hourly direct service to Prague from around 3:30am to 8pm.

Olomouc also provides easy access to the Moravian city of **Brno**, roughly 1-2 hours southwest. Direct buses to Brno (roughly 1 hour) leave Olomouc every 1-2 hours between 6am and 7:30pm on **Regiojet** (89 CZK), or every 2-3 hours between 2am and 10:45pm on **Flixbus** (75-175 CZK), with one daily bus on **LeoExpress** around 5am daily. Indirect Czech national rail service from Olomouc to Brno (around 2 hours) is also available between 7am and 7pm (80-100 CZK). Caution: when using the national railway service (www.cd.cz), make sure your train goes to either Brno dolní nádraží or Brno hl. n. and not the outlying suburban station of Brno-Královo Pole.

ESSENTIALS

Getting There

Travelers arriving via air can fly into Prague's **Vaclav Havel International Airport** (Aviatická, www.prg.aero).

FROM THE UNITED STATES

Finding a direct flight into Prague from anywhere in the US is tough. You can find sporadic non-stop service, especially in summer, from Newark

on **United Airlines** (www.united.com), from Philadelphia or Chicago on **American Airlines** (www.aa.com), or from New York (JFK) on **Delta Airlines** (www.delta.com), with flight times around 8.5 hours. Otherwise, transferring in a major hub like London, Amsterdam, or Frankfurt is more common.

FROM EUROPE

The great thing about traveling in Central Europe is you have an abundant selection when it comes to which mode of transport to pick. You can go by bus, train, car, or plane.

BY AIR

Low-cost airlines are an option if you're traveling from further afield, like the UK. Airlines like **EasyJet** (www.easyjet.com), **WizzAir** (www.wizzair.com), and **Ryanair** (www.ryanair.com) offer inexpensive flights to Prague's airport from many European destinations. It takes between 2 to 2.5 hours to reach Central Europe from London by plane.

BY TRAIN

Traveling by train through the Czech Republic is efficient, affordable, and filled with gorgeous views. You can compare options on private carriers like **Regiojet** (www.regiojet.com) or **LeoExpress** (www.leoexpress.com) with modern cars and amenities, or take your chances with the Czech national rail service (www.cd.cz), which features a mix of older and newer trains.

If you're feeling adventurous—or simply hate flying—you also have the option of traveling to Central Europe from the UK by train. You can take the **Eurostar** (www.eurostar.com) to Brussels (train tickets for this leg only are usually around €100-200), which go every two hours from London St. Pancras Station. However, from Brussels you will need to go to either Frankfurt or Cologne and change trains again to journey onto Prague, with the total journey time (with the fewest connections) lasting 15-20 hours. Tickets for onward journeys from Brussels could also cost an extra €150-250. This is not the most budget-friendly nor the most efficient way to travel, but definitely the most adventurous!

international trains and buses arrive at Praha hlavní nádraží

BY BUS

Buses can be the cheaper option, and although they may not be as comfortable as a train, buses like **Regiojet** (www.regiojet.com), **Eurolines** (www.eurolines.eu), and **FlixBus** (www.flixbus.com) are quite comfortable, with varying levels of refreshments, entertainment, Wi-Fi, and toilets onboard. This works best from neighboring countries, unless you're a pro at sleeping in cramped quarters.

It is possible to take a bus from London, but **RegioJet** (www.regiojet.com)'s daily bus services to Prague will cost you €50-70 (often more than a budget flight) and almost 20 hours.

BY CAR

Europe has a well-connected highway network, so depending on how far you're planning to drive, it's relatively easy to reach Central Europe. Highways are smooth and well maintained throughout the region, but you may find some roads in the countryside in poorer condition, and the D1 motorway between Prague and Brno in particular has a reputation for traffic jams. Note that you must use winter tires during the winter if you're planning to drive across Central Europe, as the roads can get icy and slippery.

Border Crossings

Ever since the Schengen Agreement removed border controls between the members of the EU states, traveling by car throughout Europe has gotten easier. Some countries may check at the border at random, so always have your papers—like your passport or ID, license (International Drivers Permit, if applicable), registration, insurance papers—to hand over. Peak seasons may lead to waits at the border.

Safety

In the winter, mountain passes may be slow, or even closed off if the weather is bad. If you're driving through the Alps to get to Prague, it's best to keep an eye on the news and drive at low speeds when on smaller roads. You must also fit your car with winter tires or all-season tires between the months of November and April. Speaking of winter driving conditions, you should also carry snow chains with you during the winter. Weather conditions tend to be the worst from December to February, but it's not impossible to have snow hit as early as October or as late as April. And—all year round—if you're planning on driving through Germany note that some highways won't have speed limits, so expect some crazy road runners.

Car Rentals

If you want to head out on an epic road trip from one European country to another with a rental car, you'll want to pick a company like **Europcar** (www.europcar.com), **Sixt** (www.sixt.com), or **Hertz** (www.hertz.com), who have offices in other countries that allow you just to drop the car off. These will include a "drop fee," an extra added charge to return the car to another office. Talk to your rental company about your itinerary. You can find the best rental deal with price comparison sites like **Skyscanner** (www.skyscanner.com) or **Kayak** (www.kayak.com). The minimum age to rent a car in Prague is 21. Some companies require you to be at least 25 years of age, so confirm with your rental car company.

If you prefer to cross Europe by car but don't have a license or prefer not to drive, you can also try the car-sharing service **Bla Bla Car** (www.blablacar.com), a carpooling service that matches up drivers and passengers at reasonable prices.

FROM AUSTRALIA AND NEW ZEALAND

There are no direct flights from Australia and New Zealand to Prague. The quickest and most direct route is to connect through Bangkok, Doha,

Dubai, or Shanghai. Emirates (www.emirates.com) and Qatar (www.qatarairways.com) serve most of the flights from Australia and New Zealand, which take around 22 hours or more, including transfers. Air China (www.airchina.com) and Thai Airways (www.thaiairways.com) also have services connecting the region to Oceania.

FROM SOUTH AFRICA

There are no direct flights from South Africa to Prague. The easiest way is to fly with Emirates or Qatar Airways and change in Dubai or Doha. Flights take around 15 to 18 hours or more. Some routes also go through Paris Charles de Gaulle with Air France, or through Zurich with Swiss Airlines en route from Johannesburg.

Getting Around

CITY TRANSPORT

Prague's public transport system is efficient, affordable, and reliable in any weather. The city has a well-connected subway service that runs until midnight, plus a vast network of tram lines and buses that run 24 hours a day, with limited routes during late-night service. Prague's public transport system is managed by Dopravní podnik hl. m. Prahy (www.dpp.cz), and the same tickets are valid across all three forms of transport. Tickets are sold in chunks of time, so you can get a single ticket with unlimited transfers for 30 minutes (24 CZK) or 90 minutes (32 CZK). You can also purchase unlimited transport passes for 24 hours (110 CZK) or 72 hours (310 CZK). One option that is not available in Prague is a one-week ticket. If you are staying anywhere from 7-30 days, an unlimited one-month pass (670 CZK) is the next option. You can gift this to an unsuspecting stranger at the airport or train station if you depart before it expires.

Prague is not quite as bike-friendly as other cities in Central Europe, and drivers are not always known for giving way or stopping for crosswalks. There are numerous cycling paths once you get into the countryside (see www.czechtrails.com for details).

VALIDATING TRANSIT TICKETS

Prague uses the loyalty system when it comes to enforcing public transit tickets. It works like this: you buy a ticket or a pass, and you validate it and keep it with you. Most of the

Some ticket machines require coins.

time, there are no ticket inspectors, but if there are and you don't have a valid ticket, prepare for trouble. Ticket inspectors are usually in civilian clothes, so until they approach and show you a badge you won't realize, and they take no prisoners or excuses. If your ticket is not validated or valid, you will get fined and taken to an ATM on the spot if necessary—and the experience can ruin your trip. You need to validate your ticket when you enter the metro or get on the tram or bus. Look out for the validation boxes and double check that the validation stamp on your ticket is visible. This shows you the time it was validated so you know when your ticket expires.

To avoid any drama and enjoy the ride, buy your transport tickets in ticket offices or automated machines in the metro stations, from yellow machines near some tram stops, occasionally in corner stores (look for *potraviny* signs and ask the cashier), or from Tourist Information Centers. Some of the newer trams in Prague have the option to pay onboard with a credit card, but your credit card has to be contactless and these machines were not yet installed on all trams at the time of writing. Bus drivers are able to sell tickets at a premium as you board at the front of the bus, but expect limited levels of English and make sure to have exact change ready. You cannot buy a ticket from the drivers on the metro or on trams. Overall, searching for places to buy a single tram ticket or trying to break change for older coin-only machines can be a frustrating and time-consuming experience, so buying a one- or three-day pass on arrival is well worth the convenience.

GETTING AROUND CENTRAL EUROPE

Trains and buses are the best way to travel across the Czech Republic.

TRAIN AND BUS

The main rail companies are state-run **České Dráhy** (www.cd.cz) and private carriers **RegioJet** (www.regiojet.com) and **Leo Express** (www.leoexpress.com). There are also regular buses operated by private companies like **RegioJet** (www.regiojet.com), **Flixbus** (www.flixbus.com), and **Eurolines** (www.eurolines.eu).

Expect Czech signage in smaller towns.

CAR

Road Rules

In the Czech Republic, the minimum driving age is 18. You must drive on the right side of the road. Also take note that the Czech Republic has a strict, zero-tolerance policy for driving under the influence of alcohol, so don't risk it after even one beer.

To use the major highways, the Czech Republic requires you to purchase a vignette (a sticker) instead of stopping at toll booths. You can usually buy vignettes from gas stations. These will need to be displayed in the window of your car, unless it's an electronic one tied to your license plate.

While traveling, you'll need your passport and driver's license. If you're from the US or Canada, it may also be a good idea to get an **International Driving Permit** (IDP). This is an official translation of your license from back home. Some rental companies request this, while others are less strict. Although you won't need it in all countries, it's a good idea if you're planning on driving in Austria, Hungary, Poland, Croatia, Greece, Slovenia, or Slovakia. You can get a permit from the American Automobile Association (www.aaa.com) or the Canadian Automobile Association Office (www.caa.ca) for $20.

Visas and Officialdom

The Czech Republic resides within the EU and the Schengen Zone.

U.S. TRAVELERS

As a US citizen, you will not need an entry permit (visa) to enter the Czech Republic. You can come to the Czech Republic as a tourist for up to 90 days in any 180-day period. However, you do need a passport that is valid for at least three months after your departure from the European Union.

EU/SCHENGEN TRAVELERS

If you're from another EU state, you do not need a visa to enter any of the Schengen countries, including the Czech Republic. When you travel from one Schengen country to another, chances are you won't even have your passport or ID checked, although it's a good idea to keep it on you, as some borders still check IDs. UK travelers should check for new regulations post-Brexit.

TRAVELERS FROM AUSTRALIA AND NEW ZEALAND

Australians and New Zealanders can come to the Czech Republic visa-free for a maximum period of 90 days in any 180-day period without taking up employment. Your passport must be valid for three months beyond the planned date of departure from the Schengen area.

TRAVELERS FROM SOUTH AFRICA

South African travelers need a visa to enter the Schengen Area. You can obtain a Schengen visa from any of the Schengen Area member countries, which will allow for free movement between the whole Schengen zone. Travelers beginning their journey in Prague should apply for the Schengen Visa at the Embassy of the Czech Republic in Pretoria. It's best to apply at the embassy for the country you're planning to visit first, but make sure it's a Uniform Schengen Visa (USV) if you're planning on continuing onto any additional countries. This visa will grant entry for 90 days in a 180-day period.

Festivals and Events

IN PRAGUE

JANUARY

New Year's Day Fireworks They were replaced in Prague (as of 2019) with a video projection on the National Museum in the evening of January 1, although many private businesses along the river are still likely to put on amateur shows on December 31 at midnight. January 1 also marks the anniversary of the independent Czech Republic's peaceful split from Slovakia.

MARCH-APRIL

Masopust (the Czech version of Carnivale) is the local equivalent of Shrove Tuesday or Mardi Gras. Expect small neighborhood parades of strange characters in costume, particularly around Jiřího z Poděbrad Square in Žižkov.

Easter Markets are similar to Christmas markets, but with more pastel colors, painted eggs, and Easter whips in the weeks leading up to Easter.

Čarodejnice ("Witches Day") marks the end of winter on April 30. Families gather in city parks for the lighting of bonfires topped with wooden figures dressed in witch's clothes, plus live music and refreshment stands.

MAY

Labor Day on May 1 is also known as a day of love. Couples should find a cherry blossom tree to share a kiss beneath, ideally on Petřín Hill.

Volkswagen Marathon Weekend fills the city's bridges and streets with runners from around the world.

The Prague Spring Festival showcases symphony orchestras and young musicians, who compete for prizes in the city's concert halls.

The Prague Fringe Festival brings nine days of comedy, cabaret, music, dance, and theater to the city.

AUGUST

Prague Pride celebrates the Czech LGBTQ+ community with colorful parades and parties.

SEPTEMBER

Wine Harvests: Look for festivals bringing tasting booths to squares and parks, particularly in Vinohrady or Havlíčkovy sady.

OCTOBER

The Prague Signal Festival is a free, outdoor celebration of light installations and video shows, often projected onto Prague's historical buildings.

Prague Signal Festival of Lights

Independent Czechoslovak State Day, on October 28, is still celebrated as the founding of the country, and usually features concerts and events in Wenceslas Square.

NOVEMBER

Saint Martin's Day celebrates Saint Martin's bringing of the first snow of the season. The first taste of Svatomartinské young wine is poured at 11:11am on November 11.

International Students' Day/ Struggle for Freedom and Democracy Day, on November 17, remembers the students and protesters who fought for independence from various oppressive regimes. Protests and events in Wenceslas Square are a common occurrence.

The Mezipatra Queer Film Festival celebrates diversity in film and draws international talent and attendees to Prague and Brno for discussions, lectures, workshops, exhibitions, and parties.

DECEMBER

St. Nicholas Day Don't be surprised to see an angel, devil, and saint wandering the streets on Dec 5 to kick off the Christmas spirit.

Christmas Markets set up shop in multiple squares across Prague from the end of November till the end of December, with street food, hot wine, twinkling lights, and souvenir stands.

OUTSIDE PRAGUE

FEBRUARY-MARCH

BLIK BLIK Light Festival (Pilsen) adds glowing art installations and light shows to brighten up February days.

Queer Ball (Prague and Brno) invites the LGBTQ+ community to celebrate in style.

APRIL

Olomouc Cheese Festival (Olomouc): You can taste (and smell) the local delicacy across the Upper and Lower Squares.

MAY

Spa Season Opening (Karlovy Vary) brings a costumed King Charles IV on a white horse to bless the local springs.

Mattoni Half-Marathon (Karlovy Vary) brings crowds of runners to the otherwise peaceful streets of the spa town.

The Pilsen Liberation Festival (Pilsen) in early May draws World War II veterans to commemorate the US Army's help in defeating Nazi occupying forces, with parades and ceremonies.

Ignis Brunensis (Brno): This fireworks festival lights up the sky for multiple weekends in late May and early June.

Dvořák's Olomouc Festival (Olomouc) pays tribute to the famous Czech composer.

JUNE-JULY

Gambrinus Festival (Pilsen): A variety of beer tents and drinkers fill Náměstí Republiky for one weekend in June.

Mattoni Half-Marathon (Olomouc) draws crowds of runners to the cobblestoned streets of Moravia.

The Karlovy Vary International Film Festival (Karlovy Vary) runs for eight days in early June or late July, and screens films all over town.

Baroque Opera Festival (Olomouc) in July is filled with

elaborate costumes, wigs, makeup, and drama.

AUGUST

Marathon of Music Festival (Brno): Buskers, jazz musicians, circus arts, and other entertainers take to the streets of Brno for four days in August.

SEPTEMBER

Vary Září Festival (Karlovy Vary) brings light shows and video mapping to the city's historic buildings.

Slunce Ve Skle (Pilsen): The Purkmistr brewery and spa hosts the annual "Sun in a Glass" microbrew festival.

International Organ Festival (Olomouc) is a rare chance to hear the massive organ at St. Moritz Cathedral.

OCTOBER

Pilsner Fest (Pilsen) marks the October 5 anniversary of the first beer brewed at the Pilsner Urquell Brewery with an annual festival.

Christmas Markets in Liberec

DECEMBER

Christmas Markets (Liberec, Karlovy Vary, Pilsen, Brno, Olomouc): A holiday atmosphere, twinkling lights, and decorated trees fill the squares in almost every Czech town, with Brno and Olomouc adding activities like ice skating or Ferris wheels in recent years.

Food and Nightlife

Food in Central Europe is dominated by meat, particularly pork. Starchy ingredients like potatoes and dumplings also make up the base for lots of food in this part of the world. Vegetarian meals are rare outside of designated restaurants, and vegetables tend to come in pickled form.

MEALTIMES

Breakfast in Prague is often small—a quick pastry on the go—and the lunch hour starts early, around 11am, with daily lunch specials usually served until 2pm. You can usually expect dinner service to last until at least 10pm.

TIPPING

Tipping is not required, but is customary for good service. The general rule is to round up for small amounts (e.g., 50 CZK for a 42 CZK beer) or up to 10 percent for a nice meal. You should tell your server how much you want to pay on the spot, when handing them cash or your card (e.g., Server: "That's 565 crowns." You: "600, please."). Don't leave cash on the table. Note that your

BAR AND RESTAURANT RESERVATIONS

One quirk of the Czech Republic's restaurant and café scene is a near obsession with reservations. Yes, people often book seats to meet their friends for an afternoon coffee or a drink at a pub or cocktail bar. The growing demand for high-quality dining and the response of constant restaurant openings mean that everyone (including the locals) wants to try the latest places. Some restaurants offer online reservation systems, while others require a phone call, which hotel concierges can often help you with. The English-friendly website and mobile app **Restu.cz** (scroll to the bottom to choose your language) is also a good option for a middleman to arrange your reservation without any miscommunications about the time or number of guests.

Many pubs and restaurants are often booked with company holiday parties throughout the month of December, so double-check availability with any place you plan to visit before arriving.

credit card slip will not come with a line to add the tip.

DIETARY RESTRICTIONS

Central Europe's vegetarian scene is slowly improving, with lots of raw and vegan restaurants opening in recent years in Prague. However, in many Czech pubs, the meat-free menu is still limited to fried cheese, and vegans may struggle to find anything suitable outside of restaurants that specifically cater to their diet. Seafood, ham, bacon, lard, and even rabbit have been known to pop up on vegetarian sections in village pubs, so double-check with your server to be one hundred percent sure.

Some restaurants are better than others when it comes to dairy or gluten sensitivity. Requests to leave out certain ingredients are usually honored when possible, but substitutions or asking for ingredients on the side is not common practice and will likely be met with confusion or annoyance—especially in rural areas. Restaurants are required to list certain allergens on their menus. For severe allergies, printing a list of the specific words in Czech may help communicate your needs.

Czech cuisine: *Pečená kachní stehna* (roast duck)

PAYING YOUR BAR TAB IN THE CZECH REPUBLIC

In traditional pubs, servers often keep a tally of the drinks on a piece of paper at your table, while other venues use an automated system. Separate checks are expected, but it is the responsibility of the patrons to remember what they had and tell the server which food or drinks they want to pay for at the end of the night—something to note if you're the last one of your group to pay the bill! Credit cards are accepted in maybe 65 percent of venues, but many systems don't allow tips on cards, so carrying cash in the local currency is always a good backup plan. Euros may be accepted in some touristy pubs around the center, but usually at an abysmal exchange rate.

Accommodations

HOTELS

Hotels in Central Europe get graded on a star system running from one to five stars. Just how many stars a hotel will have depends on factors like the services and facilities available in the hotel, the infrastructure, and the overall quality. Five-star hotels will offer luxury, like the Mandarin Oriental or Augustine Hotel in Malá Strana. Three-star hotels are generally comfortable for most travelers. The term "boutique hotel" will often pop up while searching. This usually refers to a smaller hotel with 10 to 100 rooms, often with a design element that sets it apart from chain hotels. Most hotels will have en-suite bathrooms—especially for hotels three stars and above—but it's best to check before booking if you're uncertain. Hotels over three stars will usually provide basic toiletries like soap and shampoo, but conditioner is a rarity.

Hotels will ask for your ID or passport upon arrival and may also want to photocopy your documents. Sometimes a city tax will be added to your bill on top of your hotel fee, and you should check to make sure that breakfast is included in the price of the room. In the Czech Republic it's pretty common to charge extra for breakfast, especially in four- or five-star hotels. Tipping hotel staff in the Czech Republic is not expected, but 20 CZK per bag, or 100-200 CZK per stay for the cleaning staff, is still a nice way to express gratitude.

BED AND BREAKFASTS

Bed and breakfasts are usually smaller than hotels, and independently owned. Breakfast is often included in the price, and sometimes cooked by the owner. If you're looking for a place with a familial feel, then a B&B is a good choice. Rates are usually much lower than in a larger hotel, and you will get a more authentic feel of the area.

Do note, though, that some B&Bs occupy old residential apartments and houses, so bathrooms and toilets may not be located in the room and are down the hall. You can usually request en-suite accommodations when booking the B&B.

HOSTELS

Young travelers, backpackers, and those on a budget will love hostels. Most hostels offer rooms in 6- to 8-bed dorms, but some have single or double rooms at budget prices too. Some travelers also love hostels for the community spirit, as they usually come with a common room or a shared kitchen, which provides an excellent opportunity for travelers to meet and mingle. Breakfast is usually extra, if offered by the hostel. If peace, quiet, and a good night's sleep is what you're after, steer clear of the Party Hostels, usually spotted by dorm rooms of 10 beds or more, and the presence of in-house bars or clubs. However, if you want to see the city's nightlife or make friends with other travelers, they can be great.

APARTMENT RENTALS

If you prefer to self-cater or have the experience of living like a local in the city you're visiting, then an apartment rental may be the option for you. The most popular way of doing this is Airbnb, but this has caused significant controversy for pushing up the rents of locals, especially in cities like Prague. Booking.com also rents out apartments. Just note that in some apartment rentals, the toilet may be shared and located out in the hall, so do your research before you book one. Also, note that with the independence of an apartment, you won't have the support of tourist information and orientation that you would have with a hotel. Some apartment rentals in Prague or Czech cities require a phone call to a Czech phone number upon arrival or a refundable cash deposit at the beginning of your stay, so read your terms and conditions carefully.

Conduct and Customs

LOCAL HABITS

You may notice that smiles are scarce in the Czech Republic, but this doesn't mean everyone is miserable or angry. Smiles are simply saved for sincere expressions of happiness rather than everyday interactions with strangers. Some places have friendly staff, but waitstaff in traditional pubs or restaurants may be on the surly side. Although smiles are not mandatory, politeness is. Always say hello or good day in the local language whenever you go into a shop or a café, stand on the right of the escalator in the metro, and give up your seat to the elderly or pregnant women on public transport. When it comes to tipping, it's best to say how much you'd like to pay in total when paying; never just leave change on the table.

GREETINGS

Greetings are especially important in Central Europe. In the Czech Republic you would say "*dobrý den*" (pronounced "dough-BREE-den") when entering any restaurant or shop. It's also considered polite to say goodbye, or "*na shledanou*" (which sounds a bit like "NAS-clay-dawn-oh"), when leaving.

Greeting friends with kisses on each cheek is common in the Czech Republic, but this usually happens between men-women or women-women. In some cases, such as within a close family or between older men, you may see the men do it, too. Kisses are generally exchanged at the beginning and the end of most social encounters. In business settings, new acquaintances, or between two men, a handshake is often the norm.

ALCOHOL

Alcohol rules in Central Europe are more relaxed than in the States, with the legal drinking age being 18 in the Czech Republic. You may be surprised to find that the beer can be cheaper than water most of the time. That said, don't think of driving even if you've had one beer—drinking and driving is taken very seriously and can incur punishment if any blood alcohol shows up in a test.

Czech beer comes with a thick head of foam.

SMOKING

Smoking is legal from the age of 18. A lot of Czechs smoke, but it's not allowed indoors in public buildings. Up until May 2017, ashtrays were an essential part of most pubs in Prague, but the recent smoking ban has restricted cigarettes to outdoor dining areas only. Be prepared for smokers in your vicinity on city streets, parks, beer gardens, and outdoor patios at cafés and restaurants.

DRUGS

The Central European region has never had a reputation as being a drug hotbed, but dealing still happens around train stations and transport hubs. The personal possession of marijuana has been decriminalized and medical cannabis is also legal in the Czech Republic. Other drugs are illegal in the Czech Republic, and many substances offered on the streets are questionable at best. It's best to play it safe while traveling and avoid consuming or possessing drugs—even in small quantities.

PROSTITUTION

Despite being legal, Czech laws prohibit organized prostitution and sex work is not regulated. There are some 200 brothels in Prague alone but their operations are not quite legal, thanks to ambiguously written laws.

DRESS

The Czech Republic has a fairly relaxed dress code. You'll see people walking around in jeans, T-shirts, or hiking gear in Prague, where most restaurants won't enforce a strict dress code. Many people go from a workday to night out without getting dolled up in dresses, heels, or collared shirts, but a little extra effort can be fun when going to trendier nightclubs. For high-class restaurants or a night at the theater, semiformal or formal wear is preferred. It is generally respectful to cover shoulders and wear skirts below the knee in religious spaces, but this is not strictly enforced in the Czech Republic.

Health and Safety

EMERGENCY NUMBERS

The number to dial in an emergency is the same throughout continental Europe: **112.**

CRIME AND THEFT

Crime and theft in Central Europe are moderate. When it comes to violent crime, Prague is generally a safe city and, despite the famously high beer consumption, bar fights are a blissfully rare occurrence. Pickpockets perhaps present the primary risk in crowded places like the metro or crowded festivals, so keep an eye out for your belongings when out and about. In Prague, avoid changing money on the street or you'll likely end up with a currency that isn't Czech Koruna. It's important not to let your guard down, but with a little common sense you should be fine.

MEDICAL SERVICES

Vaccines are not required for the Czech Republic, but if you're traveling in the window between November to March, you may want to invest in a flu shot. Also, if you're planning to head outdoors, you may want to get a Tick-Borne Encephalitis vaccine as ticks are a growing risk in Central Europe. You can also pick up bug spray in local pharmacies, which is useful to ward off mosquitos and ticks. If you haven't been vaccinated, it's a good idea to take precautions when in parks or wooded areas—even within the city.

DRINKING WATER

The water is not only safe to drink in Prague, but it's actually pretty good, so go ahead and feel free to bottle some tap water.

PHARMACIES

Pharmacies in the Czech Republic can help you pick up any medications, vitamins, or herbal supplements you may need while traveling. Drugs like ibuprofen and paracetamol (acetaminophen) won't require a prescription in European pharmacies, but some drugs like antibiotics or sedatives will require a local prescription from a doctor of that country. In the Czech Republic, pharmacies carrying medicine are often housed in separate businesses from drugstores selling things like soap, shampoo, and toiletries.

You can spot a pharmacy by the bright green cross symbol. You can find a pharmacy that's open any time of day or night.

SECURITY

Prague, to date, has not seen any terrorist attacks, but just as in any city in Europe, it's best to be vigilant and consult your embassy for travel advice. Also, if offered, register your travel with your embassy before traveling so that you're entitled to consular help.

Practical Details

WHAT TO PACK

When it comes to packing, the best bet is to pack smart-casual attire and plenty of layers. The climate in the region is changeable, so keep a jacket or a cardigan in your bag for those days when the cooler evening chill sets in.

Expect to do a lot of walking in each city, so pack a pair of **comfortable shoes.** The Old Town in Prague has cobblestoned streets, so bear that in mind when considering footwear. Since the climate is changeable—in the summer you can go from high humidity to flash storms—pack layers and an umbrella or a raincoat. If you're going in the winter, pack warm clothes as the temperatures can fall below zero.

If you're coming from the UK or the States, make sure you pack an **adapter** so you can use your electronics in Continental Europe. Plugs in Central Europe use two round prongs with a voltage of 220V. You will definitely want a camera or at least a good quality phone to snap pics, but bring extra memory cards, because you will need them!

Finally, **earbuds or headphones** can be useful for accessing museum audio guides that you can download onto your phone.

MONEY

Most EU countries use a single currency, the Euro, but the Czech Republic still uses its own currency, the Czech Koruna. While it's potentially cumbersome for travelers visiting multiple countries, this reluctance to switch has helped to maintain the low cost of living (and traveling) in the area. Euros may be accepted (usually at terrible exchange rates) at some shops in touristy areas, but this is definitely not the norm at most restaurants, shops, or sights.

ATMs will take foreign cards, and maybe 60-75 percent of restaurants and shops will take Visa, Mastercard, or Maestro. Some places won't take American Express, so best to check before ordering. If you prefer, you can also change money at official money changers, either in banks or recommended exchange places.

Some restaurants and shops will only take **cash,** and many outdoor markets and beer gardens are cash only. It's a good idea to carry some smaller bills with you if you're planning on paying in cash. Most large supermarkets and restaurants will break larger notes, but you might get a few irritated servers or sellers if you try to pay a 45 CZK bill with a 1,000 CZK note in a smaller venue. It's also a good idea to keep some small change on you at all times, especially for public toilets.

OPENING HOURS

Shops usually open around 9am or 10am and close around 6pm, perhaps later in large shopping malls, Mondays to Saturdays. In Prague, large stores or supermarkets may stay open on Sundays, but others will close. Sometimes, smaller stores will close for lunch hours.

Museums, in general, tend to close on Mondays, but check the opening times of any place you're interested in visiting—some popular attractions open every day of the week, while others may have a rest day on Tuesday or Sunday.

PUBLIC HOLIDAYS

There are a number of Czech public holidays that visitors may not expect: **Good Friday** and **Easter Monday** may have limited shopping hours, but the long weekend also brings Easter markets to many town squares. **May 1** and **May 8** are national holidays marking Labor Day and Victory in Europe (VE) Day. Both **July 5** and **July 6** are public holidays and you are likely to find limited access to some museums and shops. **September 28** (St. Wenceslas Day), **October 28** (the foundation of Czechoslovakia), and **November 17** (commemorating the Struggle for Freedom and Democracy) are often marked with performances, events, or protests in Wenceslas Square. Christmas is celebrated on **December 24** in the Czech Republic, with additional public holidays on **December 25 and 26,** but you'll also find Christmas markets popping up around the beginning of December.

COMMUNICATIONS

PHONES AND CELL PHONES

The country code for the Czech Republic is 420. If you're calling from the US, dial the international access code 011 from a US or Canadian landline, then dial the number. From a mobile phone, use the plus sign and the country code to make calls. From the UK, just dial 00 and then the country code.

To call out of the country, dial 00 or the plus sign and the country code (for US and Canada this is 1), and then dial the area code and number.

Most smartphones will work in

arrive early or late to see Charles Bridge without crowds

Central Europe with a US, UK, or Canadian SIM card, but talk to your provider to make sure you don't rack up any unwanted roaming charges when you go abroad.

INTERNET ACCESS

You should find it easy to get online in most Czech cities. Wi-Fi is standard in most hotels and hostels. Many cafés, malls, and even hotspots in the city center should also get you online for free (although you may have to ask a server or look for a chalkboard with a password or "*heslo*" in Czech). Some free Wi-Fi services may ask you to register with an email and accept their terms and conditions.

SHIPPING AND POSTAL

If you're looking only to mail a postcard, then you may want to skip the lines at the post office and try an automated machine. To mail a package or speak to a cashier at the post office, you'll need to press a button and take a number. Postcards to the US will cost around $1-2 to mail.

ELECTRICAL SYSTEM

Czech appliances run on 220-240V, as opposed to the 110V common in the US. The Czech Republic requires Type C plugs (not grounded) with two round prongs, or Type E & F plugs (grounded) with two round prongs and a hole for the outlet. Basic adapters should work for most travelers, but US travelers may want to invest in a voltage convertor, particularly for styling tools like flat irons, curling irons, or larger electronics that can be damaged by the higher voltage.

TIME ZONE

The Czech Republic is on GMT+1 (Central European Time) or GMT+2 (Central European Summer Time). It is usually one hour ahead of the UK, six hours ahead of NYC, and nine hours ahead of Seattle. The Czech Republic is eight hours behind Sydney and ten hours behind Auckland. At the time of writing, the EU had voted to abolish Daylight Savings Time but changes by individual countries were not expected until 2021.

Traveler Advice

ACCESS FOR TRAVELERS WITH DISABILITIES

With its cobbled streets, and elevator access on only some metro stations, the Czech Republic can be a challenge for disabled travelers. Historic buildings may not have a lift, and some of the older metro stations may be stairs only. It's best to do some additional research, such as contacting the **Prague Wheelchair Users Organization** (www.pov.cz/en).

TRAVELING WITH CHILDREN

Czech culture in general is quite family-friendly. Kids get discounts on public transport and museums, and some neighborhood restaurants offer children's menus or a kid's corners with toys. Outdoor events, even beer festivals, attract parents with their little ones to relaxed environments. Some tourist offices will provide brochures with family-friendly ideas. It's worth researching museums to see if they have play areas for children.

WOMEN TRAVELING ALONE

Prague is a relatively safe city for solo female travelers, but exercise the same caution as you would in any other European city. Most downtown areas are okay to explore on your own, even at night. However, if you feel anxious walking down quiet streets after dark, then try to pick accommodations on a main road. Taxis can be a great option if you don't like taking public transport late at night, but make sure you take a licensed operator or use a smartphone app like Liftago, Uber, or Bolt. And should you go to a bar, take care never to leave your drink unattended.

SENIOR TRAVELERS

Senior travelers may struggle with the cobbled streets and the less accessible sites in the Czech Republic, but on the whole, it's a region that's great for older travelers. Prague's historical sites attract travelers of all ages, including older ones. Most museums have lifts and benches, and of course, discounts for senior citizens. Public transport in Prague is free for anyone aged 70 and over (with valid ID). Just take care not to book a hotel in the heart of a party district if you're looking for a peaceful night's sleep.

LGBTQ+ TRAVELERS

The best word for Czech attitudes toward gay and lesbian travelers is tolerance. Civil partnerships for same-sex couples are recognized, but public displays of affection, especially in smaller villages, may still draw looks. When it comes to nightlife, Prague has a vibrant cis gay scene, mostly concentrated around the Vinohrady area. **Freedom Nights** (www.djhenriette.cz/freedom-night) dance parties in Prague and Brno cater to the cis lesbian scene.

Prague has hosted an annual **Pride festival** (www.praguepride.cz) in August since 2011. Both Prague and Brno also hold **Queer Balls** (www.queerball.cz) in February or March and a **Mezipatra Queer Film Festival** (www.mezipatra.cz) in November. Useful organizations for gay and lesbian travelers include **Prague Saints** (www.praguesaints.cz), a gay travel agency in Prague, or the **STUD association** (www.stud.cz) in Brno.

Transgender travelers may feel slightly less comfortable, although usually not to a level of danger or threat. A volunteer from **Trans*parent** (www.transparentprague.cz), a local organization for the transgender community, offers the following advice: "Don't be afraid to just be yourself provided that you can do so with confidence. Czech people will rarely directly confront others, but you might get some uncomfortable stares."

TRAVELERS OF COLOR

Prague may present some discomfort or challenges for travelers of color. While the capital city is generally a liberal and open-minded place, travelers from certain ethnic or religious backgrounds, particularly those with darker skin or wearing head scarves, may experience xenophobic attitudes or unwanted attention. The current Czech President Miloš Zeman is known for making anti-immigrant statements. However, most anti-Muslim or anti-immigrant marches are met with an equal or larger march in support of diverse societies. This remains a divisive political issue across the country. There is also significant racial tension in the Czech Republic toward the Romani community, an ethnic minority representing around two percent of the population.

Outside of major cities, travelers of color may also be met with stares from a few locals—particularly in rural regions—but there is no need to be concerned about safety when visiting the day trips recommended in this book. Czechs can actually be quite modest and could simply be surprised that international travelers would want to visit their town. These destinations are popular with visitors from across the world and are generally welcoming to any travelers of color expressing an interest in their culture.

Czech Phrasebook

Czech is quite a difficult language—four genders (neuter, feminine, masculine animate, and masculine inanimate), seven cases that change word endings, formal and informal phrases—plus it includes one sound, the vicious ř, that many schoolchildren need speech therapy to master! On the bright side, the language is phonetic so you can say what you see. Some quirky letters pronounced differently than English include: au, c, č, ď, j, ř, š, ť, ž, and any vowel with an accent mark.

Some locals are delighted by foreigners speaking their language, while others quickly lose patience and get frustrated if you don't understand their responses in Czech. Asking a question in Czech will likely receive an answer in Czech, and most locals are not used to simplifying their own language for foreigners. Some Czechs in the service sector will switch to English to ensure accuracy and efficiency. In many cases, simplicity (e.g., "Liberec?" while pointing to the bus) is easier to facilitate communication. This also makes it easier for the locals to understand than the unavoidable mispronunciation of their own language or small grammatical errors that can change meanings. However, do feel free to try some Czech phrases when you have the time and a willing native speaker.

a as in "father"
á longer as in "ahhhh"
au like "ow" as in "how"
c "ts" always a soft c as in "patience" (never hard like "ck")
č "ch" as in "change"
ch like an "h" but in the back of your throat like the composer "Bach"
ď a "dy" sound
e as in "egg"
é like "ai" as in "fair"
ě like adding a "y" before the "e" as in "yes"
i as in "fit"
í like "ee" as in "free"
j like "y" in "yes"
ň like "ny" as in "menu"
o as in "oh"
ó longer "oh" as in "oooooh"
ř no English equivalent; in Czech it combines saying "**ž**" plus a rolled "**r**" simultaneously, as in the composer's name Dvořák; English speakers can get by with just saying "ž" like the "s" in "pleasure"
š "sh" as in "shampoo"
ť a "ty" sound as in architecture
u as in "soup"

ú or ů like a long "u" as in "true"; the character ú is used at the beginning of a word while ů is used in the middle

y like a short "i" as in "bit"

ý like a long "e" as in "me"

ž like "s" in "measure"

ESSENTIAL PHRASES

Hello *Dobrý den* (formal, for strangers and acquaintances; used anytime you enter a shop or restaurant)

Hi / Bye *Ahoj* or *Čau* (informal, used somewhat interchangeably but only for close friends and family)

Good morning *Dobré ráno*

Good evening *Dobrý večer*

Good night *Dobrou noc*

Goodbye *Na shledanou* (used anytime you leave a shop or restaurant)

Where are you from? *Odkud jste?*

I am from the US / England / ... *Jsem z USA / Jsem z Anglie ...*

Nice to meet you *Těší mě*

Please/You're welcome *Prosím*

Excuse me *Pardon* or *Promiňte*

Sorry *Promiňte*

Thank you *Děkuji*

Excuse me, do you speak English? *Promiňte, nemluvíte* Anglicky ?* (* In Czech the more polite sentence structure is similar to "Don't you speak English?")

Where are the restrooms? *Kde jsou toalety?*

Is there Wi-Fi? *Nemáte* Wi-Fi?* (* In Czech the more polite sentence structure is similar to "Don't you have Wi-Fi?")

What's the Wi-Fi password? *Jaké je heslo na Wi-Fi?*

Yes *Ano* (formal, and often shortened to "*no*" so be careful because "'no" in Czech means "Yes!")

No *Ne*

TRANSPORTATION

bus station *autobusové nádraží*

train station *vlakové nádraží*

Where is...? *Kde je...?*

How far is it to...? *Jak daleko je.... odsud?*

Is there a bus to Liberec / Brno / ...? *Je autobus do Liberce* / Brna* / ...?* (* Almost all Czech words, including place names, change depending on the sentence.)

Is this the bus to...? *Je to autobus na ...?*

What time does the bus/train leave? *V kolik hodin autobus / vlak odjíždí?*

Where is the subway station? *Kde je stanice metra?*

Where's the ticket office? *Kde je pokladna?*

A round-trip/single ticket to... Zpáteční / jízdenku na...

FOOD

Can I make a reservation, please? *Mohu si udělat rezervaci, prosím?*

A reservation for one/two... *Rezervace za jednu osobu / dvě osoby*

Two people at 2pm *dva lidé ve dvě odpoledne*

Do you have a reservation? *Máte rezervaci?*

Do you have an English menu? *Nemáte anglické menu?*

Are you ready to order? *Máte vybráno?*

Excuse me, may I order, please? *Promiňte můžu objednat, prosím?*

I'm vegetarian. *jsem vegetarian* (male) / *jsem vegetarianka* (female).

I'll have... please. *Dám si....prosím.*

Is everything okay? *Všechno pořádku?*

I would like to pay / We would like to pay, please. *Zaplatím / Zaplatíme, prosím.*

Cash or card? *Hotově nebo kartou?*

breakfast *snídaně*

beer *pivo*

lunch *oběd*

dinner *večeře*

menu *jídelní lístek*

wine *víno*

water *voda*

coffee *káva*

tea *čaj*

(soy / almond) milk *(sójové / mandlové) mléko*

gluten / gluten-free *lepek / bezlepkový*

fruit *ovoce*

bread *chléb*

meat *maso*

fish *ryby*

SHOPPING

money *peníze*

How much does it cost? *Kolik to stojí?*

I'm just looking around. *Jen se rozhlížím.*

HEALTH

drugstore *drogérie*

pharmacy *lékárna*

It hurts here. *Bolí mě tady.*

I have a fever. *Mám horečku.*

I have a headache. *Bolí mě hlava.*

I have a stomach ache. *Bolí mě břicho.*

I have a toothache. *Bolí mě zub.*

I feel nauseated. *Je mi nevolno.*

to vomit *zvracet*

medicine *lékařství*

antibiotic *antibiotika*

pill/tablet *pilulka / tabletka*

I need a doctor *Potřebuji lékaře*

To the hospital, please. *Do nemocnice, prosím.*

I am diabetic / pregnant. *Jsem diabetik / těhotná*

I take birth control pills. *Užívám antikoncepci.*

I am allergic to... penicillin. *Jsem alergický (male) / alergická (female) na... penicilín.*

blood type *krevní skupina*

NUMBERS

0 *nula*

1 *jeden (m.) / jedna (f.) / jedno (n.)*

2 *dva / dvě*

3 *tři*

4 *čtyři*

5 *pět*

6 *šest*

7 *sedm*

8 *osm*

9 *devět*

10 *deset*

11 *jedenáct*

12 *dvanáct*

13 *třináct*

14 *čtrnáct*

15 *patnáct*

16 *šestnáct*

17 *sedmnáct*

18 *osmnáct*

19 *devatenáct*

20 *dvacet*

21 *dvacet jedna*

30 *třicet*

40 *čtyřicet*

50 *padesát*

60 *šedesát*

70 *sedmdesát*

80 *osmdesát*

90 *devadesát*

100 *sto*

200 *dvě stě*

300 / 400 *tři / čtyři sta*

500 / 600 / 700 / 800 / 900 *pět / šest / sedm / osm / devět set*

1,000 *tisíc*

2,000 *dva tisíce*

TIME

What time is it? *Kolik je hodin?*
It's 1am / 3pm (15:00) *Je jedna hodina / Je patnáct hodin*
noon/midday *poledne*
midnight *půlnoc*
morning (early, before leaving the house) *ráno*
morning (before noon) *dopoledne*
afternoon *odpoledne*
evening *večer*
yesterday *včera*
today *dnes / dneska*
tomorrow *zítra*
now *ted'*

DAYS AND MONTHS

week *týden*
month *měsíc*
Monday *pondělí*
Tuesday *úterý*
Wednesday *středa*
Thursday *čtvrtek*
Friday *pátek*
Saturday *sobota*
Sunday *neděle*
January *leden*
February *únor*
March *březen*
April *duben*
May *květen*
June *červen*
July *červenec*
August *srpen*
September *září*
October *říjen*
November *listopad*
December *prosinec*

Index

A

B

C

D

E

F

G

H

I J

K

L

M

N

O

P

QR

S

T

UVW

Z

List of Maps

Acknowledgments

Thank you to the incredible people who helped to facilitate research trips, answered questions, and generously shared their culture with me: Diky moc to Jiři Dužar and Michaela Claudino from Czech Tourism (www.czechtourism.com) and Kateřina Pavlitová and the Prague Tourism team (www.prague.eu). The incredible Brno team of Tereza, Barbora, Pavla, Jana, and Ivo (www.gotobrno.cz), with enthusiastic tours from Pavel Dvořák and 10-Z Bunker's Pavel Paleček multiplied my love of Moravia. Děkuji to Alena in Pilsen (www.visitpilsen.eu), Eliška in Kutná Hora (www.kutnahora.cz), Kristina in Karlovy Vary (www.zivykraj.cz), and Klára from South Bohemia (www.jiznichechy.cz) for helping me experience the beauty of Český Krumlov in winter. Adam and Denisa in Olomouc (www.olomouctravel.cz) could not be more patient, and the Boho Hotel Team never fails to impress me. Janek & Honza (the Honest Guides), Jan Macuch, Martin & Viktor, and the BPH team are eternally entertaining teachers. To Lani and Jussi, Victoria and Chris, Michelle and Aleš, Rosie and Miguel, Matt, Mariel, Molly, and Zuzana, thank you for ensuring I always had a bed in so many cities and neighborhoods. There are about a million more who made this book possible (including Nikki for keeping me coherent and within word limits), so I'll end with gratitude for every kind look and patient response throughout the country, even with my eternally butchered efforts at a beautiful language.

Photo Credits

Title page photo: Olgacov | Dreamstime.com

All interiour photos © Auburn Scallon, except page 2 © (left middle) Elenakirey | Dreamstime.com; (right middle) Poooow | Dreamstime.com; page 3 © Karl Allen Lugmayer | Dreamstime.com; page 4 © (left top) Anna Guryeva | Dreamstime.com; (right middle) Rostislav Sedlacek | Dreamstime.com; (left bottom) Notistia | Dreamstime.com; page 5 © Danielschreurs | Dreamstime.com; pages 6-7 © Vladimir Sazonov | Dreamstime.com; page 9 © Fabiano Waewell | Dreamstime.com; pages 10-11 © (top) chitsanupong pengsalae | Dreamstime.com, (bottom) Mineria6 | Dreamstime.com; page 12 © (top) Radomír Režný | Dreamstime.com; (bottom) Czech National Wine Cellar/Vít Mádr; page 13 © (top) Daniela Hofrajtrová | Dreamstime.com; page 15 © (top) Gepapix | Dreamstime.com; page 16 © Sazonoff | Dreamstime.com; page 24 © (top) Nikolay Antonov | Dreamstime.com; (bottom) Kaprik | Dreamstime.com; page 26 © Lazazzera | Dreamstime.com; page 29 © (top) Kaprik | Dreamstime.com; page 30 © (top) Martinfredy | Dreamstime.com; page 34 © Pigprox | Dreamstime.com; page 36 © Dimbar76 | Dreamstime.com; page 49 © (top) Mapics | Dreamstime.com; page 63 © Igor Abramovych | Dreamstime.com; page 65 © Charles Stewart; page 67 © Felker | Dreamstime.com; page 68 © Aivita Arika | Dreamstime.com; page 69 © Nomadbeg | Dreamstime.com; page 75 © Byvalet | Dreamstime.com; page 76 © Zhu_zhu | Dreamstime.com; page 84 (bottom) Lefpap | Dreamstime.com; page 87 © Dimbar76 | Dreamstime.com; page 88 © Abxyz | Dreamstime.com; page 89 © (top) Samurkas | Dreamstime.com; (bottom) Sue Martin | Dreamstime.com; page 90 © M Pater | Dreamstime.com; page 91 © (right) Pytyczech | Dreamstime.com; page 99 © Kaprik | Dreamstime.com; page 100 © Mariangarai | Dreamstime.com; page 116 © Pytyczech | Dreamstime.com; page 161 © Marcin Łukaszewicz | Dreamstime.com; page 162 © Enrique Miguel Borque | Dreamstime.com; page 169 © (bottom) Kaprik | Dreamstime.com; page 179 © Zhu_zhu | Dreamstime.com; page 193 © Smokon | Dreamstime.com; page 196 © Xantana | Dreamstime.com; page 239 © Josef Skacel | Dreamstime.com; page 242 © Fotoatelier Seidel; page 243 © (bottom) Pigprox | Dreamstime.com; page 249 © Poooow | Dreamstime.com; page 255 © (bottom) Ventura69 | Dreamstime.com; page 275 © (top) Milangonda | Dreamstime.com; page 282 © (bottom) Czech National Wine Cellar/Vít Mádr; page 283 © Graphiapl | Dreamstime.com; page 287 © Victoria Borisch; page 305 © Kaprik | Dreamstime.com

Gear up for a bucket list vacation

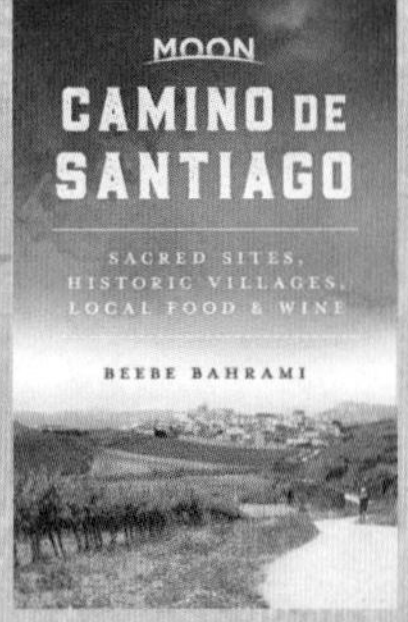

or plan your next beachy getaway!

More Guides for Urban Adventure

MAP SYMBOLS

- Expressway
- Primary Road
- Secondary Road
- Unpaved Road
- Trail
- Ferry
- Railroad
- Pedestrian Walkway
- Stairs
- City/Town
- State Capital
- National Capital
- Highlight
- Point of Interest
- Accommodation
- Restaurant/Bar
- Other Location
- Information Center
- Parking Area
- Church
- Winery
- Trailhead
- Train Station
- Airport
- Airfield
- Park
- Golf Course
- Unique Feature
- Waterfall
- Camping
- Mountain
- Ski Area
- Glacier

CONVERSION TABLES

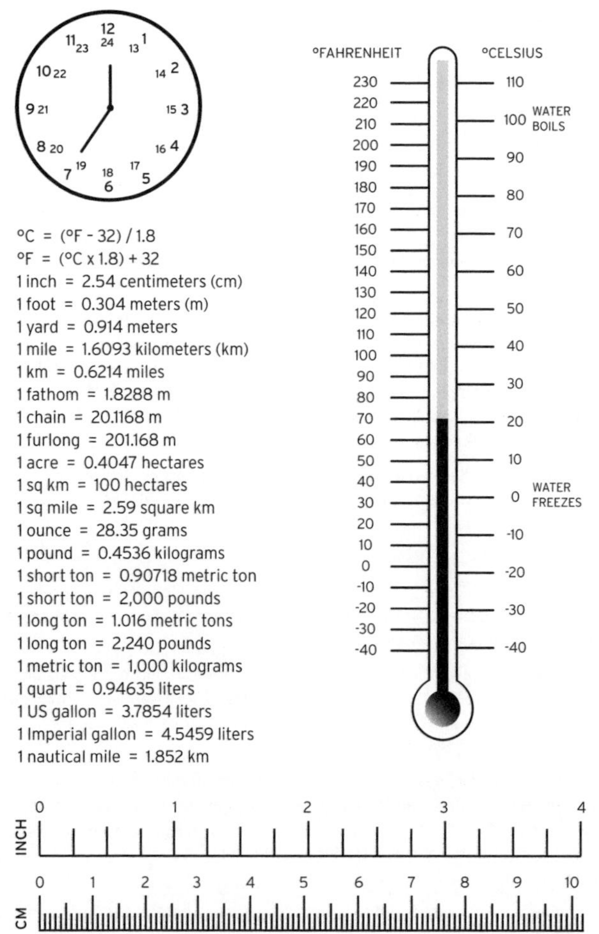

°C = (°F - 32) / 1.8
°F = (°C x 1.8) + 32
1 inch = 2.54 centimeters (cm)
1 foot = 0.304 meters (m)
1 yard = 0.914 meters
1 mile = 1.6093 kilometers (km)
1 km = 0.6214 miles
1 fathom = 1.8288 m
1 chain = 20.1168 m
1 furlong = 201.168 m
1 acre = 0.4047 hectares
1 sq km = 100 hectares
1 sq mile = 2.59 square km
1 ounce = 28.35 grams
1 pound = 0.4536 kilograms
1 short ton = 0.90718 metric ton
1 short ton = 2,000 pounds
1 long ton = 1.016 metric tons
1 long ton = 2,240 pounds
1 metric ton = 1,000 kilograms
1 quart = 0.94635 liters
1 US gallon = 3.7854 liters
1 Imperial gallon = 4.5459 liters
1 nautical mile = 1.852 km

MOON PRAGUE & BEYOND
Avalon Travel
Hachette Book Group
1700 Fourth Street
Berkeley, CA 94710, USA
www.moon.com

Editor: Nikki Ioakimedes
Managing Editor: Hannah Brezack
Copy Editor: Chris Dumas
Graphics and Production Coordinator: Lucie Ericksen
Cover Design: Faceout Studio, Charles Brock
Interior Design: Megan Jones Design
Moon Logo: Tim McGrath
Map Editor: Kat Bennett
Cartographers: Karin Dahl, John Culp
Proofreader: Lina Carmona
Indexer: Gina Guilinger

ISBN-13: 978-1-64049-824-2

Printing History
1st Edition — April 2020

5 4 3 2 1

Front cover photo: Kampa Island in Prague © Kirk Fisher / Alamy Stock Photo
Back cover photo: swans on Vltava river in Prague © Maya Afzaal | Dreamstime.com
Inside cover photo: stairs leading to the Prague Castle © UlyssePixel | Dreamstime.com

Printed in China by RR Donnelley

All recommendations, including those for sights, activities, hotels, restaurants, and shops, are based on each author's individual judgment. We do not accept payment for inclusion in our travel guides, and our authors don't accept free goods or services in exchange for positive coverage.